The Stone Court

ABC-CLIO SUPREME COURT HANDBOOKS

Peter G. Renstrom, Series Editor

ABC-CLIO SUPREME COURT HANDBOOKS

The Stone Court

Justices, Rulings, and Legacy

Peter G. Renstrom
Western Michigan University

A B C 🌊 C L I O

Santa Barbara, California • Denver, Colorado • Oxford, England

Library of Congress Cataloging-in-Publication Data

Renstrom, Peter G., 1943–
    The Stone court : justices, rulings, and legacy / Peter G. Renstrom.
      p. cm. — (ABC-CLIO Supreme Court handbooks)
    Includes bibliographical references and index.
    ISBN 1-57607-153-7 (hard : acid-free paper) — ISBN 1-57607-582-6
    (e-book : acid-free paper)
    1. United States. Supreme Court—History—20th century. 2. Stone,
Harlan Fiske, 1872–1946. 3. Constitutional history—United States.
I. Title. II. Series.
KF8742 .R48 2001
347.73'26—dc21   2001-000012

07 06 05 04 03 02 01 10 9 8 7 6 5 4 3 2 1

ABC-CLIO, Inc.
130 Cremona Drive, P.O. Box 1911
Santa Barbara, California 93116-1911

This book is printed on acid-free paper ∞ .
Manufactured in the United States of America

To my parents, Mildred and Franklin Renstrom, who lived through the Stone Court era. They withstood the misery of the Great Depression and survived the horror of world war by embracing the values of middle America. They lived by these values and passed them on to their sons. Most remarkable, if not unique, and greatly appreciated.

Contents

Series Foreword

There is an extensive literature on the U.S. Supreme Court, but it contains discussion familiar largely to the academic community and the legal profession. The ABC-CLIO Supreme Court series is designed to have value to the academic and legal communities also, but each volume is intended as well for the general reader who does not possess an extensive background on the Court or American constitutional law. The series is intended to effectively represent each of fourteen periods in the history of the Supreme Court with each of these fourteen eras defined by the chief justice beginning with John Jay in 1789. Each Court confronted constitutional and statutory questions that were of major importance to and influenced by the historical period. The Court's decisions were also influenced by the values of each of the individual justices sitting at the time. The issues, the historical period, the justices, and the Supreme Court's decisions in the most significant cases will be examined in the volumes of this series.

ABC-CLIO's Supreme Court series provides scholarly examinations of the Court as it functioned in different historical periods and with different justices. Each volume contains information necessary to understand each particular Court and an interpretative analysis by the author of each Court's record and legacy. In addition to representing the major decisions of each Court, institutional linkages are examined as well—the political connections among the Court, Congress, and the president. These relationships are important for several reasons. Although the Court retains some institutional autonomy, all the Court's justices are selected by a process that involves the other two branches. Many of the significant decisions of the Court involve the review of actions of Congress or the president. In addition, the Court frequently depends on the other two branches to secure compliance with its rulings.

The authors of the volumes in the ABC-CLIO series were selected with great care. Each author has worked extensively with the Court, the period, and the personalities about which he or she has written. ABC-CLIO wanted each of the volumes to examine several common themes, and each author agreed to work within certain guidelines. Each author was free, however, to develop the content of each volume, and many of the volumes advance new or distinctive conclusions about the Court under examination.

Each volume contains four substantive chapters. The first chapter will introduce the Court and the historical period in which it served. The second chapter will examine each of the justices who sat on the particular Court. The third chapter will represent the most significant decisions rendered by the particular Court. Among other things, the impact of the historical period and the value orientations of the individual justices will be developed. A fourth and final chapter will address the impact of each particular Court on American constitutional law—its doctrinal legacy.

Each volume contains several features designed to make the volume more valuable to those whose previous exposure to the Supreme Court and American constitutional law is limited. Each volume will have a reference section that will contain brief entries on some of the people, statutes, events, and concepts introduced in the four substantive chapters. Entries in this section are arranged alphabetically. Each volume will also contain a glossary of selected legal terms used in the text. Following each of the four chapters, a list of sources used in the chapter and suggestions for further reading will appear. Each volume will also have a comprehensive annotated bibliography. A listing of Internet sources is presented at the end of the bibliography. Finally, there will be a comprehensive subject index and a list of cases (with citation numbers) discussed in each volume. ABC-CLIO is delighted with the quality of scholarship represented in each volume and is proud to offer this series to the reading public.

Permit me to conclude with a personal note. This project has been an extraordinarily rewarding undertaking for me as series editor. Misgivings about serving in this capacity were plentiful at the outset of the project. After tending to some administrative business pertaining to the series, securing authors for each volume was the first major task. I developed a list of possible authors after reviewing previous work and obtaining valuable counsel from several recognized experts in American constitutional history. In virtually every instance, the first person on my list agreed to participate in the project. The high quality of the series was assured and enhanced as each author signed on. I could not have been more pleased. My interactions with each author have been most pleasant, and the excellence of their work will be immediately apparent to the reader. I sincerely thank each author.

Finally, a word about ABC-CLIO and its staff. ABC-CLIO was enthusiastic about the project from the beginning and has done everything necessary to make this series successful. I am very appreciative of the level of support I have received from ABC-CLIO. Alicia Merritt, senior acquisitions editor, deserves special recognition. She has held my hand throughout the project. She has facilitated making this project a reality in every conceivable way. She has encouraged me from the beginning, provided invaluable counsel, and given me latitude to operate as I wished while keeping me on track at the same time. This project would not have gotten off the ground without Alicia, and I cannot thank her enough.

—*Peter G. Renstrom*

Preface

President Franklin Roosevelt took office in 1933, in the midst of the Great Depression, and promptly declared war against the persisting consequences of the economic emergency. He died twelve years later as he began his fourth term as president. At the time of his death, the country was still at war against the Axis powers. The story of the Stone Court revolves around these two national emergencies and Roosevelt's presidency.

Roosevelt began his tenure during the Hughes Court era. Until 1937 the Hughes Court was dominated by conservative activists who were categorically unreceptive to Roosevelt's economic recovery initiatives, known collectively as the New Deal. Indeed, it was not until Roosevelt had begun his second term that direct political pressure was applied to the Court. The pressure took the form of a proposal to "reform" the federal judiciary by adding new judges for presumably worn-out older judges. It was a clumsy and transparent effort to produce the appointment opportunities that had not come to Roosevelt during his first four-year term. The Supreme Court, called the Nine Old Men in some quarters, stood to gain six new justices had Congress approved Roosevelt's proposal. Even though the plan to pack the Court was rejected, Roosevelt got his opportunity to appoint new justices almost immediately thereafter as death and retirement created the long-awaited vacancies. The new appointments came in bulk—Black, Reed, Frankfurter, Douglas, Murphy, Byrnes, and Jackson within four years. Roosevelt also elevated Justice Stone to lead what could then accurately be called Roosevelt's Court. Roosevelt finally had the Court he had been hoping for—liberal justices committed to defer to legislative judgments. Certainly Roosevelt Democrats, if not the country generally, expected great things from the Stone Court. To a significant extent, however, these expectations were unrealized.

The Stone Court left an imprint nonetheless. It affirmed the conclusion reached during the last years of the Hughes Court that the Constitution permitted the federal government to engage in extensive regulation of the national economy and private property. The Stone Court upheld this regulatory power not only to meet the necessities of wartime but also as economic policy initiatives completely independent of the war. In doing so, the Stone Court fine-tuned the restraintist orientation that had not been evident prior to 1937. It also approved the exercise of federal authority in situations previously viewed as the exclusive domain of the states. This was particularly so in cases involving what seemed to be the favored constituencies of the Stone Court, labor unions and farmers.

The Stone Court lent its support to the significant expansion of executive authority, particularly in the furtherance of foreign policy objectives. The Court declined to review many of the actions Roosevelt took during the war; when it did undertake such review, it endorsed the exercise of broader executive power. Roosevelt used executive agreements to an unprecedented extent in the conduct of foreign relations, for example, and the Stone Court recognized his ability to do so. Similarly, the Court upheld his executive orders pertaining to the exclusion of Japanese Americans from designated military zones, allowed extensive regulation of prices through an executive agency, and permitted him to create military tribunals for the purpose of trying those charged with war crimes.

The Stone Court's most significant impact came in the area of civil liberties, though its influence was muted to a degree. The Stone Court's record in this area might have been more substantial had it not been for the war. Whatever gains might be attributable to the Stone Court in advance of the cause of individual rights were overshadowed by its Japanese evacuation decisions. Still, a majority of the Stone Court justices subscribed to the view that when government actions affect fundamental rights, the courts must scrutinize them more rigorously. Although the Stone Court did not itself expand the number of Bill of Rights provisions connecting to the states through the Fourteenth Amendment, individual justices spoke to the question strongly enough to keep up the debate. The Stone Court was also sensitive to the rights of racial minorities and applied the Equal Protection Clause in ways that laid the foundation for subsequent Court rulings on segregation and discrimination. For a number of reasons, the Stone Court was unable to follow through on a new civil liberties jurisprudence. The Vinson Court, which immediately followed the Stone Court, backtracked during the cold war. The Warren Court, however, picked up on the preliminary steps taken by the Stone Court and comprehensively expanded constitutional protection of individual rights. It cannot be said that the Stone Court profoundly affected individual rights jurisprudence, but it set the stage for the Warren Court to do so. Thus, the Stone Court was something of a bridge between the constitutional interpretation before 1937 and the "new constitutionalism" that came thereafter.

I enthusiastically undertook the writing of this overview of the Stone Court. I completed my graduate degrees at Michigan State University more than thirty years ago. My doctoral dissertation was a quantitative examination of the patterns of Stone Court decision making. The current volume returns me to my professional home base in a sense, and I sincerely thank ABC-CLIO for the opportunity to revisit the Stone Court.

There are some features of this book you should keep in mind as you read. An alphabetically arranged reference section provides information on selected people, legislative acts, executive actions, and agencies to supplement discussion found in the first four chapters. At the end of the reference section is a chronology of the period 1933–1946, which represents the dates of important Court decisions, major legislative enactments, personnel changes in the Court, and other events. A glossary of legal terms follows the reference section. There are also two appendices. The first discusses the relocation of the Japanese during World War II and contains selected documents pertaining to the relocation, including the executive order from President Roosevelt that began the relocation process. The second pertains to the frequently mentioned "preferred position" doctrine proposed by Justice Harlan Stone in a footnote to his opinion in *United States v. Carolene Products Co.* (1938). The text of this important footnote appears in Appendix II. Finally, there is an extensive annotated bibliography and, appended to the bibliography, an annotated list of Internet sources on the Supreme Court.

A number of people contributed to the production of this volume. I greatly appreciate the comments and suggestions I received from my colleagues on the third floor of Friedmann Hall. They clarified my thinking time and again. In addition, I received extraordinarily helpful comments from nationally recognized political scientists and constitutional historians. Each read at least one draft chapter and freely offered insightful suggestions. As a result of their review, I am much more confident of what I offer in this volume. Certainly, remaining errors of commission or omission are mine alone. Finally, much thanks to my wife, Bobbi. She talked me through bumps in the road, and she once again spent incalculable hours with red (or green) pen in hand affecting necessary repairs to my prose. Again, thanks to you all.

— *Peter G. Renstrom*

The Stone Court

PART ONE

Justices, Rulings, and Legacy

The Stone Court and the Period

The Stone Court was the Court of World War II. It was also the Court assembled by President Franklin D. Roosevelt that served during the last four years of his presidency. The Stone Court's roots were in the political and constitutional conflict of the 1930s, and its chronic internal disharmony a product of its members' conflicting views of the Court's role. The Stone Court addressed the complex questions prompted by a world war, and its principal legacy was that it began what would later become a comprehensive expansion of constitutional protections accorded individuals.

Harlan Fiske Stone, an associate justice of the U.S. Supreme Court since 1925, was nominated by President Franklin D. Roosevelt to become chief justice on June 12, 1941. Two weeks later he was confirmed by the U.S. Senate to replace Charles Evans Hughes, who was leaving the Court after serving eleven years as chief justice. The first term of the Stone Court began in October 1941. Chief Justice Stone died on April 22, 1946, and his colleagues completed the 1945 term of the Court in June 1946. The Stone Court lasted only five years, yet it ruled on some unusually important constitutional issues.

Stone's chief justiceship coincided almost exactly with the period during which the United States was a declared participant in World War II. At the time Stone became chief justice, German and Italian military advances in Europe and North Africa had already begun. Although the United States was still neutral in a technical sense, Roosevelt committed the United States to the support of its European allies, primarily Great Britain, through such initiatives as lend-lease. In August 1941 Roosevelt and British prime minister Winston Churchill fashioned an agreement known as the Atlantic Charter, calling for the military defeat of Hitler's Germany. The charter was not a declaration of war as such by the United States but articulated objectives as though it were. The Japanese attack on Pearl Harbor on December 7, 1941, brought a formal declaration of war against Japan the following day. Four days later, on December 11, 1941, the United States declared war against both Germany and Italy. The war in Europe concluded on May 7, 1945, and the war against Japan ended September 2, 1945. Chief Justice Stone died the following April.

The coincidence of the Stone Court era and World War II might suggest that the war exclusively defined the Stone Court period. Such was not the case. Indisputably, much of the Stone Court record was shaped by the war, either directly or indirectly. Setting the historical context for the Stone Court, however, requires going back at least a decade before the war to trace the influence of the Great Depression, the first two terms of the Roosevelt presidency, his economic recovery program known as the New Deal, and the Supreme Court's response to these initiatives. The chapter that follows represents the historical context within which I examine the Stone Court. In framing this context, I identify the major factors that influenced the Supreme Court's decision making, introduce the Stone Court justices and the circumstances attaching to the nominations of each, sketch the aggregate personality of the Stone Court, and characterize Chief Justice Stone's leadership style.

The Great Depression

Herbert Hoover was elected president in November 1928; he succeeded Calvin Coolidge, who chose not to seek reelection. The prosperity of the time all but ensured Hoover's election. These were good times in the United States; people prospered and, notwithstanding national prohibition, enjoyed the Roaring Twenties. The economic conditions that brought about Hoover's election changed so dramatically by 1932 that his bid for reelection was all but impossible. Although there was no forewarning of the Great Depression, its advent exposed some serious weaknesses in the existing economic and social order. The national ordeal produced by the economic emergency would not fully abate until the country geared up for war a decade later.

Recessions occur periodically, but the Great Depression was more severe and persistent than others. A number of factors account for the severity, though historians disagree which was the most important. One factor was lack of diversification in the economy of the 1920s. Prosperity had depended too heavily on a few basic industries, such as the manufacture of cars. A second factor was the highly uneven distribution of purchasing power and, as a result, a lack of broadly based consumer demand for various products. A third problem was the credit structure of the economy. Farmers were deeply in debt—their land was mortgaged and crop prices were too low to allow them to pay off what they owed. Small banks, especially those tied to the agricultural economy, were in constant trouble in the 1920s as their customers defaulted on loans. Many of these banks eventually failed.

The stock market crash in October 1929 did not cause the Great Depression; rather, it triggered a chain of events that revealed substantial weaknesses in the U.S. economy. During the next three years, the crisis grew steadily worse, and one of the most serious problems was the virtual collapse of the banking system. Over 9,000 banks went bankrupt or closed their doors to avoid bankruptcy between 1930 and 1933. Depositors lost over $2.5 billion, and one effect was that the nation's money supply fell by more than a third. Manufacturers and retailers began reducing prices, cutting back on production, and laying off workers. By late 1931, in a misguided effort to build international confidence in the dollar, the Federal Reserve raised interest rates, which contracted the money supply even further and hastened the demise of many banks and corporations.

The economic collapse was both rapid and devastating. Industrial production plummeted by half, and the gross national product (GNP) fell 25 percent in three years. Spending to promote capital growth dropped from $16.2 billion in 1929 to less than half a billion in 1933. By 1932, more than 25 percent of the U.S. 13 million people—were unemployed, and many of those were homeless. The Great Depression brought unprecedented destruction to the economies of the United States and much of the Western world. It had far-reaching effects on American society and culture as well. Consequences of the Depression were felt by everyone in the United States, including each of those justices who sat (or would sit) on the Stone Court.

President Hoover did not immediately recognize the severity of the depression, and his response was very measured. When he realized the gravity of the economic emergency, his political views shaped and limited the options he entertained to address the situation. As secretary of commerce and as president, Hoover believed that foreign markets were essential to U.S. growth, and he suspected that an inability to expand the volume of exports had contributed to the depression. He sought to improve the country's international trade standing, but the harsh economic conditions were too widespread for this approach to be effective. Hoover eventually recommended loans to relieve the plight of home owners. He created the Reconstruction Finance Corporation and the agency through which such relief could be obtained. Hoover's recovery strategy embraced the "trickle-down" theory—the assumption that full restoration of prosperity depended on recovery at the top of the economic system first. Hoover was reluctant to bring the full force of government to the economic emergency, at least at the outset. By the time he modified his approach, what he had to offer was too little too late.

Problems in the agricultural sector were evident even as President Hoover took office in March 1929. Hoover's program for farm relief was represented in the Agricultural Marketing Act of 1929, which called for voluntary decreases in agricultural production in an effort to elevate market prices. Hoover also called for an increase in agricultural tariffs. When the broader economic depression took hold, the difficulties in U.S. agriculture grew geometrically. The marketplace contracted because consumers limited their own spending. Even if this had not been the case, most farmers could not afford to move their crops to market. By 1932, net income of farmers slipped to about one-third of what it had been in 1929. Lenders were unwilling to renew mortgages as they came due. In 1932 more than half the total farm debt was in default. The situation in industry generally mirrored the conditions in agriculture. Factory orders fell off, production slowed down, and industries laid off their workers. Unemployment rose so that by 1933 about one-third of the population lacked jobs. Workers without earnings dipped into savings, reduced their expenditures, and tried to borrow.

The congressional elections of 1930 reflected widespread disillusionment with Hoover's management both of the government and the economy. In the new Congress, the Democrats had a majority in the House. The continuation of the depression enhanced the value of the Democratic presidential nomination. Through an alliance with Speaker of the House John Nance Garner of Texas, Roosevelt was able to secure the Democratic presidential nomination. The 1932 presidential election was as much an expression of discontent with Hoover's handling of the nation's affairs as it was an endorsement of specific programs or policies Roosevelt might propose.

Although he was regarded as a progressive, Franklin Roosevelt was not a social crusader as such. As late as 1931, Roosevelt, like Hoover, subscribed to the belief that relief should remain a private and local matter. Indeed, he criticized Hoover's proposal for increased public works spending as risking dangerous government budget deficits. Both Roosevelt and the Democratic platform called for a federal budget that was annually balanced. Roosevelt would soon thereafter modify his position.

The Democratic convention of 1932 was extraordinarily upbeat. It was the common view of partisans gathered in Chicago that virtually any candidate they nominated would defeat Hoover in the November general election. Roosevelt offered convention delegates a standard-bearer who would most effectively focus the economic issues and a candidate who might draw together urban and rural constituencies. Roosevelt was able to assemble a broad coalition within the Democratic Party and win the nomination. Roosevelt appeared before the convention to deliver his acceptance speech, declaring that "bold measures were needed" and pledging himself to a "new deal for the American people," thus coining the term that would subsequently identify his legislative program.

Hoover's unpopularity virtually assured Roosevelt's election, and he won by a landslide—57.4 percent of the popular vote. In February 1933, only a month before Roosevelt's inauguration, a new crisis developed when the collapse of the U.S. banking system suddenly and rapidly accelerated. By the time Roosevelt was inaugurated, most of the nation's banks were closed and national unemployment exceeded 13 million persons.

The New Deal

During the winter of 1932–1933 the economy continued to fail. As inauguration day approached, there was a general collapse of the private financial system. Roosevelt viewed the economic situation as a dire national emergency—an emergency analogous to a war. In Roosevelt's view, the situation required bold, immediate, and wideranging federal response. Roosevelt's first task was to alleviate the panic that was threatening the financial system. Two days after taking office, Roosevelt issued a proclamation closing all U.S. banks for four days until Congress could meet in special session to consider banking reform legislation. Three days later, Roosevelt sent to Congress the Emergency Banking Act, a proposal designed primarily to protect the larger banks from being dragged down by the weakness of smaller ones. Whatever else the new law accomplished, it helped dispel the panic. On the morning after the passage of the Emergency Banking Act, Roosevelt sent another measure to Congress, the Economy Act, which, among other things, established the Federal Deposit Insurance Corporation to guarantee bank deposits and restore public confidence in the banking system.

Historians typically divide the New Deal into two stages. The first, during 1933 and early 1934, was concerned more with relief and economic recovery and less with reform. The Emergency Banking Act was the first of the New Deal measures enacted during the period known as the Hundred Days—a time of remarkable executive and legislative activity from March 9 to June 16, 1933. Among the statutes enacted during the Hundred Days were the Civilian Conservation Corps Act, Agricultural Adjustment Act, Federal Emergency Relief Act, Tennessee Valley Authority Act, Federal Securities Act, and National Industrial Recovery Act.

Some of the New Deal initiatives produced no constitutional challenges and thus were never reviewed by the Supreme Court. Creation of the Civilian Conservation Corps, for example, was a straightforward relief measure enacted by Congress using its spending authority. Other New Deal programs were more suspect from a constitutional standpoint, however. One such program was the Agricultural Adjustment Act (AAA), which Congress passed in May 1933. At the time, farmers were unable to generate much if any disposable income because of the drastically low prices for agricultural commodities. The most important and novel feature of the AAA called for reducing production of particular crops to diminish agricultural surpluses. It was a simple matter of supply and demand. Reduction in the supply of agricultural commodities would theoretically elevate price. Under the terms of the AAA, farmers who reduced production were eligible for federal subsidies. The revenue to cover the benefit payments was to come from a tax on the food-processing industry. Unlike the program introduced by Hoover in 1929, participation was not voluntary. The AAA raised several constitutional questions that were addressed by the Hughes Court in 1936.

The most extensive attempt to regulate the national economy came in the National Industrial Recovery Act (NIRA), which Congress passed in June 1933. The regulatory provisions of the NIRA were not contained in the statute itself. Rather, the substantive regulations were to reside in codes of fair competition customized for each subset of the economy. The NIRA authorized councils in each industry, representing government, management, labor, and consumers. The councils adopted enforceable codes governing all the conditions of production, including production quotas allocated to each firm. The NIRA also created a new federal agency, the National Recovery Administration (NRA). Its director, Hugh Johnson, was to coordinate negotiation of specific of codes with leaders of the nation's major industries. The codes established minimums below which no business could lower prices or wages. More than 500 codes were approved through this process.

From the outset, however, the NRA encountered serious implementation difficulties. The codes were frequently poorly written and vague, and large producers typically dominated the code-writing process, with the result that regulations worked to the disadvantage of smaller firms. Besides the operational problems, the NIRA was vulnerable to constitutional challenge on at least two points: the scope of congressional authority over interstate commerce and the delegation of legislative power. Although Congress clearly had authority to regulate interstate commerce, the codes reached production activities that occurred before commerce began. Recognition of an interstate commerce power of unprecedented breadth was thus required to sustain the NIRA on commerce clause grounds. The code-making process called for in the NIRA also transferred virtually all of the substantive rule authority to the executive branch. Delegation of legislative power to such a degree was likewise unprecedented.

Although the New Deal programs helped stabilize the economy in 1933, there was only limited recovery beyond that; many of the basic problems of the Depression remained unsolved. Franklin Roosevelt enjoyed remarkable popularity during his first two years in office. Legal challenges to New Deal initiatives had not yet made their way to the Supreme Court by early 1935, but political criticism grew in intensity. In response to the continuing economic emergency as well as the growing political pressure, Roosevelt launched an ambitious new program of legislation that has been called the "second New Deal." The proposals contained in this second round of initiatives represented something of a shift in Roosevelt's priorities, from remedying the immediate effects of the depression to changing the economic system. Roosevelt now targeted corporate interests. The second wave of legislation included the National Labor Relations (Wagner-Connery) Act, Social Security Act, Public Utility Holding Company Act, Farm Mortgage Moratorium (Frazier-Lemke) Act, and Bituminous Coal Conservation Act. These programs dramatically altered the authority of the federal government as well as its relationship to society at large. The foundations of the modern welfare state were thus in place: Federal regulation over new areas of the economy had been extended, the modern labor movement had been nurtured, and the government had become a major influence in the agricultural economy. In addition, a new political coalition had been created, and the resulting realignment dominated the U.S. political scene for several decades to follow.

The Hughes Court Response

Although the Republicans charged that Roosevelt had done grievous damage to the Constitution, it was not until early 1935 that the Hughes Court ruled on the first New Deal enactments. A dozen decisions by the Supreme Court in the 1935–1936 term invalidated all or parts of eleven New Deal measures passed by the Democratic Congress. For one of the few times in U.S. constitutional history, the Supreme Court categorically rejected the major policy initiatives of the administration in power.

The Hughes Court was a profoundly divided Court from 1934 to 1937. Four very conservative justices—Willis Van Devanter, James McReynolds, George Sutherland, and Pierce Butler—were a bloc of unyielding laissez-fairists. These justices rejected any kind of governmental intervention with the economy and voted against every piece of New Deal legislation. The Hughes Court also included a liberal bloc composed of three justices—Louis Brandeis, Harlan Stone, and Benjamin Cardozo—that was generally receptive to New Deal programs. In between were Chief Justice Hughes and Owen Roberts, whose votes could make majorities of either bloc.

The Hughes Court upheld two state laws in 1934 aimed at coping with the economic emergency. The first was a mortgage moratorium law from Minnesota that exempted property under mortgage from foreclosure during the economic depression. The Minnesota law was primarily intended to protect against the foreclosure of farmland. Chief Justice Hughes said for the five-justice majority in *Home Building & Loan Association v. Blaisdell* (1934) that emergencies might furnish the "occasion for the exercise of power." Under such circumstances, the contract clause would not restrict the legislative pursuit of a compelling public good even when the terms of mortgage contracts were undeniably altered.

The same five justices—Hughes, Stone, Cardozo, Brandeis, and Roberts—upheld a New York law establishing a maximum retail price for milk in *Nebbia v. New York* (1934). Justice Roberts suggested that a state has wide discretion in setting economic policy that reasonably promotes the public welfare. These two decisions were seen by some as an indication that the Hughes Court might uphold New Deal enactments as well. This hope was misplaced, however. It was one thing that five justices supported state, as distinct from federal, policies. It was quite another to think that such deference would transfer to federal regulatory initiatives.

The first New Deal case decided by the Hughes Court was *Panama Refining*

Co. v. Ryan (1935). By an 8–1 vote, the Court invalidated provisions of the National Industrial Recovery Act dealing with oil production. Like other sectors of the economy, the oil industry was suffering from low prices resulting from overproduction. Section 9(C) of the NIRA, known as the "hot oil" section, authorized the president to prohibit the interstate shipment of oil produced in excess of quotas fixed by the states. Over the single dissent of Justice Cardozo, the Hughes Court struck down section 9(C) on delegation of legislative power grounds. In the Court's view, Congress had not established a primary policy standard, leaving the executive branch without a clear direction to follow. The *Panama Refining* decision was a much better indicator of what was in store for the New Deal measures remaining on the Court's docket.

Less than six weeks later, the Hughes Court decided several cases known in aggregate as the "gold clause cases" (*Norman v. Baltimore & Ohio Railroad, United States v. Bankers Trust Co., Nortz v. United States*, and *Perry v. United States* [1935]). As part of the monetary reforms enacted in 1933, Congress restricted ownership and trade of gold, one objective of which was to set the stage for devaluation of the dollar. The same five justices who had upheld the state milk and mortgage moratorium statutes now found sufficient constitutional authority to allow federal prohibition of gold clauses in private contracts, among other things. The gold clause cases provided the Roosevelt administration with an endorsement of its monetary reform objectives, but it was only a partial and unenthusiastic endorsement. The feeling at the time was that the fragile five-justice coalition in these cases would fracture at the earliest opportunity.

That opportunity presented itself less than three months later when, on May 6, Justice Roberts broke away and joined the four dissenters from the milk and mortgage cases to strike down the Railroad Retirement Act of 1934, which mandated pensions for the employees of the nation's railroads. Even Hughes, Brandeis, Stone, and Cardozo agreed with the majority in *Railroad Retirement Board v. Alton Railroad Co.* (1935) that Congress had acted arbitrarily in the part of the law that extended pensions to persons no longer employed by the companies. Although striking down the act affected only railroad employees, the conclusions contained in Roberts's opinion placed a number of enactments as well as pending proposals in doubt.

Three weeks later, a unanimous Court struck down the portions of the NIRA that remained after the *Panama Refining* decision. *Schechter Poultry Corp. v. United States* (1935) invalidated the process set out in the NIRA for making codes of fair competition. Once again, the defect was excessive delegation of legislative power. The NIRA did not delegate a limited amount of authority but instead vested enormous rule-making authority within the executive branch. Even the three justices most likely to support New Deal measures, Stone, Brandeis, and Cardozo, could not support the NIRA code-making process. The process was, in Justice Cardozo's words, "delegation run riot."

The "sick chicken" case, as it was called, was a defeat for Roosevelt: From the outset of his presidency the NIRA had been the cornerstone of his economic recovery plan. More than 700 codes were crafted within two years of the enactment of the NIRA. By the time the Court decided *Schechter Poultry*, however, the regulatory framework of the NIRA was collapsing and would have been abandoned even without *Schechter*. The more disturbing aspect of the *Schechter* ruling was that the Court went beyond the delegation of legislative power issue and indicated that the federal commerce power could not reach businesses such as Schechter's. If the *Schechter* view of the commerce power remained, there would be no constitutional basis for any substantial federal regulation of the economy.

In its 1935–1936 term, the Hughes Court remained wholly unreceptive to the Roosevelt agenda. On January 6, 1936, six justices invalidated the Agricultural Adjustment Act in *United States v. Butler* (1936). Unlike the situation with the NIRA, the Roosevelt administration was fully committed to the AAA, believing it to be an effective approach for restoring price stability for agricultural products. The AAA was also strongly endorsed by the nation's farmers. The central premise of the statute was that prices would stabilize only when production was controlled—less production would reduce commodity supplies, which in turn would elevate prices. Under the AAA, the federal government would pay farmers for reducing the number of acres under production. The revenue for benefit payments was to come from a tax levied against food processors. Justice Roberts's majority opinion suggested that the general welfare clause of Article I, section 8 could sustain the kind of tax contained in the AAA, but the Court found the law unconstitutional because it attempted to regulate agriculture. In doing so, the federal law impermissibly entered the domain of the sovereign states. The taxing power aside, the Tenth Amendment and its reserve clause prevented federal regulation of agricultural production.

Two months after *Butler*, the Court struck down the Bituminous Coal Conservation (Guffey) Act of 1935 in *Carter v. Carter Coal Co.* (1936). The Guffey Act sought to address distressed conditions in the bituminous coal industry through a combination of price-fixing and labor regulations. The act created local boards that would establish codes setting minimum prices for coal. The act also provided that labor issues pertaining to wages and hours of work were to be determined through collective bargaining. In a 5–4 decision, the Court concluded that the regulations were directed primarily at problems of production, an activity distinct and prior to commerce. Thus, congressional authority to regulate interstate commerce could not provide the basis for this law.

A recurring theme of the Hughes Court's decisions on New Deal initiatives was the protection and preservation of state sovereignty. On June 1, 1936, however, the Court invalidated a state minimum wage law for women in *Morehead v. New York ex rel. Tipaldo*. *Morehead* revealed the primacy of economic laissez-faire as the basis for invalidating regulatory initiatives by government; the exercise of federal power was not the only source of forbidden regulation. Roberts joined the four dissenters from *Nebbia* and *Blaisdell,* who reasserted the "freedom of contract" concept commonly found in the substantive due process decisions. Rulings such as *Schechter, Butler, Carter,* and *Morehead* spotlighted the constitutional struggle between Roosevelt and the Supreme Court.

The Election of 1936—the "Referendum" on the New Deal

Uncertainty about the constitutionality of New Deal legislation increased the importance of the Supreme Court in the presidential election of 1936. But the Court remained a back-burner issue in the Roosevelt campaign, as he chose not to engage in Court bashing prior to the election. A direct attack on the Court by Roosevelt during the campaign might have been helpful to Republican challenger Alf Landon by reinforcing the perception of some that Roosevelt's power was approaching "dictatorial" levels. The presidential election of 1936 was seen in most quarters as a national referendum on Roosevelt and the New Deal. When Roosevelt polled just under 61 percent in the popular vote and carried every state except Vermont and Maine in the 1936 election, he and the Democrats claimed a broad mandate. The results were a clear confirmation of Roosevelt and his programs. In a message to Congress on January 6, 1937, Roosevelt said that the "judicial branch also is asked by the people to do its part in making democracy successful." It was not yet clear what this would mean.

The 1936 election marked the high point of Roosevelt's popularity. Within months, however, the New Deal was mired in serious new difficulties resulting from continuing Republican opposition, certainly, but also the president's own political errors and a major economic setback. In early 1937 the fragile economy took a serious downturn. Several million additional workers lost their jobs, and economic conditions were soon almost as bad as they had been at the outset of Roosevelt's presidency. The recession of 1937 was produced by a number of factors. Many observers at the time saw the latest economic woes as stemming from the administration's decision to reduce government spending, and the crisis prompted Roosevelt to reevaluate his policy priorities. It also prompted Roosevelt to address his difficulties with the Supreme Court.

Reforming the Courts: The Court-Packing Proposal

The Court was a major obstacle to Roosevelt and his policies. During the Hundred Days at the start of his presidency, Roosevelt placed nearly two dozen measures before Congress, and it responded by enthusiastically enacting all of them. The Hughes Court, however, imposed a judicial veto. The Court, dubbed the "Nine Old Men" by some critics, said no to virtually all of the New Deal legislation, typically by 6–3 or 5–4 votes. Roosevelt could count on the votes of only Justices Brandeis, Stone, and Cardozo. The Four Horsemen—Justices Van Devanter, Butler, McReynolds, and Sutherland—were categorically opposed to Roosevelt's initiatives. The Horsemen got the votes of Chief Justice Hughes and Justice Roberts often enough to prevail through this period. Had Roosevelt been able to replace one or two of the obstructionist justices during his first term, it is unlikely that any serious constitutional confrontation would have occurred. When Roosevelt entered his second term, however, he had been unable to replace even one justice, and frustration got the better of him.

The Hughes Court had exercised a judicial veto over the Roosevelt legislative program to an unprecedented extent, and the president felt compelled to respond. Roosevelt contemplated several options. The least attractive was to maintain the status quo. He feared that the Court's conservative naysayers would hang on indefinitely, possibly until the end of his presidency. Roosevelt was also convinced that his reelection in 1936 would not induce a "conversion" by one or more of the obstructing justices. Waiting for these justices to change their minds or leaving the Court alone had a considerable downside. Without some kind of intervention, more of his legislative agenda would surely fall victim to the Court. His advisers suggested constitutional amendments. One possible amendment would specifically authorize Congress to take the kind of regulatory action the Court found objectionable, such as regulating labor relations or agricultural production. If the Constitution were amended in this way, the Court obviously could not find such regulatory initiatives unconstitutional. Another possible amendment had a procedural focus: An amendment could limit the Court's judicial review function by allowing congressional override of any measure the Court found unconstitutional or requiring an extraordinary majority of the justices to find congressional acts unconstitutional.

Another option focused on the justices themselves, who were, of course, the root cause of Roosevelt's difficulties. This option was entertained by Roosevelt as early as January 1935 and had become his preferred response by January 1937. On February 5, 1937, Roosevelt unveiled the Judicial Reorganization Act, an unparalleled attempt by a president to influence constitutional interpretation by means of a direct assault on the Supreme Court itself. The initiative came without forewarning— Roosevelt had not hinted at such action during the campaign the previous fall, nor had he sought the counsel of his inner circle of advisers or the Democratic congressional leadership.

The proposal Roosevelt submitted would have given him the authority to appoint an additional jurist for each federal judge who, having served ten years or more, failed to retire within six months of his seventieth birthday. The additional judge would be assigned to the same court on which the seventy-year-old judge was serving. Under the proposal, no more than fifty additional judges (for the entire federal judicial system) could be appointed. The maximum size of the Supreme Court was set at fifteen. Had the plan become law, Roosevelt would have been able to move immediately to the fifteen-justice maximum, since six of the Nine Old Men were over seventy years of age. At the point the proposal was introduced, the justices' ages ranged from eighty-one (Justice Brandeis) to sixty-two (Justice Roberts), but each of the Four Horsemen and the chief justice were older than seventy.

The message behind Roosevelt's proposal was that the Court was overburdened by "insufficient personnel" and the physical disabilities of the jurists. The courts were "overworked," he claimed, and they needed additional and younger appointees to enable them to cope with their increasing caseloads. The real reason for Roosevelt's action was, of course, obvious to all: Roosevelt wanted to end the Hughes Court's veto of the New Deal programs.

Opponents of the bill at first had little hope of defeating the proposal. But opposition began to develop from an unexpected source. Conservative southern Democrats were cross-pressured by their party loyalty and their commitment to traditional views about the Constitution and the Supreme Court. The defection of Senator Burton Wheeler of Montana was serious as well. Like many Senate Democrats, Wheeler was a critic of the Court and was prepared to give Congress the authority to reverse Court decisions. He saw Roosevelt's proposal, however, as threatening the institutional independence of the federal judiciary.

On March 9, 1937, Roosevelt broadcast the first fireside chat of his second term and appealed to the American people on the judicial "reform" issue. This speech stated the central issue more candidly than did the official statements offered in support of the proposal initially. The issue was transformed from one involving adjustments to the federal judiciary to a question about the political role of the Court. In Roosevelt's view, the Hughes Court had been acting as a policymaking body, and the proposed reform of the Court would "bring to the decision of social and economic problems younger men who have had personal experience and contact with modern facts." Roosevelt promised to appoint justices "who will act as Justices, not as legislators."

Justice Brandeis, the Court's most liberal and pro–New Deal member, was deeply offended by the proposal and the accompanying rationale. Brandeis suggested to Chief Justice Hughes that a public response was in order. Soon thereafter, Hughes wrote a letter to Senator Wheeler and statistically demonstrated that the Court was fully current with its docket. The judicial "reform" proposal also fatally split the Democratic majority in the Senate and caused a storm of protest from the bench and bar. On June 14 the Senate Judiciary Committee reported the Court-packing proposal to the full Senate, but with an adverse vote of 10–8. A month later the Senate sent it back to the Judiciary Committee on a 70–20 vote. The proposal was dead, and the

Court had survived Roosevelt's political confrontation, at least in the sense that Congress had not approved a change in its size. That is not quite how the episode concluded, however.

During the several months the proposal was languishing in the Senate, two other related events took place. First, the Court decided several cases in a way more favorable to those supporting federal regulatory power. Chief Justice Hughes and Justice Roberts broke away from the Four Horsemen to produce the changed outcomes. These votes were called by some the "switch in time that saved nine." The first of these cases was decided on March 29, 1937, when the Court sustained a states minimum wage law for women in *West Coast Hotel v. Parrish*. The second ruling occurred on April 12, when the Court upheld, again by a 5–4 vote, the National Labor Relations Act of 1935 (NLRA, or Wagner Act). On May 24 the Court decided *Steward Machine Co. v. Davis* (1937) and *Helvering v. Davis* (1937). These rulings upheld the old-age tax and benefits and unemployment provisions of the Social Security Act of 1935. Hughes and Roberts later denied that their switched votes were motivated by the Court-packing proposal, but few viewed their change of mind as anything but a recognition of political realities. Although it was premature to conclude the Court's new voting alignment would be maintained, the outcomes in these cases seemed to moot the need for the Court-packing plan.

The second major event followed closely on the heels of the Court's upholding the Social Security Act in *Steward Machine* and *Helvering v. Davis*. The oldest of the Four Horsemen, seventy-eight-year-old justice Willis Van Devanter, announced in mid-May that he would retire from the Court at the end of June. He was the first anti–New Deal justice to surrender to the reality that a constitutional revolution was under way and he could not stop it. Byrnes's advice became even more compelling. The remaining Horsemen would take the same path soon thereafter. Roosevelt did not withdraw the proposal, however, and the day after Van Devanter's announcement, the Senate Judiciary Committee recommended that the Court-packing bill be rejected. Nevertheless, Roosevelt finally had his first Court vacancy. He would have eight other opportunities to pick justices over the next six years.

On one level, the Court-packing affair constituted something of a victory for Roosevelt. The Court was no longer an obstacle to New Deal reforms, particularly after the older justices began to retire. At the same time, the episode did long-lasting political damage to the Roosevelt. From 1937 on, support from southern Democrats and other conservatives for Roosevelt's programs decreased markedly. The falloff was so substantial that Roosevelt attempted to purge a number of nonsupportive Democrats in the congressional elections of 1938. For the most part, this initiative was unsuccessful, further aggravating Roosevelt's problems with Congress.

The "Other" War: From Neutrality to Intervention

Roosevelt and the country were preoccupied with economic recovery until the late 1930s. The constitutional crisis of the mid-1930s was precipitated by actions taken by Roosevelt and Congress in response to the domestic emergency caused by the Great Depression. By the latter part of the decade, however, significant foreign policy issues had taken center stage. There was strong isolationist sentiment in the country during this period, and Roosevelt did not feel compelled to confront it. Indeed, he publicly asserted that the country would remain neutral. At the same time, Roosevelt was not an isolationist but was clearly sympathetic to Britain, France, and the other Allied nations. The question was whether the United States would formally assist them and, if so, to what extent. The underlying question was whether the president or Congress would control U.S. foreign policy.

The Hughes Court addressed the issue of executive prerogatives in foreign policy in two mid-1930s cases. The Court, Roosevelt's bitter opponent on issues arising out of domestic economic policy initiatives, gave the executive something of a blank check in foreign affairs, in keeping with the long-standing view that the president possessed primary responsibility for the conduct of foreign policy. The first case, *United States v. Curtiss-Wright Export Corp.* (1936), involved review of a congressional resolution that authorized the president to prohibit arms sales to both Bolivia and Paraguay, nations at war with one another at the time. Once arms sales were prohibited, the sale of any weaponry to either country constituted a crime. The Curtiss-Wright Corporation was indicted for selling military equipment to Bolivia. The Hughes Court, with only Justice McReynolds dissenting, rejected Curtiss-Wright's contention that Congress had excessively delegated power to the executive. In doing so, Justice Sutherland recognized implied executive powers in the area of foreign policy. The constitutional limits on implied power applies "only in respect to internal affairs." Effective conduct of foreign policy requires that the president possess a "degree of discretion and freedom from statutory restriction which would not be admissible were domestic affairs alone involved" (*Curtiss-Wright*, 315–316, 320).

Several months later, the Hughes Court ruled in *United States v. Belmont* (1937) that a president may conduct foreign policy through executive agreements. An executive agreement is an agreement with another country that resembles a treaty but that does not require Senate approval to have effect. In *Belmont* the Court concluded that the conduct of foreign relations was the exclusive domain of the "political [elective] departments" of government, and was "not subject to judicial inquiry." Furthermore, the Hughes Court said that authority over external affairs "is not distributed, but vested exclusively in the national government"; within the federal government, the Court saw the president as the "sole organ of that government" (*Belmont*, 328, 331). The effect of the *Curtiss-Wright* and *Belmont* rulings made it unlikely that

Roosevelt's actions could be successfully challenged on constitutional grounds. Whatever restraint applied to Roosevelt at this time was exclusively political.

The Hitler regime furiously engaged in German rearmament, and Italy invaded Ethiopia. Concerned that the United States might intervene, Congress enacted the Neutrality Act of 1935, which significantly restricted presidential options with respect to foreign affairs. The act required, for example, an embargo on weaponry to countries engaged in warfare. The act was amended in 1937 to further restrict arms sales and financial assistance to any warring country. By this time Roosevelt felt compelled to protest the restrictions imposed on the executive and the isolationist sentiment on which the restrictions were grounded. Roosevelt believed the United States should assist the Allies to help them counter the military advantage then possessed by Germany, but he could not persuade Congress to remove or even modify the legislative restrictions. Failure to obtain congressional support did not prevent Roosevelt from taking some action nonetheless. It was Roosevelt's view that the role of commander in chief gave the president inherent power—the authority to effectively meet any international emergency by virtually any means. In September 1939 Germany invaded Poland. Once again Roosevelt asked Congress to revise the Neutrality Act, and the 1939 version of the act allowed Allied arms purchases on a cash-and-carry basis.

Whatever illusions Americans had harbored about the war in western Europe were shattered in the spring of 1940 when Germany invaded first Denmark and Norway then swept into the Netherlands, Belgium, and France. Roosevelt had already taken actions without congressional approval. For example, he used an executive agreement to circumvent the cash-and-carry provisions of the Neutrality Acts, giving Britain fifty U.S. destroyers in return for the right to build U.S. bases in British territories. Roosevelt was able to take such steps in part because American public opinion had shifted and seemed now to support these actions. Even Congress was becoming more concerned about the need to prepare for war, and in September 1940 it approved the Burke-Wadworth Act, inaugurating the first peacetime military draft in U.S. history.

In the election of 1940, Roosevelt received 55 percent of the popular vote and won 449 electoral votes to Wendell Willkie's 82. In late 1940, with the election behind him and the situation in Europe deteriorating, Roosevelt began to make profound changes in U.S. policy regarding the war. Roosevelt sought to accommodate the needs of the country's allies, nonetheless suggesting that the United States should serve as the "arsenal of democracy." The president proposed a new system for supplying Britain on a "lend-lease" basis. The United States could funnel weapons to England with no more than Britain's promise to return them when the war was over. Isolationists attacked the measure bitterly, but Congress enacted the Lend-Lease Act by a wide margin in March 1941. With lend-lease in place, Roosevelt faced the problem of attacks by German submarines in Atlantic shipping lanes. By July 1941, U.S. ships were patrolling the ocean as far east as Iceland.

Germany did not immediately respond to the actions of the United States. By September 1941, however, the situation changed. German forces had invaded the Soviet Union in June, but when the Soviets did not surrender, Roosevelt persuaded Congress to extend lend-lease privileges to the Soviet Union. This made the United States the principal producer of war materials for Germany's declared enemies on two war fronts. In addition, the U.S. Navy was protecting the shipment of those goods to Europe. In October, when Nazi submarines attacked two U.S. destroyers and inflicted casualties on American sailors, Congress voted to allow the United States to arm its merchant vessels and to sail all the way into British and Soviet ports. In effect, this commenced a naval war against Germany. In August 1941 Roosevelt met with Churchill aboard a British vessel off the coast of Newfoundland. The president made no military commitments as such, but he did join with Churchill in releasing a document that became known as the Atlantic Charter, in which the two nations set out certain "common principles" on which to base a "better future for the world." It called openly for a "final destruction" of the Nazi tyranny and for a new world order in which every nation could control its own destiny. It was, in effect, a statement of war objectives.

Meanwhile, the situation in Asia was moving toward full-fledged war. The Japanese drove into the five northern provinces of China during the summer of 1937. Japan did not formally declare war, and Roosevelt did not invoke the Neutrality Acts, but within a year Japan was making conditions almost untenable for Americans in China. Roosevelt believed that emergencies expanded presidential powers and the threat of war in Europe and in Asia allowed him to proclaim the existence of such emergencies. He declared an "unlimited" emergency, at least within the Western Hemisphere, to justify taking various defensive measures. This emergency rationale was subsequently applied across the Atlantic and the Pacific.

The debate about the war was bitter, and through the summer and fall of 1940 it was complicated by the presidential election. The Republicans met in Philadelphia in June at the time of the collapse of France. National defense suddenly became the most important issue. Roosevelt seized on this need and stole headlines from the Republican convention by appointing to his cabinet two distinguished Republicans. He made the elder statesman Henry Stimson secretary of war and Frank Knox, the 1936 vice presidential candidate and sharp critic of the New Deal, secretary of the navy.

Japan saw the European crisis as an opportunity to extend its empire. The German invasion of the Soviet Union allayed one of Japan's major fears at the time: possible intervention by the Soviets if the Japanese moved into China. The German attack prompted Japan to move against Indochina and Thailand. The short-term response from Western countries was to freeze all Japanese assets. War with Japan, however, was now seen as inevitable. The attack on Pearl Harbor almost rendered the United States impotent in the Pacific, but the nation was suddenly unified for the global war into which it had been precipitated.

It is clear that the president possesses far-reaching authority over the conduct of foreign affairs. When the power of commander in chief is added during wartime, executive authority has virtually no limit. Such was the case with Roosevelt in the months leading to Pearl Harbor and for the duration of World War II. Not only did he expand executive power through the use of executive orders, but Congress enhanced executive authority by statute as well. The Neutrality Act of 1939 and the Lend-Lease Act of 1941 are examples of legislative measures that predated Pearl Harbor. Following Pearl Harbor, Congress passed the first and second War Powers Acts, which gave Roosevelt the power to organize and reorganize government as he saw fit to enable him to meet the demands of war. Roosevelt was empowered to mobilize the country for war and then coordinate all aspects of the war effort through executive actions. Presidential control over the military was never in doubt. Such acts as the Emergency Price Control Act and War Labor Disputes Act enabled Roosevelt to exercise full control over the wartime economy.

Mobilization for war presented an array of problems. One of the most critical needs was the effective recruitment of armed forces. In the summer of 1939, the U.S. Army numbered 174,000 men. Two years later it had expanded to 1.4 million. By the end of the war, it had grown to 8.3 million, with 3.4 million more in the navy and 484,000 in the marines. In all, some 15 million men and women enrolled in the armed services. A majority of them came by way of the draft. A one-year selective service law enacted in September 1940 was extended in August 1941 and registered 31 million men. Industrial America was converted to war production and was able to supply not only U.S. military needs but those of the British, Russians, and Chinese as well.

Under conditions of world war, Roosevelt believed that besides serving as commander in chief directing military operations in the European and Pacific theaters of wars, he could manage the economy and other domestic matters with comparable authority. The Emergency Price Control Act (EPCA) of 1942 gave Roosevelt unprecedented power to regulate domestic wages and prices; the effects of the Great Depression gave way to the needs brought on by the war; presidential authority expanded by virtue of national security as it had expanded in response to the economic emergency.

The Axis had the Allies on the defensive at the outset of World War II. It took almost two years from the date of Pearl Harbor to reverse fortunes in Europe. The D-day invasion of June 1944 was the beginning of the end of the European war, although Germany did not actually surrender until May 1945. Allied successes in the Pacific essentially followed the same timetable. Victory in the battle for Okinawa in late June 1945 was the penultimate step to the conclusion of the Pacific war. Dropping the atomic bomb on Hiroshima and Nagasaki in early August 1945 brought the surrender of the Japanese.

The costs borne by Americans in World War II were enormous. Battle deaths exceeded 400,000. Almost 700,000 more Americans were wounded and another

140,000 missing or captured. The United States spent in excess of $300 billion on the war. The Supreme Court was a nonplayer in the decision making about the conduct of the war and would have deferred to executive authority had it been asked. There were, however, several sets of war-related issues that reached the Stone Court during the war.

The executive branch had been given extensive authority to regulate private property under the Emergency Price Control Act of 1942. Orders from the Office of Price Administration (OPA), the agency through which the act was implemented, were challenged in several cases that reached the Stone Court, but the regulatory actions were sustained in all cases. There were also cases stemming from administration of the Selective Service Act. Again, in virtually every instance the Stone Court deferred to the determinations of the executive branch. The Court also reviewed the cases involving denaturalization orders issued against Nazi sympathizers. Here the Stone Court was less deferential to government efforts to strip such persons of their citizenship.

A number of criminal prosecutions on charges of treason, espionage, and war crimes involved noncitizens as defendants. Although the Stone Court noted that such criminal defendants are entitled to basic legal rights, the Court recognized broad power of the executive to create special military tribunals to hear such cases. Finally, there was the matter of Japanese residing in the United States. Most of these residents were citizens, but the attack on Pearl Harbor prompted anti-Japanese sentiment that reached the level of hysteria. The government moved against these people, initially through an executive order from President Roosevelt, subjecting them first to curfew restrictions and later to relocation. The Stone Court reviewed several cases involving relocation and chose not interfere with the action, at least until the government was ready to abandon the policy.

Assembling the Stone Court

The selection of justices serving on the Stone Court unfolded in an unusual fashion. Two of the justices, Stone and Roberts, had served on the Supreme Court for more than a decade when Stone became chief justice. President Hoover nominated Benjamin Cardozo for the Court in February 1932. The next nomination of a Supreme Court justice would not occur until June 1937, when Justice Willis Van Devanter left the Court. This period of more than five years spanned all of Roosevelt's first term. At a time when he needed the Court's support, Roosevelt was unable to make the personnel changes necessary to obtain it. This was perhaps the most important factor prompting Roosevelt to pursue his Court-packing scheme.

Once Van Devanter retired, Roosevelt was given more than ample opportunity to reshape the Court. Following Hugo Black's nomination in August 1937, Roosevelt nominated three additional justices in the next nineteen months. By June 1941 the number of nominations had increased to seven, including Stone's elevation to chief justice. In other words, a span of almost five and a half years when no new justices were appointed was followed immediately by a period of less than four years when eight changes were made to the Court. Only George Washington nominated more people for the Court than Roosevelt did during these four years. Unlike those in other eras, none of Roosevelt's nominations were politically troublesome or stirred much controversy, with the exception of the furor over Black's association with the Ku Klux Klan. Furthermore, the Democrats controlled the Senate, thus ensuring that virtually any Roosevelt nominee for the Court would be confirmed. They were distinguished men by anyone's standards: Black and Felix Frankfurter have generally been ranked as great by Court experts, and William O. Douglas, Robert Jackson, and Wiley Rutledge as near great—a record of professional approbation for Court appointees no other president has attained.

The first Stone Court justice appointed to the Court was Stone himself. He was nominated by President Calvin Coolidge on January 25, 1925. Stone was an academic when he came to Washington in 1924 at the call of his classmate Calvin Coolidge, who was attempting to clean up the mess from the Teapot Dome scandal that had occurred late in President Warren Harding's tenure. Coolidge wanted Stone to replace Attorney General Harry M. Daugherty, whose Justice Department had not distinguished itself in investigating Teapot Dome. Stone's performance as attorney general was exemplary. When Joseph McKenna left the Court in 1925, many expected Coolidge to nominate a westerner, but Stone's help with Coolidge's reelection in 1924 and the independence he exhibited as attorney general made him the obvious choice. The nomination was met with all-but-universal approbation.

Senator Burton Wheeler of Montana did not support Stone because he would not drop a case brought against Wheeler by Stone's predecessor. Unanimous Senate confirmation was impossible as a result, but Stone was easily confirmed 71–6. At one point prior to the confirmation vote, it was suggested that the Stone nomination be withdrawn, but Coolidge refused to consider it. The Senate recommitted the matter to the Judiciary Committee, where Stone made a personal appearance, the first Court nominee ever to do so. Stone was grilled extensively by several hostile committee members, but he handled the questioning deftly, and the committee recommended his confirmation without dissent.

The decision to nominate Stone was Coolidge's alone, although several others claimed credit, including Chief Justice William Howard Taft. According to Henry Abraham, Stone's nomination was "entirely natural" in that Stone was exceptionally well qualified and had a long-standing association with Coolidge. Stone seemed a safe appointment for Coolidge. He had been a corporation lawyer in his private practice and had "excellent Republican credentials" (Abraham 1992, 194–195). Yet Stone's performance on the Court probably would have disappointed Coolidge. Within a year of his appointment, Stone joined Justices Oliver Wendell Holmes and Brandeis as dissenters in a number of Taft Court cases. Dissent rates on the Taft Court were generally low, but Stone's dissent rate of 5.6 percent over the last three years of Taft's chief justiceship was third highest, behind Holmes and Brandeis (Goldman 1991, 100). Stone's alignment with Holmes and Brandeis, later Brandeis and Cardozo, led some to characterize him as a liberal, mainly because they voted opposite from the ultraconservative Hughes Court majority. Stone wasn't a liberal but was "fiercely independent" (Abraham 1992, 197).

Stone was expected to closely follow the lead of Chief Justice Taft. By his second year, however, he had begun to "slide away from Taft's shadow" and often attempted to distance himself from the conservative Four Horsemen (Johnson 1994, 426). During the 1935–1936 terms of the Hughes Court, the period just preceding the advent of the Roosevelt Court, Stone supported government regulation of the economy in 97.7 percent of the cases involving that issue. Only Cardozo's support rate of 97.9 percent was higher, with Brandeis a close third at 95.8 percent. In this same period, Chief Justice Hughes supported such regulation in 66.7 percent of the cases and Justice Roberts in 50 percent. By comparison, the so-called Four Horsemen voted in support of economic regulation in less than one case in four—Van Devanter at 25.5 percent, Sutherland 20.8 percent, Butler 12.5 percent, and McReynolds 10.4 percent (Goldman 1991, 101).

Roosevelt elevated Stone to chief justice with some reluctance. Roosevelt preferred Robert Jackson, a New Deal loyalist of long standing, and he was aware that Jackson wanted the chief justiceship very much. Roosevelt discussed the replacement with Hughes, however, who suggested that Stone's record gave him "first claim." Stone's five years as chief justice were less than satisfactory; he did not compare favorably with those identified as "strong" chief justices. This view of Stone was certainly affected by the particularly fragmented Court over which Stone presided. Stone differed from his colleagues on the right (during the Hughes Court era) who interposed their own social and economic predilections under the guise of interpreting the Constitution. During his tenure as chief justice, Stone was "at odds with colleagues on the left who were equally set on using their judicial office to further some political preference" (Mason 1995, 1102).

Owen Roberts was the second of Herbert Hoover's appointees to the Court. Hoover favored prospective nominees with prior judicial experience; Roberts was his only selection who had no such experience. Following his selection of Charles Evans Hughes to replace Chief Justice Taft, Hoover's chance to nominate another justice came with the death of Justice Edward Sanford. Hoover looked to the South for a successor, as Sanford had been from Tennessee. He chose a well-known and well-liked North Carolina Republican, Judge John J. Parker of the U.S. Court of Appeals for the

Fourth Circuit. Parker was rejected in a 41–39 Senate vote, however, in a decision Henry Abraham has suggested was both "unfair and regrettable" (Abraham 1992, 202). Parker had upheld a yellow-dog contract (an employment contract that prevents workers from joining a union) and had allegedly made an insensitive remark about minorities participating in politics. The defeat of Parker brought about the nomination of Roberts. Hoover sought a candidate who would not "stir factional feeling" in the Senate, and Roberts fully met this political condition.

Roberts was a Pennsylvanian who represented railroads in his private practice and otherwise possessed "impeccable Republican credentials." He served as the government's special prosecutor for the Teapot Dome oil scandals. Roberts received national recognition for his performance in this capacity. His nomination to the Court in 1930 was applauded by all parts of the political spectrum. As it turned out, Roberts did not please either political wing.

Roberts was a political centrist or neutralist who occasionally supported liberal policy preferences. More often, he aligned with the ultraconservative Four Horsemen on economic regulation issues, at least prior to 1937. In the 1935 and 1936 terms of the Hughes Court, Roberts voted in support of federal economic regulations in half the cases. This placed him in the statistical middle of the Court during those two terms, with sizable support rate gaps on either side of him. Hughes, with a 66.7 percent support rate, was closest on his left, and Van Devanter, at 25.5 percent, was closest on his right. Roberts and Hughes began to align themselves more frequently with the proregulation justices following the Court-packing episode in 1937. Although Roberts was instrumental in effecting the Court's doctrinal change on economic regulation issues in 1937, he reverted to more and more conservative responses to such federal initiatives as the Court underwent its extensive personnel changes between 1937 and 1941. He became the Stone Court justice least receptive to federal regulatory measures.

Roberts became embittered during his last years on the bench. He had seemed to vacillate during his tenure on the Court, but by the time he retired in 1945 he was isolated to the right of everyone. During his last term, he dissented from the Court's decisions in about one-third of the cases. While on the Hughes Court, he was driven back toward more conservative positions by the "vehemence of Black's judicial radicalism, while the subtleties of Frankfurter's argumentation did not equip him to deal on equal terms with others in the intellectual melee of Stone's Court." His "handicap as a constitutional lawgiver" was his inability to break with the past while "entertaining a sympathy for the arguments favoring change." He spent his time on the Court "seeking a firm continuity from the old legality to the new, never understanding how the revolution of 1933–37 had destroyed the possibility of continuity" (Swindler 1974, 134).

Hugo Black was Roosevelt's first nominee. Roosevelt was seeking justices who subscribed, at least generally, to libertarian objectives. Roosevelt also was seeking justices who were unquestionably loyal to the political and economic principles underlying the New Deal. When Justice Willis Van Devanter retired, the leading candidate to replace him was Senator Joseph T. Robinson of Arkansas, Democratic majority leader of the Senate. Robinson faithfully supported every New Deal proposal and was the point man in the attempt to pass Roosevelt's Court-packing proposal. While the proposal was still pending before the Senate, Robinson was stricken with a fatal heart attack. Roosevelt then instructed Attorney General Homer Cummings to come up with a list of other possible nominees. The list that emerged contained the names of several men who would all eventually join the Court: Solicitor General Stanley Reed, Senator Sherman Minton (D-IN), Senator Hugo Black (D-AL), and Assistant Attorney General Robert Jackson.

The need to appoint an economic liberal was the highest priority for Roosevelt's first nomination. The Hughes Court had begun to take a new direction on issues relating to federal economic regulation in 1937, but the new majority contained only five votes and was extremely fragile in that it depended on the continued votes of Hughes and Roberts. The difficulty facing Roosevelt was securing Senate confirmation for his selection. Even though the Democrats controlled Senate, many of these were southern conservatives who did not share Black's populist views. There were also a number of Democrats who remained bitter over Roosevelt's Court-packing proposal. Not only did some see the plan as an attempt to strong-arm the Court, but they were bothered that Roosevelt introduced it without consulting any of the Senate Democrats. Roosevelt and his political advisers hoped that the nomination of one of the Senate's own members might help reduce some of the problems in securing confirmation. Nonetheless, the nomination was viewed in some quarters as Roosevelt's revenge for the defeat of the Court-packing proposal.

Black did not possess obvious judicial qualifications. Some critics had reservations about his limited legal experience during the time preceding his entry into electoral politics. Others viewed Black as too partisan, too liberal, and too much of a populist. In addition, he had once been a member in the Ku Klux Klan (KKK), which prompted concerns among political liberals. Finally, there were some in the Senate who felt Black's nomination was nothing but a reward for his backing of the Court "reform" bill. Although support on this particular measure may have been relevant in Roosevelt's considerations, it was more important that Black had clearly demonstrated his wholehearted support of the New Deal programs.

Black was the only Roosevelt nominee to generate an unusual level of controversy, although he was eventually confirmed by a 63–16 vote. The debate surrounding Black's nomination aside, Roosevelt was able to fully achieve his objectives with this appointment. It appeared that way to former president Herbert Hoover, who remarked following the confirmation vote that the Court was now "one ninth packed." The issue of Black's former membership in the KKK did not go away. Black eventually took to national radio and explained the circumstances of his membership and the subsequent abandonment of his association with the Klan. This strategy was effective, and the issue then faded from public consciousness.

Black replaced one of the New Deal's staunchest opponents in Justice Van Devanter, and his vote was the first step in solidifying a more dependable, Roosevelt-friendly majority on the Court—Black added a firm vote to the pro–New Deal trio of Cardozo, Stone, and Brandeis. During his first term, Black agreed with Justices Cardozo and Stone in 85 percent of the Court's nonunanimous decisions. The following two terms produced interagreement rates at or above 90 percent among the Roosevelt appointees, which now included Justices Reed, Frankfurter, and Douglas as well as Stone. In the final term of the Hughes Court, Black and Douglas voted together in all of the nonunanimous decisions. A second liberal activist (though slightly less so) bloc of Murphy, Frankfurter, Reed, and Stone was evident during this period as well (Goldman 1991, 113).

Roosevelt's second opportunity to nominate a justice came only six months after Black was confirmed. George Sutherland, another of the laissez-fairist Four Horsemen, retired from the Court in January 1938. Roosevelt's choice to fill the Sutherland vacancy was Stanley F. Reed, who, as solicitor general, had argued many of the New Deal cases before the Court on behalf of the Roosevelt administration. Roosevelt had considered Reed for the nomination that went to Hugo Black. Reed's unswerving commitment to Roosevelt's political agenda made him the immediate front-runner for the Sutherland seat.

Reed was an attractive candidate for Roosevelt for several reasons. He was young, had a solid legal reputation, was not controversial, and was from a border state (Kentucky). All of these characteristics were of substantial value to Roosevelt as he faced the Senate for the second time with a Supreme Court nominee. Roosevelt had failed to consult his advisers and members of the Senate with the Court-packing proposal and the nomination of Hugo Black. This time Roosevelt heeded the recommendation of those he consulted and nominated Reed. He was confirmed by voice vote of the Senate on January 25, 1938, and sworn in six days later. The confirmation of Reed marked the second time in six months that Roosevelt was able to replace one of the obstructionist Four Horsemen. Roosevelt now had a solid liberal majority on the Court even if Hughes or Roberts defected. In his first three terms, Reed aligned himself with the other Roosevelt nominees and Justice Stone in the nonunanimous rulings of the Hughes Court.

Felix Frankfurter joined the Court a year after Reed, filling the vacancy created by the death of Benjamin Cardozo. Frankfurter did not produce an immediate gain for Roosevelt in that he replaced Cardozo, who had generally supported New Deal proposals before 1937. Roosevelt had known Frankfurter for a number of years and had considered him an exceptionally well qualified candidate for the Court long before

Cardozo's death. The possibility of a Frankfurter nomination, however, was seriously affected by considerations of political constituency. Roosevelt told Frankfurter that he would have to nominate someone from the West. Roosevelt also thought it impossible to nominate Frankfurter, who was Jewish, to a Court that still included two Jewish justices (Brandeis and Cardozo). Frankfurter understood and began to prepare a list of viable candidates on Roosevelt's behalf. But substantial support was generated for Frankfurter, some of which was orchestrated by Frankfurter himself and his protégés in Roosevelt's brain trust. The pressure on Roosevelt to nominate Frankfurter "became intense," and many, such as Justice Stone, Attorney General Jackson, Roosevelt's inner circle and cabinet including Harold Ickes and Harry Hopkins, and Senator George Norris, urged Roosevelt to set aside constituency considerations and nominate Frankfurter anyway. Jackson advocated nomination of Frankfurter if for no other reason than he could interpret the Constitution with scholarship and with sufficient assurance to face Hughes in conference and hold his own in discussion. Roosevelt yielded, indicating to his advisers that there "isn't anybody in the West . . . who is of sufficient stature" (Abraham 1992, 221).

Frankfurter was the first nominee since Stone to appear before the Senate Judiciary Committee. Despite some opposition from those who tried to represent Frankfurter as a communist, he was confirmed by unanimous voice vote in the Senate. Frankfurter brought his professorial background to the Court. The role of teacher was most evident on the Stone Court, as Stone was reluctant to limit conference debate. As a result, Frankfurter would often hold forth, often to the annoyance of his colleagues. In his first term on the Court (1938), Frankfurter voted with the other Roosevelt appointees; Black, Douglas, Reed, and Frankfurter acted as a liberal bloc in more than 90 percent of the nonunanimous decisions. By the time Stone became chief justice three years later, however, Frankfurter and Reed had repositioned themselves and become part of a less liberal and less cohesive bloc. This more centrist bloc included Justices Frankfurter, Reed, Stone, Jackson, and Roberts. Although the bloc comprised five justices, it did not consistently control the decisional outcomes. Its interagreement rates were in the mid-60 percent range, and one or another member of this bloc would frequently break off and join the liberals. Which justice might break away depended on the specific issue contained in particular cases. Although Frankfurter occasionally left the centrist bloc in specific cases, he shared little common ground with the liberal activist bloc during the Stone Court period.

Four weeks after the Frankfurter nomination, Justice Brandeis retired, creating the fourth vacancy on the Court in a little more than three and one-half years. As a matter of political constituency, Roosevelt was still interested in nominating a westerner. William O. Douglas, then chair of the Securities and Exchange Commission (SEC), was born in Minnesota and raised in Washington, although he completed law school at Columbia and joined the Yale law faculty. He was in Roosevelt's eyes a "two-thirds

Easterner," but he was a Roosevelt favorite and an insider. A number of people lobbied hard for Douglas, including the outgoing Justice Brandeis, who wanted Douglas "there in his place." Douglas felt it was Brandeis's support that was "ultimately decisive" with Roosevelt, although certainly Douglas's chances were enhanced by Idaho senator William Borah's claiming Douglas as one of the West's own. When Roosevelt summoned Douglas to the White House, Douglas feared that the president wished to appoint him chair of the Federal Communications Commission, a position Douglas did not want. Instead, Roosevelt told him his name would be sent to the Senate for the Supreme Court vacancy. The Senate confirmed Douglas four weeks later by a 62–4 vote. The four opposition votes were all from Republicans, but Republicans who characterized Douglas as a "reactionary tool of Wall Street," something he never was. At forty, he was the youngest nominee for the Court since Joseph Story, who was confirmed in 1811 at the age of thirty-two.

Justices Douglas and Black connected immediately. During the first two terms of Douglas's tenure, the Roosevelt appointees generally voted together. By the 1940 term, however, Stone, Murphy, Reed, and Frankfurter had begun to vote less often with Black and Douglas. In that 1940 term, Black and Douglas voted together in every nonunanimous decision of the Court. With the appointment of Justice Rutledge, a four-justice liberal cluster of Black, Douglas, Murphy, and Rutledge was evident for the duration of the Stone Court.

Roosevelt did not hesitate when Pierce Butler died on November 16, 1939. That same day Roosevelt told Attorney General Frank Murphy of his intentions to place him on the Court, although the official nomination did not take place until January 4, 1940. Senate confirmation occurred several days later. Murphy was reluctant to accept the nomination at first, feeling "utterly inadequate" to join the Court. A "strong and articulate" advocate of federal aid during the depression, Murphy was known as a crusading New Deal liberal and had served as an assistant U.S. attorney, a judge in Detroit, and mayor of Detroit. Roosevelt sent him to the Philippines as governor, but in 1936 he gave up that post to assist with Roosevelt's reelection campaign. Also in 1936 Murphy was elected governor of Michigan. He lost in his bid for reelection two years later and was almost immediately appointed U.S. attorney general by Roosevelt. Murphy's priorities while heading the Justice Department did not always coincide with those of Roosevelt or some of his key advisers. Some suggested that Murphy's appointment to the Court was a "kick upstairs"—a promotion to get him out of the Justice Department. Murphy was the most liberal of the Stone Court justices. This was particularly evident in civil liberties cases, in which Murphy supported individual rights claims even more often than Justices Black and Douglas.

By the time Roosevelt won his third term, the post-1937 "revolution" was cemented in place. Roosevelt had nominated five new justices during his second term. The replacement of Cardozo and Brandeis did not affect decisional outcomes, as these two justices supported most of the components of the New Deal program and demonstrated sensitivity to individual liberties issues. The other appointments—Black, Reed, and Murphy—all represented net gains for Roosevelt, as they replaced three of the Four Horsemen, the reactionary opponents of the New Deal. The last of the Four Horsemen, and maybe its most tenacious and reactionary member, James McReynolds, retired in 1941. Given the personnel changes, McReynolds correctly concluded there was no point in staying and fighting the fight that had been over for several years.

Most Court observers thought the McReynolds's seat would go to Attorney General Robert Jackson. Jackson had been attorney general for only a year, however, and Roosevelt did not want to replace him so soon. There was also substantial political pressure from influential southern Senate members to nominate Senator James Byrnes of South Carolina. Byrnes was considerably more conservative than the other Roosevelt nominees, but with the Court heavily committed to Roosevelt's priorities already, it really did not matter much.

Robert Jackson's nomination to the Court finally came in June 1941, but he was not offered the chief justiceship he wanted. Although Chief Justice Hughes gave Jackson a favorable recommendation, as mentioned above, Hughes argued that Stone was next in line for the chief justiceship. Roosevelt also sought counsel from Frankfurter, who said he preferred Jackson on "personal grounds," but from a "national interest" standpoint he saw no reason to prefer Jackson to Stone. When Roosevelt discussed the matter with Jackson, he deferred to the "persuasiveness of Frankfurter's logic" (Abraham 1992, 234). Jackson also anticipated that the sixty-nine-year-old Stone would be chief justice for only a short time and that the position would be his eventually. Confirmation of Jackson took a little longer than expected because of the opposition from Senator Millard Tydings of Maryland, who was unhappy with Jackson for not prosecuting columnist Drew Pearson for alleged libel against Tydings. The Senate Judiciary Committee unanimously recommended him after only a few moments' debate, however, and Jackson was confirmed with only Tydings voting against him.

Controversy developed around Jackson at the end rather than the beginning of the Stone Court period. He retained his wish to be chief justice, and he had a second opportunity when Stone died in 1946. But his feud with Justice Black, on doctrine as well as on a personal level, prompted Harry Truman to go outside the Court for a new chief justice. He chose Frederick Vinson. When Jackson returned from the Nazi war trials, he separated himself from the liberal activists (Black, Douglas, Murphy, and Rutledge), aligned himself with Frankfurter, and voted in a more conservative manner on national security and state criminal process cases, although he remained an advocate of judicial restraint on economic regulation issues.

The Stone Court from 1941 to 1942 (left to right front row): Stanley F. Reed, Owen J. Roberts, Harlan Fiske Stone, Hugo L. Black, and Felix Frankfurter; (left to right back row): James F. Byrnes, William O. Douglas, Frank Murphy, and Robert H. Jackson (Harris & Ewing, Collection of the Supreme Court of the United States)

In October 1942 Justice Byrnes resigned to take a more active administrative role in the conduct of the war. Byrnes's resignation brought Roosevelt his ninth and last opportunity to nominate a justice to the Supreme Court. Widely mentioned candidates were Kentucky Senator Alben Barkley, Solicitor General Charles Fahy, Judge John J. Parker of the U.S. Court of Appleals for the Fourth Circuit, and Roosevelt adviser Dean Acheson. Because Attorney General Francis Biddle was not interested in moving to the Court, Roosevelt instructed him to find a suitable candidate from west of the Mississippi. Biddle recommended Wiley Rutledge, who had been considered earlier but was instead groomed for later nomination by serving for a time on the U.S. Court of Appeals for the District of Columbia. Although Rutledge was only a marginal westerner, he had more claim to the region than Douglas. He was also the only Roosevelt nominee with federal judicial experience. Roosevelt had never met Rutledge, but a White House conversation satisfied Roosevelt that Rutledge was solidly committed to his philosophy. Confirmation of Rutledge came on a unanimous voice vote.

The last member of the Stone Court was nominated by President Harry Truman, who had succeeded to the presidency in early 1945 on the death of Roosevelt. The vacancy was created by the resignation of Justice Roberts. Truman was prone to reward loyalty, and that prompted him to make a number of "crony appointments," including his four nominees to the Supreme Court. Harold Burton had served in the

The Stone Court from 1943 to 1944 (left to right front row): Stanley F. Reed, Owen J. Roberts, Harlan Fiske Stone, Hugo L. Black, and Felix Frankfurter; (left to right back row): Robert H. Jackson, William O. Douglas, Frank Murphy, and Wiley Rutledge (Acme Newspictures, Collection of the Supreme Court of the United States)

Senate with Truman and was a member of the Truman War Investigation Committee, which had catapulted Truman to national prominence. The nomination was motivated by a close personal and political relationship between Truman and Burton. There were political reasons for Burton's selection as well. Foremost was that Truman felt national unity was best served by designating a Republican to replace Roberts, a GOP justice from Pennsylvania. In Truman's view, Burton had also demonstrated the appropriate temperament for a judge. Finally, Truman expected that the Democratic governor of Ohio would replace the Republican Burton with a Democrat (which he did). Burton was unanimously confirmed by the Senate on the day he was nominated by Truman.

The Stone Court: An Aggregate Profile

The Supreme Court fundamentally redefined central provisions of the U.S. Constitution beginning in 1937. Indeed, these changes were (and still are) characterized as "revolutionary" by some observers of the Court. Justice Stone, though an important participant, did not become chief justice until the revolution was well under way, if not largely concluded.

At the core of the revolution was the removal of long-recognized limits on the authority of the federal government to regulate the economy and social welfare. There were other components of the revolution as well. Certainly one was the attention directed toward the relationship of the individual to government authority, marking the beginning of what became modern civil liberties doctrine. Sheldon Goldman has suggested that this period was the first to reveal recognizable voting alignments—patterns of bloc voting not evident previously. This phenomenon was accompanied by, if not the product of, heightened levels of division and unprecedented levels of dissent. Table 1.1 reflects what Goldman called "dramatic" changes in individual dissent rates. Justices Stone and Roberts were the only justices to sit across all three periods represented in Table 1.1, and the dissent rate for each, particularly for Roberts, increases within each time span. More important are the markedly elevated dissent rates of the Roosevelt-appointed justices. These justices had the votes to control case outcomes during the Stone Court period, and yet the dissent rates rose as the number of Roosevelt appointees grew larger. Table 1.1 clearly reflects the "division and discord" observed by Melvin Urofsky.

Table 1.1 Dissent Rates: Hughes and Stone Courts

	1931–1935	1936–1940	1941–1945
Stone	8.2	2.9	12.9
Roberts	1.8	9.2	23.1+
Black	—	8.1+	14.5
Reed	—	3.3+	10.5
Frankfurter	—	1.5+	14.7
Douglas	—	6.1+	15.3
Murphy	—	2.3+	13.0
Byrnes	—	—	7.4+
Jackson	—	—	10.4+
Rutledge	—	—	12.9+
Full Court	15.7	27.3	48.6

+ did not sit for full period; based on terms served
Source: Goldman, p. 124.

The extent to which the Stone Court was fractured is evident from Table 1.2. The number of nonunanimous decisions increased by about 30 percent from the last term of the Hughes Court through the first term of the Stone Court. The proportion of split votes during the last three terms of the Stone Court approached 60 percent of the rulings and were more than double the proportion of split votes in the last Hughes Court term. The number of 5–4 decisions also rose substantially. There were three 5–4 decisions in the final term of the Hughes Court compared with sixteen such decisions the next year in the first Stone Court term. By the 1944 term, there were thirty votes with the 5–4 split. That number may have continued to increase, but 5–4 votes were impos-

Table 1.2 Disagreement on the Supreme Court, 1940–1946 Terms

Term	Total Votes	Opinions	Non-Unanimous Opinions		Dissenting Votes	
			Number	Percent	Number	Per Opinion
1940	169	47	27.8	117	.69	3
(Hughes Court)						
1941	162	59	36.4	160	.99	16
1942	171	75	43.9	176	1.03	10
1943	137	80	58.4	194	1.42	16
1944	163	94	57.7	245	1.50	30
1945	137	77	56.2	156	1.14	—
1946	144	92	63.9	246	1.71	26
(Vinson Court)						

—Eight justices for the entire term—Jackson at the war trials in Germany
Source: Pritchett, p. 25.

Table 1.3 Individual Justice Dissent Rates (in percent), 1941–1945 Terms

	1941	1942	1943	1944	1945
Stone	14	9	12	19	15
Roberts	16	18	30	36	—
Black	13	13	14	19	13
Reed	9	10	13	10	11
Frankfurter	10	12	16	15	22
Douglas	17	14	16	15	16
Murphy	11	17	15	15	10
Jackson	7	11	17	11	—
Rutledge	—	3	12	14	16
Burton	—	—	—	—	15

Source: Pritchett, p. 45.

sible during the 1945 term, as the Stone Court was an eight-justice Court while Justice Jackson was in Germany for the entire year to participate in the Nazi war trials.

Individual dissent rates of Stone Court justices appear in Table 1.3. Each justice was among the minority in a number of cases throughout the Stone Court era. For most of the justices, dissent rates were quite comparable—between 10 and 20 percent. Frankfurter's tendency to part company with the other Roosevelt justices was becoming apparent in the final term of the Stone Court. The most frequent dissenter during this period was Roberts, who by the 1943 term was largely estranged from the remainder of the Court.

Stone and Hughes: A Comparison

Chief justices bring widely divergent leadership styles and capabilities to the position. History has clearly shown that they are not equally well suited to handle the demands of the chief justiceship. Chief Justices Hughes and Stone are good examples of the differences. Unlike many chief justices, both Hughes and Stone served on the Supreme Court as associate justices, giving both the opportunity to observe and learn from others. Before resigning to accept the Republican nomination for president in 1916, Hughes sat on the Court for six years as an associate justice under the chief justiceship of Edward White. White was himself an associate justice for sixteen years before being elevated to chief justice by President Taft in 1910. White served another eleven years as chief justice. He is generally highly regarded by those who rank performance on the Court—White rates as one of the "near great" justices. At the same time, White neither directed conferences nor managed the Court's docket effectively. Hughes learned from his observations and diligently sought to avoid performing in a similar manner. Hughes believed that a "well organized and efficient Court could not only manage its docket, but increase its power at the same time" (White 1976, 203). Preservation of the Court's power and prestige were Hughes's primary objectives as chief justice, resulting in his controlling approach to the decision-making processes of the Court.

Hughes led his Court. He set the pace of Court conferences by forcefully offering his views before other justices could speak. No justice spoke out of turn. Hughes did not tolerate debate on subjects not directly related to the case at hand, and he typically brought matters to a quick vote without prolonged debate. Hughes was a superb administrator who fully utilized the prerogatives of office, including the opinion assignment power, to achieve his objectives. Alpheus T. Mason argued that by employing "the methods of a military commander Hughes made his administration a model of efficiency" (Mason 1956, 789).

Hughes was the "embodiment of the modern chief justice" (White 1976, 204). He was conspicuously efficient, ideologically receptive to progress and reform, aloof from partisan politics, of immense public stature with wide-ranging contacts in all branches of government and influential sectors of private enterprise, possessed of superior quantities as an intellectual technician, and experienced as a justice. He seemed to match all the needs of the office (White 1976, 204).

Nonetheless, the Court under Hughes "isolated itself from the mood of the nation and revealed itself as being polarized and rancorous" (White 1976, 205). Although Hughes was not responsible for the polarization on his Court, he was largely unable to eliminate these problems.

Chief Justice Stone was elevated to the chief justiceship well into his tenure on the Court. He served as an associate justice for the last five terms of the Taft Court and the eleven years that Hughes was chief justice. He was a part of the minority for most of these years. In 1937 the Court changed course, and Stone became part of the new majority of justices who were generally sympathetic to the legislative initiatives of Roosevelt. Stone became chief justice of a Court that seemed to share judicial and political outlook—most were the appointees of Franklin Roosevelt. Nevertheless, the justices were badly fragmented essentially from the outset of Stone's tenure.

Stone had a vastly different personality and temperament from Hughes. In the words of Mason, "Stone was not born to command equals." Although an enormously able man, Stone was not a dominating personality and was unwilling and probably incapable of imposing discipline on his colleagues; he would not "hammer a minority into line as some of his predecessors did" (Mason 1956, 796). He refused to exert authority, "to see himself, despite his role as first among equals, as superior in any sense to his colleagues on the Court," and he did not use his power to assign opinions to achieve an objective such as a united Court (White 1976, 217).

Stone had his own notions of how conferences should be run, and he believed that Hughes had restricted conference discussion too greatly. Stone saw each case as requiring full discussion, and he sought to transform the Court's conferences into wide-ranging debates. As a result, discussion was full and uninhibited but too often unfocused as well. Stone offered little direction during conferences, and the vacuum this created was too often filled by Justice Frankfurter. Although the Stone Court decided as many cases as did the Hughes Court, it took much more conference time to do so. Stone did not subscribe to the view held by Taft and Hughes that a chief justice should "mass the Court." That is, Stone would not apply pressure in an attempt to accomplish unanimous votes. Indeed, Stone made no effort to create unanimity where it did not already exist.

Stone was well liked by his colleagues, but that did not make him an effective chief justice. At the same time, Stone faced a combination of particular problems his predecessors did not have to confront. His Court consisted of new, inexperienced, and ideologically driven justices. Besides the other Hughes Court holdover, Owen Roberts, none of the other associate justices had any judicial experience when Stone began his tenure as chief justice. As a consequence, these justices were only minimally familiar with the practices of the Court. In addition, the rapid turnover after 1937 meant that there were few senior justices to whom the new justices might turn for guidance. Many of the new justices shared the activism associated with Roosevelt and the New Deal. Like Stone, the new justices tended to defer to rather than veto legislative judgments, but this view was largely confined to economic regulatory policy. Where civil liberties were concerned, most of the new justices did not believe such deference was appropriate. This could set them at odds with Stone in some circumstances.

Another obstacle for Stone was the unusual array of strong personalities on his bench and the conflicts that stemmed from this. Justice Frankfurter was in part responsible for the prolonged conferences and the difficulties Stone had as chief justice. Justice Jackson clashed repeatedly with Justice Black, with whom he had a particularly visible confrontation over resolution of the *Jewell Ridge* case in June 1945. Their feud took on even larger proportions following Stone's death at the time Truman was seeking a successor as chief justice. The undercurrent of bickering during Stone's tenure involved nearly everyone. For example, Murphy and Roberts were at odds with each other, and both Murphy and Douglas took Black's side in the feud with Jackson. Stone at one point lamented in a letter to a friend, "I have had much difficulty in herding my collection of fleas, and they have been so busy disagreeing with each other that I have found it necessary to take on the writing of more opinions than I really should have" (Mason 1956, 605).

Even what should have been a simple farewell letter to Justice Roberts at his retirement in June 1945 turned into confrontation. Justice Black objected to a few lines of praise written by Chief Justice Stone. Stone eventually acquiesced to Black's rewriting the letter, but on learning of the change Frankfurter then plagued Stone until a copy of the original letter was sent to the other justices. Ultimately, both Frankfurter and Jackson refused to sign Black's rewritten version, and Black subsequently withdrew his signature from his own letter. A conference on the matter did not resolve the problem, and no formal retirement letter was ever sent to Roberts. The difficulty with Stone, according to Jackson, was that he "dreaded conflict and his dread was so strong that it seemed to me that he feared taking action which would bring it about" (Mason 1956, 769).

As did Hughes, Stone also encountered problems produced by factors outside his control. Stone's Court confronted some complex new issues that prior Courts had not faced. This was especially true with cases involving individual rights, issues made even more complex by World War II. Stone's leadership style, however, diminished the chances that his Court could find consensus on such matters.

With the exception of James Byrnes, the Roosevelt appointees to the Court were, for the most part, liberal activists. Roosevelt's appointees were also enormously talented and insightful. As a group, these justices ought to have been able to find common ground in liberal issues of the day such as civil rights, freedom of expression, and the promotion of the interests of labor unions, but the Stone Court justices found ways to fracture even on these questions. Early in his tenure as chief justice, Stone himself noted that any expectations that this group of justices "would have minds with but a single thought and hearts that beat as one were speedily dissipated" (White 1976, 221). Furthermore, Stone rejected making attempts to "convert" others to his views; the Court under Stone would not be "molded" by the preferences of the chief justice. Stone was willing to exchange efficiency in disposing of the Court's cases for the "painstaking consideration" of issues raised by the cases. Stone's "combination of personal diffidence and intellectual combativeness, when commingled with the vibrancy and contentiousness of others on his Court, formed a catalyst for divisiveness" (White 1976, 227–228).

References

Abraham, Henry J. *Justices and Presidents: A Political History of Appointments to the Supreme Court*. 3rd edition. New York: Oxford University Press, 1992.

Goldman, Sheldon. *Constitutional Law: Cases and Essays*. 2nd edition. New York: HarperCollins, 1991.

Johnson, John W. "Harlan Fiske Stone." In Melvin I. Urofsky, ed., *The Supreme Court Justices: A Biographical Dictionary*. New York: Garland, 1994, pp. 425–434.

Mason, Alpheus T. "Harlan Fiske Stone." In Leon Friedman and Fred L. Israel, eds., *The Justices of the United States Supreme Court, 1789–1995: Their Lives and Major Opinions*. New York: Chelsea House, 1995, pp. 1099–1116.

———. *Harlan Fiske Stone: Pillar of the Law*. New York: Viking, 1956.

Pritchett, C. Herman. *The Roosevelt Court: A Study in Judicial Politics and Values, 1937–47*. New York: Macmillan, 1948.

Swindler, William F. *Court and Constitution in the Twentieth Century*. Indianapolis, Ind.: Bobbs-Merrill, 1974.

White, G. Edward. *The American Judicial Tradition: Profiles of Leading American Judges*. Oxford: Oxford University Press, 1976.

2

The Justices

Eleven justices served on the Stone Court. Seven of these justices, all nominated by President Franklin D. Roosevelt, served for the entire five-term period. Justice Harlan F. Stone, for whom this period is named, was initially nominated by President Calvin Coolidge in 1925 but was elevated to chief justice by Roosevelt in 1941. The other six Roosevelt appointees to serve all five years were Hugo L. Black, Felix Frankfurter, William O. Douglas, Frank Murphy, Stanley F. Reed, and Robert H. Jackson. Justice Owen J. Roberts was nominated by President Herbert Hoover in 1930 and carried over from the Hughes Court. James F. Byrnes was nominated by Roosevelt in 1941 but served for only the first term of the Stone Court. Byrnes resigned from the Court in 1942 and was succeeded by Roosevelt nominee Wiley B. Rutledge. Justice Roberts resigned prior to the final year of the Stone Court, and President Harry Truman replaced him with Harold H. Burton.

The eleven Stone Court justices are discussed individually in the remainder of this chapter, ordered by date of appointment to the Supreme Court. Table 2.1 presents each justice's birth date, date of appointment, nominating president, age at appointment, age span during the Stone Court period, and justice being replaced.

Table 2.1 Stone Court Justices

	Birth Year	App't. Year	App't. Pres.	App't. Age	Age Span on Stone Court	Replaced
Black	1886	1937	FDR	51	55-59	Van Devanter
Burton	1888	1945	Truman	57	57-58	Roberts
Byrnes	1879	1941	FDR	62	62-63	McReynolds
Douglas	1898	1939	FDR	40	43-47	Brandeis
Frankfurter	1882	1939	FDR	56	59-64	Cardozo
Jackson	1892	1941	FDR	49	49-54	Stone
Murphy	1890	1940	FDR	49	51-56	Butler
Reed	1884	1938	FDR	53	57-62	Sutherland
Roberts	1875	1930	Hoover	55	66-69	Sanford
Rutledge	1894	1943	FDR	48	48-50	Byrnes
Stone	1872	1925	Coolidge & FDR	52	69-74	Hughes

Source: Renstrom, p. 66

Harlan Fiske Stone (Harris & Ewing, Collection of the Supreme Court of the United States)

The Coolidge Appointment

Harlan Fiske Stone

President Calvin Coolidge nominated Harlan Fiske Stone to replace Justice Joseph McKenna, who left the Court in late 1924. Thus Stone himself was the first of the Stone Court justices to join the Court. Stone was the first Supreme Court nominee to appear before the Senate committee considering his qualifications. Stone effectively responded to the questions posed by the committee's members and was subsequently confirmed by a 71–6 vote by the full Senate on February 5, 1925. When Taft resigned in 1930, many expected Stone to succeed him. Taft, however, fearing that Stone would be unable to "mass" the Court—persuade the justices to join a single opinion—influenced Hoover to appoint Charles Evans Hughes instead. Stone served as an associate justice until June 12, 1941, when President Franklin Roosevelt nominated him to succeed Hughes as chief justice. Stone was confirmed as chief justice in the Senate by voice vote on June 27, 1941, and he served in that capacity until his death on April 22, 1946.

Stone was born in Chesterfield, New Hampshire, on November 11, 1872. He took his B.A. and M.A. degrees from Amherst College before completing his law degree at Columbia University in 1898. During his youth, he was a friend of Calvin Coolidge, and the two attended Amherst together. Stone was admitted to the bar of New York and began a successful corporate law practice. Stone also became a professor of law at Columbia and later served thirteen years as dean of the Columbia Law School before returning to private practice in 1923. During this same period, Coolidge succeeded to the presidency on the death of Warren Harding. He brought Stone to Washington in 1924 to replace U.S. Attorney General Harry Daugherty, whose tenure as head of the Justice Department had been severely marred by corruption, including the Teapot Dome scandal. Coolidge not only wanted the scandal fully investigated but wanted someone with a squeaky-clean reputation. Stone clearly filled the bill. Although he held the position of attorney general for just a year, Stone was able to effect substantial organizational changes in the Justice Department.

Stone joined a conservative Court in 1925. William Howard Taft was chief justice of the Court, which included the Four Horsemen—Justices Pierce Butler, James McReynolds, George Sutherland, and Willis Van Devanter, whose views led them to categorically oppose virtually all the initiatives of the New Deal a decade later. Many expected Stone to join the conservative majority. Almost immediately, however, Stone became the third member of the Court's moderate-liberal bloc, aligning himself with Oliver Wendell Holmes and Louis Brandeis. As a member of the Hughes Court, Stone was often found with Justices Brandeis and Benjamin Cardozo on the minority side in many significant economic regulation rulings. As was true of Holmes and Brandeis, Stone subscribed to the judicial self-restraint view: He believed that policy matters are the exclusive domain of the legislative branch, and Stone sought not to substitute his own policy preferences for those of elected legislators.

One of Stone's most powerful opinions was his dissent in *United States v. Butler*, a case that clearly reflected his judicial philosophy of self-restraint. To Stone, the majority in *Butler* read the Constitution too narrowly. In an emergency such as the economic depression, courts ought not question the means by which Congress chooses to carry into operation its delegated powers. The power of courts to declare a statute unconstitutional should examine only the legislative power to enact statutes, not whether the laws establish sound policy. Further, although executive and legislative actions are subject to judicial review, such review must be limited by the Court's self-imposed restraint. Stone remained on the minority side of most split decisions until the Court's doctrinal shift of 1937. As a result of this change, Stone became part of the moderate-liberal majority for the remainder of the Hughes Court period.

During the infamous Court-packing controversy of 1937, Stone indicated to Roosevelt that he did not support changing the Court's size. At the same time, he understood Roosevelt's frustration with the Court and was active behind the scenes in urging appointment of justices with the judicial philosophy of Brandeis, Cardozo, and himself. After 1937 the Court essentially deferred to economic regulation initiatives at both the federal and state levels. The new consensus on government power to regulate the economy did not generalize to all other constitutional issues, however. Cases containing civil liberties questions became more frequent as World War II neared, and these issues would prove to be even more divisive than economic questions. The Roosevelt appointees on the Court were more than willing to speak their minds on these matters, causing Stone to refer to justices such as Black, Douglas, and Murphy as "wild horses." Stone's relations with most of the Roosevelt-appointed justices, both before and after his elevation to chief justice, was strained at best.

During his first term as chief justice, Stone agreed with Justices Black and Douglas in only 25 percent and 23 percent of the Court's decisions, respectively. His highest agreement rate was 70 percent with Justice Roberts. In 1943 Stone's agreement percentage was highest with Justices Reed (78 percent) and Frankfurter (70 percent). Stone's agreement level with Roberts dropped to 49 percent in 1943 and rose to above 50 percent with the liberal activist members of the Court. Justice Jackson was in Germany for the war trials during Stone's last term, and the Court functioned with only eight members. During this last term, Stone agreed most often with Justices Reed (80 percent) and Burton (78 percent). The agreement rate with the liberal activist bloc was in the 40 percent range (Renstrom 1972, 294–295).

One of Stone's greatest contributions to American law came in his majority opinion in *United States v. Carolene Products Co.* (1938). What made this opinion significant was the famous "footnote four," where Stone suggested that the Court should subject statutes dealing with civil liberties and discrimination issues to more searching examinations than laws pertaining to economic matters. This opinion clearly suggested a double standard. It affirmed the economic self-restraint position with which Stone was identified. Paradoxically, the *Carolene Products* opinion indicated that statutes that restrict individual rights should be subject to closer scrutiny because the rights protection provisions of the Bill of Rights occupy a "preferred position." The doctrine still retains analytic value in considerations of constitutional limits on government.

Stone's 1941 opinion in *United States v. Darby Lumber Co.* examined the Fair Labor Standards Act (FLSA) of 1938, viewed by many as the last major piece of New Deal legislation passed by Congress. The ruling reversed *Hammer v. Dagenhart* (1918), and Stone's opinion abandoned the previously operative distinction between manufacturing and commerce. The goods produced and marketed by the lumber company, Stone concluded, were part of a stream of commerce and thus could be regulated under the commerce power. The *Darby* opinion also rejected the doctrine of dual federalism from Tenth Amendment jurisprudence. Stone wrote that the Tenth Amendment "states but a truism that all is retained which has not been surrendered" (*Darby Lumber*, 124).

One of Stone's most noteworthy civil liberties opinions was delivered in *Minersville School District v. Gobitis* (1940). The Court ruled in *Gobitis* that there were some patriotic expressions that the nation could legitimately ask of its citizens, one of them being the salute of the flag. Compulsory participation in the flag salute exercise was challenged by Jehovah's Witnesses on the grounds of free exercise of religion. Justice Frankfurter said for the majority that "conscientious scruples" cannot relieve citizens from obedience to "general law not aimed at the promotion or restriction of religious beliefs" (*Gobitis*, 597). Stone was the only member of the Court to disagree. He concluded that if First Amendment guarantees are to "have any meaning they must be deemed to withhold from the state any authority to compel belief or expression of it where that expression violates religious convictions, whatever may be the legislative view of the desirability of such compulsion" (Johnson 1994, 431–432). The position Stone advanced in *Gobitis* was sufficiently compelling that when the Court reexamined the compulsory flag salute issue less than three years later, five members of the Court joined Stone to overrule *Gobitis* in *West Virginia State Board of Education v. Barnette* (1943).

As sensitive as Stone was to civil liberties, he failed to weigh in against the egregious internment of the Japanese. As an individual justice, wrote John P. Frank, "Stone was one of the great dynamic contributors to American law," but as chief justice he was "strikingly unsuccessful." Although his appointment to head the Court was universally praised, he proved ineffective in the post. He disliked administrative work and lacked the skills necessary to unify his Court and keep differences under control. Stone's Court was the most frequently divided, the most openly quarrelsome in history. The conflict included personal sniping and bickering as well as substantive differences on issues. By the end of Stone's tenure, critics asserted that the divisiveness had caused a decline in the Court's dignity and authority.

In many ways the chief justiceship was an unhappy ending to an otherwise illustrious public life. Part of Stone's difficulty as chief justice was his tolerance for disagreement. In the minds of some Court colleagues, he let conferences over pending cases and certiorari petitions continue far too long. The Stone Court did not generally observe the normal Court protocol of allowing the justices to speak in turn in ascending levels of seniority. As a result, the discussions went in many different directions. Another problem was that Stone did not have the ability and perhaps the inclination to indulge the egos of some of his colleagues. Justice Jackson believed that Stone's problem was, paradoxically, that he dreaded conflict and wished to avoid it even at high cost. Yet his willingness to permit dissension to continue unintentionally abetted the already high degree of conflict that was inevitable given the positions and personalities of the "wild horses" (Johnson 1994, 433).

Stone cannot be classed as a great chief justice if that term includes the capacity to lead the Court. He was incapable of applying the type of pressure that Taft and Hughes could exert in the conferences. He either could not or would not rely on comradeship or persuasiveness or political loyalties to bind his colleagues to him. He would not even seek to create this illusion for the public. The difference between the way Hughes or Taft ran the Court and the lack of management exhibited by Stone was striking (Asch 1971, 138). Stone was almost sixty-nine when he succeeded Hughes in the center chair. He would live for not quite five more years. Those years proved less satisfactory, less happy than his sixteen as associate justice. Experts rank Stone as one of the great justices to sit on the Court. Stone was not bold, but principled. He was a legal scholar who was able to apply effectively this scholarship to the practical demands of Supreme Court decisionmaking. His opinions were generally compelling, particularly when he wrote in support of individual rights and democratic processes. He was a justice of accomplishment and his contributions to American constitutional law were substantial. Such an assessment, however, is based largely on his performance as an associate justice. His greatness was obscured during his five years as chief justice by the highly divided Court over which he presided. As John W. Johnson aptly suggests, "In many ways, the chief justiceship was an unhappy denouement to an otherwise illustrious public life" (Johnson 1994, 433).

The Hoover Appointment

Owen Josephus Roberts

A vacancy on the Supreme Court opened up in March 1930 on the death of Justice Edward Sanford. President Herbert Hoover nominated U.S. Court of Appeals judge

Owen Josephus Roberts (Harris & Ewing, Collection of the Supreme Court of the United States)

John J. Parker of North Carolina for the position. Parker was opposed by both labor unions and civil rights organizations, and his nomination was eventually defeated in the Senate. Owen Josephus Roberts presented none of the political liabilities that accompanied the Parker nomination, and Hoover sent his name to the Senate within forty-eight hours of the Parker vote. Roberts had no previous judicial experience and was not seeking the nomination, but he was nonetheless unanimously confirmed by voice vote of the Senate on May 5, 1930. Roberts was the only Stone Court justice not nominated (renominated in Stone's case) by Franklin Roosevelt.

Roberts was born in Philadelphia on May 2, 1875. Privately educated, Roberts graduated from the University of Pennsylvania at the age of twenty and entered law school at the same institution. He served as editor of the law review and graduated with highest honors from law school in 1898. For about twenty years, he ran a private practice in Philadelphia that specialized in corporate law; among his clients was the Pennsylvania Railroad. In addition, Roberts served as a part-time member of the faculty at the University of Pennsylvania Law School. Following World War I, Roberts was appointed special deputy attorney general, and he prosecuted federal criminal defendants under the Espionage Act. He later accepted an appointment from President Calvin Coolidge as special counsel to investigate the oil lease scandal known as Teapot Dome. Roberts not only successfully prosecuted the principal participants in the incident, including Secretary of the Interior Albert B. Fall, but was able to secure revocation of the fraudulently obtained oil leases. Roberts's performance as special counsel in the Teapot Domes cases was nationally visible and widely praised.

The Court Roberts joined was more fundamentally split than the Stone Court. On the one side were four nonnegotiable conservatives, and on the other three justices who were largely supportive of the New Deal regulatory initiatives. Roberts and Chief Justice Charles Evans Hughes, who joined the Court at nearly the same time, were frequently the decisive votes on cases raising constitutional questions about federal and state regulatory authority. Roberts tended to vote with the conservatives at the outset of his Court service but did not fully share the ideological orientation of the Court's laissez-fairists. What is often seen as his refusal to consistently align himself with either side, however, may have been the absence of a coherent judicial philosophy. Indeed, there are those who suggest that "by temperament, he was not suited to the appellate bench" (Hall 1994, 383). There were occasions prior to 1937 when Roberts and Hughes voted to uphold the exercise of governmental regulatory power. Most notable among these were *Nebbia v. New York* (1934), where the Court upheld a state price control regulation on retail milk sales, and *Home Building & Loan Association v. Blaisdell* (1934), in which the Court upheld a state law placing a moratorium on foreclosures for failure to make mortgage payments.

More often, however, Roberts voted with the conservatives to nullify many New Deal as well as state regulatory initiatives. The majority opinion for which

Roberts is best known during this period came in *United States v. Butler* (1936), which struck down the Agricultural Adjustment Act of 1933. Central to Roosevelt's economic recovery strategy, the AAA sought to stabilize prices for agricultural commodities and the purchasing power of farmers by having farmers cut production of certain commodities enough to increase market prices. Farmers who agreed to reduce production received a government subsidy for the acreage they took out of production. The funds used to pay for these subsidies came from a tax levied on food processors, businesses who prepared agricultural commodities for the market. Roberts suggested that the federal government possessed the authority to levy such a tax on behalf of the general welfare, but the AAA was unconstitutional because it impermissibly encroached on the powers of the states; regardless of the extent of the federal power to tax and spend, that power could not be used to usurp local control of agriculture.

Roosevelt's frustration with such decisions as *Butler* prompted him to introduce his Court-packing proposal in a transparent attempt to obtain more favorable decisions from the Court. A month after this judicial "reform" proposal was submitted to Congress, the Hughes Court rulings changed direction and began to affirm rather than veto New Deal policies. Roberts and Hughes were the justices whose votes reversed and produced the new outcomes.

As pivotal as Roberts's votes were to the 1937 turnaround, Roosevelt was soon able to nominate a group of pro–New Deal justices to the Court, ending the period during which Roberts's votes were decisive. In his last several terms on the Court, Roberts reverted to his earlier, more conservative positions and was frequently found on the minority side of these cases. Of 191 nonunanimous cases Pritchett labeled "economic," involving such issues as federal regulatory authority, labor, restraint of trade, and state economic regulation, 111, or 58 percent, of these decision upheld governmental intervention in the economy. Roberts was among the majority in only 12 percent (23) of these cases (Pritchett 1948, 257). With the exception of Stone's first year as chief justice, when Roberts agreed with him in 70 percent of the decisions, Roberts had no interagreement score higher than 62 percent (with Frankfurter) during the four years he served on the Stone Court. His break from the liberal activists (Black, Douglas, Murphy, and Rutledge) in nonunanimous cases occurred in almost 80 percent of the decisions. In his last term, for example, Roberts agreed only 9 percent of the time with Black, 20 percent with Douglas and Rutledge, and 25 percent with Murphy (Renstrom 1972, 295–299).

Several Stone Court justices supported civil liberties and civil rights claims more consistently than Roberts. He was responsible, however, for several important civil liberties opinions for the Court. For example, in *Cantwell v. Connecticut* (1940), Roberts offered justification for applying to the states the free exercise clause of the First Amendment. He also suggested in *Cantwell* that the First Amendment contains an absolute freedom of belief. Roberts's support of Cantwell, a Jehovah's Witness, did not generalize to other cases involving the Witnesses or most other civil liberties cases. Roberts voted against the Witness's free exercise claims in the two compulsory flag salute cases. Roberts also wrote the opinion of the Court in *Betts v. Brady* (1942), a decision that held that states need not provide counsel to indigent felony defendants in the absence of "special circumstances."

His most noteworthy individual rights opinion was his dissent in *Korematsu v. United States* (1944), where he condemned the basis for relocating Japanese Americans on the West Coast. The evacuation of Japanese Americans, in his view, was undertaken without any "evidence or inquiry" about loyalty to the United States. Rather, the Japanese Americans were relocated solely on the basis of ancestry, an action Roberts saw as plainly unconstitutional.

Roberts resigned from the Court on July 31, 1945, after fifteen years of service. His last four years were on the Stone Court, and they were his unhappiest. He often found himself on the minority side of the Court's decisions. During his final term alone, Roberts dissented in more than fifty Stone Court rulings, his opinions focusing on what he considered the majority's "wholesale deviation" from judicial precedent and established doctrine.

Assessment of Roberts's decade and a half on the Court is difficult. Henry J. Abraham suggested that there was an almost "terpsichorean quality about this benign, conscientious jurist who established a probably difficult-to-equal record of inconsistency in his voting on the bench" (Abraham 1992, 203). In retirement Roberts pursued a variety of interests important to him—world federation, the Boy Scouts, and the state bar of Pennsylvania among others. He also served three years as dean of the University of Pennsylvania Law School. He left that position in 1951 and lived the remaining years of his life on his Pennsylvania farm. He died on May 17, 1955.

The Roosevelt Appointments

Hugo Lafayette Black

Hugo Lafayette Black was the first of President Franklin Roosevelt's eight Supreme Court nominations, picked when Justice Willis Van Devanter retired in 1937. Black was confirmed by his Senate colleagues on August 17, 1937, by a 63–16 vote.

Black was born in a rural area of Alabama on February 27, 1886. His family settled in the community of Ashland, where Black received his early education. After attending Birmingham Medical College for a year, Black changed his career path and decided to pursue law. He enrolled at the University of Alabama Law School at the age of eighteen and went into private practice in Ashland following graduation. Shortly thereafter, Black moved to Birmingham and developed a practice around

Hugo Lafayette Black (Harris & Ewing, Collection of the Supreme Court of the United States)

labor and personal injury law. For a time, Black served as a police court judge on a part-time basis, and from 1915 to 1917 Black was the county prosecutor. After a brief period in the military during World War I, he resumed his law practice. In 1926 Black successfully ran for the U.S. Senate, and he served almost two full terms in the Senate before his appointment to the Supreme Court. Black believed that Congress, largely through its authority over interstate commerce, had the power to intervene aggressively in response to the economic emergency that followed the Great Depression. Accordingly, Black was a leading advocate of the measures contained in Roosevelt's New Deal program. He was particularly interested in protecting employees in the workplace. The Fair Labor Standards Act of 1938, enacted after Black joined the Supreme Court, was based extensively on proposals regarding hours of work Black had introduced five years earlier. Black also supported Roosevelt's Court-packing proposal.

A month after Black's confirmation, it was reported in the media that Black had been a member of the Ku Klux Klan while in private practice in the early 1920s. Black responded in a national radio broadcast in which he acknowledged his association with the Klan and indicated that he had long since resigned from the organization. The controversy soon subsided, and Black commenced what was to be a thirty-four-year tenure on the Court. Black resigned from the Court on September 17, 1971, after suffering a severe stroke, and he died eight days later.

Although Black had been in the U.S. Senate for more than ten years prior to his appointment to the Court, he possessed a well-developed judicial philosophy at the point he joined the Court. Sidney Asch called him a "fighting liberal" and the "intellectual dean" of the New Deal Court (Asch 1971, 189). He certainly was one of the Court's most influential justices. Indeed, Black provided intellectual leadership to the Court throughout his tenure, even though he did not share the academic credentials of such colleagues as Stone, Frankfurter, or Douglas.

Black was a "self-styled strict constructionist" and a textual literalist (Asch 1971, 190). He saw the Constitution as providing a fundamental basis for government action, and he took its words literally. This approach led him to view the powers of Congress as extensive, certainly extensive enough to engage in comprehensive regulation of the national economy and the establishment of the modern welfare state. Although he believed the judiciary must preserve explicit constitutional directives, he saw the judicial branch as having no authority to modify by interpretation the Constitution's provision. The Court, he said, "has no power to add or subtract from the procedures set forth by the Founders. . . . I shall not at any time surrender my belief that the document itself should be our guide, not our own concept of what is fair, decent, and right" (Asch 1971, 191).

This literalism produced an absolutist view with respect to certain constitutional rights while at the same time allowing Black to extend substantial latitude to government, particularly in the area of criminal process. Black rejected the notion of the "living" or evolving Constitution, believing instead that its meaning is fixed. He considered it imperative to repair erroneous interpretations of the Constitution by removing "encrustations on the Constitution written by Court majorities over the generations." He felt that cases should be adjudicated on the basis of the historical meaning of the terms of the Constitution as well as defining the intent of the framers. He had an "unshakable commitment to ridding the books of gratuitous and erroneous precedent by goal-oriented substantive due process Court majorities" (Ball 1996, 108–109). In Black's view, judges should not exercise great discretion or make substantive policy judgments. Rather, a literal reading of the Constitution established absolutes that judges were to maintain.

Black was at the center of the internal friction on the Stone Court. His "principal jurisprudential antagonist" (Yarbrough 1988, 2) was Felix Frankfurter; theirs was a fundamental clash of wills. They differed most essentially over the proper role of the Court. Frankfurter believed the Court ought maintain a lower profile and defer to the elective branches. Black shared this perspective to a degree, but his literalist views frequently led him to engage in judicial intervention, particularly with respect to individual rights. The doctrinal differences between Black and Frankfurter were magnified by their dramatically different personal styles.

Justice Black was a member of the liberal activist bloc of the Stone Court. In nonunanimous rulings during the 1941 term, he agreed most often with Justice Douglas; the two voted together in 95 percent of the nonunanimous cases. Black voted with Justice Murphy in 78 percent of the cases during this same year. Rutledge was added to this group during the 1943 term, and the four justices all had agreement ratios with each other ranging from 72 to 86 percent. The agreement levels began to diminish during the 1946 term; Black's agreement levels with Justices Douglas, Murphy, and Rutledge fell to 71 percent, 67 percent, and 59 percent, respectively (Renstrom 1972, 295–299).

Black was generally deferential to the policy judgments of legislative bodies. It was Black's view that courts ought not examine the reasonableness of legislative judgments, federal or state. He said in *Southern Pacific Railroad Co. v. Arizona* (1945) that representatives "elected by the people to make their laws can best determine the policies which govern the people" (*Southern Pacific*, 789). It was this deference to legislative authority that prompted Senator Black to support Roosevelt's Court-packing plan in 1937. From the beginning of his tenure on the Court, Black played a "key role in the implementation of doctrines of judicial self-restraint that worked to move the Court away from interposition in social and economic matters of state." He "vigorously defended the principle of the supremacy of the legislature in the American political system and strongly argued for a much more limited, constitutionally prescribed role in American politics for the Supreme Court" (Ball 1996, 108–109).

Justice Black's deference to legislative judgments and his commitment to the protection of constitutional rights came into conflict during World War II. Black was among the majority when the Court upheld exclusion of the Japanese from "military areas" on the West Coast. The Japanese were not, in Black's view, excluded because of "hostility" toward their race but rather because "properly constituted military authorities feared an invasion of our West Coast and felt constrained to take proper security measures" (*Korematsu*, 223). The *Korematsu* decision was an "easy one" for Black, and he never anguished over what one critic called the "most Klanlike" opinion he ever wrote. The country was at war. The president and his military commanders could do whatever was necessary to assure victory against the enemy. The Japanese exclusion cases "clearly illustrate Black's belief in the supremacy of legislative-executive lawmaking for the national community" (Ball 1996, 113).

Black believed that the federal power to regulate interstate commerce enabled Congress to comprehensively address economic problems if they affected the national economy either directly or indirectly. In his view the commerce clause gave Congress complete, unrestricted power to regulate interstate commerce. Indeed, during his lengthy tenure on the Court, Black never voted to invalidate a federal law challenged on commerce power grounds. Furthermore, he also believed that federal courts lacked any constitutional authority to strike down such initiatives. During the five terms of the Stone Court, the justices rendered 165 nonunanimous decisions involving some form of federal or state economic regulations. The Stone Court upheld just over 61 percent of these initiatives. Justice Black voted in support of these regulatory initiatives in 93.3 percent of these cases, ranking him first in such voting among justices of the Stone Court (modified from Pritchett 1948, 257).

Black's view that the courts possessed only limited authority to review federal statutes based on the commerce power transferred to state economic initiatives as well. Black fully supported the Court's abandonment of the substantive due process approach to reviewing state economic regulations. The more conservative justices sitting on the Court prior to Black's appointment had used this approach to strike down many state regulatory laws. Black rejected substantive due process, favoring instead more deference to state legislative judgments. It was Black's belief that the Court had no authority to review the reasonableness of regulatory legislation. He argued that the Fourteenth Amendment language referring to "persons" meant only people and did not extend to businesses or corporations.

Black was a relentless defender of individual rights, which was manifest in a number of issues. He believed that the Bill of Rights should fully apply to the states through the Fourteenth Amendment. His total incorporationist argument in *Adamson v. California* (1947) is regarded as the most compelling exposition of that view. Although a majority of the Court did not embrace total incorporation, in the 1960s Black was responsible, at least in part, for the Warren Court's nationalization of the rights of the accused provisions contained in the Fifth, Sixth, and Eighth Amendments.

Black rejected the "balancing" approach to rights protection, particularly as it was used in First Amendment cases. Rather, he read the "Congress shall make no law" language in the First Amendment as providing an absolute protection for "pure" speech. Although government could impose some restrictions on the timing and location of expressive activities, it could not regulate expressive content. Black was a vigorous advocate of the right of the people to freely express their views without government censorship of any kind. For Black, there should be no governmental interference with a person's use of First Amendment practices until the speech evolved into some form of conduct, action that could be constitutionally restricted by government—local or national. It was on this basis that Black concluded the government could not impose regulations on obscenity, for example. Black drew the line between speech and certain conduct associated with speech. He was "mortally afraid" of street protesters, believing that violent conduct would threaten the very essence of representative democracy and would, if left unchecked, lead to the destruction of freedom. He feared that organized protests of civil rights groups and the opponents of the Vietnam War would produce uncontrollable disorder (Ball 1996, 115).

Black split with his liberal colleagues on some equal protection issues. He joined the Warren Court majority in *Brown* but believed the equal protection clause should not be interpreted broadly to invalidate state actions that did not have a direct connection to race. Although race discrimination cases required strict scrutiny, all other classifications should be examined using a less stringent test. Unless there was an invidious or capricious use of governmental power that discriminated on the basis of race, "ill-advised or merely stupid legislative actions" should not be overturned by federal judges (Ball 1996, 118). Black thus distanced himself from other Warren Court justices such as Douglas, Brennan, and Marshall, who would have extended strict scrutiny to a number of classifications besides race.

Black's view of the right to privacy was analogous to his view on equal protection. In *Griswold v. Connecticut* (1965), the Court recognized a constitutional right of privacy, but Black strongly dissented, saying he found no explicit language in the Constitution guarding an individual's privacy. Black believed the Bill of Rights protections were sufficient and rejected Douglas's view that protections must be extensively expanded by judicial interpretation. Black's literal-textual interpretive approach led to an absolutist application of First Amendment guarantees. At the same time, his approach limited his willingness to support certain claims of rights violations.

Black had serious and personal differences with Justice Jackson. These differences evolved over time and eventually went beyond the purely ideological. Jackson was publicly critical of Black's participation in a 1945 case, *Jewell Ridge Coal Corp. v. Local No. 6167 of the United Mine Workers of America* (1945). Black's former law partner argued the case on behalf of the union, and Jackson was of the view that Black should not have participated in the case. Black not only participated but provided the decisive fifth vote for the United Mine Workers. By 1943 Black and Jackson "typified the rival polarities" that had emerged since 1939 on issues other than economic and social engineering by governments.

Stanley Forman Reed

George Sutherland, another of the anti–New Deal justices, left the Court in 1938 and presented Roosevelt with his second opportunity to nominate a justice. Stanley Forman Reed had been under serious consideration for the Van Devanter vacancy a year earlier, and he was the logical choice to succeed Sutherland. He met all Roosevelt's criteria for a Court nominee, and he was clearly committed to Roosevelt's domestic policy agenda. He was unanimously confirmed by the Senate on January 25, 1938.

Reed was born to a locally prominent family in the small town of Minerva, Kentucky. He earned two B.A. degrees, one from Kentucky Wesleyan College and the other from Yale University. Reed began law school at the University of Virginia but returned to Kentucky after a year. Although he resumed law school at Columbia University, he did not complete his degree there either. Instead, he spent a year in Paris and continued his legal studies at the Sorbonne. He concluded his legal education back in Kentucky by reading with a local attorney. He was admitted to the bar and began a legal practice then quickly became engaged in Kentucky politics. He served in the state legislature for four years beginning in 1912. He also played an active role on the congressional campaigns of Fred Vinson, who would eventually serve as chief justice during Reed's tenure on the Court. Following a period of military service, Reed joined a law firm in Maysville, Kentucky, and eventually became a partner. Among his principal corporate clients was Burley Tobacco Growers Cooperative Association. Reed was instrumental in organizing the cooperative and subsequently acted as its legal counsel. Notwithstanding his Democratic partisan affiliation, it was Reed's association with the cooperative that led to his appointment as counsel to the Federal Farm Board (FFB), an entity established during the Hoover administration to respond to the particular problems of agriculture in the post-depression period.

Just prior to the end of his term as president, Hoover appointed Reed as general counsel to the Reconstruction Finance Corporation (RFC), one of the organizations created to address the economic depression. The RFC made federal money available in the form of loans to various businesses, including agriculture. Reed was retained as general counsel to the RFC when Franklin Roosevelt succeeded Hoover, and the functions of the RFC were expanded. One of the RFC initiatives designed to raise the prices of agricultural commodities was to nullify provisions of private contracts requiring payment in gold. The authority of the government to pursue this and other

Stanley Forman Reed (Harris & Ewing, Collection of the Supreme Court of the United States)

related policies was challenged in the courts, and Reed was made a special assistant to the attorney general to participate in the presentation of the government's side before the Supreme Court in what were known as the gold clause cases (1935). The Court ruled in favor of the RFC in what was regarded as a significant New Deal success. Soon thereafter Roosevelt nominated Reed to serve as solicitor general, a position he held for three years. As solicitor general, Reed was the Roosevelt administration's principal advocate on New Deal policies under review by the Hughes Court. Reed believed that the government had a profound and positive role in managing the nation's economy. This view was evident when Reed acted as a supporter for interventionist economic policies and was reflected in Reed's progovernment predisposition while on the Supreme Court. He was particularly deferential to congressional judgments. If congressional intent was clear, that governed his review of statutes and administrative actions.

Reed frequently aligned himself with the Stone Court's more liberal justices, at least on economic regulation issues, but he was more often viewed as a center justice. More evident at the outset of his tenure on the Court was an orientation toward judicial restraint and general deference toward executive and legislative authority. In other words, Reed was "less likely to favor the use of judicial power, and more inclined to support the government and public order against claims of individual right and freedom" (Pritchett 1995, 1181). In this respect, Reed shared common ground with Hugo Black and Roosevelt appointees who came immediately after him.

Reed was in complete accord with the policy priorities of the Roosevelt administration, and his deference on those issues was expected. He supported a broad interpretation of congressional commerce power. He wrote the Court's opinion in *United States v. Appalachian Electric Power Co.* (1940), which substantially expanded federal authority over inland waterways by means of changing the test used in determining navigability. He argued that the appraisal of navigability must include improvements that might be made to allow commercial navigation to occur. The power of Congress over commerce is "not hampered because of the necessity for reasonable improvements to make an interstate waterway available for traffic" (*Appalachian Electric*, 408). He also joined the Court's ruling to uphold provisions of the Fair Labor Standards Act in *United States v. Darby Lumber Co.* (1941). In *Darby* the Court unanimously concluded that, among other things, the commerce power allowed Congress to prohibit items from moving in interstate commerce if they were, for example, produced by child labor. The Court saw the commerce power as complete and believed the congressional motives in its exercise were beyond judicial review. Reed agreed.

Reed's expansive view of federal commerce power also frequently prompted him to invalidate state laws that came into conflict with interstate commerce. In *Southern Pacific Railroad Co. v. Arizona* (1945), for example, he was part of the majority that struck down a state law that limited the length of trains because the regulation unnecessarily burdened interstate commerce. Similarly, Reed wrote the Court's opinion in *Cloverleaf Butter Co. v. Patterson* (1942), a case that limited state regulatory authority because federal regulation so extensively occupied the field as to preempt any state initiatives. At the same time, Reed was reluctant to extend provisions of the federal Bill of Rights to the states through the due process clause of the Fourteenth Amendment.

Reed generally deferred to executive judgments as well, or in Pritchett's words, "avoided challenges to the exercise of executive power" (Pritchett 1995, 1185). The strongest evidence of Reed's executive deference position is seen in his disagreement with the Vinson Court ruling in *Youngstown Sheet & Tube Co. v. Sawyer* (1952). In *Youngstown* a six-justice majority invalidated President Truman's seizing control of the country's steel mills during the Korean War. Reed joined Chief Justice Vinson's dissent and would have allowed the action taken by Truman on the basis of inherent power the president possesses in crisis situations.

Reed's record on civil liberties issues was somewhat mixed. He supported governmental regulation generally, even in situations where regulation impinged on individual rights. Reed was from an affluent southern family, and when viewed in this context his civil liberties record is not altogether surprising, especially in cases involving national security issues. Reed was unreceptive to civil liberties claims of those convicted of war-related crimes. He voted to uphold a treason conviction in *Cramer v. United States* (1945) but did so from a dissenting position. Similarly, he dissented in *Hartzel v. United States* (1944), when the Court struck down the conviction of a person who had sent pro-Nazi materials to military officers and persons registered for the draft. It was Reed's view that a trial court could have reasonably concluded that Hartzel's intent was to cause insubordination in the armed services.

Reed also distanced himself from what he saw as the absolutist positions taken by the Court's most liberal members. In *Martin v. Struthers* (1943), for example, he dissented from the Court's ruling that communities could not restrict the door-to-door distribution of printed materials. Reed viewed the regulation as "trivial" rather than one that effectively suppressed expression. He was also unreceptive to the First Amendment claims of the Jehovah's Witnesses. He was among the Court's majority in upholding both the compulsory flag salute exercise in public schools in *Minersville School District v. Gobitis* (1940) and the municipal license taxes on door-to-door peddlers in *Jones v. Opelika* (1942). When the Court reversed itself on both issues soon thereafter in *West Virginia State Board of Education v. Barnette* (1943) and *Murdock v. Pennsylvania* (1943), Reed strongly disagreed.

Reed opposed racial segregation, albeit reluctantly. He wrote the Court's opinion in *Smith v. Allwright* (1944), when the Court struck down the so-called white primary practice of selecting nominating candidates for public office. Reed joined the majority in *Morgan v. Virginia* (1946), as the Court held that racial segregation of interstate carriers unconstitutionally interfered with the federal government's authority to regulate interstate commerce. He also withdrew a dissent in *Brown v. Board of Education* (1954), the school desegregation case, to allow the Court to resolve the case through a single opinion.

According to C. Herman Pritchett, Reed had a positive view of government. Reed favored "equipping the government with adequate powers for economic control and social welfare" because it was an entity "not to be feared." His reluctance to support many of the individual rights claims coming before the Court was largely driven by his view of government—"aberrant individuals or groups" should not prevail over government acting in pursuit of the general good. He also believed that judicial power should not be used to second-guess legislative or executive judgments. To the contrary, he believed in "giving the political branches of government the power and the responsibility for governing" (Pritchett 1995, 1197).

Reed served under four chief justices, and the Court's membership changed extensively during his tenure. Reed was basically a judicial moderate but shifted back and forth between the majority and minority side because of the personnel changes on the Court. His votes were also affected by the different kinds of issues the Court ruled on during the 1940s and early 1950s. According to Henry J. Abraham, Reed was the "least glamorous and least mercurial" of the Roosevelt appointees who "faithfully backed" Roosevelt's domestic economic program. He is labeled a judicial conservative by some probably because he was opposed to "government by judges," moved more "slowly and cautiously" than most of his colleagues, and was "reluctant to side with his more liberal associates in their escalating rulings that favored individuals vis-à-vis government" (Abraham 1992, 219). When viewed across the full range of issues that came before the Court on which he served, his record appears more moderate than conservative. Reed retired from the Court at the age of seventy-two on February 2, 1957, after nineteen years of service. Because his health was still good, he frequently sat on cases for the Court of Appeals for the District of Columbia, a practice he continued until he was in his mid-eighties. He also served for a brief period as chair of the newly created Civil Rights Commission. Reed died on April 1, 1980.

Felix Frankfurter

Felix Frankfurter became the third Roosevelt Court justice when Roosevelt nominated him to replace Justice Benjamin N. Cardozo on January 5, 1939. His nomination was widely acclaimed, and he was confirmed by voice vote in the Senate less than two weeks later, on January 17. Frankfurter retired from the Court on August 28, 1962, after suffering a heart attack. He died on February 22, 1965.

Felix Frankfurter was born in Vienna, Austria, on November 15, 1882, and emigrated to the United States in 1894. He received his undergraduate education at City

Felix Frankfurter (Harris & Ewing, Collection of the Supreme Court of the United States)

College of New York, graduating in 1902. He earned his law degree from Harvard Law School in 1906 and began his legal career as an assistant U.S. attorney in New York. He subsequently served as assistant to Secretary of War Henry Stimson until 1914, when he returned to Harvard Law School as a member of the faculty. His extraordinary performance as a law professor earned him a national reputation as a legal scholar, and he was a recognized authority on the federal judiciary in particular.

Frankfurter engaged in activities away from Harvard that established strongly liberal credentials. He argued such cases as *Bunting v. Oregon* (1917) and *Adkins v. Children's Hospital* (1923) before the Supreme Court, advocating on behalf of a state maximum hour law and a federal minimum wage law, respectively. He also was active with the National Association for the Advancement of Colored People (NAACP) and the American Civil Liberties Union (ACLU) and conducted the appeals on behalf of Nicola Sacco and Bartolomeo Vanzetti, two anarchists convicted of murder. During the 1920s Frankfurter regularly used the *New Republic* as a forum for criticizing the judicial vetoes of the Taft Court. Frankfurter had numerous opportunities to leave Harvard but chose to remain there for twenty-five years. He would not, for example, allow his nomination to the Massachusetts Supreme Court in 1932, and he declined President Franklin D. Roosevelt's offer to become solicitor general the following year. While at Harvard, he became a member of Roosevelt's inner circle of advisers during the 1930s. He actively engaged in writing provisions for some of the early New Deal legislation. Indeed, in Michael Parrish's words, his "fingerprints were all over landmark pieces of legislation" such as the Norris-LaGuardia Act, Securities Act of 1933, and the Public Utility Holding Company Act of 1935 (Parrish 1994, 171). As the size of the federal government ballooned with the New Deal agencies, many of Frankfurter's students from Harvard were placed in key administrative positions.

Frankfurter had a lengthy and extremely close relationship with Oliver Wendell Holmes, and the two shared a commitment to judicial self-restraint. Indeed, Frankfurter succeeded Holmes as the Court's primary advocate of this approach to judicial decision making. He rejected the view that constitutional provisions were intended to be adapted to the "social arrangements and beliefs of a particular epoch" (Cushman 1993, 390). Even the vagueness of some of the provisions do not give courts authority to nullify the actions of the elective branches of government. The judicial opinions Frankfurter wrote were thoughtfully developed and solidly supported his conclusions. His judgments generally adhered to precedents as well. He belonged to no "jurisprudential coterie of the Court," although he most frequently joined Justice Robert Jackson and later Justice John M. Harlan in the Warren Court era (Cushman 1993, 390). Frankfurter had been criticized by those on the right as too radical, but in the most controversial cases that came before the Stone Court his positions were more conservative than Roosevelt anticipated (Asch 1971, 162). Michael Parrish has observed that Supreme Court justices have a "habit of disappointing, amazing, and confounding" the presidents who nominated them as well as those who supported or opposed their nominations, and he saw "few clearer examples of this axiom than Frankfurter" (Parrish 1994, 171).

Frankfurter's extrajudicial political activities, especially during World War II, were suspect from a separation of powers standpoint. Although there are historical precedents for interaction between justices and the elective branches, Frankfurter's extrajudicial involvements were unusual in scope and volume. Frankfurter assisted White House lawyers with drafting the executive agreement that transferred U.S. destroyers to Britain in exchange for leases on British naval bases, and he drafted sections of the Lend-Lease Act. Fortunately for Frankfurter, legal issues stemming from these matters never came before the Court. The same cannot be said of his role in a case involving German saboteurs, (*Ex parte Quirin [1942]*). President Roosevelt wanted all enemy aliens tried before a military tribunal rather than civilian courts. Secretary of War Henry Stimson consulted with Frankfurter about how to constitute such a military court. Frankfurter recommended that it be composed exclusively of regular officers and exclude any civilian leaders. He later vigorously defended this military tribunal when it was reviewed by the Court. Frankfurter played a major role in shaping Chief Justice Stone's opinion that rejected the saboteurs' habeas corpus plea in *Ex parte Quirin* (1942). Frankfurter's interactions with the executive branch ended with Roosevelt's death in 1945, when he lost access to both the White House and key agencies of the executive branch.

Historians have been critical of Frankfurter and his Court service. The publication of his own personal notes and letters suggest Frankfurter was both vain and insecure. Almost universally, scholars conclude that Frankfurter was a failure or at least a major disappointment. He was a justice who, in Joseph Lash's phrase, became "uncoupled from the locomotive of history" sometime during World War II and left little in the way of an enduring doctrinal legacy. Except for Justice McReynolds, it is "difficult to recollect a member of the Court who had worse personal relations with his colleagues" (Parrish 1994, 177). The Court's most "controversial and unhappy member," he operated best when "weaving crochet patterns of legalism on the fingers of the case." Not only did the ex-professor remain "notoriously a professor, lecturing and heckling attorneys and Court colleagues alike, he also remained a rather narrow academician, engrossed in the trivia of formal legal propriety" (Rodell 1955, 271). Frankfurter's particular kind of judicial restraint became passé as the Warren Court's agenda shifted to the expansion of civil rights and civil liberties.

Frankfurter's constitutional adversary, Justice Hugo Black, criticized Frankfurter's approach to constitutional rights protection as dangerously subjective, and one that led to an "accordion-like meaning of due process" (Parrish 1994, 180). Unlike Justice Black, Frankfurter was as deferential to legislative judgments across the board—he rejected the "preferred position" concept, seeing no meaningful difference between statutes involving economic regulation and those involving individual rights. Nonetheless, Frankfurter left a legacy that includes the primacy of judicial restraint in a democratic political system and the value of the U.S. federal-state governance structure. A "passionate believer in the democratic process with an abiding regard for the British concept of legislative supremacy," he would dedicate his twenty-three years on the Court to the proposition that the "people should govern, but that it was up to their elected representatives in the legislature, not to the appointed judiciary, to make laws" (Abraham 1992, 222). Albert Sacks has suggested that Frankfurter believed the genius of the Constitution was found in its "grand, general language creating a foundation for social ordering" (Sacks 1995, 2709). In contrast to Justice Black, Frankfurter rejected absolutes. He regarded many of the Hughes Court's decisions invalidating New Deal initiatives as abusive exercises of judicial power. The Court's proper role, in Frankfurter's view, should be nonpolitical, and justices must restrain themselves in order to fulfill its function in our governmental scheme and forestall external attempts to limits its authority. Frankfurter did not see judicial restraint as judicial "paralysis"; rather, judges must exercise judgment. On social and economic regulation, the "vague and amorphous restrictions of the due process clause had to be lifted, and rationally supportable legislation allowed to function" (Sacks 1995, 2409).

Procedural questions, at least in federal criminal cases, required a more active judicial role. Frankfurter was more activist in federal criminal cases where the Court had supervisory authority over lower federal courts and where relatively specific constitutional clauses were available to guide the justices. This activism did not carry over to state criminal cases, however, as seen in such cases as *Wolf v. Colorado* (1949). Frankfurter also rejected the view that speech and press were absolutes to be protected against all conflicting interests. Nor would he embrace the general approach that treated speech and press as "preferred" freedoms, the restriction of which was even presumptively invalid unless justified. He insisted on a case-by-case approach free of categorical prepossession and yet recognized speech as having special values in our system (Sacks 1995, 2408–2411). Frankfurter's jurisprudential philosophy enabled him to fully support the New Deal programs. But when it came to the interpretation of the Bill of Rights, Black and the other liberal activists, especially Douglas, Murphy, and Rutledge, would often part company—for Frankfurter brought the same principled sense of judicial restraint to legislation concerning human rights as he did to legislation concerning economic-proprietarian issues (Abraham 1992, 223).

Frankfurter's scrupulous adherence to his duty as a judge despite his personal policy preferences is best illustrated by his dissent in the second flag salute case (*Barnette*). Frankfurter, of course, would not have voted for such a law had he been a legislator because it compelled saluting the flag even by those, like the Jehovah's Witnesses, who regarded the act as paying homage to a graven image. But as a jurist he could not bring himself to join the majority opinion that the compulsory flag salute amounted to an unconstitutional invasion of the free exercise of religion and freedom of expression guaranteed by the First Amendment. Frankfurter's conception of the judicial function is also clearly evident in the legislative redistricting cases, where he consistently maintained his noninterventionist position.

William Orville Douglas

William O. Douglas became Franklin Roosevelt's fourth Supreme Court nominee in an eighteen-month period. He was nominated on March 20, 1939, and confirmed by the Senate in a 62–4 vote on April 4, 1939. He replaced Justice Louis D. Brandeis on the Court.

Douglas, born October 16, 1898, in Maine, Minnesota, suffered a number of hardships during his youth. When he was only six, his father died. Douglas also contracted polio. Despite these obstacles, Douglas was able to work his way through Whitman College in Washington and graduate with honors. After graduation he traveled across the country on freight trains, frequenting "hobo jungles" along the way and arriving in New York City with only six cents in his pocket. During his tenure on the Supreme Court, Douglas never lost his sensitivity for the poor and powerless. After a short period as a schoolteacher, Douglas entered Columbia Law School, where he graduated second in his class in 1925.

He spent the next several years dividing his time between a private practice, in which he specialized in corporate finance, and part-time teaching at Columbia Law School. Douglas began teaching full time in 1928 when he took a position as a member of the law faculty at Yale. While there Douglas was influenced by the legal realists at Yale who viewed law as a vehicle for bringing about social change. He cultivated his expertise in corporate law and finance as well. As a recognized expert, he was asked to do some investigative work for the Securities and Exchange Commission (SEC). In 1936 President Franklin D. Roosevelt appointed Douglas to the SEC, and he became its chair the following year. During his tenure with the SEC, Douglas became part of Roosevelt's inner circle and was the leading candidate for the Supreme Court when Brandeis left the Court in 1939.

Even after he joined the Court, Douglas remained politically connected to the Roosevelt White House. Before Roosevelt decided to run for a third term in 1940, Douglas was regarded as a possible candidate for president. Once Roosevelt entered the race, he seriously considered Douglas as his running mate. Four years later Roosevelt decided to replace Vice President Henry Wallace on the ticket and again deliberated the possibility of naming Douglas as candidate. In 1946 President Truman offered to nominate him to the position of interior secretary. Douglas declined. Two years later his name surfaced once more as a possible presidential candidate. He took himself out of the running but weighed at some length Truman's invitation to become

William Orville Douglas (Harris & Ewing, Collection of the Supreme Court of the United States)

his running mate in the 1948 election. He eventually turned down the offer, choosing to remain on the Court. Douglas was forty at the time of his nomination to the Court, making him the youngest nominee in more than 125 years. Douglas suffered a stroke on December 31, 1974. He retired from the Court less than a year later, on November 12, 1975, after thirty-six years of service, the longest tenure of any Supreme Court justice. Douglas died on January 19, 1980.

Douglas was a liberal activist justice. He saw the Court as a political institution with both the authority and the obligation to review the actions of the other two branches and apply constitutional checks when necessary. He saw his judicial role as deciding legal questions based on facts examined in particular contexts. Since his decisions were driven in large part by context or circumstances, his conclusions changed as well. Douglas continually reexamined his own positions and changed his mind on constitutional issues more often than did his colleagues, annoying some of them, particularly Justice Frankfurter. It also meant he was less inclined to adhere to previous decisions. His switched vote in the second compulsory flag salute case is illustrative. Douglas saw law as the product of social forces and the priorities of those who function in the legal system. Douglas was also a legal functionalist, regarding law as a means of achieving broad social objectives. Douglas rejected orthodoxy in any form, and although some aspects of the legal realist view were generally appealing to him, he resisted fully embracing its doctrine. It is for this reason that Douglas is often characterized as both highly independent and results-oriented.

Since Douglas came to the Court from the Securities and Exchange Commission, it is not surprising that he tended to favor the regulatory initiatives of the New Deal and, further, deferred to the judgment of regulatory agencies. He immediately paired with Justice Black in deciding all types of cases, and during his first three years on the Court the two voted the same way in every economic regulation case (Asch 1971, 212). In the five-term Stone Court period, Douglas supported federal and state regulatory initiatives in 82 percent of the 191 nonunanimous decisions on economic issues. Douglas's support level was the same as Murphy's and ranked only behind Black's 88 percent support rate (Pritchett 1948, 257). By comparison, the Court as a whole supported 58 percent of the regulatory initiatives of this kind during this same time.

Douglas became an unrelenting advocate of civil liberties by the 1950s, but during the Stone Court era Douglas was less receptive to individual rights claims than were Justices Murphy and Rutledge. This was most evident in cases where Douglas supported some wartime actions of the national government despite the possible adverse consequences for individual rights. He supported 94 percent of the individual rights claims arising out of state cases but only 33 percent of similar claims raised in federal cases. This diverse response was a direct result of his support of federal actions relating directly to the war, such as the relocation of the Japanese on the West

Coast and the criminal prosecution of those accused of sabotage or espionage. Douglas's 63 percent individual rights support rate ranked him fourth on the Stone Court behind Murphy (94 percent), Rutledge (83 percent), and Black (66 percent). The Stone Court as a whole decided 49 percent of these same cases in favor of those asserting individual liberty claims during this period (Pritchett 1948, 254). The four-justice bloc including Douglas clearly differed from the remainder of the Stone Court on individual rights issues.

Two of the Japanese relocation cases best reflect the influence of context on Douglas's decision making and his early inclination to see individual rights as conditional. Under review in *Hirabayashi v. United States* (1943) and *Korematsu v. United States* (1944) were the constitutionality of actions taken by military authorities to relocate and confine many Japanese on the West Coast. Douglas voted to uphold the curfew order imposed on those of Japanese ancestry in *Hirabayashi* and more broadly supported the relocation program in *Korematsu*. In these cases Douglas found that national emergency interests stemming from the war outweighed the individual rights interests of persons of Japanese descent. He referred to the situation the military faced after Pearl Harbor as "grave," and he rejected the option of requiring the military to examine individually all persons of Japanese ancestry to detain only those whose loyalty could not be established. Processes used in peacetime "do not necessarily fit wartime needs," Douglas concluded; where the "peril is great and the time short," temporary treatment on a group basis may be the "only practicable expedient" (*Korematsu*, 106).

Douglas became the civil liberties anchor of the Court during the Vinson justiceship and after. Justices Murphy and Rutledge were gone from the Court and in their places were Justices Sherman Minton and Tom Clark, both of whom were largely unreceptive to civil liberties claims. Douglas and Black usually were found as a dissenting minority of two in many individual rights cases of the period. Douglas moved to a position of virtual absolutism with respect to constitutional protections of individual rights during the Warren Court period. He also separated himself from longtime ally Justice Black, who was unwilling to modify some of his views, particularly on First Amendment expression rights, to meet the circumstances of the 1960s. During this time Douglas was a member of the liberal activist majority. Although he voted with the bloc in virtually every case, he often wrote concurring opinions that expressed views that went beyond the Court's rationale for particular rulings. In close to 96 percent of all cases "involving a line drawn between the rights of the individual and those of society, he sided with the former" (Abraham 1992, 227).

Douglas was a strong advocate of incorporating all the Bill of Rights guarantees to the states, but he was also willing to strike down policies even in the absence of explicit language from the Bill of Rights. He fully embraced the notion of a "living," or evolving, Constitution. The best example, of course, is the Warren Court ruling in *Griswold v. Connecticut* (1965) striking down a state law that prohibited the sale of contraceptives. Douglas said for the Court in *Griswold* that "penumbras" are formed by "emanations" from Bill of Rights language that enlarge the areas afforded constitutional protection. In *Griswold* several Bill of Rights provisions created overlapping "penumbras" to establish a constitutional right of privacy. The Connecticut birth control law was struck down because it interfered with a right to marital privacy.

Douglas left the Court in 1975. He had become its strongest proponent for the broadest interpretation of constitutional rights. The adaptive, ends-oriented approach he brought to the Court remained fully evident throughout his tenure. He clearly reflected the liberal activism of the Warren Court, and he often provoked highly critical response. This was particularly true during his last several years, when the Court became much more conservative and Douglas was no longer on the majority side of the Court's rulings. During his term on the Burger Court, many of his dissents contained unorthodox if not extreme legal arguments. As a result, these dissents were not well received in the academic and legal communities. He also provoked political reaction: On three separate occasions Congress considered his impeachment.

William Francis Murphy

William Francis (Frank) Murphy was Franklin Roosevelt's fifth and most reluctant nominee for the Supreme Court—it was a position Murphy did not seek and about which he had substantial self-doubts. When Justice Pierce Butler, a persistent opponent of the New Deal, left the Court, Roosevelt nominated his attorney general, Frank Murphy. Although some members of the Senate had reservations about Murphy, he was unanimously confirmed by voice vote on January 15, 1940.

Frank Murphy was born in Sand Beach, Michigan, on April 13, 1890, to a devoutly Catholic and politically active family. He received his law degree from the University of Michigan in 1914 and joined a Detroit law firm until his military service in World War I. On his discharge from the service, he was appointed an assistant U.S. attorney for the Eastern District of Michigan. A brief period of private practice followed, but Murphy soon returned to public life. Law and politics were opposite sides of the same coin for Murphy, and he combined the two with his election as judge of Detroit's Recorder's Court in 1923. During his tenure on Recorder's Court, he was instrumental in effecting fundamental changes in its operations. All the while he entertained political ambitions, including the presidency.

His record as a trial judge demonstrated unusual sensitivity to the interests of racial minorities and those of limited economic resources. He was able to coalesce these constituencies with others and was elected mayor of Detroit in 1930. His response to the extensive economic distress of the depression was to fashion a public assistance program at the local level. He also played a significant role in Franklin Roosevelt's election to the presidency in 1932. Soon after Roosevelt's inauguration,

William Francis (Frank) Murphy (Pach Brothers, Collection of the Supreme Court of the United States)

Murphy was appointed governor-general of the Philippines. During his tenure he brought about significant economic reforms and strongly supported Philippine independence. He returned from the Philippines in time to be elected governor of Michigan in 1936. As governor, he was immediately faced with a sit-down strike of automobile workers. He called out the National Guard to maintain order while bringing about resolution to the labor-management dispute. Both sides in the dispute, however, thought that Murphy had been too sympathetic to the interests of the other. Murphy was not able to reassemble his political coalition from 1936, and he was defeated in his bid for reelection.

Murphy's defeat in his gubernatorial campaign resulted in a change of venue, a move to Washington, D.C. Roosevelt appointed him attorney general in 1939. Among his other priorities in the post, Murphy aggressively sought to protect the interests of organized labor and racial minorities. The intensity of this pursuit created some friction inside the Roosevelt administration and prompted Roosevelt to nominate him for the Supreme Court, at least in part to remove Murphy and his agenda from the Justice Department.

He sat on the highest bench for about a decade and has been characterized as the most liberal justice ever to serve on the Court. He was deeply influenced by the political militancy of his father and the unyielding social values reflected in his mother's Catholicism. Murphy viewed law as a means by which the ends of freedom and justice might be advanced. According to Peter Irons, Murphy subscribed to a "visceral" jurisprudence and his opinions, particularly the dissents, "swept aside technical 'niceties' in a quest for justice and 'human dignity'" (Irons 1994, 331). Murphy's ten years on the Court are most effectively represented from this vantage point.

Two broad observations apply to Murphy's record as a Stone Court justice. First, the Stone Court divided into two groups—the judicial activists and the judicial self-restraintists. Murphy was clearly among the former. He eventually aligned himself with Justices Black, Douglas, and Rutledge, but initially he was more inclined to join the Court's majorities and not rock the boat. During his first two terms, he frequently looked to Chief Justice Hughes and Justice Frankfurter for guidance in deciding cases. By the 1941 term, Murphy's more natural philosophical inclinations began to emerge, and in 78 percent of the nonunanimous decisions he aligned himself with Black and 72 percent of the time with Douglas, then the Court's most prominent liberal activists. By contrast, he voted with Stone and Jackson in 48 percent of these cases and with Roberts in only 34 percent. These interagreement levels were maintained through the 1944 term. In the 1945 term, the interagreement levels with Douglas and Black fell into the mid-60 percent range. The span of his agreement rates narrowed as well. Murphy agreed with the new Stone Court member, Harold Burton, least often—in 45 percent of the cases. The previous term Murphy had agreed with Justice Roberts, who was replaced by Burton, in only 25 percent of the Court's decisions.

Second, Murphy was more receptive to claims of individual rights violations than any justice on the Stone Court. The Stone Court supported the personal liberty position in 49 percent of the eighty-two nonunanimous decisions in this five-year span. Murphy, by comparison, supported the personal liberty position in 94 percent of these cases, a position he had to express through a dissent in almost half of the cases. Justices Frankfurter, Jackson, Roberts, and Reed voted in support of the individual rights claim in only 30 percent of these cases during this period. Justices Black and Douglas voted in support of individual rights positions in less than two-thirds of these cases.

Murphy's self-doubts about his capacity to function as a jurist did not prevent him from having a clear judicial philosophy—he fully subscribed to the "preferred position" view of constitutional rights, that is, rights occupy a preferred, or elevated, position relative to other constitutional provisions. The preferred position view is given effect by subjecting any law that impinges on a protected right to extremely close or searching scrutiny. Murphy clearly signaled the priority he assigned to constitutional rights in *Thornhill v. Alabama* (1940), his first major opinion for the Court. In *Thornhill* Murphy "launched one of the Court's boldest and most controversial experiments with freedom of expression—the doctrine that constitutional guarantees of free communication include peaceful picketing" (Howard 1968, 238). A law that imposes penal sanctions for picketing readily lends itself to harsh and discriminatory enforcement by local prosecuting officials against particular groups deemed to merit their displeasure. This results in a continuous and pervasive restraint on all freedoms of discussion that might reasonably be regarded as within its purview (*Thornhill*, 97–98).

The war led Murphy uncharacteristically to take the government's side against individual rights claims, albeit infrequently. He joined the Court in upholding the compulsory saluting of the flag in schools in *Minersville School District v. Gobitis* (1940), for example. Murphy was prepared to dissent in this case but was persuaded by Frankfurter's appeal to his patriotism to join the majority opinion. Similarly, he voted with the Court in upholding the curfew provisions of Roosevelt's executive order directed at those of Japanese ancestry following the attack on Pearl Harbor. The decision subordinated obvious discrimination against Japanese Americans to "military necessity." As in the first flag salute case, Murphy had written a dissent but again yielded to Frankfurter's appeal to national security and patriotism. Murphy voted with the majority, but his concurring opinion retained some of the strong language from his draft dissent.

The constitutional issues raised in *Gobitis* and *Hirabayashi* quickly returned to the Court, giving Murphy the opportunity to "correct" the positions he had taken originally. Indeed, enough other justices changed their minds in the second flag salute case, *West Virginia State Board of Education v. Barnette* (1943), to overrule *Gobitis*. Justice Jackson's majority opinion in *Barnette* focused the Jehovah Witnesses' free expression, as distinct from religious, interests. Murphy, however, specifically grounded his concurring opinion on religious freedom. He said that "reflection" had convinced him that he had "no loftier duty or responsibility than to uphold . . . spiritual freedom to its farthest reaches." He also expressed skepticism that patriotism and national unity could be advanced by mandatory flag salute exercises. Rather, it is in the "freedom and the example of persuasion, not in force and compulsion, that the real unity of America lies" (*Barnette*, 645–646). The Court did not reverse itself on the relocation of the Japanese before the war ended, but Murphy did in unmistakable terms. He suggested, among other things, that the Court's ruling constituted the "legalization of racism." Murphy's dissent in *Korematsu* is regarded by many as the strongest opinion he authored during his ten years on the Court.

It was Murphy's view that constitutional protections extended even to the most despised. Three war-related prosecutions are illustrative. William Schneiderman was a member of the Communist Party and embraced its political agenda. Twelve years after his naturalization, the government sought to reclaim his citizenship on the grounds that he had "fraudulently" taken his oath of allegiance as a precondition for citizenship. The government argued that he could not have truthfully claimed to support the principles of the Constitution and then participate in the activities of a party committed to the violent overthrow of the government. Murphy wrote for the Court in *Schneiderman v. United States* (1943) that the government could not "turn the clock back twelve years" in order to strip him of the "priceless benefits" of citizenship for engaging in protected activities. Murphy similarly agreed that Harry Bridges ought not be deported. Bridges was head of the International Longshoreman's union and was seen by many as having troublesome connections to the Communists. For a number of years, efforts to have Bridges, a native Australian, deported for alleged illegal "affiliation" with the Communists were unsuccessful. Congress then changed the law giving the Justice Department greater power in deportation cases, and Bridges was ordered deported under the new law. The Stone Court set aside the orders in *Bridges v. Wixom* (1945), however, on procedural due process grounds.

Murphy was livid that the Court treated the case as presenting "wholly administrative" questions, and he refused to join the majority opinion. Instead, he referred to the long-term efforts to deport Bridges as a "monument to man's intolerance of man." He suggested that there had never been such a "concentrated and relentless" crusade to deport someone for daring to "exercise the freedom that belongs to him as a human being and that is guaranteed to him by the Constitution" (Howard 1968, 349). Finally, Murphy was adamant that procedural guarantees of the Constitution extend to all persons, even enemy military officers. General Tomoyuki Yamashita was prosecuted before a military tribunal for war crimes at the end of the war. It was alleged that his troops committed various and extensive atrocities in the Philippines. It was Murphy's view in *In re Yamashita* (1946) that due process guarantees extend even to war crimes defendants. The protections afforded by the Bill of Rights "rise above any status of belligerency or outlawry." Such rights "survive any popular passion or frenzy of the moment. No court or legislature or executive, not even the mightiest army in the world, can ever destroy them." Fred Rodell has written that no justice "in all Court history—not Holmes, not Stone, not Black, not Douglas—was so consistent and passionate a judicial crusader for civil liberties for everyone; for Nazi spies and for Japanese generals, in peacetime and in wartime, as Murphy" (Rodell 1955, 278).

According to Abraham, Murphy would "all-but-inevitably side with the underdog" (Abraham 1992, 230). Many of the positions taken by Murphy, often in dissent, presaged the decisions that would come from the Warren Court in the 1950s and 1960s. Murphy would have enthusiastically embraced the civil liberties priorities of the Warren Court. As early as 1942, Murphy began to experience health problems, and during his last three years on the Court he was hospitalized several times. Soon after the completion of the 1948 term of the Court, he suffered a fatal heart attack and died on July 19, 1949.

James F. Byrnes

James F. Byrnes was strongly considered for the vice presidential nomination in 1940, but Roosevelt chose to pay off his political IOUs to Byrnes with a Supreme Court seat instead. When Chief Justice Hughes left the Court in 1941, Roosevelt elevated Harlan F. Stone to the chief justiceship and nominated Byrnes to fill the Stone vacancy on June 12, 1941. The Senate approved the nomination by voice vote the same day. Byrnes, Roosevelt's most conservative nomination for the Court, became the sixth new justice Roosevelt had placed on the highest bench. By the time Byrnes was appointed to the Court, it was already a safely pro–New Deal body.

Byrnes was born in Charleston, South Carolina, on May 2, 1882. At the age of fourteen, after only seven years of formal education, Byrnes took a job clerking for a prestigious Charleston law firm. While working in this capacity, he read extensively in the law, and was admitted to the South Carolina bar in 1903. He opened a law practice, became co-owner and editor of the local newspaper, and soon thereafter began his political career as well. He was elected prosecuting attorney in 1908 and elected to Congress two years later. A Democrat, Byrnes pursued a relatively progressive agenda during his fourteen years in the House and was highly supportive of the policy initiatives of President Woodrow Wilson. Byrnes lost a bid for the U.S. Senate seat from South Carolina in 1924 and resumed his legal practice in Spartanburg, South Carolina. Six years later Byrnes again sought election to the Senate and unseated the person who had defeated him in 1924.

Byrnes had become a close friend of Franklin Roosevelt during his tenure in the House, and he was one of Roosevelt's principal political advisers during the presi-

James F. Byrnes (Harris & Ewing, Collection of the Supreme Court of the United States)

dential campaign in 1932. A fiscal conservative, Byrnes nonetheless successfully guided many New Deal proposals to passage in the Senate during Roosevelt's first term. Byrnes was a political pragmatist and earned a reputation as an effective compromiser. He viewed political issues as debates about policy options rather than non-negotiable political principles. Although Byrnes's enthusiasm waned during Roosevelt's second term, he continued to provide Roosevelt with political counsel and broker selected legislation in the Senate. Most important in Roosevelt's second term was Byrnes's role in securing passage of the Administrative Reorganization Act of 1939, which, among other things, expanded the presidency by authorizing the establishment of the Executive Office of the President.

Byrnes also advised Roosevelt that persisting with the Court-packing proposal was unnecessary because of Justice Van Devanter's resignation from the Court. Van Devanter was one of the hard-line opponents of the New Deal, and his retirement assured that the pro–New Dealers could consistently sustain a majority. Byrnes supposedly phrased his advice on the Court-packing issue by asking Roosevelt, "Why run for a train after you've caught it?" Byrnes's support of the New Deal domestic agenda diminished after 1936. Indeed, he saw his role as "counterbalancing" the "radical ideas" of the "extreme liberals" who surrounded Roosevelt (Murphy 1995, 1266). At the same time, Byrnes was instrumental in securing the adoption of many of Roosevelt's proposals in the area of foreign policy and national security, thus indebting Roosevelt to a substantial extent. Most significant, Roosevelt asked Byrnes to act as floor manager in the Senate for the administration's "most important prewar defense legislation, the Lend-Lease Act" (Robertson 1994, 296).

Byrnes served on the Court for only one year. Although he had been generally supportive of the New Deal's economic recovery objectives, he withheld support from the liberal New Deal initiatives on such policy issues as welfare, labor, and race. This accurately foreshadowed his inclinations as a judicial conservative. His voting agreement scores with both his liberal and conservative colleagues were not significantly different. His highest interagreement scores in the nonunanimous cases decided in the 1941 term were with Justices Jackson (68.7 percent) and Frankfurter (67.2 percent). By contrast, he agreed with Justice Douglas least often, at 52.6 percent (Renstrom 1972, 295). The range of his agreement numbers from high to low was unusually narrow.

In the single term he served on the Court, Byrnes wrote sixteen opinions, all of them majority opinions. Byrnes is best known for his opinion in *Edwards v. California* (1941), which reveals his differences with the Stone Court's liberal activists. *Edwards* involved a California statute that made it a misdemeanor to bring or assist in relocating an indigent nonresident into the state. Edwards, a California resident, brought his wife's brother, an unemployed resident of Texas, to California. Shortly thereafter, the brother-in-law sought financial assistance from the government. Edwards was convicted of violating the California law and was given a six-month suspended sentence.

The Stone Court unanimously struck down the statute but divided on the reasons for doing so; four justices chose not to join Byrnes's opinion, which focused on federal authority over interstate commerce. California could not prohibit bringing an indigent person into the state, said Byrnes, without establishing an unconstitutional "barrier to interstate commerce." Byrnes suggested that while the Court ought not review either the wisdom or appropriateness of state legislative initiatives, state police power is limited by the federal Constitution nonetheless. No state may "isolate itself from difficulties common to all of them by restraining the transportation of persons and property across its borders." Byrnes saw the "express purpose and inevitable effect" of the California law to prohibit the transportation of indigents into the state. The burden this imposed on interstate commerce was "intended and immediate, . . . the plain and sole function of the statute" (*Edwards*, 173–174). Justices Douglas, Black, and Murphy agreed that California law was unconstitutional but saw the right of persons to cross state lines as occupying a "more protected position in our constitutional system than does the movement of cattle, fruit, steel and coal across state lines." Unlike Byrnes, the dissenters saw the right of free movement as an incident of state citizenship and would have used the privileges and immunities clause of the Fourteenth Amendment to strike down the California law.

Byrnes also wrote the Court's opinion in *Taylor v. Georgia* (1942), where the Court struck down a state law prohibiting a person who accepted advance payment for work to leave until the advance was repaid. Byrnes said for the Court that was "coerced labor" that violated both the Thirteenth Amendment and a federal peonage law. The *Edwards* and *Taylor* cases were somewhat atypical, however. More frequently Byrnes was unreceptive to libertarian arguments. For example, he was among the majority in rejecting coerced confession claims in *Lisenba v. California* (1941) and assistance of counsel arguments in *Betts v. Brady* (1942). Byrnes's record on claims arising out of the First Amendment was strikingly similar. He disagreed with the Court's decision in *Bridges v. California* (1941) to permit the news media to make highly critical editorial comments about a judge while a case was still before him. Byrnes supported limitations on unions' right to freely engage in picketing in cases such as *Carpenters' and Joiners' Union v. Ritter's Café* (1942), and he voted in *Chaplinsky v. New Hampshire* (1942) to uphold a breach of peace conviction against a person who engaged in provocative speech. Byrnes supported civil liberties claims less often than his colleagues, ranking ahead of only Justice Roberts during the 1941 term.

Byrnes continued to provide political counsel to Roosevelt even while he was on the Court. Indeed, he was the behind-the-scenes sponsor of the First and Second War Powers Acts passed by Congress in March 1942 (Robertson 1994, 312). He was an extremely skilled politician, and his mind "sought consensus rather than new constructions and was fundamentally impatient with judicial procedures" (Robertson 1994, 303). Unlike the other justices, Byrnes seldom engaged in debates, ideological or otherwise, over the wording of opinions. This trait was an apparent holdover from his Senate career, where he was "more interested in the outcome of a vote than in the ideological speeches" that preceded voting.

Following the attack on Pearl Harbor, Byrnes wished to play a more active role in the war effort. He couldn't stand the "abstractions of jurisprudence at a time like this," preferring instead to "be in it." In part because of this feeling, it was "incontrovertible that his one term on the Supreme Court was the unhappiest of his public life" (Robertson 1994, 304). Thus when Roosevelt asked him to take on a substantial executive role during the war, Byrnes did not hesitate in resigning from the Court. He first became director of the Office of Economic Stabilization and then director of the Office of War Mobilization (OWM), a position that gave Byrnes authority directly to manage the domestic war effort. The magnitude of this role led Byrnes to become known as the "assistant president." Byrnes sought the vice presidential nomination in 1944 but was not selected. This rejection troubled him greatly, and it ultimately led him to resign as director of OWM. He intended to return to his law practice in South Carolina, but Roosevelt died and Harry Truman succeeded to the presidency. Truman asked Byrnes to stay on as his secretary of state, and he served in that capacity until early 1947, when a deteriorating relationship with Truman and health problems prompted Byrnes return to South Carolina.

Byrnes's departure from Washington enabled him to speak critically about what he saw as the liberal excesses of the Truman administration. Although he could no longer support Truman, he did not participate in the Dixiecrat revolt in 1948, when a number of southern Democrats broke away from the party largely over fundamental civil rights differences. Byrnes reentered the political arena in 1950, successfully campaigning for governor of South Carolina. During his four-year term, he sought to implement what must be regarded as moderate civil rights policies, at least for South Carolina in the 1950s. Following his tenure as governor, Byrnes largely retired from public life. He did, however, take part in the criticism of the Warren Court and its activism, particularly its school desegregation rulings.

Robert Houghwout Jackson

Robert Houghwout Jackson was a front-runner for a place on the Supreme Court but was passed over three times by President Roosevelt. When Harlan F. Stone was elevated to chief justice on the retirement of Charles Evans Hughes, Jackson was nominated on June 12, 1941, to fill Stone's seat. Jackson was confirmed by voice vote of the Senate on July 7, 1941.

Robert H. Jackson was born in Spring Creek, Pennsylvania, on February 13, 1892. His formal education did not go beyond high school, although he attended Albany Law School for a short time. Jackson studied law by the apprenticeship

Robert Houghwout Jackson (Harris & Ewing, Collection of the Supreme Court of the United States)

method through his affiliation with a law firm in Jamestown, New York. He was admitted to the bar in 1913 and began a successful private practice. As a Democrat, Jackson had some contact with Franklin D. Roosevelt during the 1920s. He was offered appointment to the New York Public Service Commission by then Governor Roosevelt but declined. Jackson's public role was limited to his service as Jamestown corporation counsel. In 1934 Roosevelt offered Jackson the post of general counsel to the Bureau of Internal Revenue; Jackson accepted. Between 1936 and 1941, Jackson became in succession assistant U.S. attorney general, solicitor general, and U.S. attorney general. He was considered a possible presidential candidate in 1940 until Roosevelt decided to seek an unprecedented third term.

In 1945 Jackson took an eighteen-month leave from the Court to serve as chief prosecutor for the United States at the Nuremberg war crimes trials. Jackson would have preferred to play a more active role in the country's war effort than serving on the Court, which may explain his willingness to participate in the Nuremberg trials. Indeed, Jackson regarded the Nuremberg period as the "most constructive" of his legal career, "infinitely more important than [his] work on the Supreme Court."

When Chief Justice Stone died, it was thought that Jackson might succeed him. Jackson certainly aspired to be chief justice, but "tragically, his path was blocked in considerable measure by a doctrinal and personal feud with Justice Black," who threatened to leave the Court if Jackson were named (Abraham 1992, 235). Truman ultimately chose Fred Vinson to succeed Stone. Jackson released a statement from Nuremberg revealing the nature and basis of his strife with Justice Black. The two had philosophical differences on a number of issues, but the heart of their dispute was Black's failure to recuse himself from hearing a case where one of the parties was represented by counsel who twenty years before had been Black's partner. The disagreement about disqualification was aggravated because the case, *Jewell Ridge Coal Corp. v. Local No. 6167 of the United Mine Workers of America* (1945), was decided by a 5–4 vote. However strong his position might have been on the merits of the recusal dispute with Black, Jackson never fully recovered from the decision to make the conflict public. Daniel A. Farber suggested that the "repercussions of this ugly public fight poisoned Jackson's later years on the Court." Furthermore, "his absence from the Court for an entire term compounded his difficulties with his colleagues" upon his return (Mason 1956, 714–719). Jackson remained on the Court until his death on October 9, 1954.

Jackson was, in Fred Rodell's view, a "most gifted wielder of words." The opinion often mentioned as containing his best prose is *West Virginia State Board of Education v. Barnette* (1943), the second flag salute decision. Three years earlier the Court had held in *Minersville School District v. Gobitis* (1940) that Jehovah's Witnesses could be expelled from a public school for refusing on religious grounds to participate in flag salute ceremonies. By 1943, however, the Court came to a different conclusion, and Jackson offered the rationale. He deemphasized the religious motive of the Witnesses and instead argued the more general communicative dimension of the Witnesses' refusal to salute the flag. He acknowledged that the case was made difficult "not because the principles of its decision are obscure, but because the flag involved is our own." Nonetheless, the freedom to hold different views is not "limited to things that do not matter much. That would be a mere shadow of freedom." Rather, the test is the right to "differ as to things that touch the heart of the existing order." He concluded by saying that "if there is any fixed star in our constitutional constellation, it is that no official, high or petty, can prescribe what shall be orthodox in politics, nationalism, religion, or other matters of opinion or force citizens to confess by word or act their faith therein" (*Barnette*, 641–642). The *Barnette* ruling proved particularly significant in that it reflected the redirection of the Court from economic to individual freedoms issues.

The views Jackson expressed in the *Barnette* opinion did not in his case generalize to other individual rights issues. Rather, he more typically was amenable to government regulation of expression if such expression produced sufficient danger or threat to the public interest. During his four terms on the Stone Court, Jackson supported individual rights claims in 30 percent of the cases. His predisposition to defer to governmental authority in civil liberties cases, particularly those involving First Amendment rights, became evident after his return from Nuremberg during the cold war. Illustrative of this position is his vote to uphold the Smith Act convictions of Communist Party members in *Dennis v. United States* (1951). He was also inclined to allow states to administer their criminal justice processes without federal judicial intervention.

Jackson was something of a judicial maverick—not as predictable as Black and Frankfurter, who possessed more fixed judicial philosophies. Despite his capacity to compose masterful opinions, Jackson was nonetheless neither an intellectual nor political leader on the Court. He was known for his commitment to judicial self-restraint, and his deference to federal legislative authority allowed him to play a substantial role in redefining federal and state regulatory power. The Court had begun to recognize greater federal authority to regulate the economy by the time Jackson became a justice, but his opinion in *Wickard v. Filburn* (1942) made it clear just how extensive the federal commerce power had become. In *Wickard* the Court upheld wheat production and marketing quotas contained in the Agricultural Adjustment Act of 1938. The law was designed to stabilize agricultural production and commodity prices by limiting the number of acres that farmers could put into production. Filburn operated a small farm in Ohio and grew wheat on 11.9 acres over his allotment. Filburn had not attempted to market any of his wheat but had used it exclusively for his own consumption. Jackson wrote for a unanimous Court that the commerce power enabled Congress to regulate even that part of agricultural production not destined for the market. Jackson abandoned the distinction between direct and indirect effects, suggesting instead that the commerce power extends to those intrastate activities that so affect interstate commerce or the "exertion of the power of Congress over it." Wheat grown for personal consumption would have a "substantial influence on price and market conditions," because being in a marketable condition, the wheat grown for home consumption "overhangs the market" and may be "induced" to flow into the market by rising prices (*Wickard*, 128). Recognition of federal regulatory authority such as that reflected in *Wickard* posed fundamental questions about the coexistence of federal and state regulatory power. According to G. Edward White, the essential issue was whether a "spirit of judicial permissiveness toward state economic regulation could be maintained in the face of the increased presence of the federal government." Federalism was a "doctrine that could justify both local and national primacy, depending on the emphasis of the framers" (White 1976, 243). Jackson was of the view that on the question of economic federalism the framers had preferred "one commercial and economic unit and not a collection of parasitic states preying on each other's commerce." At the same time, Jackson saw areas where state primacy was favored. Federalism required a "measure of judicial deference to the states in their efforts to maintain security and order within their boundaries" (White 1976, 244). It is largely for this reason that Jackson's record on civil liberties issues did not resemble those of Black, Douglas, Murphy, or Rutledge.

Jackson "mirrored the contradictory jurisprudential impulses of the times." He maintained a "vividly personalized" approach to judging while at the same time developing a theory of adjudication that "emphasized the importance of internalized restraints on judges" (White 1976, 231). He was known for his forceful, direct, and plain-talk opinions. Near the end of his tenure on the Court, he attacked the "cult of libertarian judicial activists" whose views he thought encouraged the belief that the "judges may be left to correct the result of public indifference to issues of liberty." This view led Jackson to serve as a "counterweight to militant liberalism" as a member of the Stone Court and an "aid to those who tolerated curtailment of civil liberties when national security was allegedly involved" during the cold war that followed (White 1976, 246).

Wiley Blount Rutledge Jr.

When Justice Byrnes left the Court to become Roosevelt's administrator of domestic economic regulations during the war, Wiley Blount Rutledge Jr. was nominated on January 11, 1943, to fill the vacancy. He was confirmed by a voice vote in the Senate on February 8, 1943. Rutledge was Roosevelt's last appointment to the Court and the only one with prior judicial experience. He served for a little more than six years until

Wiley Blount Rutledge Jr. (Harris & Ewing, Collection of the Supreme Court of the United States)

his untimely death at the age of fifty-five from a cerebral hemorrhage on September 10, 1949.

Rutledge was born in Cloverport, Kentucky, on July 20, 1894. The son of a fundamentalist minister, Rutledge spent his youth in a number of locations in North Carolina, Kentucky, and Tennessee. He began his undergraduate career at Marysville College but completed his degree at the University of Wisconsin. Rutledge wished to enter law school at Wisconsin but was unable to do so for financial reasons. Instead, he moved to Bloomington, Indiana, and taught high school while attending Indiana Law School.

He contracted tuberculosis, however, and was hospitalized for a lengthy period. For the next three years, Rutledge lived in Albuquerque, New Mexico, where he taught and had administrative responsibilities for the board of education. Having fully recovered his health, he moved to Boulder, Colorado, to resume his law studies, receiving his LL.B. from the University of Colorado in 1922. He spent two years in private practice in Boulder before taking a faculty appointment at the University of Colorado Law School, the first of a number of academic positions Rutledge would hold. In 1926 he went to Washington University and became dean of the law school in 1930. Five years later Rutledge became dean of the University of Iowa College of Law.

Rutledge was an enthusiastic supporter of President Franklin D. Roosevelt and the New Deal, and he was highly vocal in his criticism of the Supreme Court decisions invalidating many of the essential elements of it. In addition, Attorney General Francis Biddle assured Roosevelt that Rutledge was a "bona fide libertarian." These views plus his endorsement of Roosevelt's Court-packing proposal convinced Roosevelt, who nominated him to the U.S. Court of Appeals for the District of Columbia in 1939.

Rutledge saw Article 1 of the U.S. Constitution as vesting Congress with broad authority, and he consistently voted to use the interstate commerce and taxing powers to expand the federal regulatory role over the economy. During his tenure on the court of appeals, Rutledge was supportive of the increased regulatory power vested in federal administrative agencies, particularly the National Labor Relations Board (NLRB). At the same time, he was highly suspicious of governmental power when it impinged upon individual rights. Rutledge was a liberal activist and immediately joined Chief Justice Stone and Justices Black, Douglas, and Murphy as a voting bloc controlling most of the decisional outcomes in individual rights cases. It was this bloc that gave at least partial effect to the "preferred position" doctrine introduced by Stone in *United States v. Carolene Products Co.* (1938).

Next to Justice Murphy, Rutledge was the Court's most consistent supporter of cases involving claims of constitutional rights violations. He supported claims from criminal defendants of procedural violations in more than 90 percent of the cases, and he supported claimed First Amendment violations in almost 80 percent of those cases (Nash 1994, 392). He also subscribed to the position that the due process clause of the Fourteenth Amendment conveyed all of the Bill of Rights restrictions to the states. Furthermore, it was Rutledge's view, shared by Justice Murphy, that beyond the protections afforded by the Bill of Rights itself the Fourteenth Amendment brought additional substantive protections as well, and that these protections broadened restraints on state authority. By the time Rutledge died, the liberal activists were no longer the majority. Many of the positions represented in his opinions during his terms on the Vinson Court were eventually embraced by the Warren Court.

Rutledge averaged slightly less than thirty opinions per year during his six terms on the Court. The most enduring of these opinions were written in individual rights cases. Rutledge and Murphy gave the Bill of Rights provisions about criminal rights particularly expansive interpretation. Rutledge ruled against the government in most cases containing self-incrimination or Fourth Amendment violations, and he voted in support of every right to counsel claim asserted by a criminal defendant. Rutledge maintained his commitment to procedural fairness even when the criminal defendants were political subversives or military enemies. In *Schneiderman v. United States* (1943), for example, Rutledge opposed the revocation of a Communist Party member's naturalization. He concluded that if naturalization decisions could be reexamined years after they were made, "no naturalized person's citizenship is or can be secured" (*Schneiderman*, 128). Similarly, Rutledge vigorously dissented from the Court's decision to uphold the war crimes conviction of a Japanese general in *In re Yamashita* (1946). The Court deferred to the military commission that tried Yamashita and chose not to review the commission's findings, but Rutledge was highly critical of the failure to incorporate protective procedural requirements. In particular, he focused on the admissibility of evidence that could not have been used in a civilian trial. In his view the procedures used by the commission were a "most flagrant" departure from the "whole British-American tradition of the common law and the Constitution" (*Yamashita*, 55).

Both Rutledge's recognition of the "preferred position" concept and his general commitment to the support of labor are revealed in *Thomas v. Collins* (1945). Texas law required that union organizers obtain an "organizer's card" from the state before soliciting prospective union members. Thomas, president of the United Auto Workers (UAW), went to Texas and spoke at a meeting where he clearly invited nonunion members to join the union even though he had not secured an organizer's card. The Court struck down the Texas law on a 5–4 vote, and Rutledge offered the Court's rationale: The statute was unconstitutional for two reasons. First, the restriction was overbroad, thus allowing Texas to punish protected speech. Texas had conceded that Thomas was free to "laud unionism" as he wished but not solicit new members. Rutledge failed to see how speaking favorably about unionism could be distinguished from at least implicit invitation to join. The effect of the Texas restriction was to prohibit both solicitation of members and speech "in advocacy of the cause of trade unionism." Second, the Court found no "clear and present danger" to the public to justify the restriction. A restriction "so destructive of the right of public discussion, without greater or more imminent danger to the public interest than existed in this case, is compatible with the freedoms secured by the First Amendment." If exercising the right of free speech and assembly "cannot be made a crime," Rutledge continued, "we do not think this can be accomplished by the device of requiring previous registration as a condition for exercising them" (*Thomas*, 534–535). *Thomas v. Collins* thus set out a broad principle that licensing in the area of free speech would be allowed only if the public interest were gravely threatened.

Rutledge's impact on the Court was limited by his brief tenure. He was able to demonstrate, nonetheless, that he was a sound legal scholar who exhibited a mastery of the law. He wrote effectively on a range of complex legal issues and was regarded as one of the Supreme Court's "near great" justices.

The Truman Appointment

Harold Hitz Burton

Harold Hitz Burton was the only member of the Stone Court appointed by President Harry Truman. Justice Roberts resigned from the Supreme Court on July 31, 1945, and Truman nominated Burton on September 19, 1945. Truman's choice of Burton was attributable at least in part to cronyism, but the nomination served Truman well in several ways. The only Republican remaining on the Court following Roberts's resignation was Chief Justice Stone, and Truman was under some pressure from members of Congress to nominate another Republican. Furthermore, Truman's experience convinced him that Burton would be neither highly partisan nor ideologically driven. In other words, Truman believed that Burton's moderate approach to politics would carry over to the Court. As important, the nomination of a Senate member would reduce the confirmation process to a mere formality. The expectation of easy confirmation was borne out immediately: The Senate by unanimous voice vote confirmed Burton on the same day he was nominated. Indeed, the confirmation went so quickly that those senators "who wished to speak in his favor . . . spoke after confirmation" (Berry 1978, 25). Although Truman and Burton were friends, Burton was "closer politically to Eisenhower," who "actively sought Burton's advice on appointments to the lower court vacancies" (Rudko 1988, 45).

Burton was born in Jamaica Plain, Massachusetts, on June 22, 1888, but spent much of his early childhood in Switzerland. He graduated Phi Beta Kappa from Bowdoin College and received his LL.B. from Harvard Law School in 1912. Burton began his legal practice in Cleveland, then moved to Idaho and later Utah, acting as legal

Harold Hitz Burton (Harris & Ewing, Collection of the Supreme Court of the United States)

counsel for several utilities. Following distinguished service in the military during World War I, Burton returned to Cleveland to resume private practice. During this period he taught corporate law at Western Reserve University Law School. He also became heavily engaged in local politics.

Burton was a Republican but a political moderate. When he sought elective office, his middle-of-the-road approach enabled him effectively to appeal to voters of both parties. Burton served a term in the Ohio legislature before becoming Cleveland's director of law from 1929 to 1932. In 1935 Burton was elected mayor of Cleveland; he was subsequently reelected twice. As the mayor of a large city, he had to address the extensive consequences of the depression. Despite his Republican affiliation, he backed many of Roosevelt's New Deal initiatives.

In 1940 Burton was elected to the U.S. Senate. His record on domestic issues was predictably moderate. Notwithstanding the considerable isolationist sentiment that existed at the time, Burton strongly supported Roosevelt's interventionist foreign policy. During his Senate tenure, he served on the Senate Committee on the Conduct of the War, chaired by Senator Harry Truman, and the two developed a close working relationship. He was also a sponsor of the Ball-Burton-Hill-Hatch resolution, which provided the foundation for the United States to join the United Nations following World War II.

Burton's impact on the Stone Court was limited, as he sat for only its final term. In addition, the substitution of Burton for Roberts did not substantially affect the doctrinal priorities of the Court. This was especially true with respect to civil liberties issues, for Burton "merely carried on Robert's tendencies" (Kirkendall 1995, 1326). He joined the Stone Court when it was even more severely divided between those favoring judicial activism and those favoring judicial self-restraint. Burton was more often found with the restraintists, but as Eric W. Rise has pointed out, he "deferred to legislative judgments because he agreed with them, not necessarily because he believed the political branches had the exclusive power to formulate public policy" (Rise 1994, 77). He did not bring a well-developed judicial philosophy to the Court. Instead, he favored deciding cases on the narrowest possible grounds. This approach limited his own visibility on a Court dominated by such high-profile justices as Frankfurter, Black, Douglas, Jackson, Murphy, and Rutledge. His meticulous attention to detail, his pragmatism, his constant attempt to decide cases objectively, and his narrowly focused opinions minimized the likelihood that he would fashion new constitutional doctrine. Writing "came hard to Burton," and he "painfully mulled over every possible precedent." He regarded dissenting opinions largely as "vain shows of erudition," and he carefully confined his dissents to discussion of those essentials that might prevail in the future (Berry 1978, 31).

In addition to the differences of view over the appropriate role for the Court, the Stone Court was divided on various civil liberties issues. These two issues are intertwined in *Duncan v. Kahanamoku* (1946). Under terms of the Hawaiian Organic Act, the governor of Hawaii issued a proclamation placing the territory under martial law following the Japanese attack on Pearl Harbor. The Supreme Court set aside the convictions and sentences of two civilians whose cases were handled by military rather than civilian courts. Burton would have sustained the actions of the military tribunals, noting the "extraordinary conditions" created by the attack on Pearl Harbor, which turned the islands into a "white-hot center of war," and warning against the "dangers of over-expansion of judicial control into the fields allotted to agencies of legislation and executive action" (*Duncan*, 340). The conduct of war under the Constitution is "largely an executive function." When the actions of military authorities are under review, it is necessary for reviewing courts to "put themselves as nearly as possible in the place of those who had the constitutional responsibility for immediate executive action." For the Supreme Court to "intrude its judgment" into spheres of discretion reserved for the chief executive is to "invite disregard of that judgment under a claim of constitutional right to do so" (*Duncan*, 342–343).

Burton's separation from the majority on civil liberties and civil rights issues during the 1945 term of the Court can also be seen in *Marsh v. Alabama* (1946). The Court ruled in *Marsh* that Jehovah's Witnesses could distribute religious pamphlets in a company-owned town. Burton joined the dissent of Justice Reed, in which Reed said that the Court's ruling "establishes as a principle . . . that one may remain on private property against the will of the owner and contrary to the law of the state so long as the only objection to his presence is that he is exercising an asserted right to spread there his religious views" (*Marsh*, 512). He also dissented *Tucker v. Texas* (1946), a case that closely paralleled *Marsh* and extended the Witnesses' right to distribute religious materials in government housing projects.

Burton was reluctant to rule against government authority even against claims that had civil rights implications. He was the only dissenter in *Morgan v. Virginia* (1946), as the Court struck down a Virginia law that required racially segregated seating on interstate buses. In Burton's view the primary question in *Morgan* was not the issue of segregation but the state law's impact on interstate commerce. He disagreed with the Court's conclusion that the law imposed such a burden on interstate commerce as to "outweigh the contribution made by the statute to the state's interest in its public welfare." Once again Burton was troubled by the willingness of the majority to engage in judicial intervention. The law represented the "tested public policy of Virginia regularly enacted, long maintained, and currently observed." The declared interests of Virginia should not be "laid aside summarily by the Court in the absence of Congressional action." It is only Congress and not the courts, said Burton, "that can supply affirmative national uniformity of action" (*Morgan*, 394).

The Stone Court disposed 170 cases in the 1945 term. Burton authored the majority opinion in five of those cases. He also issued one concurring and five dissenting opinions during his first term on the Court. Almost 60 percent of the Court's rulings his first term were nonunanimous, which makes interagreement ratios between pairs of justices particularly revealing. It was also a Court of only eight justices for the entire term, as Justice Jackson was on leave at the Nuremberg war crimes trials. During his first term (1945) on the Court, Burton voted with Justice Reed in 80 percent of the nonunanimous cases and with Chief Justice Stone in 78 percent of the decisions. In contrast, Burton agreed with Justices Rutledge and Douglas, two of the liberal activists on the Court, in less than half of the cases, 45 percent and 49 percent, respectively (Renstrom 1972, 299). If Burton is to be characterized in ideological terms, he "probably should be labeled a middle-of-the-roader with a conservative slant" (Berry 1978, 13).

Burton's first seven years on the Court came during Truman's presidency, and he typically supported Truman's policy objectives. This was especially true in the area of national security. He was among the Court's majorities in such cases as *American Communications Association v. Douds* (1950) and *Dennis v. United States* (1951), which upheld anti-Communist objectives of the Taft-Hartley and Smith Acts, respectively. Burton was also among the majority, however, ruling against Truman's use of executive power in the steel seizure case of *Youngstown Sheet & Tube Co. v. Sawyer* (1952). Across the entirety of the Vinson Court period, Burton supported civil liberties claims in 26 percent of the cases.

When Chief Justice Stone was replaced by Vinson and Justice Jackson returned to the Court from the Nuremberg war trials, Burton became part of the restraintist majority with Vinson, Frankfurter, Reed, and Jackson. This majority solidified in 1949 when Justices Murphy and Rutledge died and were replaced by Truman appointees Tom C. Clark and Sherman Minton. This change in the Court's composition enabled Burton to become a somewhat more influential member of the Court. Burton was well respected by his colleagues, and the strength of his personality and his technical approach occasionally facilitated consensus-building on the Vinson Court, an effect he did not have during his single year on the Stone Court. What influence Burton possessed during the Vinson Court years diminished substantially when Warren succeeded Vinson as chief justice.

Health problems prompted Burton to resign from the Court on October 13, 1958, although he later occasionally sat on cases that came before the Court of Appeals for the District of Columbia. Although he left a Court "still torn by internal conflict," Burton remained a "center of serenity . . . even as he watched tensions from within and attacks from without grow in intensity during the final stages of his illness" (Berry 1978, 230). He believed he could decide most cases without any attention to "personal philosophy or practical circumstances," and he adopted this approach even though his personal background "molded him into a generally conservative mind-set" (Berry 1978, 231). There were, as he saw it, certain givens in the constitutional system: States' rights should not be invaded by federal power; criminals should not be acquitted because of procedural niceties; contracts should be interpreted in such a way as to protect free enterprise; labor unions should not be more powerful than employers; congressional statutes should be interpreted in such a way as to maximize congressional authority; the president should not be permitted to run roughshod over Congress but should have freedom to act, particularly when it comes to making war; the Supreme Court should only decide those cases which were necessary (Berry 1978, 231).

Burton spent thirteen years on the Court. At the outset he seemed out of his depth and appeared to function by submerging himself in the detail of previous Court rulings. It is probably because of this early performance that he is regarded by some observers as one of the less able justices to sit on the Court. This view is too harsh, however, particularly while Vinson was chief justice. As the stature of the Court declined somewhat during the cold war, Burton's standing grew. Nonetheless, Burton was "essentially a devotee of the self-restraint, when-in-doubt-don't school of jurisprudence, and he was far happier in the role of follower than leader" (Abraham 1992, 243).

References

Abraham, Henry J. *Justices and Presidents: A Political History of Appointments to the Supreme Court.* 3rd edition. New York: Oxford University Press, 1992.

Asch, Sidney H. *The Supreme Court and Its Great Justices.* New York: Arco, 1971.

Ball, Howard. *Hugo L. Black: Cold Steel Warrior.* New York: Oxford University Press, 1996.

Berry, Mary Frances. *Stability, Security, and Continuity: Mr. Justice Burton and Decision-Making in the Supreme Court 1945–1958.* Westport, Conn.: Greenwood Press, 1978.

Cushman, Clare, ed. *The Supreme Court Justices: Illustrated Biographies, 1789–1993.* Washington, D.C.: Congressional Quarterly Press, 1993.

Hall, Kermit L. "Owen Josephus Roberts." In Melvin I. Urofsky, ed., *The Supreme Court Justices: A Biographical Dictionary.* New York: Garland, 1994, pp. 383–387.

Howard, J. Woodford. *Mr. Justice Murphy: A Political Biography.* Princeton, N.J.: Princeton University Press, 1968.

Irons, Peter. "Francis (Frank) William Murphy." In Melvin I. Urofsky, ed., *The Supreme Court Justices: A Biographical Dictionary.* New York: Garland, 1994, pp. 331–336.

Johnson, John W. "Harlan Fiske Stone." In Melvin I. Urofsky, ed., *The Supreme Court*

Justices: A Biographical Dictionary. New York: Garland, 1994, pp. 425–434.

Kirkendall, Richard. "Harold Burton." In Leon Friedman and Fred L. Israel, eds., *The Justices of the United States Supreme Court, 1789–1995: Their Lives and Major Opinions.* New York: Chelsea House, 1995, pp. 1322–1333.

Mason, Alpheus T. "Harlan Fiske Stone." In Leon Friedman and Fred L. Israel, eds., *The Justices of the United States Supreme Court, 1789–1995: Their Lives and Major Opinions.* New York: Chelsea House, 1995, pp. 1099–1116.

———. *Harlan Fiske Stone: Pillar of the Law.* New York: Viking, 1956.

Murphy, Walter F. "James F. Byrnes." In Leon Friedman and Fred L. Israel, eds., *The Justices of the United States Supreme Court, 1789–1995: Their Lives and Major Opinions.* New York: Chelsea House, 1995, pp. 1263–1281.

Nash, A. E. Kier. "Wiley Blount Rutledge." In Melvin I. Urofsky, ed., *The Supreme Court Justices: A Biographical Dictionary.* New York: Garland, 1994, pp. 391–393.

Parrish, Michael E. "Felix Frankfurter." In Melvin I. Urofsky, ed., *The Supreme Court Justices: A Biographical Dictionary.* New York: Garland, 1994, pp. 171–181.

Pritchett, C. Herman. *The Roosevelt Court: A Study in Judicial Politics and Values, 1937–47.* New York: Macmillan, 1948.

———. "Stanley Reed." In Leon Friedman and Fred L. Israel, eds., *The Justices of the United States Supreme Court, 1789–1995: Their Lives and Major Opinions.* New York: Chelsea House, 1995, pp. 1181–1198.

Renstrom, Peter G. "The Dimensionality of Decision Making of the 1941–45 Stone Court: A Computer-Dependent Analysis of Supreme Court Behavior." Ph.D. dissertation, Michigan State University, 1972.

Rise, Eric W. "Harold Hitz Burton." In Melvin I. Urofsky, ed., *The Supreme Court Justices: A Biographical Dictionary.* New York: Garland, 1994, pp. 77–80.

Robertson, David. *Sly and Able: A Political Biography of James F. Byrnes.* New York: W. W. Norton, 1994.

Rodell, Fred. *Nine Men: A Political History of the Supreme Court of the United States from 1790 to 1955.* New York: Vintage Books, 1955.

Rudko, Frances Howell. *Truman's Court: A Study in Judicial Restraint.* New York: Greenwood Press, 1988.

Sacks, Albert M. "Felix Frankfurter." In Leon Friedman and Fred L. Israel, eds., *The Justices of the United States Supreme Court, 1789–1995: Their Lives and Major Opinions.* New York: Chelsea House, 1995, pp. 2401–2417.

White, G. Edward. *The American Judicial Tradition: Profiles of Leading American Judges.* Oxford: Oxford University Press, 1976.

Yarbrough, Tinsley E. *Mr. Justice Black and His Critics.* Durham: Duke University Press, 1988.

3

Significant Decisions

The Stone Court is often called "Roosevelt's Court" because President Franklin D. Roosevelt nominated eight of its nine members. Although it might be expected that the Roosevelt-appointed justices would share common views on most constitutional issues, fewer than half the rulings of the Stone Court were unanimous, leading Melvin I. Urofsky to entitle his discussion of Chief Justice Stone and his successor, Chief Justice Fred M. Vinson, as an era marked by "division and discord. The division among the Roosevelt appointees reflects both the significance and complexity of the constitutional issues that reached the Stone Court.

Several categories of constitutional questions stand out, albeit to varying degrees of importance. First, the Stone Court became extensively involved with individual liberties issues. The civil liberties cases decided by the Stone Court separate into two broad groups—cases that raised civil liberties questions independent of World War II and cases with civil liberties issues arising out of that national emergency. Cases in the former group most probably would have been addressed by the Stone Court even in the absence of World War II, whereas the latter group would not have been before the Stone Court but for the war. Although the Stone Court's civil liberties record does not approach that of the Warren Court, it served as a transitional court on individual rights issues, setting the stage for the Warren era, which began a decade later.

Second, the Stone Court had to respond to difficult questions about the exercise of federal regulatory power. As with the civil liberties cases, some of these cases stemmed from the war whereas others did not. The war required the Stone Court to address the extent to which the national government's capacity to regulate private property might expand during wartime. These cases involve the scope of federal power during a war emergency, most notably the boundaries of presidential war power. The Stone Court also reviewed cases raising questions about federal regulatory power, which had no particular wartime dimension. For example, there were some New Deal issues that carried over from the Hughes Court, cases involving federal initiatives to regulate the national economy. Although many of the most important constitutional questions had been resolved during the Hughes era, the Stone Court provided closure for economic regulation issues resulting from the New Deal.

There were also a number of cases raising questions about organized labor as a major actor in the national economy.

Superimposed across these broad categories were questions about federal judicial power—the proper role of federal courts in the overall scheme of governance and the scope of judicial review—and the issue of the appropriate division of authority between the federal and state levels of government. The discussion that follows attempts to represent the Stone Court's most important responses to these issues. To begin, however, I offer a brief statistical overview.

The number of cases that reached the Stone Court in its five terms was greater than the number of cases the Hughes Court reviewed during its last five terms. A similar increase occurred during the first five years of the Vinson Court between 1946 and 1950. Table 3.1 compares the five-year Stone Court averages of new cases filed and total cases on the docket with the averages from the last five years of the Hughes Court and first five years of the Vinson Court. The docket numbers shown in Table 3.1 represent the cases seeking review by the Supreme Court.

The number of cases granted review by the Supreme Court and disposed with signed opinions are shown in Table 3.2. The Stone Court disposed of just under 180 cases per year on average, a rate comparable to the last five terms of the Hughes Court and about forty cases per year above the rate for the first five years of the Vinson Court.

Finally, the high level of division on the Stone Court is reflected in Table 3.3. Fewer than half of the Stone Court's decisions were unanimous (46.37 percent). By comparison, more than 70 percent of the Hughes Court's rulings from 1936 to 1940 were unanimous. The Vinson Court, which followed the Stone Court, was even more fragmented, achieving unanimity in fewer than 30 percent of its cases.

The substantive issues raised in the Stone Court's cases differed, at least in proportion, from earlier eras. The Court's deference to legislative judgments is reflected in a lower number of cases involving federal regulatory initiatives. Cases involving constitutional questions about the First Amendment, rights of the accused, and equal protection appeared in significantly larger numbers.

Individual Rights

A major component of the Stone Court era was the development of constitutional law that was more protective of individual rights. The Stone Court's individual rights rulings were, at least in part, influenced by two jurisprudential themes: extension of Bill of Rights guarantees to the states and the "preferred position" doctrine.

Whether federal Bill of Rights provisions limit state governments as well as the federal government is known as the "incorporation" question. The initial response to

Table 3.1 Caseload Comparisons (Five-term Averages)

	New Cases	%Change	Total Docket	%Change
Hughes Court\				
(1936–1940 Terms)	966.2	—	1070	—
Stone Court				
(1941–1945 Terms)	1142.4	+18.24	1278.2	+19.46
Vinson Court				
(1946–1950 Terms)	1344.2	+17.66	1497.8	+17.18

Source: Epstein, Segal, Spaeth and Walker, pp. 59—60

Table 3.2 Total Cases Disposed and Signed Opinions (Five-term Averages)

	Signed Opinions	Cases Disposed
Hughes Court (1936–1940 Terms)	148.6	176
Stone Court (1941–1945 Terms)	143.6	178.8
Vinson Court (1946–1950 Terms)	108.8	140.4

Source: Epstein, Segal, Spaeth and Walker, p. 72

Table 3.3 Unanimous Decisions and One-Vote Decisions (Five-year Averages)

	Signed Opinions	Unanimous Rulings	Percent Unanimous	One-Vote Decisions	Percent One-Vote
Hughes Court					
(1936–1940 Terms)	148.4	105.2	70.9	6.2	4.2
Stone Court					
(1941–1945 Terms)	143.6	66.6	46.4	15.6	10.9
Vinson Court					
(1946–1950 Terms)	108.8	31.2	28.7	19.6	18.0

Source: Epstein, Segal, Spaeth, and Walker, pp. 147, 162

the question came in *Barron v. Baltimore* (1833), and it was the Court's judgment that the Bill of Rights "constrained only government created by the [Constitution], and not the distinct governments," meaning the states. *Barron* was decided prior to the ratification of the Fourteenth Amendment in 1868. The due process clause of the Fourteenth Amendment prohibits the states from denying "life, liberty, or property" without due process of law. The interpretive question left to the Court after ratification was whether specific components of the Bill of Rights were embraced by the term "liberty" and made applicable at the state level.

The Court was reluctant to interpret the Fourteenth Amendment in a way that diminished state sovereignty but came to modify its position over time. The pivotal case was *Palko v. Connecticut* (1937), in which the Hughes Court elected to resolve the incorporation question on a "selective" basis. That is, the Court would determine whether particular rights contained in the Bill of Rights are, in the words of Justice Cardozo, "implicit in the concept of ordered liberty." Application of this standard would occur on a right-by-right basis, and although the line dividing the higher-order rights from others "may seem to be wavering and broken," Justice Cardozo reassured his audience that there "emerges the perception of a rationalizing principle which gives to discrete instances a proper order and coherence" (*Palko*, 325). If a right is determined to meet this criterion, it limits actions at the state level regardless of the factual circumstances of specific cases. The selective approach created what Henry Abraham called an "honor roll" of rights, with rights designated as fundamental ("honor-roll" worthy) made wholly operative at the state level (Abraham 1994, 107). *Palko* provided the theoretical framework for the incorporation process thereafter.

The Stone Court added no right to the incorporation "honor roll," but a number of its justices supported incorporation. The Stone Court justices were fully aware that by 1941 most of the First Amendment already had been extended to the states through the incorporation process. In *Gitlow v. New York* (1925), the Court incorporated the free speech provision. The free press, right to assemble, right to petition government, and free exercise of religion provisions followed in *Near v. Minnesota* (1931), *DeJonge v. Oregon* (1937), *Hague v. C.I.O.* (1939), and *Cantwell v. Connecticut* (1940). Thus, as the Stone Court reviewed First Amendment cases from the states, it already had been determined that the states were subject to the same constitutional restraints that applied to the federal government. The significance of this set of precedents for the Stone Court was magnified in some First Amendment cases when coupled to the "preferred position" doctrine.

The "preferred position" doctrine defines a role orientation introduced by Justice Stone in *United States v. Carolene Products Co.* (1938). Stone suggested in a *Carolene* footnote that deference to legislative judgment in matters of economic regulation might not be applicable to cases arising under the Bill of Rights. In other words, the "usual presumption" supporting legislation is overridden by the "preferred place," or elevated position, given to the freedoms secured by the Bill of Rights. (The text of Justice Stone's *Carolene Products* footnote four appears in Appendix II.) That priority gives Bill of Rights liberties, according to Justice Rutledge, "a sanctity and a sanction not permitting dubious intrusions" (*Thomas v. Collins*, 235). The "preferred position" view was accepted by a majority of the Stone Court from the time Justice Rutledge joined the Court until the end of Stone's tenure as chief justice, a period of less than three years. The influence of this doctrine and the effects of incorporation can be seen most clearly in some of the Stone Court's First Amendment decisions, most notably in cases involving religious exercise, free speech, and assembly.

First Amendment Issues

Free Exercise of Religion

The First Amendment forbids the Congress from making laws that prohibit the free exercise of religion. With the exception of a post–Civil War attempt to prohibit polygamy in U.S. territories, a law unsuccessfully challenged by the Mormons, the federal government was not the source of policy that impaired the free exercise rights of religious minorities. The same could not be said about policy originating at the state level. Among the religious sects that were adversely affected by a variety of state laws were the Jehovah's Witnesses. Starting in the late 1930s, the Witnesses turned to the courts for relief, and the Stone Court addressed a number of their complaints. Indeed, the Stone Court came to the support of religious minorities to an unprecedented extent, deciding twenty-one free exercise cases in its five terms (a number of these cases were consolidated and concluded through ten signed opinions). All but one of these cases involved the Jehovah's Witnesses and their particular methods of evangelism. The Stone Court ruled for the free exercise claims in seven of the ten opinions (covering sixteen of the twenty-one cases), and in one of the remaining three the Court reversed itself within a year (*Jones v. Opelika* [1942] and its two companion cases). Justice Murphy supported the free exercise claims in all twenty-one cases. Justices Black and Stone agreed with the free exercise arguments in all twenty-one cases except *Prince v. Massachusetts* (1944). Justice Rutledge voted in favor of these claims in seventeen of the eighteen cases in which he participated with *Prince*, again producing the atypical vote. Chief Justice Stone was the fifth and decisive vote in eighteen of the twenty-one cases. Although Justice Frankfurter countenanced the asserted free exercise violations in only four of the twenty-one cases, two of those supporting votes produced 5–4 majorities for the Witnesses. Justices Roberts and Jackson voted against free exercise claims in seventeen of nineteen cases, while Justice Reed failed to support a free exercise claim in any of the cases.

Two Hughes Court decisions, both involving the Witnesses as well, are helpful in framing the responses of the Stone Court. In the first, *Cantwell v. Connecticut* (1940), the Hughes Court struck down a Connecticut law that prohibited solicitation of money for religious causes without the approval of a local government official. The ruling marked the first time the Court had concluded that the states were subject to the limits of the free exercise clause. The Court then invalidated the regulation because it vested the government official with authority to censor the means a religious sect might utilize to sustain itself financially. The importance of the *Cantwell* case cannot be overstated. Virtually none of the governmental policies that intersected with religious practices were initiated by the national government. Rather, they came from the state or local level. By ruling that the free exercise clause of the First Amendment applied to these levels of government, *Cantwell* opened the gates for the Court to review free exercise claims targeting the actions of state or local governments.

The same year, the Hughes Court decided against the Witnesses in the compulsory flag salute case of *Minersville School District v. Gobitis* (1940). It was the Court's conclusion in *Gobitis*, with only Justice Stone disagreeing, that the local school board's requirement was entitled to the same deference as a legislative enactment. For the Court to strike down the flag salute requirement, suggested Justice Frankfurter, "would amount to no less than the pronouncement of a pedagogical and psychological dogma in a field where courts possess no marked and certainly no controlling competence." Frankfurter also suggested that religious freedom was not absolute. To the contrary, he said that "conscientious scruples have not, in the course of the long struggle for religious toleration, relieved the individual from obedience to a general law not aimed at the promotion or restriction of religious beliefs" (*Gobitis*, 594, 597). There clearly was no "preferred position" thinking evident in *Gobitis* except in Stone's dissent. Several of the justices on Frankfurter's side of the case, particularly Justice Murphy, were very uncomfortable with their votes. The public response was critical of the ruling as well. *Gobitis* was destined to a short shelf life.

Several of the Stone Court's free exercise cases involved license taxes, fees imposed on persons who peddle, sell, or canvas. The first of these cases was *Jones v. Opelika* (1942) and two other consolidated cases—*Bowden v. Fort Smith* and *Jobin v. Arizona*. The question in these cases was whether a license tax could be enforced against religious literature. In a 5–4 ruling, the Stone Court upheld the license tax on the grounds that it was nondiscriminatory and imposed no special burden on persons selling religious literature. The Witnesses were like other sellers and could not be exempted from the tax because their merchandise was religious in character. Justice Reed said for the Court that subjecting any religious group to a "reasonable fee for their money-making activities does not require a finding that the licensed acts are purely commercial"—a book agent cannot escape the license tax by arguing that it is a "tax on knowledge" (*Jones I*, 596–597). Chief Justice Stone and Justices Black, Douglas, and Murphy dissented, asserting that the command of the "preferred position" doctrine extends to any form of taxation that can be used to control or suppress. The dissenters were concerned that the Court's ruling affirmed *Gobitis*, a decision about which some justices were now having second thoughts. Indeed, Justice Black's dissent indicated that he, Douglas, and Murphy believed that *Gobitis* had been wrongly decided. They would have occasion to "correct" their *Gobitis* vote a year later.

The license tax issue returned to the Stone Court in the next year as well, but not before Justice Rutledge had replaced Justice Byrnes. In *Murdock v. Pennsylvania, Jones v. Opelika (Jones II), Douglas v. Jeannette*, and *Follette v. McCormick*, the Court struck down license taxes. Rutledge added the decisive fifth vote. Justice Douglas offered the Court's rationale and dusted off the argument that religious freedom occupies a "preferred position." *Murdock* marked the first time this view was embraced by a majority of the Court in a religious freedom case. On the merits, the Court concluded that hand distribution of religious tracts is an "age-old form of missionary evangelism" and occupies the "same high estate under the First Amendment as do worship in the churches and preaching from the pulpit" (*Murdock*, 109). The "mere fact" that the religious literature is sold rather than given away does not "transform evangelism into a commercial enterprise"; if it did, then the "passing of the collection plate in church would make the church service a commercial project" (*Murdock*, 111).

The power to tax brings with it the power to suppress. Those who can tax the selling of religious literature, Douglas said, "can make its exercise so costly as to deprive it of the resources necessary for its maintenance" (*Murdock*, 112). The Court also concluded that the nondiscriminatory character of the tax was "immaterial." A license tax ordinance does not acquire constitutional validity simply because it classifies "privileges protected by the First Amendment along with the wares and merchandise of hucksters and peddlers and treats them all alike" (*Murdock*, 115).

The four justices now in the minority reiterated the Court's position in *Jones I*. Justice Reed deferred to the state's judgment that selling merchandise, even religious merchandise, was a taxable activity. When a price is put on the articles that are being distributed, the "sacred character" of the transaction has been lost and the "evangelist becomes also a book agent" (*Murdock*, 132). Justice Frankfurter returned to his *Gobitis* rationale—individuals cannot be made exempt from taxation merely because their actions involve the exercise of a constitutional right: "A clergyman, no less than a judge, is a citizen" (*Murdock*, 135).

The Stone Court extended the *Murdock* reasoning in *Follett v. McCormick* (1944). The town of McCormick argued that *Murdock* was applicable only to itinerant preachers, but the Court ruled in *Follett* that it also applied to evangelists or preachers in their hometowns. The Court failed to see why such a license tax was any less unconstitutional when exacted from those who confine themselves to their own village or town. The dissenters, Justices Roberts, Frankfurter, and Jackson, were adamant that the tax was a generally applicable revenue measure and must apply to all community residents: Follett was made exempt from a tax all others must pay and as a result enjoyed a "subsidy" for his religion.

The Stone Court made two other important free exercise rulings in 1943. First, the Court acted on Justice Black's comment in *Jones I* that *Gobitis* had been "wrongly decided." It reversed *Gobitis* in *West Virginia State Board of Education v. Barnette* by a 6–3 vote. Justice Jackson, who seldom subordinated legislative judgments to claims of religious freedom, based the decision on the "clear and present danger" test. This standard is often used in free speech cases, and the free speech perspective provided the foundation for Jackson's reasoning in reversing *Gobitis*. Refusal to salute the flag was a "form of utterance." The compulsory flag salute was invoked without any contention that remaining passive during a flag salute ritual would actually create sufficient danger to justify the impairment of expression. The Court acknowledged that government may attempt to foster national unity, but compulsory participation in flag salute ceremonies was an impermissible means for pursuing that objective. The Witnesses were not forcing their beliefs on anyone through their nonparticipation in the flag salute exercise. To the contrary, the government was compelling the Witnesses to adhere to its views.

The Court was also dubious about the efficacy of required participation in saluting the flag. To believe that patriotism "will not flourish if patriotic ceremonies are voluntary and spontaneous instead of a compulsory routine is to make an unflattering estimate of the appeal of our institutions to free minds." Jackson brought his argument to a close with a flourish: "If there is any fixed star in our constitutional constellation, it is that no official, high or petty, can prescribe what shall be orthodox in politics, nationalism, religion, or other matters of opinion" (*Barnette*, 641–642).

Justice Frankfurter had authored the Court's opinion in *Gobitis* and strongly objected to its being overruled in *Barnette*. Justices, he believed, can never justify writing "private notions" into the Constitution, no matter how deeply cherished. Even the narrow judicial authority to "nullify legislation has been viewed with a jealous eye [because it can be used to] prevent the full play of the democratic process" (*Barnette*, 650). In his view the scope of "political power" of the states was before the Court in this case, and the exercise of this power should generally receive the Court's deference. State legislative power should not be seen as "wanting whenever a general nondiscriminatory civil regulation . . . touches conscientious scruples or religious beliefs of an individual or group" (*Barnette*, 651).

In its second important free exercise ruling in 1943, *Martin v. Struthers*, the Court struck down a municipal ban on door-to-door distribution of handbills, circulars, advertisements, or other literature. The Court determined that individual householders possessed the prerogative to accept visitors to their door rather than having the decision made for them by government. Although door-to-door distributors of literature may be a nuisance to many, they may also have information of value to some householders. The right to free speech was viewed as including the right to distribute literature as well as the "right to receive it, and the right may not be withdrawn even if it leaves a minor nuisance for a community" in its wake (*Martin*, 143). Justices Reed, Roberts, Frankfurter, and Jackson, for their part, found no First Amendment violation in this "trivial" regulation.

One of the two free exercise cases that failed to produce a favorable outcome for the Witnesses after *Jones I* was *Prince v. Massachusetts* (1944). This case involved a nine-year-old child who, with her aunt, sold religious literature on a street corner. Under terms of a Massachusetts law, girls under the age of eighteen were prohibited from selling anything on the streets. By an 8–1 vote, the Stone Court upheld the regulation as reasonably directed at protecting the interests of children. Justices Douglas, Black, and Rutledge were virtually automatic free exercise votes, yet all three voted against the Witnesses in *Prince*, the single case in which they supported a regulation that affected free exercise of religion. Only Justice Murphy, the sole dissenter in *Prince*, maintained that the regulation impermissibly impaired religious freedom.

Justice Rutledge indicated that it was "cardinal with us that the custody, care and nurture of the child reside first in the parents, whose primary function and freedom included the preparation for obligations the state can neither support nor hinder." At the same time, the family is not "beyond regulation in the public interest," and neither the rights of religion nor of parenthood are "beyond limitation." Acting on behalf of the child's well-being, the state as *parens patriae* "may restrict the parent's control" by requiring school attendance or prohibiting child labor, among other ways (*Prince*, 166). The regulation prohibiting "street preaching" by children was deemed to be reasonable. Proselytizing in the community can be difficult even for adults, and the activity can produce situations that are "wholly inappropriate for children, especially of tender years, to face." Parents and other adults may be free to "become martyrs themselves," but it does not follow that they are free to "make martyrs of their children before they have reached the age . . . when they can make that choice for themselves" (*Prince*, 170). But Murphy was unconvinced that the state had shown the "existence of any grave or immediate danger to any interest which it may lawfully protect; there was no proof that the youngster constituted a "serious menace to the public" *(Prince*, 174).

During the last term of the Stone Court, the "preferred position" justices decided in favor of the Witnesses in two similar free exercise cases. In *Marsh v. Alabama* (1946), the Court determined that a criminal punishment could not be imposed for the distribution of religious literature on the premises of a company town contrary to the wishes of the town's management. Marsh, a Jehovah's Witness, was prosecuted for remaining on the town's so-called business block after having been told she could not distribute her literature without a permit. A five-justice majority rejected the contention that the company's private property interests resolved the issue. To the contrary, Justice Black said that when an owner opens private property to public use, property rights may be "circumscribed by the . . . rights of those who use it" (*Marsh*, 506). The Court found no constitutional difference between a municipality and a privately owned town. In either case the public has an "identical interest" in having the "channels of communication remain open." Again referring to the "preferred position" occupied by speech and religion rights, Black said the "right to exercise the liberties safeguarded by the First Amendment lies at the foundation of free government by free men" (*Marsh*, 509–510). Justice Reed, with Stone and Justice Burton, objected to the proposition that one may remain on private property "against the will of the owner and contrary to the law of the state so long as the only objection to his presence is that he is exercising an asserted right to spread there his religious views" (*Marsh*, 512). A virtually identical ruling came in *Tucker v. Texas* (1946), a case involving a village owned by the federal government that provided housing for persons engaged in national defense activities. Justice Black suggested that the only difference from *Marsh* was governmental rather than private ownership, and that difference "does not affect the result" (*Tucker*, 520).

Speech and Association

The Stone Court left a far greater mark with its religious freedom decisions than it did with its free speech rulings. The "preferred position" doctrine notwithstanding, the Stone Court made it evident that expression is not immune to restriction under the police power of the sovereign states. The pattern of responses by individual Stone Court justices resembled that found for the religion cases. Justices Black, Douglas, and Murphy were most receptive to claims of free speech violations, as they were in religious freedom cases. Neither Chief Justice Stone nor Justice Rutledge, crucial votes in the religious freedom cases, were as willing to provide the fourth and fifth votes in free speech cases.

Perhaps the best example of a speech restriction upheld by the Stone Court is *Chaplinsky v. New Hampshire* (1942). A New Hampshire law provided that no person "shall address any offensive, derisive or annoying word" to any other person who is lawfully in any public place, nor "call him by any offensive or derisive name, nor make any noise or exclamation in his presence and hearing with intent to deride, offend or annoy him, or to prevent him from pursuing his lawful business or occupation." Walter Chaplinsky created a public disturbance with a provocative speech in which he denounced all religion as a "racket." When threatened with arrest by local police, Chaplinsky called an officer a "God damned racketeer," and a "damned Fascist," among other things. He was arrested and convicted for violation of the state law. Chaplinsky failed to secure a vote from even the most receptive free speech justices, and as a result the Stone Court unanimously upheld his conviction.

Justice Murphy began the Court's opinion with the familiar premise that the right of free speech "is not absolute at all times and under all circumstances." Rather, there are certain "well-defined and narrowly limited classes of speech," which are "no essential part of any exposition of ideas, and are of such slight social value as a step to truth that any benefit that may be derived from them is clearly outweighed by the social interest in order and morality" (*Chaplinsky*, 572). These classes of speech include the lewd and obscene, the profane, the libelous, and insulting or "fighting" words. The last of these classes, "fighting words," are those that by their very utterance "inflict injury or tend to incite an immediate breach of peace." Resorting to epithets or personal abuse "is not in any proper sense communication of information or opinion safeguarded by the Constitution, and its punishment as a criminal act would raise no question under that instrument." The New Hampshire statute, suggested Murphy, does no more than prohibit "face-to-face words plainly likely to cause breach of the peace by the addressee, words whose speaking constitute a breach of the peace by the speaker" (*Chaplinsky*, 573).

The attempt to deport Australian-born union leader Harry Bridges produced a different result, although the Stone Court's ruling was not grounded on associational considerations as such. A federal statute allowed the deportation of aliens who were members of or affiliated with any organization that believes in the overthrow by force of the government of the United States. The government contended that Bridges, head of the Marine Workers Industrial Union, was affiliated with the Communist Party, an association that met the statutory deportation requirements. The Stone Court disagreed in a 5–4 decision.

Justice Douglas suggested that Congress had not intended, by its use of the term "affiliation," to impose such hardship on an alien for "slight or insubstantial reasons." On examination of the record, the Court concluded that utterances made by Bridges were entitled to protection. His statements revealed a "militant advocacy of the cause of trade unionism, but they did not teach or advocate or advise the subversive conduct condemned by the statute." Douglas acknowledged that Bridges's objectives were "energetically radical," but the government failed to establish that the methods he used to pursue those objectives were "other than [those that] the framework of democratic and constitutional government permits" (*Bridges v. Wixom*, 149). Douglas focused on the evidence the government used to support its deportation case. The incriminating statements against Bridges were taken from unsworn witnesses, which made them inadmissible. Use of ex parte statements was highly prejudicial to Bridges. The Court concluded that because Bridges's deportation order was based on a "misconstruction of the term 'affiliation'" and an unfair hearing on his membership in the Communist Party, the order must be nullified (*Bridges v. Wixom*, 156).

In a concurring opinion, Justice Murphy was more outspoken. He argued that the case record "will stand forever as a monument to man's intolerance of man." Seldom if ever in the history of this nation, he continued, has there been "such a concentrated and relentless crusade to deport an individual because he dared to exercise the freedom that belongs to him as a human being and that is guaranteed to him by the Constitution" (*Bridges v. Wixom*, 157). Chief Justice Stone, joined by Justices Roberts and Frankfurter, dissented. In their view, the *Bridges* case presented no "novel questions." More important, Congress possessed plenary power over the deportation of aliens and had explicitly directed that any alien who affiliates with a subversive organization is to be deported. They deferred to the administrative judgment calling for Bridges's deportation (*Bridges v. Wixom*, 166–167).

Assembly and Picketing

The Hughes Court determined that peaceful picketing was comparable to other forms of protected speech, and in *Thornhill v. Alabama* (1940) it struck down a state law that categorically prohibited picketing. The Stone Court carried this further, in part because it agreed with the picketing-is-speech premise but also because it was generally supportive of labor interests. A more detailed discussion of the Stone Court's picketing cases appears later in this chapter, in the section on labor unions. Comment here is limited to two early picketing cases, one of which qualified *Thornhill* while the other upheld state restrictions on such activity.

Thornhill played into the policy preferences of many of the Stone Court justices—it involved both the First Amendment and labor unions. In *Bakery and Pastry Drivers Local v. Wohl* (1942), however, the Court struck down an injunction issued by a state court against picketing. The *Wohl* ruling qualified *Thornhill* to the extent that it distinguished between the message of the picketers and the conduct associated with picketing. The latter may be reasonably regulated, whereas the former may not. A state is not required, said Justice Jackson, "to tolerate in all places and all circumstances even peaceful picketing by an individual" (*Bakery and Pastry Drivers Local*, 775). Although the Court unanimously struck down a state court injunction against picketing workers, Justices Douglas, Black, and Murphy expressed strong concern that Jackson's opinion moved too far from *Thornhill*. Under *Thornhill*, restriction of picketing can occur only where a clear and present danger of "substantive evil" is demonstrated. Clear and present danger, said Douglas, is not "inherent in the activities of every person who approaches the premises of an employer and publicizes the facts of a labor dispute." Dissemination of information about a labor dispute is protected speech, and a state may not "define labor dispute so narrowly as to accomplish indirectly what it may not accomplish directly" (*Bakery and Pastry Drivers Local*, 776).

The same day, the Court decided *Carpenters' and Joiners' Union v. Ritter's Café* (1942). This case produced a 5–4 split on the Court, with the majority upholding a state court injunction restricting picketing to the specific location in which a labor dispute takes place. Ritter engaged a contractor to construct a building in Houston, Texas. Under terms of the agreement, the contractor was allowed to make his own arrangements regarding the project workforce. The contractor proceeded to hire nonunion carpenters and painters. Ritter also owned a café located approximately a mile and a half away from the construction site, and the new building was wholly unconnected with the café business. All of the café employees were members of the Hotel and Restaurant Employees International. There was neither an existing dispute between Ritter and his café employees or their union, nor did the carpenters and joiners union have any dispute with Ritter over the operation of his café. But members of the Carpenters' and Joiners' Union picketed Ritter's Café in an attempt to persuade Ritter to require the contractor to use exclusively members of the defendant unions on the construction project. At the same time, the Hotel and Restaurant Employees Union called Ritter's café workers out on strike and withdrew the union card from his restaurant. Union truck drivers refused to cross the picket line to deliver food and other supplies to the restaurant, and members of all trade unions withheld patronage of Ritter's Café, which suffered an approximate 60 percent drop in business. A state court found the union's activities constituted a violation of state antitrust law and enjoined picketing at the café, although the injunction did not prohibit picketing elsewhere nor communication of the facts of the dispute by other means.

Justice Frankfurter drew on *Thornhill* and reaffirmed that the right to "communicate peaceably to the public facts of a legitimate dispute is not lost merely because a labor dispute is involved or because the communication takes the form of picketing, even when the communication does not concern a dispute between an employer and those directly employed by him" (*Ritter's Café*, 725). Nonetheless, a labor dispute as the context for exercising free speech "does not give that freedom any greater constitutional sanction or render it completely inviolable." Rather, a state retains authority to impose reasonable regulations on behalf of the public interest. In this case, Texas had undertaken to "localize industrial conflict" by prohibiting the use of such tactics as picketing "directed at a business wholly outside the economic context of the real dispute." Recognition of peaceful picketing as an exercise of free speech, Frankfurter concluded, "does not imply that the states must be without power to confine the sphere of communication to that directly related to the dispute." The Court refused to "write into the Constitution the notion that every instance of peaceful picketing—anywhere and under any circumstances—is necessarily a phase of the controversy which provoked the picketing." Such a view, suggested Frankfurter, would compel the states to "allow the disputants in a particular industrial episode to conscript neutrals having no relation to either the dispute or the industry in which it arose" (*Ritter's Café*, 726–728). Furthermore, workers involved in this dispute had other modes of communication available to them.

Justices Black, Douglas, and Murphy thought the picketing should not have been enjoined. The union members sought to convey truthful information and violence was not threatened. The dissenters could see no reason why "members of the public should be deprived of any opportunity to get information which might enable them to use their influence to tip the scales in favor of the side they think is right." Justice Reed dissented separately, saying that the philosophy underlying the Court's conclusion gave a state "the right to bar from picket lines workers who are not a part of the industry picketed" (*Ritter's Café*, 739), a restriction he thought impermissible on free speech grounds. The line distinguishing protected expression from expression that could be regulated was something of a blur following these rulings, as the Court struggled with "pure" expression and communication by means of picketing—speech requiring an action by those wishing to communicate.

In *Thomas v. Collins* (1945), the Stone Court ruled that labor-organizing activity could not be subjected to a state permit system. This ruling was primarily about free expression but also reflected the Stone Court's strong sympathy toward the interests of unions. A Texas law required that all union organizers obtain an "organizer's card" from the state before attempting to solicit new members. R. J. Thomas, the president of the United Auto Workers, violated both the state law and a temporary restraining order by addressing a union meeting without registering with the state. The Stone Court ruled for Thomas in a 5–4 decision.

Justice Rutledge spoke for the majority and characterized the statute as imposing a prior restraint on Thomas's right of free speech and assembly. In doing so, Rutledge invoked the "preferred position" doctrine. He spoke of the judicial "duty" to determine where individual freedoms end and a state's regulatory power begins. Although drawing such a line is "always delicate," it is more so where the "usual presumption supporting legislation is balanced by the preferred place given in our scheme to the great, the indispensable democratic freedoms secured by the First Amendment." As a result, attempts to limit those liberties "must be justified by clear public interest, threatened not doubtfully or remotely, but by clear and present danger." Indeed, only the "gravest abuses, endangering paramount interests, give occasion for permissible limitation." The state clearly has power to regulate labor unions with a view to protecting the public interest; unions cannot claim "special immunity from regulation." Such regulation, however, whether aimed at fraud or other abuses, "must not trespass upon the domain set apart for free speech and free assembly" (*Thomas*, 529–530).

Thomas's objective in going to Texas was to assert the advantages of unionizing and to persuade workers to join. How Thomas might "laud unionism," as Texas conceded he was free to do, "yet not imply an invitation, is hard to conceive." His audience, in Rutledge's view, had the capacity for making rational connections. That audience would understand that the president of the UAW and vice president of the Congress of Industrial Organizations (CIO), by addressing an organization meeting, "was not urging merely a philosophic attachment to abstract principles of unionism, disconnected from the business immediately at hand." When legislation or its application can confine labor leaders on such occasions to "innocuous and abstract discussion of the virtues of trade unions," the right of "public discussion" is impaired (*Thomas*, 535).

Justice Jackson observed in a concurring opinion that the purpose of the First Amendment is to "foreclose public authority from assuming a guardianship of the public mind through regulating the press, speech, and religion." This liberty was not protected, he continued, "because the forefathers expected its use would always be agreeable to those in authority or that its exercise always be wise, temperate, or useful to society." Texas did not wait to see what Thomas would say or do. This gave Jackson the inescapable impression that the injunction, sought before Thomas had even reached Texas, was an effort to "forestall him from speaking at all and that the contempt is based in part on the fact that he did make a public labor speech" (*Thomas*, 545, 548).

Freedom of the Press

The Stone Court was largely supportive of federal efforts to regulate the economy, and a number of its rulings involved the issue of whether these economic regulations could apply to the media. The Stone Court's first free press case, however, was of a different kind. There were two cases, actually—one involving a large metropolitan newspaper and the other involving one of the period's most controversial figures, labor leader Harry Bridges. The two cases were decided jointly.

The *Los Angeles Times* and Bridges were both cited for contempt by a California court. The newspaper had published an editorial urging prison sentences for two persons the *Times* characterized as union "goon squad" members, who had been convicted of assaulting nonunion truck drivers. Bridges's contempt was based on a letter he wrote the secretary of labor threatening a labor strike if a state court decision adverse to his union were enforced. The *Times* editorial was published and Bridges's letter sent while the court was still deciding on the sentences of the union members. The Stone Court reversed the contempt citations in *Bridges v. California* and *Times-Mirror Co. v. Superior Court* (1941).

Justice Black spoke for the five-justice majority. He noted initially that California had no law prohibiting comment outside the courtroom on a pending case. As a result, Black looked to the "clear and present danger" test for guidance. This standard requires that a "substantive evil" must be extremely serious and its likelihood extremely high "before utterances can be punished" (*Bridges/Times-Mirror*, 260). The substantive evil the state court sought to avert with the contempt citations was twofold: disrespect for the judiciary and disorderly and unfair administration of justice. Black rejected the assumption that respect for the judiciary can be won by shielding judges from published criticism. No matter how limited, enforced silence in the "name of preserving the dignity of the bench, would probably engender resentment, suspicion, and contempt much more than it would enhance respect" (*Bridges/Times-Mirror*, 270).

The second targeted evil disorderly and unfair administration of justice, "is more plausibly associated with restricting publications, which touch upon pending litigation." The Court did not start, however, with the premise that publication of the content involved here actually threatened to "change the nature of legal trials." Black also rejected the premise that preservation of judicial impartiality required that judges have a contempt power by which they can "close all channels of public expression to all matters which touch upon pending cases." In view of the *Times-Mirror*'s continued and militant opposition to unions, it was "inconceivable" that any judge in the Los Angeles area "would expect anything but adverse criticism" from the newspaper if the sentence for the union members on trial were merely a term of probation. The *Times* editorial, given the "most intimidating construction . . . did no more than threaten future adverse criticism, which was reasonably to be expected anyway in the event of a lenient disposition of the pending case" (*Bridges/Times-Mirror*, 271, 273).

Justice Frankfurter, joined by Chief Justice Stone and Justices Roberts and Byrnes, dissented. It was a dissent Frankfurter had not expected to write. The *Bridges* case had been before the Court the previous year, but Frankfurter took so long in writing the opinion for a 6–3 vote against Bridges that that the case was reargued in the 1941 term. This time Murphy switched his vote to Bridges. Justice Jackson, not on the Court when the case was first argued, joined Murphy and Justices Black, Douglas, and Reed, who were the three dissenters initially, to change the original outcome.

Frankfurter contended that our "whole history repels the view" that it is an exercise of a civil liberty secured by the Bill of Rights for a "leader of a large following or for a powerful metropolitan newspaper to attempt to overawe a judge in a matter immediately pending before him." The administration of justice by an impartial judiciary has been basic to our conception of freedom. A trial, however, is not a "free trade in ideas" (*Bridges/Times-Mirror*, 282). Frankfurter acknowledged that freedom of public expression is "indispensable to the democratic process," but the right to free speech is not absolute. In these cases the substantive evil to be eliminated was interference with impartial adjudication.

The dissenters concluded that California should not be denied the right to free its courts from such "coercive, extraneous influences" (*Bridges/Times-Mirror*, 296). The outcome in *Bridges* marked the beginning of the split between Frankfurter and several other Roosevelt-appointed justices. This split became more pronounced following the appointment of Justice Rutledge, as was evident in the free exercise of religion cases, in which the Court abandoned Frankfurter's *Gobitis* and *Jones I* reasoning.

The Stone Court was typically protective of First Amendment rights. It also was inclined to bring workers within the reach of such federal labor laws as the Wagner Act and the Fair Labor Standards Act. These two preferences came into tension when federal labor regulations were applied to the media. *Mabee v. White Plains Publishing Co.* (1946) is illustrative. The key question in *Mabee* was whether the White Plains Publishing Company was engaged in interstate commerce, thus meeting the precondition for making it subject to the provisions of the FLSA. White Plains published a newspaper with a daily circulation of 9,000–11,000. The company did not attempt to attract out-of-state circulation, but about half of 1 percent of its daily publication regularly went out of state. Employees of White Plains sought to recover, among other things, overtime compensation from the publisher under terms of the FLSA.

The Stone Court ruled for the employees, with only Justice Murphy dissenting. Justice Douglas pointed out that Congress made no distinction about the volume of shipments produced for and placed into commerce. Although the Court assumed that shipments of insubstantial amounts of goods were not intended to be included under the FLSA, there was reason to assume that regular shipments in commerce were to be "included or excluded dependent on their size." On the First Amendment issue, Douglas said that the press has business aspects that create "no special immunity from laws applicable to business in general" (*Mabee*, 181–182). Justice Murphy was of the view that a company that produces 99.5 percent of its products for local commerce is essentially and realistically a local business. On similar grounds, the Court upheld a ruling that vendors who distribute daily papers on the streets were employees of the publishers in *Oklahoma Press Publishing Co. v. Walling* (1946).

Although the Stone Court frequently deferred to federal regulatory agencies, it occasionally reversed agency decisions on procedural grounds. In *Federal Communications Commission v. National Broadcasting Co.* (1943), for example, the Court ruled that the Federal Communications Commission (FCC) erred in granting a Boston radio station permission to operate on a frequency already assigned to a Denver station. The Court focused on the procedural failure of the FCC to allow the Denver station to appear at the hearing. Similarly, the Court held in *Ashbacker Radio Corp. v. Federal Communications Commission* (1945) that the FCC could not grant a license to one of two applicants without a hearing.

Finally, the Court ruled in *Associated Press v. United States* (1945) that operating bylaws of the Associated Press (AP) restrained trade in violation of the Sherman Antitrust Act. The AP sold news to member newspapers. Its bylaws prohibited AP members from reselling news to nonmembers. Further, the bylaws contained restrictive provisions that made it difficult for nonmembers to gain membership, particularly where a new member would directly compete with an old member. When the AP refused to grant membership to the *Chicago Sun*, the federal government initiated proceedings under the Sherman Act. A five-justice majority upheld the Sherman Act conviction against the AP's free press claim. Justice Black said that the First Amendment, "far from providing an argument against application of the Sherman Act, here provides powerful reasons to the contrary." Although freedom to publish is protected by the First Amendment, "freedom to combine to keep others from publishing is not" (*Associated Press*, 20).

Rights of the Accused

The Stone Court decided almost fifty cases raising constitutional issues about procedural fairness in criminal cases (conventional criminal cases that had no direct connection to the war). The Stone Court upheld convictions in more than 60 percent of these. Only Justices Murphy, Black, and Douglas consistently supported defendants claiming procedural rights violations. Justice Murphy voted to uphold convictions in only 16.7 percent of these cases, Black in 30.5 percent, and Douglas in 29.6 percent.

In other words, these justices voted to set aside convictions because of procedural error in 83.3 percent, 69.5 percent, and 70.4 percent of the cases, respectively. Justice Rutledge was next in rank on these issues, but he voted to affirm convictions in just under half (48.1 percent) of the cases in which he participated. The remaining justices voted to uphold convictions in 64–75 percent of the cases (Renstrom 1972, 219, 223, 226, 251, 260). These numbers suggest that the Stone Court was decidedly less libertarian about criminal procedure questions than other individual rights issues.

An underlying issue in many criminal cases was the matter of incorporation. Justice Black believed that adoption of the Fourteenth Amendment had made the entire Bill of Rights applicable to the states. He hoped to establish fixed standards that would minimize the need for judges to make subjective judgments on a case-by-case basis. Justice Frankfurter, in contrast, rejected the incorporation argument, preferring instead to address these matters on a case-by-case, due process basis. Only those state criminal process practices that "shock the conscience" would violate provisions of the federal Bill of Rights. The Stone Court was largely unwilling to enter the domain of state criminal process, much less impose significant constitutional restrictions stemming from a total incorporation position. In other words, the Frankfurter bloc was successful in maintaining the authority of the sovereign states on matters involving the criminal process.

Self-Incrimination and Coerced Confessions

Confessions are inadmissible at trial if they are involuntary or obtained by threats or physical abuse. One of the ongoing problems in enforcing such a rule is to prove that the accused was, in fact, coerced in some way. The landmark Warren Court ruling of *Miranda v. Arizona* (1966) was more than two decades off, which meant that custodial interrogations typically took place in private, and reviewing courts were typically presented with claims by the suspect that compulsion was perceived and a denial from the police that any misconduct occurred. The Wickersham Commission, established by President Herbert Hoover to investigate police practices, wished to eliminate physical torture or "third-degree" situations and proposed shortening the period during which the police hold prisoners before they appeared before a magistrate. This was the approach the Stone Court chose in *McNabb v. United States* (1943).

The convictions in *McNabb* were set aside without reaching the question of whether the statements were involuntary. The primary reason for excluding McNabb's statements was that they had been offered while he was unlawfully detained. Federal law requires that arrested persons must be promptly taken before a judicial officer. In McNabb's case the arresting officers "assumed functions which Congress has explicitly denied them" by subjecting McNabb to procedures "wholly incompatible" with the duties of law enforcement officers and procedures, which tend to "undermine the integrity of the criminal proceeding" (*McNabb*, 342). The Court extended the exclusionary rule, based in large part on its supervisory authority over the administration of justice in the federal courts, to statements made by suspects whose arraignment was unnecessarily delayed.

Coercive police conduct was even more difficult for the Court to handle in cases arising in state courts. It had long been true that even with the Fourteenth Amendment, states were left a considerable area of autonomy in managing criminal processes. During the Hughes era, however, the Court had made it plain that this autonomy was not limitless, especially in cases involving alleged coerced confessions. The Court had no difficulty in holding, in *Brown v. Mississippi* (1936), that such fundamental rights were denied by a state trial in which the only evidence was brutally extorted confessions. The basic problem was that unless coercion is provable, and it often cannot be, coercive conduct could go on largely undisturbed inside police stations. Several cases were enough like *Brown* so that the Hughes Court had no difficulty in concluding that confessions were involuntary and therefore inadmissible. Black said in *Chambers v. Florida* (1940) that the "rack, the thumbscrew, the wheel, solitary confinement, protracted questioning and cross questioning, and other ingenious forms of entrapment of the helpless or unpopular had left their wake of mutilated bodies and shattered minds along the way to the cross, the guillotine, the stake and the hangman's noose" (*Chambers*, 237).

In *Lisenba v. California* (1941) the Court confronted a different situation. Law enforcement officers had kept a prisoner incommunicado for a long period and committed various illegal acts in the course of questioning him. Yet there remained substantial doubt that the defendant was actually broken by police misconduct. The Stone Court upheld the state finding that his confession was voluntary, a ruling consistent with the common law concept that coerced confessions are excluded only because they may be unreliable. Justice Roberts, speaking for the seven-justice majority, said that although evidence may be "shocking to the sensibilities, that reason alone does not render its reception a violation of due process." Roberts expressed disapproval at any mistreatment of persons in police custody. He said that the Court will scrutinize carefully the record where a prisoner is "held incommunicado," subjected to police questioning, and deprived assistance of counsel. Nonetheless, the Court did not find the police misconduct in this case serious enough to constitute a deprivation of due process.

Justices Black and Douglas, however, felt this traditional approach to the issue left huge loopholes for arbitrary police conduct. They were interested in going beyond the question of evidence reliability to examine police misconduct. By 1944 the two dissenters became part of a majority in *Ashcraft v. Tennessee* (1944) to rule that a confession was inadmissible if the product of an "inherently coercive" interrogation without considering whether the defendant's "will had been overborne by the questioning." This case involved a murder suspect who offered a confession after undergoing thirty-six hours of continuous interrogation with bright lights shining in his face. Although the majority was satisfied that *Ashcraft* had been subjected to a coercive interrogation, Justices Roberts and Frankfurter dissented by distinguishing between "persistent and prolonged" questioning and the use of the "third degree." Interrogation, they concluded, is not inherently coercive, whereas use of violence is categorically barred by the Constitution. One can see in Justice Black's majority opinion in *Ashcraft* the thinking that would provide the basis for *Miranda v. Arizona* (1966).

The shift to this new focus was evident in *Malinski v. New York* (1945) as well. Malinski and two others had been arrested in connection to an investigation of a police officer's murder. The police took Malinski to a hotel, where they subjected him to questioning until he provided a confession. A second confession, substantially the same as the first, was obtained several days later. The Court found the first confession to be involuntary and reversed his conviction. The Court threw out the initial confession because the procedures used in obtaining it "offend those canons of decency and fairness which express the notions of justice of English-speaking peoples," even though it was not shown that Malinski had actually "broken because of the pressure" (*Malinski*, 416). At the same time, Justices Douglas, Black, and Frankfurter, three of the five justices who voted to reverse Malinski's conviction, affirmed the conviction of one of Malinski's accomplices, who was convicted at a trial that admitted Malinski's second confession into evidence.

Assistance of Counsel

Perhaps the best examples of the Stone Court's relatively restrained approach to procedural rights are the right to counsel cases. The issue presented no difficulties in federal criminal proceedings, since the Hughes Court had held in *Johnson v. Zerbst* (1938) that the Sixth Amendment secured the right of a federal defendant not only to employ a lawyer but also to have counsel appointed if the accused lacked the resources to retain his or her own defense attorney. There was no equivalent rule for indigent defendants in state courts, and the Stone Court did little to change that. As early as 1932 the Hughes Court had held in *Powell v. Alabama* that the Fourteenth Amendment required appointment of counsel in capital cases if defendants were too poor to hire their own lawyers and too ignorant to conduct their own defenses.

The *Powell* and *Zerbst* rulings prompted some to believe that the Stone Court might require the states to provide counsel in all criminal cases. But in *Betts v. Brady* (1942) the Court ruled that counsel need not be appointed in noncapital state felony cases that presented no "special circumstances." Justices Douglas and Murphy joined Justice Black's strongly worded dissent. *Betts* revealed a fundamental split among the Stone Court's justices. The two sides entertained different views on whether the Sixth

Amendment right to counsel ought to be extended to state cases; how fundamental the assistance of counsel clause was to fair trials; and, if fundamental, whether it was required in all felony cases or only capital cases. The majority of justices, including Frankfurter and Stone, wanted a flexible and subjective standard that would permit the Court to decide these questions on a case-by-case basis. The dissenters viewed assistance of counsel as fundamental to fair trials and advocated a categorical rule providing for counsel in all felony cases.

The fairness standard was utilized by a majority of justices in *Betts*. From this perspective, state criminal trials where defendants were not provided counsel were not inherently unfair. At the same time, the Court recognized exceptions—counsel must always be supplied in state trials that presented "special circumstances," a category that included all capital cases. Justice Roberts wrote for the Court in *Betts* that a survey of then current state practice on this issue revealed that a "great majority" did not consider appointment of counsel a fundamental right "essential to a fair trial" (*Betts*, 471). Roberts suggested that the matter was one for state legislatures to resolve but pointed out that trial courts could always appoint counsel if deemed necessary in the "interest of fairness." He categorically rejected an all-purpose rule requiring states to provide counsel in all felonies, saying the states "should not be straight-jacketed in this respect" (*Betts*, 472). Roberts concluded that although the Fourteenth Amendment prohibits conviction of one whose trial is offensive to the fundamental ideas of fairness, it does not "embod[y] an inexorable command that no trial for any offense, or in any court, can be fairly conducted and justice accorded a defendant who is not represented by counsel" (*Betts*, 473). Although the "special circumstances" proviso was broadened following *Betts*, the basic holding in *Betts* governed assistance of counsel jurisprudence until it was formally overruled by the Warren Court in *Gideon v. Wainwright* (1963).

The Stone Court refused to require that a criminal defendant retain counsel in *Adams v. United States ex rel. McCann* (1942). Gene McCann had been indicted on six counts of mail fraud. He insisted on conducting his own defense even after the trial court advised that he secure defense counsel. McCann proceeded without counsel nonetheless, opted to waive a jury trial in favor of a bench trial, and was convicted. The Court of Appeals set aside McCann's conviction, concluding that an accused without counsel cannot surrender his right to a jury trial. The Supreme Court disagreed, ruling instead that so long as a defendant makes a "free and intelligent" choice, there is nothing in the Constitution to prevent an accused from waiving his right to obtain counsel. Justice Frankfurter said that nothing in the Bill of Rights precludes a defendant, "in obedience to the dictates of self-interest . . . from surrendering his liberty by admitting his guilt." The Constitution, he continued, does not compel a defendant to "stand trial against his wishes," and absent any statutory requirement to the contrary, "no social policy calls for the adoption by the courts of an inexorable rule that guilt must be determined only by trial and not by admission." It is one thing for a court to determine if an accused is capable of making an intelligent and informed judgment. It is quite another to suggest that the Constitution "unqualifiedly deems an accused incompetent unless he does have the advice of counsel" (*McCann*, 276). Justice Douglas, in a dissent joined by Justices Black and Murphy, said he did not believe the Court "could safely assume that in absence of legal advice a waiver by a layman of his constitutional right to a jury trial was intelligent and competent" (*McCann*, 282).

Notwithstanding the *Betts* and *Adams* rulings, there were other and more protective assistance of counsel decisions. *Glasser v. United States* (1942) and *Rice v. Olson* (1945) are illustrative. Daniel Glasser was indicted with several others on charges of conspiracy to defraud the United States. He was represented by defense counsel of his choice. Over his objection, however, the trial court appointed his attorney to represent one of the codefendants. Following his conviction, he appealed on the grounds that he had been denied counsel. The Supreme Court agreed in a 6–2 decision. Justice Douglas said a trial court must refrain from "embarrassing defense counsel by even suggesting that counsel undertake to concurrently represent interests which might diverge from those of his first client." This is particularly important in conspiracy cases, Douglas observed, where each defendant must be "given the benefit of undivided assistance of his counsel without the court's becoming party to encumbering that assistance" (*Glasser*, 76). Beyond the obvious conflict of interest, the "additional burden of representing another party may conceivably impair counsel's effectiveness." Justice Frankfurter and Chief Justice Stone saw the record differently. Although Glasser may have objected to joint representation initially, he "plainly acquiesced" in the arrangement. It was "clear," Frankfurter suggested, that the final arrangement as to representation was "voluntarily assumed by both parties" (*Glasser*, 75, 91).

Rice, a Native American, pleaded guilty to state burglary charges without consulting with an attorney. Rice argued that he had not waived his right to counsel in any way, but the state court concluded that a waiver of counsel was implicit in his plea of guilt. Justice Black spoke for a six-justice majority and rejected the proposition that one who pleads guilty without the benefit of counsel has "thereby competently waived his constitutional right to counsel, even though he may have sorely needed and been unable to obtain legal aid." A defendant who pleads guilty, Black continued, "is entitled to the benefit of counsel, and a request for counsel is not necessary." Rather, it is enough that a defendant charged with a serious offense is "incapable adequately of making his defense, that he is unable to get counsel, and that he does not intelligently and understandingly waive counsel" (*Rice v. Olson*, 788–789).

When Rutledge joined the Stone Court at the beginning of the 1944 term, the liberal bloc was able to secure majorities in the three other right to counsel cases decided that year—*Hawk v. Olson*, *House v. Mayo*, and *Tomkins v. Missouri*. Nonetheless, the

Stone Court retained the *Betts* ruling and its scope-limiting "special circumstances" approach. More than any other rights of the accused issue, the Stone Court's assistance of counsel rulings reflected the principal obstacle to incorporating more than First Amendment guarantees to the states. Only the states possessed the police power, and most justices were as reluctant to interfere with the states as they were about the business of administering justice. Indeed, the *Betts* majority saw incorporation as destructive of the federal system.

Searches and Seizures

The Fourth Amendment issues examined by the Stone Court produced no particularly important rulings. The Stone Court refused to enlarge any privacy protection based on the Fourth Amendment even in federal courts. As for state practices, there were no cases of consequence. The double standard employed by the Supreme Court in reviewing federal and state convictions was detectable in Fourth Amendment cases as it was on other rights of the accused issues.

The most noteworthy Fourth Amendment ruling was perhaps *Goldman v. United States* (1942), where a sharply divided Court held that evidence acquired by using a detectaphone (a device that, when placed against a wall, allows one to overhear conversations on the other side) was admissible. Section 605 of the Federal Communications Act barred the interception of messages transmitted through the air or by wire. The Court ruled the federal statute was not violated since the listener had merely eavesdropped. In resolving Goldman's claim in this way, the Stone Court affirmed a proposition found in *Olmstead v. United States* (1928) that the Fourth Amendment cannot be violated without trespass, without physical entry into the place where people are overheard. Since the intercepted conversation in *Goldman* was neither transmitted by air or wire, the Court concluded that section 605 did not apply. Justice Roberts said that the Communications Act targeted the "means of communication" and not the "secrecy of the conversation" (*Goldman*, 133). Justice Murphy dissented in *Goldman*, saying that the search of one's home or office need not require physical entry in order to activate Fourth Amendment protection. Technology, he suggested, had developed "far more effective devices" by which a person's privacy could be invaded than the "direct and obvious methods of oppression which were detested by our forebears and which inspired the Fourth Amendment" (*Goldman*, 139). Chief Justice Stone and Justice Frankfurter indicated they would have joined the Court had it chosen to overrule *Olmstead*, but since that did not occur, they instead reiterated the arguments from Justices Holmes and Brandeis's *Olmstead* dissents.

The Court examined a closely related electronic surveillance issue in *Goldstein v. United States* (1942). Federal agents obtained information from a wiretap, which was admitted as evidence in Goldstein's trial. Goldstein was not a party to the intercepted conversation, however. The Court concluded that because Goldstein had not participated in the conversation, he had no standing to challenge the use of the evidence. Justices Stone, Frankfurter, and Murphy dissented in *Goldstein* for essentially the same reasons they dissented in *Goldman*.

Trial by Jury

Trial by jury is, in the eyes of many, an essential institution of democratic political systems. Nonetheless, the Stone Court was no more inclined to extend the Sixth Amendment right to a jury trial to the states than it had been with the assistance of counsel provision. The two situations were not altogether comparable, however; although few states provided counsel to indigent defendants in the 1940s, a great majority of them permitted criminal defendants to have jury trials as a matter of state law. The one jury issue addressed by the Stone Court related to jury composition—whether jury selection processes produced jurors who represented a cross-section of the community. In theory at least, a jury must represent the community at large and must not be an institution of any special group or class. If one population group is systematically excluded from jury service, this requirement is not met. By this reasoning, the exclusion from federal jury lists of all persons who work for a daily wage was held improper in *Thiel v. Southern Pacific Co.* (1946). A similar decision was reached the same year in *Ballard v. United States* (1946) with regard to a jury panel from which women were systematically excluded. "Jury competence," the Court concluded in *Thiel*, is an "individual rather than a group or class matter." Indeed, that fact "lies at the very heart of the jury system." To disregard it is to "open the door to class distinctions and discriminations which are abhorrent to the democratic ideals of trial by jury" (*Thiel*, 220). Additional discussion of this issue is included in the next section of this chapter.

Discrimination

Racial Discrimination

The post-1937 Court differed from its predecessors in its willingness to give fuller effect to the constitutional guarantee of equal protection, particularly for discrimination on the basis of race. The claims of unlawful discrimination examined by the Stone Court arose out of several diverse situations. The Stone Court's most widely known equal protection decision put an end to racially exclusive primary elections, but it made other important rulings as well. The race discrimination cases also involved the reach of federal civil rights laws, methods of jury selection, and segregation in interstate transportation. The Stone Court struck down a state law designed to keep indigents from moving into the state and examined claimed political inequality resulting from failure to redraw legislative district lines. The Stone Court broke significant new ground with its equal protection decisions.

Soon after the Civil War, Congress passed a number of civil rights laws. These laws remained largely unused for decades but were dusted off for selective implementation in the early 1940s. The Hughes Court's ruling in *United States v. Classic* (1941) did not involve minority rights as such but addressed closely related issues. Classic and other white election officials were accused of falsely counting votes in a congressional Democratic primary in New Orleans. They were indicted under two of the Civil War–era federal laws, one of which (section 241) punished conspiracy to interfere with a right secured by the federal Constitution or laws, while the other (section 242) punished anyone who "under color of law" willfully deprived an inhabitant of such a right. The government contended that the defendants had violated section 241 by conspiring to deny the right to vote and have one's vote counted and that they violated section 242 by using public office (the "color of law") to deny the right to vote. Among the significant conclusions reached by the Hughes Court in *Classic* was that Congress has the authority to protect the right to vote in congressional elections from interference by private persons. As important, the Court ruled that the federal law could reach primary elections because primaries could not be detached from the election process as a whole; *Classic* fused the primary and general election into a single process for choosing public officials. Once the Court came to this view, racially discriminatory primary practices could be addressed. The Stone Court took on the "white primary" practice in *Smith v. Allwright* (1944).

Although *Classic* changed the constitutional landscape, it did not dislodge the Hughes Court's ruling in *Grovey v. Townsend* (1935). A Democratic Party resolution adopted in 1932 specified that "all white citizens" qualified to vote under state law are eligible for membership in the Texas Democratic Party, and *Grovey* allowed the exclusion of minorities from party-run primaries and conventions. In *Grovey* the Hughes Court saw primaries as separable from the rest of the election process and concluded that parties are private rather than state actors, a status that gives parties exclusive control over their memberships.

The *Grovey* decision was anomalous following *Classic*, an anomaly the Stone Court removed in *Smith v. Allwright* (1944). The Court held in *Smith* that although primaries are operated by political parties, these primaries are nonetheless conducted under state authority. In other words, the political parties act as agents of the state when they determine who participates in primaries. The statutory system in Texas placed the name of those nominated in party primaries on the general election ballot. Since political parties, albeit private entities in other contexts, determined who would appear on the general election ballot, they took on the character of state agencies because of the duties imposed upon them by state law. Such duties "do not become matters of private law because they are performed by a political party." To the contrary, when primaries become "part of the machinery for choosing officials" (*Smith*, 663–664), the same tests to determine the character of discrimination must be applied to both the primary and the general election. Membership in a party may be no concern of a state as such, but when, as here, membership is also the essential qualification for voting in a primary to select nominees for a general election, the state "makes the action of the party the action of the state" (*Smith*, 665). Only Justice Roberts disagreed. As the author of the *Grovey* opinion, he was greatly distressed that the Court abandoned the unanimously established precedent handed down only nine years earlier.

Screws v. United States (1945) examined the broader effectiveness of the same federal civil rights law at issue in *Classic*. Screws, a local sheriff, had been convicted under section 242 for the beating death an African American held in his custody. The Stone Court concluded that the "under color of law" language reaches those officials who break state laws. The outcome in *Screws* indicated that the justices were prepared to allow federal civil rights law to reach state and local officials such as Sheriff Screws. The Court concluded that the federal law was not unconstitutionally imprecise or vague in its requirement that the prosecution demonstrate "willful" deprivation of a person's constitutional rights. A person who so willfully acts—acts with specific intent to deprive someone of his or her constitutionally protected rights—does exactly what the federal law forbids. The impact of the *Screws* ruling was less than immediately clear, however. The Court concluded that when this federal law is applied in actual cases, the trial court must clearly instruct jurors on the meaning of the term "willfully." It was the Stone Court's judgment that such jury instructions had not been given in Screws's case and that he was entitled to a new trial. Even though Screws won a new trial, the Court's ruling expanded the scope of federal civil rights laws.

The Stone Court decided several cases involving claims of discriminatory jury selection. The claim in *Hill v. Texas* (1942) was that African Americans had been "systematically excluded" from grand jury service in Dallas County, Texas. In unanimously reversing Hill's sexual assault conviction, Chief Justice Stone stated that "no chance or accident could hardly have accounted for the continuous omission of negroes from the grand jury lists for so long a period as sixteen years or more." Indeed, it is the duty of both the Court and the states to ensure that a criminal defendant "shall enjoy the protection which the Constitution guarantees" (*Hill*, 406). State criminal defendants are thus entitled to jury selection methods that do not discriminate on the basis of race. Furthermore, the Court held that Hill was not obligated to demonstrate discrimination in his case specifically but simply make out a prima facie case of the discriminatory exclusion of blacks as a general policy.

The county out of which the *Hill* case had come quickly developed an evasive policy that technically complied with *Hill*. The jury commissioners placed a single minority person on grand juries. A prosecution that began with an indictment from such a grand jury was before the Court in *Akins v. Texas* (1945). The county's jury commissioners admitted that the limitation of minority representation to a single juror was intentional. Nonetheless, the Stone Court, in a 6–3 decision, concluded that this tactic was constitutionally sufficient. Quite remarkably, the Court determined that "purposeful discrimination" was not demonstrated by a showing that minority membership on any single grand jury was limited to one. Defendants are not, said Justice Reed, "entitled to demand representatives of their racial inheritance upon juries before whom they are tried" (*Akins*, 403). In other words, the mere inequality in the number of minorities selected did not in itself show unlawful discrimination. The Stone Court's ruling in *Akins* was not long-lived; it was overruled by the Vinson Court in *Cassell v. Texas* (1950).

The Stone Court decided one other case involving jury composition, although race was not at issue. In *Thiel v. Southern Pacific Co.* (1946), the Court held that excluding prospective jurors on the basis of economic status was unconstitutional. Thiel had filed a civil claim against Southern Pacific. The case went to trial, but in creating a jury pool for the trial the court clerk had excluded all day laborers because local judges typically excused such individuals from actual jury service on economic hardship grounds. As a result of excluding all day laborers from the jury list in this case, half of the remaining jury pool were businessmen and their wives. In a 7–2 decision, the Stone Court set aside the judgment for Southern Pacific. It concluded that general principles underlying the jury selection process would clearly "outlaw" the exclusion of day laborers. Justice Murphy said for the majority that juror competence "is not limited to those who earn their livelihood on other than a daily basis." Jury service is a "duty as well as a privilege" of citizenship. A "blanket exclusion" of all daily wage earners, "however well intentioned and however justified by prior actions of trial judges, must be counted among those tendencies which undermine and weaken the institution of the jury trial" (*Thiel*, 223–224). Justice Frankfurter, joined by Reed, dissented. He argued that there was no constitutional question present in the case but only a question of judicial administration. The challenged practice was not a "covert attempt to benefit the propertied, but a practice designed, wisely or unwisely, to relieve the economically least secure from the financial burden which jury service involves." A group may be excluded for reasons that are "relevant not to their fitness but to competing considerations of public interests," as is the exclusion of doctors, among others. Frankfurter thought it obvious that these "accepted general considerations must have much leeway in application" (*Thiel*, 227).

The Stone Court considered the effects of state segregation laws on interstate travel. In 1941 the Hughes Court held that the Interstate Commerce Act compelled a railroad to supply presumably equal but racially segregated sleeper accommodations for racial minorities in *Mitchell v. United States* (1941). Five years later the Stone Court went further in *Morgan v. Virginia* (1946), ruling that enforced segregation of interstate bus passengers impeded commerce by forcing travelers to move from one seat to another as the bus proceeded from one state to another. The Court resolved this case by examining statutes in other states even though they had not come into play in Morgan's travels. The Court considered it important to determine whether there were "cumulative effects" from these other state laws, which "may make local regulation impracticable" (*Morgan*, 382). It was evident to all the justices except Burton that seating arrangements for different races in interstate travel "require a single, uniform rule to promote and protect national travel" (*Morgan*, 386). Justice Burton disagreed, saying that where "conditions are diverse," solutions to problems arising from them "may well come through the application of diversified treatment matching the diversified needs as determined by our local governments." Accordingly, uniformity of treatment is appropriate "where a substantial uniformity of conditions exists" (*Morgan*, 394). *Morgan* would have been a stronger ruling had it been grounded on the Fourteenth Amendment. Even though the Stone Court chose not to invoke the equal protection clause, *Morgan* sent somewhat of a signal of things to come on the segregation issue.

Discrimination by labor unions presented slightly different questions for the Stone Court. As "private associations," they could not be brought within the reach of the Fourteenth Amendment. The Court interpreted the Railway Labor Act, however, to prohibit discriminatory union practices by the Brotherhood of Locomotive Firemen and Enginemen. The Court struck down a labor agreement in *Steele v. Louisville and Nashville Railroad Co.* (1944) because the act conferred on the brotherhood a legal obligation to represent all railroad workers. Although the union could exclude minority workers from union membership, the act required that the union represent all railroad workers in collective bargaining, "regardless of their union affiliations or want of them" (*Steele*, 200). Shortly after deciding *Steele*, the Court ruled in *Railway Mail Association v. Corsi* (1945) that a racially exclusive union was not immune from provisions of a state civil rights law forbidding any union from denying membership or equal privileges because of race, creed, or color.

Sterilization and Discrimination against Indigents

The Stone Court's intention to confront unlawful discrimination was evident in *Edwards v. California* (1941). The case involved state law that made it a misdemeanor if any "person, firm or corporation, or officer or agent thereof . . . knowingly brings or assists in bringing" an indigent person into the state. Laws of this kind were not uncommon at the time—about half the states had such "anti-Okie" laws on the books in 1940. Edwards was found to have violated the law when he brought his destitute brother-in-law from Texas into California. The Stone Court unanimously struck down the law as an unconstitutional barrier to interstate movement.

Justice Byrnes spoke for the Court in the most important opinion of his brief tenure as a justice. He acknowledged that the Court's function is not to pass on the "wisdom, need, or appropriateness" of legislative initiatives by the states to solve difficult problems. This does not mean, however, that there are "no boundaries to the permissible area of State legislative activity." Such boundaries exist, and "none is more certain than the prohibition against attempts on the part of any single state to isolate itself from difficulties common to all of them by restraining the transportation of persons and property across its borders" (*Edwards*, 173). Byrnes found it "difficult to conceive" of a state law more "squarely in conflict" with this proposition than the California law. Its "express purpose and inevitable effect" is to prohibit the transportation of indigent persons into California. The burden upon interstate commerce, the Court concluded, is "intended and immediate; it is the plain and sole function of the statute." Furthermore, California's law was an "open invitation to retaliatory measures," leading the Court to conclude that states could not engage in regulation that affected interstate commerce in this way (*Edwards*, 174).

Several members of the Court agreed the California law was unconstitutional but would have preferred resolving the case on other than interstate commerce grounds. In a concurring opinion joined by Justices Black and Murphy, Justice Douglas contended that the right of people to move freely among the states "occupies a more protected position in our constitutional system than does the movement of cattle, fruit, steel and coal across state lines." The right to move freely is "an incident of national citizenship protected by the privileges and immunities clause of the Fourteenth Amendment against state interference" (*Edwards*, 177–178). If a state were able to impose the type of restriction involved in *Edwards*, it would "introduce a caste system utterly incompatible with the spirit of our system of government." It would permit those who were "stigmatized" by labeling them as indigents or paupers to be "relegated to an inferior class of citizenship" and prevent citizens from "seeking new horizons in other states" simply because they were poor (*Edwards*, 181). Justice Byrnes and others were concerned, however, that grounding the decision in either the equal protection or privileges and immunities clause could prompt future Courts to resume a substantive due process–like review of state policies—and that the Court could then effectively veto virtually any state legislation.

Justice Jackson issued a concurring opinion in *Edwards* that paralleled the view of Douglas. The Byrnes's opinion neither "fit easily" into Jackson's sense of what commerce is nor sufficiently protected citizenship interests. Jackson distinguished reasons that a state might legitimately restrict access, such as "crime or contagion." The "mere state of being without funds," however, is a "neutral fact—constitutionally an irrelevance, like race, creed or color." Jackson, with the eloquence for which he was known, concluded:

> Any measure that would divide our citizenry on the basis of property into one class free to move from state to state and another class that is poverty-bound to the place where it has suffered misfortune is not only at war with the habit and custom by which our country has expanded, but is also a short-sighted blow at the security of property itself. Property can have no more dangerous, even if unwitting, enemy than one who would make its possession a pretext for unequal or exclusive civil rights. Where those rights are divided from national citizenship no state may impose such a test, and whether the Congress could do so we are not called upon to inquire. (*Edwards*, 185)

An important development in the field of individual rights concerned heightened judicial scrutiny where encroachments on fundamental human rights are involved. In *Skinner v. Oklahoma* (1942), for example, the Court struck down a state law requiring the sterilization of persons convicted a third time of a crime involving "moral turpitude." Skinner had been convicted first of stealing chickens and then twice for armed robbery. The case presented the same kind of problem for the Court it faced in *Edwards*, and the Stone Court was similarly reluctant to use the due process clause to nullify state laws given the history with substantive due process rulings in property rights cases. But the law did not apply equally to all felony level offenses since it contained an exception for persons convicted of embezzlement. Douglas said sterilization of those who have "thrice committed grand larceny with immunity for those who are embezzlers is a clear, pointed, unmistakable discrimination." Although pointing out that states had broad powers to classify in lawmaking, Douglas asserted that procreation is a "fundamental right" and involves one of the "basic civil rights of man." Oklahoma made no attempt, Douglas continued, to "say that he who commits larceny by trespass or trick or fraud has biologically inheritable traits which he who commits embezzlement lacks." If sterilized, the felon is "forever deprived of a basic liberty." Under such circumstances, it is "essential" that the Court "strict[ly] scrutin[ize]" a classification used in a sterilization law, "lest unwittingly or otherwise, invidious discriminations are made against groups or types of individuals in violation of the constitutional guaranty of just and equal laws" (*Skinner*, 541–542).

Chief Justice Stone and Justice Jackson registered their reservations in concurring opinions about pursuit of a "eugenic plan to eliminate from the race characteristics that are only vaguely identified and which in our present state of knowledge are uncertain as to transmissibility" (*Skinner*, 546). They were also concerned that a convicted felon be given an opportunity to rebut the facts offered by the state that might justify so drastic a measure.

Political Equality: Legislative District Lines

Once a state receives its apportionment of representatives in the U.S. House, there remains the problem of dividing states into districts from which members of the House are elected. The task of establishing congressional districts is left to the states, subject to direction from Congress. Although Congress has required states to avoid districting in ways that advantage or disadvantage political parties, a practice called gerrymandering, it largely left this aspect of districting to state discretion. But many states had developed population disparities across districts, often the product of failure to redraw district lines altogether. The Stone Court reviewed a complaint brought by a group of Illinois voters alleging that their congressional districts had much larger populations than other districts in the state. The Illinois legislature had not redrawn the lines since 1901, and population shifts had produced substantially disparate populations by the mid-1940s. Chief Justice Stone died just before the Court decided this case, and Justice Jackson was involved with the war trials in Germany, so only seven justices addressed this question in *Colegrove v. Green* (1946). By a 4–3 vote, the Court chose not to intervene.

Justice Frankfurter spoke for Justices Reed and Burton in addition to himself. He invoked the "political question" doctrine and concluded that the Illinois voters asked the Court "what is beyond its competence to grant." This issue had historically been regarded as of a "peculiarly political nature and therefore not meet for judicial determination." Besides presenting a "political question," the remedial options of the judiciary were limited. The courts might remove the existing boundaries, but cannot, said Frankfurter, "affirmatively remap the Illinois districts so as to bring them more in conformity with the standards of fairness for a representative system" (*Colegrove*, 552–553). The only option would be to have congressional elections in Illinois conducted on an at-large basis—electing representatives from a single statewide ballot containing the names of all candidates. Frankfurter saw this as worse than maintaining the status quo.

The redistricting issue present in *Colegrove* gave Frankfurter the opportunity once again to expound on the role of courts in the American political system. Intervention into this dispute could bring the courts into "immediate and active" relations with political parties and party contests. The Supreme Court has traditionally remained aloof from such cases. More than aloof, it is "hostile to a democratic system to involve the judiciary in the politics of the people." In Frankfurter's view, it was no "less pernicious" to legalize judicial intervention into judicial disputes by "dress[ing them] up in the abstract phrases of the law." The better remedy "ultimately lies with the people" (*Colegrove*, 554). Frankfurter concluded with one of his classic statements on judicial self-restraint, at least when "political questions" were at hand:

> To sustain this action would cut very deep into the very being of Congress. Court ought not enter this political thicket. The remedy for unfairness in districting is to secure State legislatures that will apportion properly, or to invoke the ample pow-

ers of Congress. The Constitution has many commands that are not enforceable by courts because they clearly fall outside the conditions and purposes that circumscribe judicial action. The Constitution has left the performance of many duties in our governmental scheme to depend on the fidelity of the executive and legislative action and, ultimately, on the vigilance of the people in exercising their political rights. (*Colegrove*, 556)

The decisive fourth vote in *Colegrove* came from Justice Rutledge. Unlike the three other justices opposing the Court's intervention, Rutledge presumed the redistricting issue contained in *Colegrove* was as a general matter appropriate for judicial consideration. At the same time, he viewed this as such a "delicate" question that the Court ought to exercise its jurisdiction "only in the most compelling circumstances" (*Colegrove*, 565). He did not think *Colegrove* presented such circumstances.

Justices Black, Douglas, and Murphy dissented in *Colegrove*. Justice Black found it difficult to see why the 1901 Illinois districting statute did not deny petitioners equal protection of the laws. The population differences across Illinois congressional districts diminished the effectiveness and value of citizens' votes. Such a "gross inequality in the voting power of citizens irrefutably demonstrates a complete lack of effort to make an equitable apportionment." Although the Constitution did not explicitly require that congressional districts must contain equal populations, the right to vote and have that vote counted, said Black, "clearly imply the policy that state election systems, no matter what their form, should be designed to give approximately equal weight to each vote cast" (*Colegrove*, 569, 570). A state can neither directly deny eligible voters access to the ballot nor "destroy the effectiveness" of their votes. It cannot accomplish this result any more "in the name of 'apportionment' than under any other name." The dissenters did not agree that judicial intervention was inappropriate under the "political question" doctrine. Rather, *Colegrove* involved a state law that "abridged the constitutional rights of citizens to cast votes in such a way as to obtain the kind of congressional representation the Constitution guarantees them" (*Colegrove*, 572). In their view, the "political question" doctrine should not insulate unconstitutional practices from the Court's scrutiny.

One might have expected the Court to revisit and possibly reverse *Colegrove* in the wake of the 4–3 vote, and with the fourth vote from Rutledge so soft on the political question point. Sixteen years passed, however, before the Warren Court abandoned *Colegrove* in *Baker v. Carr* (1962).

Civil Liberties and the War

World War II introduced factors not present in conventional criminal cases, and these war-related cases raised a number of substantial constitutional or statutory questions. Several Stone Court cases examined the issue of whether enemy belligerents are entitled to constitutional protections. There were also cases based on alleged violations of the Espionage Act of 1917 and the Selective Service Act of 1940. These cases raised, among others, important evidentiary questions. Finally, there were a number of cases concerning denaturalization. The cases involving civil liberties raised significantly more challenging constitutional issues. The major rulings in these classes of cases follow.

War Crimes

In June 1942 a German submarine dropped eight saboteurs off the U.S. East Coast. They brought a variety of supplies, such as explosives that would allow them to inflict great damage. They also had enough money to cover their expenses and detailed lists of potential targets—factories, railroad centers, bridges, power plants, and other war facilities in the United States. Before they were able to accomplish any of their objectives, they were captured. President Roosevelt issued a proclamation denying the saboteurs access to civil courts and directing that they be tried by military tribunals instead. A second order followed creating a military commission of eight army officers to try the saboteurs, ordering the attorney general to prosecute them, and designating two army officers to act as defense counsel. President Roosevelt depended heavily on the advice of Secretary of War Henry Stimson on the matter of how to handle these prosecutions. There is evidence that suggests Stimson, in turn, sought the counsel of his protégé Justice Frankfurter, and it appears that the recommendation to create a commission composed exclusively of military officers came from Frankfurter (Urofsky 1997, 60).

Four charges stating offenses under the law of war were filed against each of the saboteurs. At the outset of the proceedings, the defense challenged the constitutionality of Roosevelt's orders and the jurisdiction of the military commission. While the trial was in progress, the defendants sought habeas corpus review. The Stone Court heard and rejected the arguments of the defendants but chose not to issue a full opinion at that time. The trial resumed and the saboteurs were convicted and executed. Chief Justice Stone's opinion in *Quirin* was published three months after the Court first ruled against the saboteurs and provided the Court's reasons for upholding Roosevelt's order that the saboteurs be tried by the specially constituted military commission.

The main contention of the defendants was that the president was without statutory or constitutional authority to order trial by a military tribunal. If that were true, then the saboteurs would have been entitled to trial in a civil court with all the procedural safeguards that come with civilian trials. The government responded by asserting that the defendants could not access civilian courts because they entered the United States as enemy belligerents and because Roosevelt's order precluded access to civilian courts. Stone fully deferred to executive authority during wartime but suggested that nothing in the president's order could "foreclose consideration by the courts . . . that the Constitution and laws of the United States constitutionally enacted forbid their trial by military commission." Constitutional safeguards for the protection of all persons accused of crimes, he warned, are "not to be disregarded in order to inflict merited punishment on some who are guilty." Nonetheless, the president ordered the detention and trial of the saboteurs under his commander-in-chief power in time of war and grave public danger, and those orders are "not to be set aside by the courts without the clear conviction that they are in conflict with the Constitution or laws of Congress constitutionally enacted" (*Quirin*, 25–26).

The Constitution vests the president with the authority to wage war and to carry into effect all laws passed by Congress for the conduct of war. This authority includes "punishing offenses against the law of nations, including those which pertain to the conduct of war." The articles of war also recognize military commissions as appropriate tribunals for the trial and punishment of offenses against the law of war not ordinarily tried by court-martial. Further, Congress had explicitly provided that military tribunals "shall have jurisdiction to try offenders or offenses against the law of war in appropriate cases" (*Quirin*, 28–29). The Court recognized that those who during time of war "pass surreptitiously from enemy territory into our own, discarding their uniforms upon entry, for the commission of hostile acts involving destruction of life or property, have the status of unlawful combatants punishable as such by military commission" (*Quirin*, 35).

Trial by jury was a familiar part of the machinery of criminal trials in the civil courts at the time the Constitution was ratified. Trial by jury, however, was "unknown to military tribunals, which are not courts in the sense of the Judiciary Article." The Sixth Amendment, "while guaranteeing the continuance of certain incidents of trial by jury which Article III, Section 2 had left unmentioned, did not enlarge the right to jury trial as it had been established by that Article." As a result, said Stone, the Court "cannot say that Congress in preparing the Sixth Amendment intended to extend trial by jury to the cases of alien or citizen offenders against the law of war otherwise triable by military commission" (*Quirin*, 39–40). The Court was unanimous in its conclusion (Justice Murphy not participating) that the constitutional provision in question did not provide any basis for issuing a writ of habeas corpus. Roosevelt's proclamation convening the commission was a lawful order.

The *Quirin* decision was significant in that it reaffirmed the breadth of presidential war power. The Stone Court ruled that President Roosevelt, drawing on his authority as commander in chief, statutory law, and the articles of war, had sufficient power to proceed as he did in the case of the saboteurs. The Court also reiterated the conclusion that military authorities could proceed against enemy belligerents without adhering to constitutional protections afforded defendants in civilian courts. Finally, the Court made it clear that it would not interfere in this kind of proceeding, although habeas corpus review remained possible to persons convicted by military tribunals.

In contrast to the ruling in *Quirin*, the Stone Court's scrutiny over the application of wartime penalties was evident in the first treason case arising from World War II. The case of Anthony Cramer, a naturalized citizen of German birth, was directly connected to *Quirin;* Cramer was a close friend of Werner Thiel, one of the saboteurs convicted with Quirin. Thiel was an ardent Nazi who had returned to Germany from the United States in 1941. When he returned on his mission of sabotage, he contacted Cramer in New York. Cramer met Thiel and another of the saboteurs and agreed to safeguard his money. Cramer admitted that he assumed Thiel had secretly returned to the United States on some kind of mission for Germany. Cramer was prosecuted and convicted of treason in a federal district court. The Constitution provides in Article 3, section 3 that treason against the United States "shall consist only in levying war against them, or in adhering to their enemies, giving them aid and comfort." It further provides that no person "shall be convicted of treason unless on the testimony of two witnesses to the same overt act, or on confession in open court."

In a 5–4 decision, the Stone Court concluded in *Cramer v. United States* (1945) that there was insufficient evidence to convict Cramer of treason. Justice Jackson wrote for the five-justice majority and discussed Cramer's actions in the specific context of the treason charges. The crime of treason consists of two elements, said Jackson, "adherence to the enemy, and rendering him aid and comfort." He noted that Cramer had retained "strong affection" for Germany, refused to work on materials produced for the war against Germany, and "openly opposed participation by this country in the war against Germany" (*Cramer*, 4). A citizen "intellectually or emotionally" may favor the enemy and harbor convictions "disloyal to their country's policy or interest, but so long as he commits no act of aid and comfort to the enemy, there is no treason." Similarly, a citizen may take actions that "aid and comfort the enemy" such as "making a speech critical of the government or opposing its measures, profiteering, striking in defense plants or essential work, and the hundred other things which impair our cohesion and diminish our strength," but if there is "no adherence to the enemy, . . . no intent to betray, there is no treason" (*Cramer*, 29).

According to Jackson, the Court's problem in this case "begins where the Constitution ends." The Constitution fails to specify what "relation the indispensable overt act must sustain of the elements of the offense." In the Court's view, the defendant must not only intend to act but must "intend to betray his country by means of the act" (*Cramer*, 31). Jackson acknowledged that Cramer met and spoke with Thiel and offered counsel; he gave aid and comfort. There was, however, neither the testimony of two witnesses about what they said to each other, as required under Article

3, section 3, nor a showing that Cramer gave them any information of value to their mission. Further, Cramer made no effort to conceal his meeting, and he furnished the saboteurs no shelter or anything that could be called "substance or supplies." The inference of intent to betray the country from such acts is "very different from the intent manifest by drinking and talking together" (*Cramer*, 39).

The framers' effort to "compress into two sentences the law of one of the most intricate of crimes gives a superficial appearance of clarity and simplicity which proves illusory when it is put to practical application." There are few subjects, Jackson continued, on which the "temptation to utter abstract interpretive generalizations is greater or on which they are more to be distrusted." The protection of the two-witness requirement on overt acts may be "wholly unrelated to the real controversial factors in a case." The provision was adopted, however, "not merely in spite of the difficulties put in the way of prosecution but because of them" (*Cramer*, 48). As a result, the Court concluded that the overt acts are "insufficient as proved" to support Cramer's conviction.

Justice Douglas, joined by Chief Justice Stone and Justices Black and Reed, dissented. The dissenters argued that the Court's opinion was based on an "untenable" constitutional interpretation. It was their view that the jury had "ample evidence" to conclude that Cramer had harbored treasonable intent. Criminal intent exists if an act gives aid and comfort to a person known or believed to be an enemy; there must be criminal intent since the person "intended to do the act forbidden by law" (*Cramer*, 49, 54–55). The effect of the Court's ruling in *Cramer* was to make treason a very difficult charge to prove. The dissenters felt the ruling stacked the deck in the alleged traitor's favor.

A second treason prosecution resulted from the German saboteur case. Hans Haupt, father of one of the saboteurs, was convicted of treason for providing shelter for his son and attempting to get him a job in a defense-related factory. The Vinson Court upheld his conviction in *Haupt v. United States* (1947). The Court, with Jackson again providing the rationale, concluded there could be no question that Haupt's acts provided "aid and comfort" to the son's mission of sabotage. Haupt's actions had the "unmistakable quality which was found lacking in the *Cramer* case of forwarding the saboteur in his mission" (*Haupt*, 636).

In late 1945 the Stone Court returned to the issue of trial by military commission in the *Yamashita* case. The question in *Yamashita* differed from the issue in *Quirin* because the trial occurred after World War II had ended. The Court reviewed the trial of Japanese general Tomoyuki Yamashita, known as the "Tiger of Malaya," and others for their failure to restrain their troops from committing atrocities against Americans and Filipinos. As in *Quirin*, the Court reiterated that military proceedings may be reviewed on habeas corpus. The Court then ruled, in a 6–2 decision, that the military commission constituted by General Douglas MacArthur to try Yamashita was established in accordance with federal law that provided for military trials of enemy combatants charged with violating the law of war.

Yamashita challenged his conviction on the grounds both that the commission was created unlawfully and that no military commission could try his case after the cessation of hostilities. Chief Justice Stone offered the Court's conclusion that the commission had been created in "complete conformity" to federal law "sanctioning the creation of such tribunals for the trial of offenses against the law of war by enemy combatants" (*Yamashita*, 11). The Court then turned to the question of whether the military tribunal could be directed to try Yamashita after the cessation of hostilities. The Court could not say that there is "no authority to convene a commission after hostilities have ended" even to try violations committed before their cessation, "at least until peace has been officially recognized by treaty or proclamation of the political branch of the Government." In fact, Stone continued, in "most instances the practical administration of the system of military justice under the law of war would fail if such authority were thought to end with the cessation of hostilities." The extent to which the power to prosecute violations of the law of war "shall be exercised before peace is declared rests, not with the courts, but with the political branch of the Government." Accordingly, the military tribunal's procedures, the evidence admitted, and its conclusions are simply not, Stone said, "subject to review by civilian courts" (*Yamashita*, 24).

Justices Murphy and Rutledge each issued strongly worded dissents. The Fifth Amendment guarantee of due process of law, said Murphy applies to "any person" who is accused of crime by the federal government or any of its agencies. No exception is made, Murphy continued, as to those who are "accused of war crimes or as to those who possess the status of enemy belligerent." Indeed, such an exception would be "contrary to the whole philosophy of human rights which makes the Constitution the great living document it is." According to Murphy,

> The rights protected by the due process requirement belong not alone to members of those nations that excel on the battlefield or that subscribe to the democratic ideology. They belong to every person in the world, victor or vanquished, whatever may be his race, color or beliefs. They survive any popular passion or frenzy of the moment. The existence of these rights is not always respected; they are often trampled under by those who are motivated by hatred, aggression or fear. (*Yamashita*, 26)

Soon after the Civil War, the Court had held in *Ex parte Milligan* (1866) that military trials were prohibited by the Constitution where civilian courts were "open and functioning." Nonetheless, the Stone Court concluded in both *Quirin* and *Yamashita* that enemy belligerents are not entitled to constitutional protections, a conclusion to which Justices Murphy and Rutledge reacted with alarm. Although exhibiting strong commitment to civil liberties generally, the Stone Court's rulings in *Quirin* and *Yamashita* reflected the view that certain interests, such as national security, can override the protection of individual rights.

Throughout the war years, there was a concerted effort to avoid the level of political repression that had existed during World War I. This was certainly true with respect to German and Italian populations. The Stone Court played a significant role in this effort. The remainder of this section on sanctioning war-related conduct is developed chronologically. To do so, it is necessary to return to early 1943 and the Court's ruling in *Viereck v. United States*.

George Viereck was convicted of willfully failing to disclose all information required under the Foreign Agents Registration Act. The purpose of the law was to identify agents of foreign governments who might "engage in subversive acts or in spreading propaganda." The compulsory registration was designed to "make public record of the nature of their employment." The question in *Viereck* was whether the act required persons to report activities of their own as distinct from those activities undertaken on behalf of a foreign government. By a 5–2 vote, the Court ruled that an agent was obligated to report only those actions taken on behalf of foreign principals. Chief Justice Stone suggested that if private actions were to be within reach of the statute, the law's language should have unambiguously said so. Although Congress had a legitimate interest in regulating agents of foreign principals by directing them to register and furnish such information, the Court "cannot add to its provisions other requirements merely because we think they might more successfully have effectuated that purpose" (*Viereck*, 243–244). In an interesting twist, Justices Black and Douglas disagreed. They read the statute as including actions taken by Viereck in pursuit of his own as distinguished from a foreign government's agenda.

Several months after *Viereck*, the Court decided *Schneiderman v. United States* (1943). Federal law permits the "cancellation" of naturalized citizenship if the certificate of naturalization was obtained by fraud or other illegal act. William Schneiderman became a naturalized citizen in 1927 after having resided in the United States for almost twenty years. At the time of his naturalization proceeding, he was a member of the Communist Party. The Justice Department initiated citizenship revocation proceedings against Schneiderman in 1939 on the ground that as a Communist, he could not have "attached to the principles" of the United States and be "well disposed to the good order and happiness" of the United States. Wendell Willkie, the Republican opponent of President Roosevelt in 1940, represented Schneiderman and argued that adhering to abstract political views did not necessarily constitute absence of true allegiance. The Stone Court reversed the decision to revoke Schneiderman's citizenship in a 6–3 ruling.

Justice Murphy, who spoke for the majority, was troubled by the length of time that had elapsed from Schneiderman's naturalization and the initiation of proceedings to revoke that citizenship. The government, he suggested, was seeking to "turn the clock back twelve years . . . and to deprive him of the priceless benefits that derive from [citizenship]" (*Schneiderman*, 122). Murphy pointed out that when Schneiderman was naturalized, Communist belief or affiliation was not proscribed by federal law. Rather, the applicable federal law only forbid the naturalization of persons who did not believe in organized government or were members of organizations "teaching such disbelief" (*Schneiderman*, 132). Although acknowledging congressional authority to set the conditions of citizenship, the Court rejected the argument that revocation of citizenship could be based on political belief; belief that the constitutional system can be improved cannot suffice to show "lack of attachment to the principles of the Constitution." Expression of desires to improve the Constitution "should not be judged by conformity to prevailing thought." If there is any constitutional principle that "more imperatively calls for attachment than any other," said Murphy, "it is the principle of free thought—not free thought for those who agree with us but freedom for the thought that we hate" (*Schneiderman*, 138). In any event, the Court concluded that the government had not carried its burden of proof by evidence, which does not leave in doubt that Schneiderman was not in fact "attached to the principles of the Constitution."

The dissenters, Chief Justice Stone and Justices Frankfurter and Roberts, split with the majority on two basic points. First, they believed the Court should not review congressional judgment in establishing conditions of citizenship. Second, the dissenters viewed Schneiderman's affiliation with the Communist Party as antithetical to attaching to constitutional principles. Chief Justice Stone said it was a principle of our Constitution "that change in the organization of our government is to be effected by the orderly procedures ordained by the Constitution and not by force or fraud" (*Schneiderman*, 181).

The same predisposition to subject citizenship cases to the broadest judicial review was manifested in draft cases as well. The Court's rulings on the draft began in 1944 in the case of *Falbo v. United States*. Falbo had been classified by his draft board as a conscientious objector and ordered to report for "work of national importance." He refused to obey the order on the ground that he was an ordained minister, which, in his view, entitled him to total exemption from the draft. Unlike *Schneiderman*, however, the Court ruled that judicial intervention was not called for here. Justice Black suggested that when the Selective Service Act was passed in 1940, Congress was faced with the "urgent necessity of integrating all the nation's people and forces for national defense." As a result, Congress was seeking to "mobilize national manpower" as quickly as possible. The Court was convinced that Congress had not intended judicial intervention before an individual is accepted for national service. Rather, a draft board order was only an "intermediate step in a process which would not reach its conclusion until the selectee was actually accepted by the Army,

Navy, or civilian public service camp." The statute nowhere provided for judicial review, and the circumstances under which the act was adopted "lend no support to a view which would allow litigious interruption of the process of selection which Congress created." Had Congress intended to authorize interruption of the draft process by intermediate challenges of orders to report, concluded Black, "it would have said so" (*Falbo*, 553–554).

The Court applied in *Falbo* the rule that administrative remedies must be exhausted before judicial review is available. Need to adhere to such a practice is particularly appropriate in a situation of heightened urgency. Only Justice Murphy disagreed. He saw this case as "another aspect of the perplexing problem of reconciling basic principles of justice with military needs in wartime." In Murphy's view, effective prosecution of the war did not demand that Falbo be denied a full hearing. Speedy and effective mobilization of armed forces is "neither impeded nor augmented by the availability of judicial review of local board orders in criminal proceedings" (*Falbo*, 555, 560).

Baumgartner v. United States (1944) provided the occasion for the Stone Court to reverse another denaturalization finding. Baumgartner was a German-born engineer who served as a German officer during World War I. He came to the United States in 1927 and was naturalized in 1932. Almost immediately Baumgartner expressed his support of the Nazi regime in Germany and was an active member of the German-American Bund. The Stone Court unanimously ruled that the government had failed to demonstrate that Baumgartner had not fully renounced his prior German citizenship—that he had reservations about declaring his complete allegiance to the United States. Justice Frankfurter wrote the majority opinion but did not embrace the "clear, unequivocal, and convincing" standard Murphy had used in *Schneiderman*.

Frankfurter pointed out that Congress had required as a condition of citizenship that an alien renounce foreign allegiance and swear allegiance to this country and its Constitution. Allegiance to this country and its laws was intended to reflect full commitment to those political and legal institutions that are the enduring features of American political society. Frankfurter distinguished between the evidence required to grant citizenship in the first place and evidence required to denaturalize a citizen. Denaturalization calls for "weighty proof," and the Court must be particularly "watchful that citizenship once bestowed should not be in jeopardy nor in fear of exercising its American freedom through a too easy finding that citizenship was disloyally acquired." There was no such "weighty proof" in Baumgartner's case. Whatever "political leanings" he might have had in 1932, "Hitler did not come to power until after he forswore his allegiance to the German nation" (*Baumgartner*, 676).

Justices Murphy, joined by Black, Douglas, and Rutledge, wrote a separate concurring opinion. They wished to resolve the case on the basis of the *Schneiderman* standard. American citizenship is not a right granted "condition subsequent," said

Murphy, that requires the naturalized citizen to "refrain from uttering any remark or adopting an attitude favorable to his original homeland or those there in power, no matter how distasteful such conduct may be to most of us." A naturalized citizen, he concluded, "is not required to imprison himself in an intellectual or spiritual straight jacket." Moreover, the naturalized citizen does not lose the "precious right of citizenship because he subsequently dares to criticize his adopted government in vituperative or defamatory terms." The naturalized citizen "has as much right as the natural born to exercise the cherished freedoms of speech, press, and religion" (*Baumgartner*, 679–680).

Two years after *Baumgartner*, the Court reviewed a similar situation in *Knauer v. United States* (1946). Knauer had come to this country in 1925 at the age of thirty and became a citizen in 1937. Unlike *Baumgartner*, however, the evidence against Knauer showed that before, at the time of, and after his naturalization, he had followed a course of conduct designed to promote the Nazi cause in this country. He was not, the Court concluded, "an underling caught up in the enthusiasm of a movement, driven by ties of blood and old associations to extreme attitudes, and perhaps unaware of the conflict of allegiance implicit in his actions." Rather, Douglas characterized Knauer as an "astute person, . . . a leader." His activities portrayed a "shrewd, calculating, and vigilant promotion of an alien cause." The Court concluded that "when Knauer forswore allegiance to Hitler and the German Reich, he swore falsely" (*Knauer*, 668–669). Douglas emphasized that the evidence against Knauer was "much more than political utterances." Rather, the record "portray[ed] a program of action to further Hitler's cause."

Rutledge and Murphy, in dissent, agreed that if any man deserved revocation of citizenship, Knauer did. They were unable to accept that the federal government had the authority to denaturalize, however. If such power exists, then all naturalized citizens are "second-class citizens"—any process that takes away citizenship "for causes and by procedures not applicable to native-born citizens places them in a separate and an inferior class" (*Knauer*, 677).

The Espionage Act of 1917 provided the basis for a number of federal prosecutions in World War I. The Stone Court narrowly interpreted the Espionage Act, however, in an attempt to prevent the kind of politically oppressive results that occurred during the earlier world war. The principal Espionage Act case of World War II, *Hartzel v. United States* (1944), involved an American citizen who had expressed hope for a German victory before this country entered the war and who wrote articles in 1942 describing U.S. participation in the war as a betrayal of the United States. More specifically, Hartzel had circulated articles vilifying Jews, the English, and the president of the United States, calling for an alliance with Germany and conversion of the war into a race struggle. He mailed out some 600 copies of these articles, some going to army officers and others to persons registered under selective service. He was convicted under the Espionage Act for seeking "willfully" to cause insubordination or disloyalty in the military forces and to obstruct enlistment. In a 5–4 decision, the Court set aside the conviction.

Justice Murphy wrote for the majority, which focused exclusively on whether there was sufficient evidence to support the jury's decisions that Hartzel willfully attempted to cause insubordination, disloyalty, mutiny, and refusal of duty in the armed forces and obstructed the recruiting and enlistment service of the United States. The Court concluded that Hartzel lacked such "willful intent" at the time he composed and mailed the pamphlets. Although the pamphlets contained "such iniquitous doctrines" that under certain circumstances could provide the means for purposeful undermining of the "morale and loyalty of the armed forces and those of draft age," they cannot by themselves be taken as proof beyond a reasonable doubt that Hartzel had the "narrow intent" requisite for an Espionage Act conviction. Instead, the Court saw Hartzel's purpose as obtaining the names of prominent individuals and organizations and to "propagate his ideas among them." Distribution of his pamphlets to the selected individuals and organizations, Murphy suggested, was "quite consistent with a mere intent to influence public opinion and to circulate malicious political propaganda among outstanding personages, whether they be in the armed forces or not" (*Hartzel*, 687–688). Murphy concluded that unless there is sufficient evidence from which a jury could infer beyond a reasonable doubt that Hartzel intended to bring about the specific results banned by the act, an American citizen "has the right to discuss these matters either by temperate reasoning or by immoderate and vicious invective without running afoul of the Act" (*Hartzel*, 689).

Justice Reed, joined by Justices Frankfurter, Douglas, and Jackson, dissented. Reed asserted that papers or speeches "may contain incitements" for the military to be insubordinate "without a specific call upon the armed forces so to act." The dissenters took the position that Hartzel's pamphlets revealed the requisite intent to sustain a conviction. The jury was entitled to weigh that those to whom his articles were sent were "hand-picked and composed a select group. These actions speak as loud as the words" (*Hartzel*, 692). Similarly, placing the pamphlets in military hands was an attempt to cause insubordination among the troops. Reed suggested that the circumstances under which the pamphlets were distributed were "important and entitled to weight." The right of free speech is "vital," Reed said, but the necessity of finding beyond a reasonable doubt the "intent to produce the prohibited result affords abundant protection to those whose criticism is directed to legitimate ends" (*Hartzel*, 694).

In similar fashion the Court in *Keegan v. United States* (1945) reversed the Selective Training and Service Act convictions of twenty-four leaders of the German-American Bund on grounds of insufficient evidence. The professed purpose of the organization was to keep alive the German spirit among persons of German blood in the United States. One of the group's "commands" (command 37) provided that Bund members and German Americans, if they "properly can . . . [should] refuse to do military service" until the draft law is upheld in a test case against claims it was discriminatory. The Bund members were charged with conspiracy to counsel persons to "evade, resist, and refuse service" in the U.S. military. Justice Roberts, speaking for the five-justice majority, suggested that the objective of the Bund was to create public opinion favorable to the Hitler regime and to the German National Socialist state. Merely promulgating and communicating command 37 did not constitute counsel to evade the draft, and the petitioner's "general disposition" toward the government of the United States and the Selective Service Act "did not make the command such" (*Keegan*, 494–495).

Justice Black, in a concurring opinion, pointed to a seeming inconsistency in the government's case. The government had tried to prove that the defendants counseled the members of the Bund to evade the Selective Service Act. The government's case rested on the premise that Bund members were subject to the draft under the act. The act, however, contained language that stripped Bund members of their citizenship, which made them ineligible for the draft as well. If Bund members were not subject to draft, Black argued, no person "could be convicted for advising Bund members to this effect." Chief Justice Stone, joined by Justices Reed, Douglas, and Jackson, dissented. They saw the evidence as demonstrating the government's contention that Keegan and the others "had the inclination and the purpose to persuade Bund members to obstruct the operation" of the Selective Service Act and that command 37 "was their chosen means to accomplish that end" (*Keegan*, 501).

The government's decade-long effort to deport labor leader Harry Bridges came to an end in *Bridges v. Wixom* (1945). He was first investigated for possible deportation as early as 1934, but there were insufficient grounds for action at that time. Four years later deportation proceedings were formally initiated alleging that Bridges was affiliated with the Communist Party. If such affiliation could be shown, Bridges could be deported because the party advocated the violent overthrow of the government. Dean Landis of the Harvard Law School, acting as special examiner for the government, concluded that there was insufficient evidence to show Bridges was a current member of the party. Labor Secretary Frances Perkins, whose department had jurisdiction over deportation matters, agreed, and the charges were dismissed in January 1940.

Those who wished to deport Bridges did not accept Perkins's judgment as final, however. The House of Representatives proceeded to adopt a special bill directing the attorney general, "notwithstanding any other provisions of law," to deport Harry Bridges because his continued presence in the United States was deemed "hurtful" by Congress. When this bill was not reported out of a Senate committee, Congress amended the deportation law to permit the deportation of aliens who at any time since entering the country had been members of or affiliated with an organization believing in the overthrow of the government by force or violence. Action to deport

Bridges was then begun under the amended statute. A special examiner concluded that Bridges had affiliated with the Communist Party and subscribed to the party's unlawful objectives. The examiner's findings were overturned by the Board of Immigration Appeals, but Attorney General Francis Biddle, who was at that point responsible for deportation proceedings, reversed the appeals board and ordered deportation. Bridges failed to get the deportation set aside in the lower courts but won a 5–3 decision from the Stone Court.

Justice Douglas said that the facts of the case showed little more than a course of conduct that "reveals cooperation with Communist groups for the attainment of wholly lawful objectives," such as seeking to organize labor and raise wages. Indeed, the association Bridges had with Communist groups "seem[ed] to indicate no more than cooperative measures to attain objectives which were wholly legitimate" (*Bridges v. Wixom*, 145). In addition, incriminating statements used to support the contention that Bridges was an actual member of the Communist Party were unsworn, making them inadmissible. Although deportation is not a criminal proceeding as such, it imposes a great hardship and deprives an individual of the right to live and work in this country. Accordingly, "meticulous care" must be taken to be certain that the deportation process meets the "essential standards of fairness" (*Bridges v. Wixom*, 154).

Justice Murphy, who wrote his own concurring opinion in *Bridges v. Wixom*, suggested that the government's ongoing campaign against Bridges was both excessive and unwarranted. He characterized the government's attempts to deport Bridges as a "concentrated and relentless crusade" against someone who attempted to do no more than exercise his constitutionally protected right of expression (*Bridges v. Wixom*, 157).

Murphy would have preferred to declare the deportation statute unconstitutional on First Amendment grounds. Chief Justice Stone, joined by Justices Roberts and Frankfurter, deferred to the "plenary power" of Congress over deportation. Congress chose to confer the conduct of deportation proceedings to the attorney general, "with no provision for direct review of his action by the courts." The dissenters would have deferred to the attorney general's judgment in this case and upheld the deportation order (*Bridges v. Wixom*, 167).

Two years after the Stone Court's ruling in *Falbo v. United States* (1944), it reexamined the scope of judicial review available in draft cases in *Estep v. United States* (1946). Two Jehovah's Witnesses claimed ministerial exemption from the draft. Their local boards refused to grant the exception and instead classified both as available for military service. Estep reported for but refused to submit to induction and was convicted of violating the Selective Service Act. He sought review both of his criminal conviction and the local draft board's original classification. But the act did not provide for judicial review of local boards' classification decisions. To the contrary, a provision of the act declared that decisions of the local boards "shall be final." The Stone Court found, however, that congressional silence on the matter of review was not conclusive. The Court did not believe that Congress had "intended that criminal sanctions were to be applied to orders issued by local boards no matter how flagrantly they violated the rules and regulations which define their jurisdiction." Thus, the Court could not infer that Congress "departed so far from the traditional concepts of a fair trial when it made the actions of the local boards 'final' as to provide that a citizen of this country should go to jail for not obeying an unlawful order of an administrative agency" (*Estep*, 121–122).

Congress used the term "final" to limit but not preclude judicial review. Decisions of local boards "in conformity" with the regulations are final in virtually all cases. Although judicial review can occur, it is confined to those cases where "there is no basis in fact for the classification which it gave the registrant" (*Estep*, 122).

Justice Murphy issued a strongly worded concurring opinion. The lower court rulings denying judicial review "communicated to Estep that he had disobeyed an allegedly illegal order for which he must be punished without benefit of the judicial review mandated by the Constitution." In Murphy's view, absence of judicial review essentially condemns a man without a fair hearing. Justice Frankfurter concurred with the result in this particular case but thought Congress had intended to lodge "exclusive discretion" with the Selective Service System in most cases. Justice Burton and Chief Justice Stone agreed in part with Frankfurter's reasoning. They were of the view, however, that Estep's wish to challenge his classification required that he first comply with the draft law and submit to induction. Compliance would have positioned him to seek habeas corpus review. By refusing induction, Estep forfeited that review. *Gibson v. United States*, decided later in 1946 by the Vinson Court, reaffirmed the Court's determination to keep the draft system under judicial control.

The Stone Court reviewed two cases involving conscientious objector draft status. The first was *In re Summers* (1945). Summers, lawfully classified as a conscientious objector, was refused admission to the Illinois bar because the examiners concluded that his religious scruples seemed "inconsistent" with the obligation of an attorney practicing in Illinois to take an oath supporting the state constitution. A provision in the Illinois constitution required that all "able-bodied" men residing in the state serve in the state militia. Summers was willing to take the oath, but bar examiners ruled he could not do so in good faith.

The Stone Court ruled that Summers had not been deprived of his religious freedom. The Court based its judgment on *United States v. Schwimmer* (1929) and *United States v. Macintosh* (1931), where the Court had permitted denial of naturalized citizenship to conscientious objectors. Admittedly, the state could not exclude members of a particular religious group from the bar, but the refusal to admit Summers was based on his unwillingness to serve in the state militia, a statutory condition of admission to the bar in Illinois. Justices Black, Douglas, Murphy, and Rutledge saw the exclusion of Summers from the bar as a direct assault on his religious freedom and contended that both *Schwimmer* and *Macintosh* had been wrongly decided.

A year after *Summers*, the Stone Court overruled *Macintosh* and *Schwimmer* in *Girouard v. United States* (1946). Girouard was a Seventh-Day Adventist who refused to bear arms, although he was willing to serve in noncombat roles. Justice Douglas, speaking for the five-justice majority, pointed out that Congress had not made a promise to bear arms a prerequisite to citizenship and that the Court should not read such a requirement into federal law by implication. Neither had Congress acted affirmatively to embrace the rule from *Schwimmer* and *Macintosh*. The Naturalization Act of 1940 reenacted the preexisting provision on the oath required of aliens before citizenship could be granted. The oath did not require an explicit promise to bear arms. Similarly, the naturalization provisions of the second War Powers Act permitted citizenship for noncombatants prevented from bearing arms by religious convictions. The oath required of aliens under the Naturalization Act was seen as virtually identical to the oath required of public officials. Girouard's religious scruples would not have disqualified him from holding office, and Douglas doubted Congress would "set a stricter standard for aliens seeking admission to citizenship than it did for officials who make and enforce the laws of the nation and administer its affairs" (*Girouard*, 66). Douglas acknowledged the importance of bearing arms but said that serving in a combat role is "not the only way in which our institutions may be supported and defended, even in times of great peril." Further, he argued that refusal to bear arms is "not necessarily a sign of disloyalty or lack of attachment to our institutions" (*Girouard*, 64).

Chief Justice Stone dissented from the *Girouard* decision even though he had disagreed with *Macintosh* when it was decided in 1931. The issue in *Girouard* was whether Congress had rejected the Court's rulings in *Schwimmer* and *Macintosh*. Unlike the majority, Stone was convinced that Congress had since that time "adopted and confirmed" the construction of the naturalization laws given by the Court in the earlier cases. As a result, he felt constrained to adhere to the principles of the earlier decisions, even though they were personally objectionable to him. Justices Reed and Frankfurter joined him in this view.

Martial Law

Immediately following the attack on Pearl Harbor, the governor of Hawaii placed the territory of Hawaii under martial law, suspended the writ of habeas corpus, and delegated to the commanding general of the Hawaiian Department his own authority as governor as well as all judicial authority in the territory. These steps were taken under the Hawaiian Organic Act of 1900, which authorized such action "in case of rebellion or invasion, or imminent danger thereof, when the public safety demands it." The commanding general proclaimed himself military governor of Hawaii and set up a military regime superseding the civil government. Among other things, he established military courts to try civilians in cases involving offenses against the laws of the United States or the territory of Hawaii or the rules and orders of the military authorities. Sentences imposed by these tribunals were not subject to review by the regular federal courts, and all regular civil and criminal courts were closed. Ultimately, the Stone Court ruled that military government in Hawaii had been illegal, although it did not do so until after the war ended.

Duncan v. Kahanamoku (1946) involved criminal convictions of civilian residents of Hawaii, including Lloyd Duncan, by the military courts established under the martial law declaration. Duncan was charged with fighting with two marines more than two years after the Pearl Harbor attack. He was convicted in a case heard by a military tribunal and sentenced to six months' imprisonment. His attorney filed a habeas corpus petition in a federal court, which found the military exigency in Hawaii had diminished to the point that Duncan was entitled to civilian trial. The district court decision was reversed by the Court of Appeals, however, leading to review by the Stone Court.

After much delay, the Court held, on a 6–2 vote, that the establishment of military tribunals in Hawaii to try civilians had been illegal. Black's opinion for the majority acknowledged that Congress could empower the governor of Hawaii to declare martial law but further concluded that Congress "did not wish to exceed the boundaries between military and civilian powers" (*Duncan*, 324). Black offered strong words about the role of courts in the U.S. system of government. Courts and procedural safeguards are "indispensable" to the protection of liberties valued by the constitutional founders. As Black put it,

> Our system of government clearly is the antithesis of total military rule, and the founders of this country are not likely to have contemplated complete military dominance within the limits of a Territory made part of this country and not recently taken from an enemy. . . . For that reason, we have maintained legislatures chosen by citizens or their representatives and courts and juries to try those who violate legislative enactments. We have always been especially concerned about the potential evils of summary criminal trials and have guarded them by provisions embodied in the Constitution itself. Legislatures and courts are not merely cherished American institutions; they are indispensable to our government. (*Duncan*, 322)

Justice Murphy would have preferred to go further—to find military trials of civilians unconstitutional under any circumstance. The civilian courts were open in Hawaii when Duncan was tried. To retreat from the "open court" rule established in *Ex parte Milligan* (1866), he said, "is to open the door to rampant militarism and the glorification of war, which have destroyed so many nations in history." The Court must be on "constant guard against excessive use of any power, military or otherwise, that results in the needless destruction of our rights and liberties" (*Duncan*, 335). Chief Justice Stone also concurred, suggesting that although military trials might displace civilian trials while the threat of invasion is high, the civilian courts were capable of functioning in Hawaii at the time Duncan was tried.

Justice Burton offered a dissent that was joined by Frankfurter. He argued that the Constitution made the conduct of war an executive function, and a function that should be allowed broad discretion. Indeed, the executive discretion to determine policy is intended to be "supreme" under the Constitution. Executive power is generally "positive" in character, and it is "essential that the opportunity for well directed positive action be preserved and vigorously used if the Government is to serve the best interests of the people" (*Duncan*, 343). Burton said that it was "all too easy" in hindsight to ignore that "those were critical days when the United States could afford no military mistakes and when the safety and control of Hawaii . . . was essential." The more reasonable perspective, he suggested, was to examine the decision to declare martial law in the context in which it was made. Acting as they were in the "fog of war," the military commanders were "entitled to a wide range of discretion if they were to meet the obligations imposed on them." It is not justifiable, Burton continued, "to tear Hawaii out from the context of the war as whole. Our military policy there, as elsewhere, had to be guided by its relation to the global war" (*Duncan*, 351–352).

Evacuation of the Japanese

The Stone Court attempted to strike a balance between support for the war effort and sensitivity to the rights of individuals or groups regarded as "dangerous" to the national security. The Japanese exclusion cases found the Stone Court approving highly suspect restrictions on persons of Japanese ancestry. These cases projected a message that military exigency may provide authorities with expanded power to subject persons to curfew, at a minimum, and the possibility of incarceration, even without proof of the disloyalty. The evacuation of the Japanese is discussed at length because the Stone Court's rulings were of an unfortunately defining character. In addition, virtually each Stone Court justice expressed his views in one or more opinions. Their responses to the evacuation program provide valuable contrasts in constitutional interpretation.

The basic law authorizing the detention of all persons, including citizens of the United States, "friendly aliens," and enemy aliens alike, for the duration of the war was Executive Order 9066 issued by President Roosevelt on February 19, 1942. The order authorized the secretary of war and designated military authorities to identify and prescribe those "military areas" from which all persons may be "excluded, expelled, restricted, or otherwise subjected to regulations the appropriate military authorities might impose at their discretion." No direct sanctions were explicitly defined in the executive order, but the clear implication included military arrest and confinement. To implement the order, Secretary of War Henry Stimson designated Lieutenant General John L. DeWitt as military commander of the Western Defense Command. DeWitt issued a number of public proclamations pursuant to Executive Order 9066.

Roosevelt issued Executive Order 9102 on March 18, 1942, establishing the War Relocation Authority (WRA). The authority and its director were to "formulate and effectuate a program for the removal, relocation, maintenance and supervision" of such persons as indicated in Executive Order 9066. Three days later Congress specifically ratified Executive Order 9066 by statute and provided that those violating the law would be guilty of a misdemeanor and subject to fine and/or imprisonment upon conviction. (The text of several evacuation documents, including Executive Orders 9066 and 9102 and the March 21 statute, are provided in Appendix I.)

DeWitt designated the whole West Coast within forty miles of the coast as Military Area Number 1. On March 2, 1942, he ordered immediate implementation of a curfew for the entire area. In the months that followed, 112,000 Japanese Americans on the Pacific Coast were detained and transported to War Relocation Centers. Included in this number were approximately 70,000 native-born U.S. citizens. No evidence of disloyalty was required before subjecting those of Japanese ancestry to the evacuation program.

Four cases challenging the authority of the government and the military to take these actions reached the Stone Court. The first two cases were brought by Gordon Hirabayashi and Minoru Yasui. Hirabayashi, a twenty-four-year-old University of Washington student, had been raised in a Quaker family, was a member of the University Quaker Meeting, and was registered as a conscientious objector with the draft board. Hirabayashi initially obeyed the curfew but subsequently decided not to comply with the order and surrendered himself to the FBI in Seattle. Hirabayashi had no legal training and was represented by the ACLU.

Hours after the curfew went into effect, Minoru Yasui, the other curfew challenger, presented himself to the Portland, Oregon, police and demanded that he be arrested. Yasui was a leader of the Japanese American Citizens League (JACL), an organization established to represent the citizenship rights of Japanese Americans. An attorney who had been employed by the Japanese consulate in Chicago, he resigned the consulate position the day after Pearl Harbor and immediately offered his services to the army, only to be rejected for active service like many other Nisei (U.S. citizens of Japanese parentage) at the time.

Both Hirabayashi and Yasui were convicted of curfew violations in separate federal court proceedings. Hirabayashi was also convicted for failing to report to a designated "registration station" as the first step in his relocation, and he was given concurrent three-month sentences for these offenses. Since the sentences were concurrent, either or both convictions could be reviewed on appeal. The Stone Court took advantage of the concurrent sentence to isolate the curfew order, clearly a less severe interference with constitutional liberties than the forced evacuation and relocation. Although Yasui's case was reviewed separately by the Stone Court, the outcome on the curfew violation was identical to the ruling in *Hirabayashi*. Chief Justice Stone's opinion summarily indicated that Yasui's conviction "must be sustained for the reasons stated in the *Hirabayashi* case." The lower court had concluded additionally that Yasui had renounced his citizenship by violating the curfew order. The Stone Court vacated the portion of the lower court decision respecting the renunciation of citizenship and addressed only his curfew violation.

The Stone Court unanimously upheld the curfew in *Hirabayashi* and *Yasui*. Although all nine justices voted to uphold the convictions, serious differences of view existed among them on the underlying constitutional issues. It was argued that the president and Congress must be given the widest latitude to effectively respond to the war. National security was at stake, and that overrode any other consideration. Counterarguments were framed around the race-based character of the relocation program—only those of Japanese ancestry were targeted, and none of the people subjected to relocation were formally accused of crime or allowed to establish their loyalty to the United States. Justices Douglas and Murphy had the most serious reservations about the curfew, and both were pressured by their colleagues to make the vote unanimous. Even so, Douglas, Murphy, and Rutledge issued concurring opinions that distanced themselves from Stone's opinion of the Court.

Chief Justice Stone saw two central questions under review by the Court. The first was whether Congress and the executive had constitutional authority to impose the curfew restriction. Second, the Court needed to determine whether Congress and the president could delegate to a designated military commander the authority to implement Executive Order 9066, including the authority to impose a curfew. Stone's opinion was completely deferential to presidential and congressional authority to respond to the exigencies of war. The war power of the national government, Stone suggested, is the "power to wage war successfully," and this power "embraces every phase of the national defense." The Constitution commits to the president and Congress the exercise of the war power "in all the vicissitudes and conditions of warfare." In doing so, the Constitution has "necessarily given them wide scope for the exercise of judgment and discretion" in responding to wartime emergencies. It is not, Stone argued, "for any court to sit in review of the wisdom of their action or substitute its judgment for theirs" (*Hirabayashi*, 93–94). Furthermore, actions taken by the president or Congress must be examined "in light of the conditions which existed at the time," not from the vantage point of hindsight. In the Court's view, those who were responsible for the nation's defense "had ample ground" to conclude the military danger was both real and expansive.

Congress and the executive, for a variety of reasons, could also have reasonably concluded that some citizens of Japanese ancestry residing on the West Coast retained "attachment" to Japan and its institutions. As a result, the Court could not "reject as unfounded" the judgment of military authorities and Congress that "there were disloyal members of that population." The Court could not say that the war-making branches of the government did not have ground for believing that in a "critical hour such persons could not readily be isolated and separately dealt with." The presence of some disloyal Japanese within the larger Japanese community constituted, in the view of the military, a "menace to the national defense and safety, which demanded that prompt and adequate measures be taken to guard against it" (*Hirabayashi*, 99).

Stone then reached the core of the curfew cases. Neither *Hirabayashi* nor *Yasui* denied that imposition of a curfew during wartime was an "appropriate measure against sabotage." Stone called the curfew an "obvious protection against the perpetration of sabotage [which is] most readily committed during the hours of darkness." If the curfew was a reasonable use of the war power, Stone asserted, "its validity is not impaired because it has restricted the citizen's liberty." Military control of people living in a "dangerous zone in wartime . . . necessarily involves some infringement of individual liberty" (*Hirabayashi*, 100).

Finally, there was the most troublesome question—whether the curfew unlawfully discriminated against those of Japanese ancestry. Stone addressed the issue from the war emergency perspective. Congress "may hit at particular danger where it is seen, without providing for others which are not so evident or urgent." If government takes particular measures for the public safety in the "crisis of war and threatened invasion," based on facts and circumstances that suggest that a group of one national extraction may "menace that safety more than others, is not wholly beyond the limits of the Constitution and is not to be condemned merely because in other and most circumstances racial distinctions are irrelevant" (*Hirabayashi*, 100–101). The "fact" that attack on the continental United States was threatened by Japan rather than another enemy power "set these citizens apart from others who have no particular associations with Japan." Stone concluded his opinion by suggesting that the Constitution is a "continuously operating charter of government [that] does not demand the impossible or the impractical." The "essentials" of the legislative function are preserved when Congress designates a representative to make a determination that implements a legislatively defined objective. In his view, that had taken place in this instance.

Justice Douglas deferred to the war emergency once he was satisfied that the measures taken against the Japanese would be temporary. Douglas observed that the military had a "grave problem on its hands" following the attack on Pearl Harbor. The threat of Japanese invasion of the West Coast was "not fanciful but real." He addressed the argument that a better policy would have been to separate loyal Japanese from disloyal Japanese residents on an individual basis. The "wisdom or expediency of the decision which was made is not for us to review." Peacetime procedures, he argued, "do not necessarily fit wartime needs." Where the "peril is great and the time is short," Douglas concluded, "temporary treatment on a group basis may be the only practicable expedient whatever the ultimate percentage of those who are detained for cause." Nor should the military be "required to wait until espionage or sabotage becomes effective before it moves" (*Hirabayashi*, 105, 107). The weight given the military exigency is perhaps best reflected in the strong words of Douglas— a justice not easily deflected from the primacy of individual rights protection.

Justice Murphy's opinion was a concurring opinion in name only; it read more like a dissent. He acknowledged that restrictive actions against the Japanese were taken in "complete good faith" and on the basis of genuine concern about public safety and military security. He also recognized that the Court needed to extend great deference to the judgment of Congress and the military authorities as to what is necessary for the effective prosecution of the war. At the same time, the Court cannot forget that "there are constitutional boundaries which it is our duty to uphold." Distinctions based on color and ancestry are "utterly inconsistent with our tradition and ideals"; they are "at variance with the principles for which we are now waging war." He painfully suggested that with this decision the Court took the unprecedented action of approving a "substantial restriction" on personal liberty "based upon the accident of race or ancestry." This, he believed, bore a "melancholy resemblance" to the treatment of the Jews in Germany. The consequence of creating two classes of citizens on the basis of ancestry "goes to the very brink of constitutional power." A regulation like the curfew applicable solely to citizens of a particular racial extraction cannot be regarded as in accord with the requirement of due process of law contained in the Fifth Amendment "[e]xcept under conditions of great emergency" (*Hirabayashi*, 110–111). Given the critical military situation that existed on the Pacific Coast, military authorities should not be "required to conform to standards of regulatory action appropriate to normal times." In supporting the curfew, however, Murphy did not wish to be understood as intimating that the military authorities in time of war are "subject to no restraints whatsoever, or that they are free to impose any restrictions they choose on the rights and liberties of individual citizens or groups in those places which may be designated as military areas" (*Hirabayashi*, 112–113).

Rutledge echoed some of Murphy's concerns in his concurring opinion. He wished to make it clear that the Court's ruling should not be interpreted as wholly insulating from review all military judgments made during wartime emergencies. Although deference may typically be in order, there are limits beyond which the military officer cannot go, and if he "oversteps" those limits, the courts retain power to "protect the civilian citizen" (*Hirabayashi*, 114).

The curfew was a limited restriction compared to full-scale evacuation and detention. This was clearly evident from the Court's reluctance to address evacuation in *Hirabayashi*. The broader constitutional questions could not be avoided indefinitely, however, and the petition of Fred Korematsu placed the exclusion issue squarely before the Court. Korematsu was convicted for violating General DeWitt's Civilian Exclusion Order Number 34 by remaining in a military area following the issuance of DeWitt's exclusion order.

Korematsu was a Japanese American shipyard welder in the San Francisco Bay area, and he certainly did not intend to become the test case for the exclusion orders. When his family reported to the Tanforan Assembly Center for relocation, Korematsu stayed behind to be with his girlfriend, who was of Italian descent. Korematsu had previously attempted to enlist in the U.S. Army but had been turned down because of stomach ulcers. He was discharged from his shipyard job when the local union revoked his membership on nationality grounds. He was not a dual citizen, did not speak Japanese, and most of his acquaintances were Caucasian. Indeed, about a month before the evacuation orders were issued, Korematsu had undergone plastic surgery to make him look less Asian. It was his intention to go to Arizona with his girlfriend to be married without anyone's realizing he was a Japanese American (tenBroek et al. 1970, 236).

The divisions that existed behind the ostensibly unanimous curfew ruling in *Hirabayashi* took center stage in *Korematsu*. Justice Black's opinion for the six-justice majority suggested that the Court had already implicitly affirmed the broader exclusion orders in *Hirabayashi*. In light of the principles underlying the curfew decision, the Court was "unable to conclude that it was beyond the war power of Congress and the Executive to exclude those of Japanese ancestry from the West Coast war area at the time they did" (*Korematsu*, 218). Black acknowledged that "all legal restrictions which curtail the civil rights of a single racial group are immediately suspect." Nonetheless, the suspect character of such restrictions does not make them all unconstitutional. Courts need to subject such restrictions to the "most rigid scrutiny," but "pressing public necessity may sometimes justify the existence of such restrictions; racial antagonism never can" (*Korematsu*, 216).

Black conceded that exclusion from the area in which one's home is located is a "far greater deprivation" than confinement to one's residence during nighttime hours. Nothing short of apprehension by authorities of the "gravest imminent danger to the public safety can constitutionally justify either." Nevertheless, exclusion from a threatened area, no less than curfew, has "a definite and close relationship to the prevention of espionage and sabotage." In this case the military authorities concluded that the curfew alone "provided inadequate protection" and ordered exclusion. As in

Hirabayashi, Black said the Court could not "reject as unfounded" the judgment of the military authorities and Congress that there were "disloyal members" of the Japanese population, whose numbers and strength could not be "precisely and quickly ascertained." Like the curfew, exclusion of those of Japanese ancestry was deemed necessary for the very reason that an indeterminate number resided in the designated military areas (*Korematsu*, 218–219).

The Court upheld the exclusion order "as of the time it was made and when the petitioner violated it." In doing so, Black suggested that the Court was not "unmindful of the hardships imposed by it upon a large group of American citizens." At the same time, "hardships are part of war, and war is an aggregation of hardships." The burden on every citizen is "always heavier" in time of war. Compulsory exclusion of citizens from their homes, "except under circumstances of direst emergency and peril, is inconsistent with our basic governmental institutions." The bottom line, however, was that when hostile forces threaten the nation, the "power to protect must be commensurate with the threatened danger" (*Korematsu*, 219–220).

The Court's sensitivity to the discriminatory aspects of the exclusion order occupied Black's concluding paragraph. The outcome in this case would be "simple" if it involved the detention of a loyal citizen in a concentration camp because of racial prejudice. Magnifying the racial prejudice component, without reference to the real military dangers that were presented, "merely confuse[d] the issue," in Black's view. Korematsu was not excluded from the military area "because of hostility to him or his race." Instead, Korematsu was excluded

> because we are at war with the Japanese Empire, because the properly constituted military authorities feared an invasion of our West Coast and felt constrained to take proper security measures, because they decided that the military urgency of the situation demanded that all citizens of Japanese ancestry be segregated from the West Coast temporarily, and finally, because Congress reposing its confidence in this time of war in our military leaders—as inevitably it must—determined that they should have the power to do just this. (*Korematsu*, 223)

Chief Justice Stone and Justices Douglas, Reed, and Rutledge joined Black's opinion. Justice Frankfurter was the sixth vote to uphold the exclusion order. He used his concurring opinion to emphasize that the validity of the order under the war power must be judged "wholly in the context of war"; the action should not be "stigmatized as lawless because like action in times of peace would be lawless" (*Korematsu*, 224).

Justice Murphy's dissent is often quoted because it contains the sharpest rhetoric. Justice Roberts's dissent, however, is notable because he was perhaps the least likely member of the Stone Court to object so strongly. He saw a "clear violation" of constitutional rights. He distinguished the curfew and exclusion orders by saying that

Korematsu did not involve only "keeping people off the streets at night." Rather, it was a case of convicting a citizen for violating the exclusion "based on his ancestry, and solely because of his ancestry, without evidence or inquiry concerning his loyalty" (*Korematsu*, 225–226).

Justice Jackson also dissented. He took issue with both the nationality basis and the blanket enforcement of the exclusion program against everyone of Japanese ancestry. Jackson suggested that if any fundamental assumption underlies our system, it is that "guilt is personal and not inheritable." Jackson recognized that it would be "impracticable and dangerous idealism" to expect that each specific military command will "conform to conventional tests of constitutionality." He argued, however, that if all military expedients cannot be confined by the Constitution, the Constitution should at least not be "distort[ed] . . . to approve all that the military may deem expedient" (*Korematsu*, 244).

Justice Murphy's vote in *Korematsu* was consistent with his opinion in *Hirabayashi* even though he voted to support the curfew in that case. Appeals to patriotism and national unity notwithstanding, Murphy could not be dissuaded in *Korematsu* from registering his vote as well as his words against exclusion. Individuals must not be "left impoverished of their constitutional rights on a plea of military necessity that has neither substance nor support." He could not sustain exclusion in the absence of martial law; it was his view that the level of military necessity required for the declaration of martial law was required for exclusion as well. Absent such military necessity, the exclusion of all persons of Japanese ancestry was both unjustified and discriminatory—it "goes over the very brink of constitutional power and falls into the ugly abyss of racism." The judicial test of whether government, on a plea of military necessity, can deprive individuals of their constitutional rights is whether the deprivation is reasonably related to a public danger that is so "immediate, imminent, and impending as not to admit of delay and not to permit the intervention of ordinary constitutional processes to alleviate the danger" (*Korematsu*, 234).

The exclusion order, in Murphy's view, also deprived the excluded individuals of their constitutional rights to "live and work where they will, to establish a home where they choose and to move about freely." By "excommunicating" Japanese Americans without hearings, the exclusion order deprived them of their constitutional rights without procedural due process. In support of this "blanket condemnation" of all persons of Japanese descent, no reliable evidence was provided to show that such individuals were "generally disloyal" or had conducted themselves in ways that made them a "special menace" to defense installations or war industries. In Murphy's view, the government failed to demonstrate the nexus between the "group characteristics" of Japanese Americans and the "dangers of invasion, sabotage, and espionage." Instead, justification for exclusion of the Japanese rested on "questionable racial and sociological grounds not ordinarily within the realm of expert military judgment" and "an accumulation of much of the misinformation, half-truths, and insinuations that for years have been directed against the Japanese Americans by people with racial and economic prejudices" (*Korematsu*, 239). For these reasons, Murphy dissented from what he characterized as the "legalization of racism." Racial discrimination has "no justifiable part whatever in our democratic way of life." It is "unattractive in any setting," but it is "utterly revolting among a free people who have embraced the principles set forth in the Constitution of the United States" (*Korematsu*, 242).

The Court decided *Ex parte Endo* on the same day it ruled in *Korematsu*. Mitsuye Endo was detained for more than thirty months in the Tule Lake and Topaz Relocation Centers. The question presented in Endo's appeal was whether her application to leave the center could be denied given that she was a citizen of unquestioned loyalty. The Roosevelt administration did what it could to moot the *Endo* case by terminating the mass exclusion program on December 17, 1944, the day before the *Endo* decision was announced (Schubert 1957, 218–219).

Endo was a Sacramento-born Nisei stenographer working as a civil service employee for the California State Highway Commission when the exclusion order was applied to Sacramento. At the time of her evacuation, she had fully complied with all military orders, had not resisted in any way, and had not violated any law. Nonetheless, she found herself confined under armed guard. She challenged the relocation program in a civil lawsuit. The Court unanimously ruled that the War Relocation Authority could not detain a citizen whose loyalty had been confirmed.

Justice Douglas said for the Court that regardless of the power the WRA had to detain other classes of citizens, it had "no authority to subject citizens who are concededly loyal to its leave procedure." He distinguished the question presented in *Ex parte Milligan* (1866), where the jurisdiction of military tribunals to try persons according to the law of war was challenged in habeas corpus proceedings. Endo, by contrast, was detained by the WRA, a civilian rather than military authority. As a result, no questions of military law were involved (*Endo*, 298).

A citizen who is concededly loyal, Douglas said, "presents no problem of espionage or sabotage." Loyalty is a "matter of the heart and mind not of race, creed, or color." When the power to detain individuals is derived from the power to protect the war effort against espionage and sabotage, "detention which has no relationship to that objective is unauthorized." Presuming that the original evacuation was justified, its lawful character was "derived from the fact that it was an espionage and sabotage measure," Douglas suggested. The authority to detain a citizen as protection against espionage or sabotage "is exhausted at least when his loyalty is conceded" (*Endo*, 302). These were strong words, but they came only after the war was virtually over. Further, by December 1944, when *Endo* was decided, there was no reason why the small number of possibly disloyal Japanese Americans could not be dealt with on an individual basis. As in *Korematsu*, Murphy's concurring opinion again focused on what he saw as the racist underpinnings of the evacuation program. Racial discrimination of the kind present in these cases "bears no reasonable relation to military necessity and is utterly foreign to the ideals and traditions of the American people" (*Endo*, 308).

Most agree that the evacuation of the Japanese was, at minimum, excessive, unfortunate, and unparalleled. It ought not be a surprise that a civilian court could err on the side of deferring to military judgments under the emergency presented by World War II. Nonetheless, the Stone Court's refusal to intervene until after the war was disappointing to say the least. This was a Court whose members included justices who would later rank among the most distinguished defenders of constitutional rights. A majority of the Stone Court's justices subscribed to the "preferred position" approach to individual rights protection, an approach that requires the Court to be especially vigilant when constitutional rights are directed at "insular minorities." Even the "preferred position" approach must yield in the face of national security interests, apparently.

More difficult to defend is the Stone Court's decision to delay review of the evacuation program as long as it did. When the Court did intervene by ruling in *Endo* that loyal citizens could not be detained, the military authorities had already ended their detention. Judicial review in the evacuation cases was called "perfunctory." Apprehensions of the "gravest imminent danger to the public safety" led the Court to conclude that exclusion of the whole group was a bona fide military imperative. Deference to the justifications offered for the military action allowed the military, without effective limit, to decide when to invoke its "extraconstitutional powers" (tenBroek et al. 1970, 216–217). In the evacuation cases, the Supreme Court "carried judicial self-restraint to the point of judicial abdication" and sustained a "drastic act of military government over citizens within the country without inquiring in its factual justification" (tenBroek et al. 1970, 220). Viewed in retrospect, the Stone Court's rulings on relocation of the Japanese were clearly its low-water mark.

Government Authority in Wartime

The norm in times of war is judicial ratification of actions taken by the legislative and executive branches. The Stone Court adhered to this norm, as was distressingly apparent in the Japanese relocation cases. It is necessary, however, to distinguish actions taken in pursuit of foreign policy objectives from actions taken in pursuit of domestic policy objectives. The former were outside the Court's reach, or viewed as such by the Court. To be fair, the Stone Court had little opportunity to review these actions. For example, President Roosevelt concluded a number of executive agreements, including the "destroyers for bases" agreement, under which the United States provided Great Britain with fifty navy destroyers in exchange for leases to a number of military bases on British soil. The arrangement was of uncertain legal status, given seemingly incompatible provisions of existing federal law. Neither the agreement nor the provisions of the Lend-Lease Act of 1941, which embraced the agreement, were reviewed by the Stone Court.

Similarly, Roosevelt declared a "limited" state of national emergency in late 1939, and six months before the attack on Pearl Harbor he declared an "unlimited national emergency." Roosevelt's declarations of national emergency enabled him to draw on those powers Congress had stipulated could be exercised only in time of such emergency. Coupled with his frequent use of executive orders, Roosevelt had substantially expanded his authority to act even before the United States became an actual participant in World War II. Further, Congress passed a number of statutes that provided additional grants of power to the executive to meet the demands of the war. Among these statutes were the War Powers Acts of December 1941 and March 1942 and the Emergency Price Control Act of 1942. Based on authority of the two war powers statutes and the Executive Reorganization Act of 1939, Roosevelt had virtually a free hand to create new or modify existing agencies and regulate extensively through either. One such agency Roosevelt set up was the Office of Emergency Management (OEM), within which a number of other administrative agencies were located. The Court reviewed none of the actions taken by or through any of these agencies during the course of the war, with the exception of some price control actions stemming from the Emergency Price Control Act.

Emergency Regulation of Property

Congress authorized presidential seizures of manufacturing and production facilities in the War Labor Disputes (Smith-Connally) Act of 1943. Only one case arising from these seizures was commenced, but it never reached the Stone Court for review and thus produced no definitive ruling. That case involved the protracted struggle between Montgomery Ward and the War Labor Board, one of the agencies residing within the Office of Emergency Management. Roosevelt ordered Secretary of War Stimson to take possession of the company's properties. A federal judge, however, ruled that Montgomery Ward was engaged in distribution rather than production and thus not subject to seizure under Smith-Connally. The Court of Appeals reversed, however, and the Stone Court agreed to review the case. The Court subsequently dismissed the case on mootness grounds when the army turned the properties back over to the company.

Congress provided Roosevelt with broad powers to achieve price control and wage stabilization during the war. The Emergency Price Control Act of 1942 gave the federal government comprehensive authority to regulate prices and rents. The Office of Price Administration was created to implement provisions of the EPCA. The Stabilization Act of 1942 granted similarly broad authority to stabilize wages. These and other statutes delegating emergency authority to Roosevelt vested him with war power of unprecedented magnitude.

Following the constitutional "revolution" of 1937, neither the Hughes nor Stone Courts chose to interfere with economic regulatory initiatives of virtually any kind. Because the Court was operating in this deferential mode prior to World War II, it would have been most surprising had the Stone Court not fully supported wartime regulation of property. The principal test of the EPCA came in *Yakus v. United States* (1944), where the Court upheld the act in a 6–3 ruling. Unquestioned by the challengers in *Yakus* was congressional authority to establish price controls in response to the war emergency. Rather, it was contended that Congress had impermissibly delegated power to the Office of Price Administration. The Court disagreed, concluding that the limits on the field of OPA action were sufficiently "marked" by Congress. The statute directed that prices fixed by the price administrator "shall effectuate the declared policy of the Act to stabilize commodity prices so as to prevent wartime inflation and its enumerated disruptive causes and effects." In addition, the EPCA required that prices that are fixed by the OPA be "fair and equitable" and that "due consideration" be given to prices designated by Congress as the "base period." It was seen as sufficient to satisfy the statutory requirements that the OPA found that the prices fixed would tend to "achieve that objective and . . . conform to those standards" (*Yakus*, 423).

Chief Justice Stone distinguished the delegation of power issue in the EPCA from the problematic delegation found in the National Industrial Recovery Act, which the Court had found unconstitutionally excessive in *Schechter Poultry Corp. v. United States* (1935). The delegation defect in the NIRA was that the regulations were fashioned by representatives from the regulated industries. No such defect existed under the EPCA.

The Constitution, as a "continuously operative" charter of government, does not "demand the impossible or the impracticable," Stone suggested. Accordingly, Congress does not need to "find for itself every fact on which it desires to base legislative action." Rather, "essentials" of the legislative function are to decide on a legislative policy and how that policy is to be furthered by subsequent action. These essentials are "preserved" when Congress has specified the "basic conditions of fact," under which designated administrative agencies may implement the command. The separation of powers principle does not deny Congress the authority to allow an administrative officer such as the price administrator "ample latitude" within which the officer might determine whether the requisite conditions exist. The standards in the EPCA were "sufficiently definite and precise to enable Congress, the courts and the public to ascertain whether the Administrator, in fixing the designated prices, had conformed to those standards" (*Yakus*, 426).

The EPCA created an Emergency Court of Appeals consisting of federal district or circuit judges designated by the chief justice, and it authorized any person "aggrieved by the denial or partial denial of his protest" to file an appeal with this special court within thirty days. The emergency court had the power to issue injunctions if it found that any regulation, order, or price schedule did not accord with law or was arbitrary or capricious (*Yakus*, 428). Prior to *Yakus*, in *Lockerty v. Phillips* (1943), the Court had upheld the decision of Congress to create a special court to hear appeals involving OPA orders. Chief Justice Stone noted congressional authority under Article 3 to establish lower federal courts at its discretion and concluded that this power includes the authority to invest or withhold jurisdiction in the "exact degrees and character which to Congress may seem proper for the public good" (*Lockerty*, 187). Although *Lockerty* did not represent a broad challenge to the EPCA, its conclusion about the Emergency Court of Appeals was fully embraced in *Yakus*.

Stone reiterated the reasoning from *Lockerty* by noting that when Congress enacted the EPCA, it was mindful that the effectiveness of price control as an approach to prevent inflation could be jeopardized if the validity of prescribed maximum prices were to be subject to the "exigencies and delays" of the normal judicial process (*Yakus*, 432). Congress sought to minimize these difficulties by devising a single process for review of OPA regulations. The Court found this reasonable. Certainly the Constitution did not require that challenges "be made in one tribunal rather than another" as long as there is "an opportunity to be heard and for judicial review which satisfies the demands of due process" (*Yakus*, 443–444).

There were three dissenting justices in *Yakus*. Justice Roberts was of the view that the EPCA delegated too much legislative power to the OPA. This defect was a constant for Roberts in every EPCA case, and he never voted to affirm an OPA order or regulation in any case in which he participated. Justice Rutledge, joined by Justice Murphy, dissented on altogether different grounds. They were concerned that persons convicted of violating OPA orders were denied the procedural due process afforded in criminal cases.

On the same day it announced its decision in *Yakus*, the Court decided *Bowles v. Willingham*, which upheld the rent control provisions of the EPCA in much the same way it had permitted price control in *Yakus*. A state court issued an injunction restraining the OPA from issuing rent orders on Willingham's property. The OPA in turn brought suit in a federal court to restrain execution of the state court's order. The federal court dismissed the OPA suit, ruling that the rent orders against Willingham as well as the EPCA on which they were based were unconstitutional. The Stone Court reviewed on direct appeal and reversed the lower court with only Justice Roberts dissenting.

Justice Douglas delivered the opinion of the Court and indicated the rent control issues in *Bowles* were virtually identical with the price control issues addressed in *Yakus*. Congress both established standards for "executive action" and left with the administrator the "decision when the rent controls of the Act should be invoked" (*Bowles*, 512). The grant of discretion to the OPA was not "unbridled," as Willingham contended, but sufficiently circumscribed by Congress. The administrator could not "fix rents whenever and wherever he might like and whatever level he pleases." Rather, Congress directed that maximum rents be set in those areas "where defense activities have resulted or threaten to result in increased rentals inconsistent with the purpose of the Act." Congress provided both the standard and base period as a guide for determining what maximum rentals should be in a particular area. The rent control standards were as clear as those governing administrative determinations in other contexts (*Bowles*, 515–516). Douglas said that Congress must determine when and how to delegate authority to an officer or agency. Whether that judgment is "wise or unwise raises questions which are none of our concern" (*Bowles*, 516).

The Court found the EPCA provisions regarding judicial review adequate as well. Although the review comes after the order has been promulgated and makes no provision for staying the order, the review "satisfies the requirements of due process." Where property rights are involved, "postponement of the judicial inquiry is not a denial of due process, if the opportunity given for the ultimate judicial determination of the liability is adequate." Delay in the judicial determination of property rights, Douglas concluded, "is not uncommon where it is essential that governmental needs be immediately satisfied." The demands of national security may simply not afford "the luxuries of litigation" (*Bowles*, 521).

Justice Roberts dissented on two grounds. First, he contended that when the provisions of the EPCA were applied to rent control (or anything else), the delegation of legislative power to the administrative official was excessive. Second, after reviewing decisions of the Emergency Court of Appeals, he concluded it was "futile" for a citizen to try to "convict the Administrator of an abuse of judgment in framing his orders" and how this rendered "illusory" the judicial review process "in fact" (*Bowles*, 541). These were the same objections he registered in his *Yakus* dissent.

The more specific issue of fuel rationing was reviewed in *Steuart & Bros. v. Bowles* (1944). The second War Powers Act provided that when the president determines that defense needs will result in a shortage of a material, the president may "allocate such material . . . in such a manner . . . as he shall deem necessary or appropriate in the public interest and to promote the national defense." The president, in turn, delegated to the OPA the authority to ration fuel oil. The OPA issued a ration order for fuel oil that included a provision that violators may, by administrative suspension order, be prohibited from "receiving any transfers or deliveries of, or selling or using or otherwise disposing of fuel oil." Steuart and Brothers, a retail fuel oil dealership, was found by the OPA to have violated its rationing order by obtaining large quantities of fuel oil from its supplier without surrendering any ration coupons and by delivering many thousands of gallons of fuel oil to consumers without collecting ration coupons. The Stone Court upheld the order, with Justice Roberts again the sole dissenter, in this case without attaching an opinion.

Justice Douglas focused on the "sole question" presented in the case—whether the power to "allocate materials includes the power to issue suspension orders against retailers" (*Steuart & Bros.*, 404). Steuart and Brothers argued that the suspension orders were penalties determined by the OPA and should not be imposed "because the EPCA did not explicitly call for them." The Court saw the OPA suspension order as a means for ensuring equitable distribution of a scarce commodity rather than a device for imposing penalties. Rationing was designed to eliminate inequalities and allow the greatest number to share limited supplies. Retailers like Steuart and Brothers are the "chief if not the only conduits between the source of limited supplies and the consumers," and such retailers "bent on defying the rationing system could raise havoc" with the objectives of the rationing program. The president, Douglas suggested, is certainly empowered under the act to remove the supply of a scarce material from a "wasteful" factory and route that material to an "efficient" factory. The factory owner from whom the materials were diverted certainly would view the action as "harsh," but in wartime the national interest "cannot wait on individual claims to preference."

Douglas found it "difficult to see why the same principle is not applicable to the distribution of fuel oil." The Court concluded that the record indicated that the suspension order was based on considerations "relevant to the problem of allocation." The record also sustains the conclusion that in restricting Steuart and Brothers' quota, the OPA was "doing no more than protecting the community against distribution which measured by rationing standards was inequitable, unfair, and inefficient." If the power to allocate "did not embrace that power it would be feeble power indeed" (*Steuart & Bros.* 404, 405–406).

Federal Economic Regulation Unrelated to World War II

It is clear from the EPCA cases that the Stone Court subordinated property rights to the national needs stemming from the war. None of the challenges to the EPCA or the price orders of the OPA were successful. This same deference was seen in cases involving federal economic regulatory measures adopted independently of the war emergency. President Roosevelt selected his nominees for the Supreme Court with every expectation that once on the Court these justices would support these types of federal regulatory initiatives, war emergency or not. This expectation was not misplaced. The Stone Court typically supported federal regulatory initiatives and deferred to those administrative agencies created to implement federal regulatory policy. The Stone Court upheld various agency regulations in more than two-thirds of about 150 cases falling into this broad category. Justices Black, Douglas, and Murphy had support rates in excess of 90 percent across these cases. Rutledge followed at just over an 85 percent support level. The decisive fifth vote necessary to produce a majority in individual cases most often came from Reed (62.59 percent) and/or Jackson (54.84 percent), followed by Justice Frankfurter (47.62 percent) and Chief Justice Stone (40.82 percent). Justice Roberts categorically rejected such regulation; he was found in support in only 3 percent of these cases.

The deference the Stone Court afforded both congressional judgments about economic regulation and the administrative agencies created by Congress was evident in a number of contexts, but most were grounded on congressional power to regulate interstate commerce. Following the 1937 "revolution," the commerce power was viewed as power to regulate virtually any aspect of the national economy broadly defined. This was true even when those regulations applied to businesses protected by Bill of Rights provisions. For example, in *Associated Press v. United States* (1945), the Court upheld a Sherman Act restraint of trade conviction against a news association over a claim of free press protection. Justice Black's opinion for the five-justice majority focused on the need for the federal government to intervene where competition is impaired, even against businesses covered by the First Amendment. Limitations on the ability to buy news from a news agency like the Associated Press or one of its members "can have most serious effects on the publication of competitive newspapers," both in the present and the future. Trade restraints of this kind, Black continued, "aimed at the destruction of competition, tend to block the initiative which brings newcomers into a field of business and to frustrate the free enterprise system which it was the purpose of the Sherman Act to protect" (*Associated Press*, 13–14).

The breadth of the congressional authority over interstate commerce was evident in Justice Murphy's sweeping statements in both *North American Co. v. Securities and Exchange Commission* (1946) and *American Power & Light Co. v. Securities and Exchange Commission* (1946), where the Stone Court upheld provisions of the Public Utility Act of 1935. Murphy described the commerce power as an affirmative power commensurate with national needs. It is unrestricted by contrary state laws or private contracts. And in using this great power, Congress is not bound by technical legal conceptions. Commerce itself is an intensely practical matter. To deal with it effectively, Congress must be able to act in terms of economic and financial realities. The commerce clause gives it authority so to act (*North American Co.*, 705).

When Congress enacted the Public Holding Company Act, it was concerned with the "economic evils" that result from "uncoordinated and unintegrated" public utility holding company systems. Congress found these evils were "polluting the channels of interstate commerce." In addition to the interests of investors and consumers, Congress found that the "national welfare was thereby harmed." Further, Congress was able to trace these "evils" to the "nature and extent" of securities owned by holding companies. The commerce power enabled Congress, said Murphy, to "attempt to remove those evils by ordering the holding companies to divest themselves of the securities that made such evils possible" (*North American Co.*, 706).

Later in 1946, in the early months of the Vinson Court, Justice Murphy again spoke for the Court and reiterated an expansive view of federal commerce power. To deny that Congress has "power to eliminate evils connected with pyramided holding company systems . . . is to deny that Congress can effectively deal with problems concerning the welfare of the national economy." Rather than deny that such power resides with Congress, the Court reaffirmed the reach of Congress to "undertake to solve national problems directly and realistically." In short, Murphy said the federal commerce power "is as broad as the economic needs of the nation" (*American Power & Light*, 103–104). The Stone Court recognized a federal commerce power of this magnitude.

A major thrust of Roosevelt's domestic program was the stabilization of agricultural production and prices. The most comprehensive legislation was the Agricultural Adjustment Act of 1938, a "replacement" statute for the 1933 version of the legislation struck down by the Hughes Court in *United States v. Butler* (1936). The second AAA, upheld by the Court in *Mulford v. Smith* (1939), featured marketing quotas as a means of stabilizing agricultural prices. Under the law, Agriculture Secretary Claude Wickard set a national acreage allotment for wheat (other agricultural commodities were similarly regulated)—the number of acres of wheat that could be planted across the country. The national allotment was apportioned across the states and on to individual farmers. Roscoe Filburn operated a small farm on which he maintained some livestock. He produced small amounts of wheat, part of which he used to feed his livestock and the remainder as seed or to mill into flour for his own use. Filburn made no attempt to market any of the wheat he grew on his farm. He was told he could plant 11.1 acres of wheat or, calculated at a national yield rate average of 20.1 bushes of wheat per acre, he could produce and market about 223 bushels of wheat. Filburn planted 23 acres of wheat and produced 239 bushels of wheat more than he was allowed. Although he argued that the wheat grown in excess of his quota was wholly consumed on his land, he was fined $117.11. Filburn challenged his fine and more broadly the authority of Congress to regulate his wheat production in this way. The Stone Court unanimously upheld the regulation.

The issue in *Wickard v. Filburn* (1942) was whether federal commerce power could be used to regulate agricultural production that was never intended for interstate commerce. The Stone Court concluded it could. The marketing quotas included not only wheat that could be sold without penalty but also wheat that could be consumed on the premises. Filburn argued that the very limited amount of wheat he grew for personal consumption did not remotely affect interstate commerce. Justice Jackson responded by saying that federal commerce power reaches even those activities that appear local if a "substantial economic effect" on interstate commerce results (*Wickard*, 125).

It had already been established in *Mulford* that the commerce power allows Congress to regulate commodity prices and those practices that affect prices. The AAA was enacted to increase the market price of wheat by limiting production volumes—prices go up as supply diminishes. By growing more wheat than he was allowed, Filburn affected this supply-and-demand balance. Home-consumed wheat had a "substantial influence on price and market conditions." Because Filburn's home-consumed wheat was in a "marketable condition," it "over[hung] the market" and might have been "induced to flow into the market by rising prices." Furthermore, even if his wheat was never marketed, it met the grower's need that would otherwise lead to wheat purchases by the grower. Thus, the home-grown wheat, said Jackson, "compete[d] with wheat in commerce" (*Wickard*, 128). The *Wickard* ruling enlarged the already expanded federal commerce power by allowing Congress to reach items that are not actually moving in commerce. Jackson's sweeping rationale reflected a view of the federal commerce power that arguably was the furthest removed from the "pre-revolution" view and represented the most expansive statement of federal commerce power ever.

The Stone Court demonstrated an occasional willingness to allow states to regulate commerce when these regulations were compatible with federal commerce policy. A good example is *Parker v. Brown* (1943), where the Stone Court upheld a state-created monopoly that marketed all state-grown agricultural produce against commerce clause challenge. California adopted a policy whereby competition among agricultural producers was restricted in an attempt to stabilize distribution prices of various products. Under the program, all marketing was to be done through a state-established commission. Brown, a raisin grower, sought to enjoin implementation of the program because he was suffering financial losses under the commission-set prices. Since 90 percent of California raisins were shipped out of state, Brown challenged the California policy on commerce clause grounds. The Stone Court unanimously upheld the state program.

Chief Justice Stone delivered the opinion and set the stage by suggesting that congressional power was not exclusive but could be exercised concurrently. The grant of commerce power to Congress "did not wholly withdraw" authority to regulate "matters of local concern" on which Congress "has not spoken." As long as a state regulation serves "local ends," does not "discriminate" against interstate commerce, and is compatible with national interests, it may operate even though the interstate commerce is "materially affected" (*Parker*, 333). There may also be local regulation whose effect "coincides" with established federal policy. The California regulation was seen as such a coincidental policy. Congress had recognized the "distressed condition" of American agriculture and had authorized marketing procedures "substantially like" those in the California program. Whatever the effects of the California regulation on interstate commerce, they were effects, said Stone, Congress chose to "aid and encourage through its own agencies" (*Parker*, 367–368).

The Court considered whether states could impose conditions on the transport of interstate shipments through them in *Carter v. Virginia* (1944). Virginia required that vehicles carrying liquor through the state must use the most direct route, carry a bill of lading showing the route, post a $1,000 bond conditioned on lawful transport, and show on the bill of lading both the name of the consignee and that the consignee had a legal right to receive the liquor. The Court unanimously ruled that these restrictions were not barred by the commerce clause. Justice Reed said that although state regulation may not "unduly burden" interstate commerce, a state may take reasonable steps to "protect herself from illicit liquor traffic within her borders." Reed went on to say that in the absence of contrary federal law, a state could prohibit the transport of liquor altogether without imposing any "substantial clog of whatever cognate rights her sister states may have to determine their own policies regarding intoxicating liquors" (*Carter*, 135, 138).

Although the Stone Court accorded the states some regulatory latitude in rulings like *Parker* and *Carter*, it firmly drew the line on state laws that unreasonably impaired or burdened interstate commerce. An example of such a result is found in *Southern Pacific Railroad Co. v. Arizona* (1945). A 1912 Arizona statute prohibited the operation within the state of passenger trains longer than fourteen cars or freight trains of more than seventy cars. Arizona attempted to justify the regulation as a safety measure, but the law was strongly supported by railroad unions who felt the regulation would create additional railroad jobs. Southern Pacific challenged the law on impairment of interstate commerce grounds. In a 7–2 decision, the Court ruled that the statute impermissibly interfered with interstate commerce.

Chief Justice Stone said that in the absence of conflicting federal regulation, states possess a "residuum of power to enact laws governing matters that are local in character and effect" and whose impact does not seriously interfere with national commerce. At the same time, states do not have the authority to impede the free flow of commerce from state to state. Neither do the states have the power to regulate those aspects of national commerce that require nationally uniform regulation. The length of trains was seen as a matter requiring such national uniformity. Trains running through Arizona either had to change routes to go around the state, be "broken up and reconstituted" when they entered Arizona, or conform to the most restrictive state law from the outset (*Southern Pacific*, 773). The Court saw this as a "serious burden" on interstate commerce and was concerned that if Arizona could regulate train lengths in this way, any and all other states could do so as well.

Stone was skeptical of Arizona's argument that the law was primarily a safety measure. He said the law "affords at most slight and dubious advantage, if any, over unregulated train lengths" (*Southern Pacific*, 779). The Court also rejected Arizona's contention that its railroad restriction was similar to state laws regulating highways and highway use. Although acknowledging the interstate character of highways, the Court concluded states have more "extensive control" over highways because, unlike railroads, highways are "built, owned and maintained by the states." Justices Black and Douglas argued in dissent that Congress, not the Court, needed to determine whether a uniform national policy was appropriate in this situation. The dissenters admonished the Court to leave the choice to Congress, where it "properly belongs" (*Southern Pacific*, 789).

The self-restraint exhibited by the Stone Court to federal regulatory legislation carried over to the conclusions of fact reached by federal administrative agencies. This was evident in administrative rate-making cases because of the technical complexity of the issues. Two Federal Power Commission (FPC) utility regulation cases illustrate. In *Federal Power Commission v. Natural Gas Pipeline Co.* (1942), the Stone Court unanimously upheld an FPC order requiring the Natural Gas Pipeline Company to reduce its rates. The FPC rate reduction order followed its finding that the company's rate structure was "unjust, unreasonable, and excessive." Chief Justice Stone indicated that the interstate character of the company's operations clearly brought them within the scope of the federal commerce power. Congress in turn could delegate rate issues to agencies that possess appropriate technical competence. Furthermore, these agencies could review rates on any reasonable bases they chose. The Constitution, Stone said, "does not bind rate-making bodies" to any single formula or combination of formulas. Agencies to whom rate-making authority has been delegated "are free . . . to make the pragmatic adjustments which may be called for." Stone also pointed out that the FPC order was preceded by a hearing that afforded the company full opportunity to defend its rate. If any rate-making order, as "applied to the facts before it" and taken in its entirety, produces no "arbitrary result, the Court's inquiry is at an end" (*Natural Gas Pipeline*, 586).

Two years later the Court decided in *Federal Power Commission v. Hope Natural Gas Co.* (1944) that it would no longer scrutinize the formula by which rates were fixed as it had done since the turn of the century. A major difficulty in providing this oversight was the determination of property value. Among the considerations the Court viewed as relevant were original cost, cost of operation, market value, and replacement cost. In *Hope Natural Gas* the Court indicated that its review of rates would focus only on overall reasonableness in terms of general impact on the business and leave to the regulatory agency the task of deciding the most suitable basis for setting rates. The more limited scope of judicial review heightened the regulatory authority of agencies like the FPC and allowed them to more fully give effect to their technical expertise. Justice Douglas, one of three justices who had expressed concern that Stone's opinion in *Natural Gas Pipeline* invited a return to substantive due process, wrote for the Court in *Hope Natural Gas*. He suggested that the "just and reasonable" standard is met by looking at the impact of the order, not the methodology used in arriving at the end result. If the "total effect of the rate order cannot be said to be unjust and unreasonable, judicial inquiry . . . is at an end" (*Hope Natural Gas*, 602). Justices Reed, Frankfurter, and Jackson were unwilling to go that far. They worried that Douglas's opinion had made it impossible for either Congress or the courts to hold administrative agencies accountable for either their methodology or conclusions.

The Stone Court interpreted the National Labor Relations Act broadly, thus allowing its provisions to reach virtually every sector of the economy. The exception was the insurance industry. An 1869 decision, *Paul v. Virginia*, defined the insurance industry as local and not subject to federal regulation. The Court overruled *Paul* in *United States v. South-Eastern Underwriters Association* (1944), concluding instead that the insurance industry was interstate in character and subject to the federal restrictions contained in the Sherman Act. Justices Roberts and Reed did not participate in this case, and it was decided by a 4–3 split of the remaining justices. Thus, the *South-Eastern Underwriters* ruling was far from definitive, and Congress weighed in on the issue shortly thereafter.

The association was charged with fixing fire insurance premiums in a manner that produced "arbitrary and noncompetitive" rates in a multistate area. Justice Black spoke for the majority and said that premiums collected from policyholders throughout the country "flow into these companies for investment." When claims are filed, payments flow back to the policyholders. The result, suggested Black, is a "continuous and indivisible stream of intercourse." Black suggested that the insurance business holds a "commanding position in the trade and commerce of our nation." Perhaps no other modern commercial activity "affects so many persons in all walks of life" (*South-Eastern Underwriters*, 540).

An insurance contract, considered as a "thing apart from negotiation and execution, does not itself constitute interstate commerce." That did not mean, however, that the Court was "powerless to examine the entire transaction, of which the contract was but a part, in order to determine whether there may be a chain of events which becomes interstate commerce." A nationwide business is not "deprived of its interstate character merely because it is built upon sales contracts which are local in nature." No commercial enterprise that conducts its activities across state lines has been held to be "wholly beyond the regulatory power of Congress. . . . We cannot make an exception of the business of insurance" any longer (*South-Eastern Underwriters*, 547, 553).

The effect of defining insurance as interstate commerce was immediately seen in *Polish National Alliance v. NLRB* (1944). A unanimous Court found that the NLRB was justified in finding that the Alliance's unfair labor practices would "affect commerce." Although the organization was primarily interested in promoting the contributions that Poland has made to civilization, that objective did not "subordinate its business activities to insignificance." As a result, the NLRB could reasonably conclude that the alliance's cultural and fraternal activities did not "withdraw [it] from amenability to the Wagner Act" (*Polish National Alliance*, 648).

The overruling of *Paul v. Virginia* prompted concerns that state regulation of the insurance industry, the only regulation of insurance at the time, might be nullified as impermissibly interfering with interstate commerce. To make sure that existing state insurance regulations would not be set aside on commerce clause grounds, Congress passed the McCarron Act, which authorized continuation of existing state controls until the federal government might enact superseding legislation. *Prudential Insurance Co. v. Benjamin* (1946) upheld the McCarron Act. The "obvious" purpose of Congress was to "give support to the existing and future state systems for regulating and taxing the business of industry." In taking the action it did, Congress had "full knowledge" of the nationwide existence of state systems and understood that systems "differ[ed] greatly in the scope and character of regulations imposed and of taxes exacted." The purpose of Congress in passing the McCarron Act "was evidently to throw the whole weight of its power behind the state systems, notwithstanding these variations" (*Prudential Insurance Co.*, 430).

Federalism

Intergovernmental Tax Immunity

Many of the Stone Court's rulings had direct implications for the federal system of governance. Several are noteworthy. The intergovernmental tax immunity doctrine, for example, exempts property and instruments of federal and state government from taxation by the other. The immunity doctrine had its origin in *McCulloch v. Maryland* (1819), in which the Marshall Court held that states may not subject federal entities to taxation. It was argued that without such immunity, the taxing power of one level could be used to impair or disrupt functions of the other. The doctrine had begun to erode by 1941, and the Stone Court's decisions on the issue eventually weakened the doctrine further.

One of Stone Court's tax immunity cases was *Alabama v. King & Boozer* (1941), in which a tax on profits from business done with governmental agencies was permitted. In *King & Boozer* the Court unanimously (Justice Jackson not participating) allowed a state to tax a federal contractor even though the taxes were subsequently passed on to the federal government under explicit provision of the government contracts. The state government disclaims, said Chief Justice Stone, "rightly we think," any contention that the Constitution, in the absence of legislation to the contrary, prohibits a tax exacted from contractors "merely because it is passed on economically as a part of the construction cost to the Government." If a nondiscriminatory state tax affects the costs of the materials to the government, that is "but a normal incident of the organization within the same territory of two independent taxing sovereignties" (*King & Boozer*, 8–9).

Two years later the Stone Court unanimously invoked the immunity doctrine in *Mayo v. United States* (1943). Florida had a law that comprehensively regulated the sale and distribution of commercial fertilizer. Among the regulations was a requirement that each bag of fertilizer display a stamp indicating that an inspection fee had been paid. Under terms of the Federal Soil Conservation and Domestic Allotment Act, the Agriculture Department purchased commercial fertilizer outside Florida and distributed it to consumers within the state. The fertilizer distributed under this program did not undergo inspection or bear the inspection stamp. The Florida commissioner of agriculture ordered that distribution of the unstamped bags of fertilizer be stopped. The Stone Court ruled that activities of the federal government must be "free from regulation by any state." Indeed, Justice Reed said, no other "adjustment of the competing enactments is possible." The inspection fees were "laid directly upon the United States." They are money exactions "the payment of which, if they are enforceable, would be required before executing a function of government" (*Mayo*, 445, 447). As such, the state requirement was "prohibited by the supremacy clause."

By 1946, however, the Stone Court had largely abandoned the intergovernmental tax immunity doctrine, at least as it insulated state activities from federal taxation. In *New York v. United States* (1946), the Court ruled that state activities that are not "essential" to the function of state government may be subjected to federal tax. New York established a public corporation called the Saratoga Springs Authority to bottle and sell mineral water. The authority resisted payment of a federal tax, claiming immunity as an agency of state government. The Stone Court rejected this argument in a 6–2 decision. Justice Frankfurter characterized as insufficient attempts to distinguish "historically recognized functions of a state" from activities of a kind "pursued by private enterprise." Frankfurter suggested that the Court allow Congress to exercise federal taxing authority limited only by fiscal and political factors. As long as Congress chooses to "generally tax a source of revenue by whomsoever earned, and not uniquely capable of being earned only by a State," Congress is not constitutionally forbidden to levy a tax "merely because its incidence falls also on a state." When a state "enters the market place seeking customers, . . . it takes on the character of a trader," at least for federal taxation purposes (*New York v. United States*, 580, 582). Justices Douglas and Black again dissented. They urged that states ought to be able to determine for themselves which activities were legitimate in furthering their own state's interest and believed this decision impermissibly impinged on state sovereignty. Douglas saw no difference in the immunity from federal tax a state receives when it sells its securities than when it "sells power or disposes of other natural resources" (*New York v. United States*, 591). Following the *New York v. United States* ruling, the intergovernmental tax immunity doctrine ceased to function as a significant limit on the exercise of federal taxing power.

State Taxes on Commerce

The Stone Court generally limited state taxing power when levied in such a way as to involve interstate commerce. *Northwest Airlines v. Minnesota* (1944), however, seemed to suggest otherwise. In this case the Court permitted a state tax levy against the entire fleet of an airline even though only a small portion of its daily interstate flights were within the state's airspace. Justice Frankfurter spoke for the five-justice majority. The tax was not imposed on the airline because it was engaged in interstate commerce or "aimed by indirection" against interstate commerce. Rather, it was assessed against Northwest's property residing within the state during the tax year. The relationship between Northwest and Minnesota, a relationship "existing between no other State and Northwest," and the "benefits this relationship affords are the constitutional foundation for the taxing power which Minnesota has asserted." No other state served as the "State of legal domicile as well as the home State of the fleet." Thus, on the basis of rights that "Minnesota alone originated and Minnesota continues to safeguard, she alone can tax the [personal and movable property] which is permanently attributable to Minnesota and to no other State" (*Northwest Airlines*, 294–295).

Chief Justice Stone, joined by Justices Roberts, Reed, and Rutledge, dissented. Stone saw the Minnesota tax as levied on "vehicles of interstate transportation." Interstate commerce is not free of any tax burden, and must "pay its way by sustaining its fair share of the property tax burden." But Minnesota had taxed the airline's property at full value for the entire tax year. Parts of this property, physical facilities used in interstate transportation, were still vulnerable to taxation by other states, which could result in an undue burden on interstate commerce (*Northwest Airlines*, 310–311).

The Stone Court was more likely, however, to limit state taxing power if any levy touched interstate commerce even remotely. Two decisions that followed *Northwest Airlines* are representative. The first was *Hooven & Allison Co. v. Evatt* (1945), where the Court ruled that bales of hemp imported from the Philippines and held in a manufacturer's warehouse pending their use in the manufacture of rope were not subject to state property taxation. Chief Justice Stone drew on the "original package" doctrine fashioned by Chief Justice John Marshall in *Brown v. Maryland* (1827). The doctrine directed that only after the importer removes items from their "original packages" and mixes them with the "mass of property" in the country can such items be subjected to state taxation. As in *Brown*, a five-justice majority concluded the hemp retained its status as an import subject only to action by the national government. The

Court also concluded that the Philippines was a "foreign country," at least for purposes of taxation status, by determining that items shipped into the country from the Philippines were "imports." The "national concern in protecting national commercial relations" by exempting imports from state taxation "would seem not to be essentially different or less in the case of merchandise brought in from the Philippines" (*Hooven & Allison Co.*, 678–679).

Justices Black, Douglas, and Rutledge dissented. They were joined by Justice Reed on the point that the Philippines was considered "foreign." In their view, this gave unfair advantage to territories or possessions like the Philippines over competing products of the states. Justice Murphy joined the dissenters on the original package issue. He and the others did not think that raw materials in a manufacturer's warehouse awaiting conversion to another product qualified for the original package exemption from state taxation.

Similarly, the Court ruled in *McLeod v. Dilworth* (1944) that when delivery of goods is made from outside the state as a result of a sales contract entered within the state, state taxes could not be levied. A tax on interstate sales "involves an assumption of power by a State which the Commerce Clause was meant to end." The "very purpose" of the commerce clause was to "create an area of free trade among the several States." The commerce clause exclusively vested the taxing power for any transaction forming an unbroken process of interstate commerce with Congress, not with the states, said Justice Frankfurter (*McLeod*, 330–331). Justices Douglas, Black, and Murphy disagreed. They believed receipt of goods within the state of the buyer was "as adequate a basis for the exercise of taxing power as use within the State." Furthermore, Justice Douglas saw no justification for an interpretation of the commerce clause "which puts local industry at a competitive disadvantage with interstate business" (*McLeod*, 332).

Finally, in *Nippert v. Richmond* (1946) the Court invalidated a local tax affecting salespeople who solicit orders to be filled by subsequent interstate shipment. Justice Rutledge suggested that the tax in question "inherently involves too many probabilities, and we think actualities, . . . for discrimination against interstate commerce" (*Nippert*, 434). Justices Black, Douglas, and Murphy objected, charging that the majority's reasoning was based on purely speculative judgments of potential interference with interstate commerce. Until an actual burden on interstate commerce was shown, the dissenters would have permitted levying the tax in *Nippert*.

Full Faith and Credit

The full faith and credit clause, found in Article 4, section 1, requires that each state fully accept certain official acts of all other states. Among these official actions are court decisions, at least those decisions that are final. The Stone Court twice struggled with the full faith and credit concept arising from the same underlying fact situations in *Williams v. North Carolina* (*Williams I*; 1942) and *Williams v. North Carolina* (*Williams II*; 1945). Two North Carolina residents wished to marry, but each was married to another at the time. The two went to Nevada, lived there for the six weeks necessary to establish residency under Nevada law, and obtained divorces. They married in Nevada and returned to North Carolina, where they were prosecuted and convicted for bigamous cohabitation. The underlying issue was the validity of the Nevada divorces. The case required the Court to choose between adhering to the full faith and credit principle, in which case the Nevada divorce would have to be recognized in North Carolina, or recognizing North Carolina's authority to determine its own policies regarding marriage, the Nevada divorce decree notwithstanding.

In *Williams I* (1942) the Stone Court opted for the former: that the full faith and credit clause obligated North Carolina to recognize the Nevada divorce decrees. In so ruling, the Court set aside the bigamy convictions since Williams and his wife were considered legally divorced prior to marrying each other. Justice Douglas, who wrote for seven members of the Court in *Williams I*, said that when a court of one state acting in accord with the requirements of procedural due process alters the marital state of one domiciled in that state by granting him a divorce from his absent spouse, we cannot say its decree should be excepted from the full faith and credit clause merely because its enforcement or recognition in another state would conflict with the policy of the latter (*Williams I*, 303).

Douglas concluded by saying that the question of whether Congress could create such exceptions to the full faith and credit clause would not be addressed, but he noted that Congress, in its "sweeping requirement" that court judgments be recognized in the courts of other states, "ha[d] not done so" (*Williams I*, 303).

The Douglas opinion did not address whether legal residence had been established in Nevada because Nevada's finding of domicile was not questioned, even though the other spouses had neither appeared nor been served with process in Nevada, and "recognition of such a divorce offended the policy of North Carolina" (*Williams II*, 227). It was on the legal residence issue that Justices Jackson and Murphy dissented in *Williams I*. They believed that a mere six weeks spent in Nevada could not provide the basis for a divorce decree that North Carolina had to recognize by force of the full faith and credit clause. North Carolina was the state in which Williams and his second wife had "their roots" and the state to which they returned immediately after their six weeks in Nevada. Under those circumstances, the Nevada decrees were "entitled to no extraterritorial effect when challenged in another state" (*Williams I*, 309). In the absence of "uniform law" on the matter of divorce, Murphy suggested, the Court was not obligated by the clause to "force Nevada's policy upon North Carolina any more than it [could] compel Nevada to accept North Carolina's requirements." The "fair result," he said, was to "leave each state free to regulate within its own area the rights of its own citizens" (*Williams I*, 311).

The North Carolina Supreme Court ordered a second trial of Williams to consider the issue of residency. Williams and his second wife were again convicted of bigamy. The case returned to the Supreme Court in 1944 and was decided the following year. In *Williams II* the Stone Court ruled that North Carolina could determine for itself whether Williams and his wife had legitimately established residence in Nevada and could deny giving full faith and credit to a Nevada decree if, in its view, bona fide residency had not been established. Justice Frankfurter contrasted the situation where an issue has been settled "after appropriate opportunity" to present arguments has been given to "all who had an interest in its adjudication" to the situation where those not actual parties to litigation have interests to represent. In his view, those not party to the litigation "ought not be foreclosed by the interested actions of others" from reopening an issue of law. This is especially true of a state, which is concerned with the "vindication of its own social policy and has no . . . effective means to protect that interest against the selfish action of those outside its borders." The original state of residency "should not be bound by an unfounded . . . recital in the record of a court of another State" (*Williams II*, 230).

A divorce decree is a "conclusive adjudication" of everything except the jurisdictional facts on which it is based. Residence is one of the jurisdictional facts to which Frankfurter was referring in *Williams II*. To permit the necessary finding of residency by one state "to foreclose all [other] States in the protection of their social institutions would be intolerable" (*Williams II*, 232). If a state cannot foreclose all other states by a finding that a spouse is domiciled within its bounds, "persons may . . . place themselves in situations that create unhappy consequences for them." This, said Frankfurter, is "merely one of those untoward results inevitable in a federal system in which regulation of domestic relations has been left with the States and not given to the national authority." When a person seeks a divorce outside the state in which he has resided and maintained a marriage, the person is "necessarily involved in the legal situation created by our federal system whereby one State can grant a divorce of validity in other States only if the applicant has a bona fide domicile in the State of the court purporting to dissolve the marriage" (*Williams II*, 237–238). Accordingly, it was determined that North Carolina was not required to "yield her State policy" because Nevada deemed Williams a resident when it granted the divorce decree. Instead, North Carolina was entitled to find that Williams did not acquire residency in Nevada and that the Nevada court was "without power to liberate [Williams] from amenability to the laws of North Carolina governing domestic relations" (*Williams II*, 239).

Justices Rutledge, Black, and Douglas disagreed. They saw the residency issue as a mountain of molehill proportions. Indeed, Rutledge used the word "sham" in speaking of the domicile question. Although a Nevada divorce may not reflect the values of most states, it was available to persons who wished to avail themselves of a hasty divorce, go back where they came from, and move on with their lives. The

Nevada proceedings, as disturbing as they were to many, were entitled to acceptance at face value through the full faith and credit protection. The Constitution made no mention of the term "domicile," said Rutledge, and it certainly did not direct that the question of how much credit to afford judgments of other states be left to the "caprice of juries" (*Williams II*, 245).

Between *Williams I* and *Williams II*, the Stone Court considered a different full faith and credit question in *Magnolia Petroleum Co. v. Hunt* (1943). Magnolia Petroleum employed Hunt as an oil field laborer in Louisiana. He was sent by his employer to Texas to engage in similar work and was injured on the job. Hunt secured a worker's compensation award under Texas law but subsequently obtained a worker's compensation award in Louisiana as well. In a 5–4 ruling, the Stone Court ruled that the full faith and credit clause precluded the Louisiana award after the Texas award had become final. Chief Justice Stone compared the clause to the commerce clause as a "nationally unifying force." The clause "altered the status" of the states as "independent foreign sovereignties, each free to ignore rights and obligations created under the laws or established by the judicial proceedings of the others," by making legislative decisions and court judgments "an integral part of a single nation." As a result, the full faith and credit clause bars a defendant from challenging for a second time the "validity of [a] plaintiff's right which has ripened into a judgment." At the same time, a plaintiff such as Hunt may not "for his single cause of action secure a second or a greater recovery" (*Magnolia*, 439–440). Justice Jackson, in a concurring opinion, indicated that he could not see how Louisiana could be "constitutionally free" to apply its own worker's compensation law when North Carolina, as a result of *Williams I*, was not free to "apply its own matrimonial policy to its own citizens after judgment on the subject in Nevada" (*Magnolia*, 446).

Justices Black, Douglas, Murphy, and Rutledge dissented. Justice Black argued that there should be "no constitutional barrier" preventing a state from increasing the worker's compensation award of another state in a case "in which it has jurisdiction over the participants and the social responsibility for the results." Where two states both have a "legitimate interest" in the outcomes of worker's compensation litigation, the matter of whether the second state to consider the case should "abide by the decision of the first is a question of policy which should be decided by the state legislatures and courts" (*Magnolia*, 459). Justice Douglas was more outspoken. He said that the full faith and credit clause should be enforced not "only if the outcome pleases us" but even if it does not (*Magnolia*, 447).

Executive Agreements

Presidents make extensive use of executive agreements in dealing with foreign countries because such agreements have comparable effect to treaties and they need not undergo Senate review. The Hughes Court ruled that executive agreements have the status of law in *United States v. Belmont* (1937), and the Stone Court reaffirmed this view in *United States v. Pink* (1942).

Following the Russian Revolution in 1918, the new government seized the properties of Russian insurance companies. A portion of these properties were located in New York. In response to the Soviet nationalization initiatives, New York seized assets of one of the Russian insurance companies located in the state and used the proceeds to pay policyholders residing in New York. A New York court ruling in 1931 directed the state's insurance commissioner to dispose of all remaining assets. Two years later the United States diplomatically recognized the Soviet Union and, as part of the terms by which it extended such recognition, agreed to take control of the remaining insurance company assets and distribute them among American claimants. This portion of the agreement was known as the Litvinov Assignment. A suit in a New York court to recover these assets was unsuccessful, and the case eventually came to the Stone Court. In a 5–2 decision in *Pink* (Justices Jackson and Reed not participating), the Court built upon both *Belmont* and *United States v. Curtiss-Wright Export Corp.* (1936) and concluded that the provisions of the Litvinov Assignment were binding.

Justice Douglas suggested that if the same asset assignment had been contained in a treaty, there would be "no doubt as to its validity. The same result obtains here." Presidential power to conduct foreign relations included the power, "without consent of the Senate, to determine the public policy of the United States with respect to the Russian nationalization decrees." Such executive authority is not limited to the recognition of foreign governments. It also includes "the power to determine the policy which is to govern the question of recognition" (*Pink*, 229–230). Recognition of foreign government is sometimes "conditional," and the power to remove "obstacles" to full recognition, such as settlement of claims of U.S. nationals, "certainly is a modest implied power of the President who is the sole organ of the government in the field of international relations." Recognition of the Soviet government and the Litvinov Assignment were "interdependent," and the Court would usurp the executive function if it held that that decision "was not final and conclusive in the courts" (*Pink*, 229–230). The conduct of international relations is clearly the domain of the national government. If state laws and policies do not "yield before the exercise of the external powers of the United States, then our foreign policy might be thwarted." The action of New York was seen as essentially rejecting a "part of the policy underlying recognition by this nation of Soviet Russia." No state can "rewrite our foreign policy to conform to its own domestic policies"; such power is not "accorded a State in our constitutional system" (*Pink*, 233–234).

Labor

The Stone Court was called upon to respond to more than 100 cases involving federal laws and their application to organized labor. Several federal laws figured prominently in these cases—the Sherman Antitrust Act of 1890 (as modified by the Clayton Act of 1914 and the Norris-LaGuardia Act of 1932), the National Labor Relations (Wagner) Act of 1935, and the Fair Labor Standards Act of 1938. Labor was a favored constituency of Roosevelt from the outset of his presidency, and a number of the provisions of the NLRA were first contained in the National Industrial Recovery Act, a statute struck by the Hughes Court in *Schechter Poultry Corp. v. United States* (1935).

The Sherman Act, enacted in 1890, was the oldest of these statutes. Intended to free the marketplace from restraints on trade, the act was used to prevent unlawful combinations and monopolies from adversely affecting fair competition. It was also used against unions, as certain union tactics such as boycotts and strikes were seen as restraints on trade falling within the reach of the Sherman Act. Although the Norris-LaGuardia Act of 1932 protected unions from a number of responses by management, unions remained vulnerable to Sherman Act limits under then existing precedent. The Court began to depart from these precedents and move unions (or at least certain of their actions) outside the scope of the Sherman Act. This was a change of direction initiated by the Hughes Court in the terms immediately preceding Stone's elevation to chief justice. *Apex Hosiery Co. v. Leader* (1940) and *United States v. Hutcheson* (1941), two Hughes Court decisions, provide some foundation.

Apex Hosiery Company operated a nonunion plant in Philadelphia. Its workers engaged in a sit-down strike, seized control of the plant, damaged plant property, and prevented plant management and nonstriking workers from entering the plant. The Court neither condoned the unlawful conduct of the workers nor attempted to limit prosecutions under state criminal laws. Indeed, Justice Stone said the workers, "by substituting the primitive method of trial by combat for the ordinary processes of justice and more civilized means of deciding an industrial dispute, violated the civil and penal laws of Pennsylvania which authorize the recovery of full compensation and impose criminal penalties for the wrongs done" (*Apex Hosiery*, 484). Nonetheless, the Court concluded that the workers' actions did not restrain trade within the meaning of the Sherman Act. It was "plain" that the action of the workers did not "have as its purpose restraint upon competition in the market for [Apex Hosiery's] product"; the actions were not "intended to and did not affect market price." Instead, the objective of the workers was to promote unionization of the plant, an altogether distinct objective from restraint of trade. If a local work stoppage, in the absence of market effect, violates the Sherman Act, Stone concluded, "practically every strike in modern industry" would be brought to federal courts under the Sherman Act to "remedy local law violations" (*Apex Hosiery*, 513).

In *Hutcheson* the Hughes Court protected a union president from criminal charges arising out of a dispute between two unions. The issue was whose workers would provide the workforce for a particular company. When one union was chosen, the other union called for a boycott of the company's products, among other things. Justice Frankfurter avoided dealing with those previous decisions that seemed to call for a finding against Hutcheson and his union. Rather, he argued that provisions of the Clayton Act of 1914 insulated Hutcheson from the reach of the Sherman Act. The Clayton Act was intended to neutralize some of the early and adverse Sherman Act rulings against unions, and it decriminalized secondary boycotts. The Clayton Act had limited effect, however, at least initially. Frankfurter argued in *Hutcheson* that the Norris-LaGuardia Act had revitalized the Clayton Act and its labor-protective objectives. The union's actions were "plainly within the free scope accorded to workers by [section 20 of the Clayton Act] for terminating any relation of employment, or ceasing to perform any work or labor, or recommending, advising or persuading others by peaceful means so to do" (*Hutcheson*, 233), and, as a result, no Sherman Act violation was demonstrated in *Hutcheson*.

The Stone Court initially struggled with the issue of the Sherman Act and labor unions. It gave effect to *Apex Hosiery* and *Hutcheson* in some cases but ruled against unions in others, and the line of distinction was not altogether clear. Two cases serve as examples. In *Allen-Bradley v. Local 3* (1945), a union had obtained closed-shop agreements with producers and distributors of electrical equipment in New York City. The agreements had the effect of preventing new manufacturers or distributors from entering the New York market. The pact labor entered into with manufacturers and distributors brought it within the Sherman Act. The primary objective of antitrust legislation, said Justice Black, was to "preserve business competition and to proscribe business monopoly." It would be "surprising" if Congress gave unions "complete and unreviewable authority to aid business groups to frustrate its primary objective." A business monopoly, Black concluded, "is no less such because a union participates, and such participation is a violation of the Act" (*Allen-Bradley*, 810–811). The Court acknowledged that under *Hutcheson* labor union activities could interrupt trade whether or not that interruption resulted from peaceful or violent actions. Had the restraint of trade that occurred in this case been the result of unilateral union actions, presumably *Hutcheson* would have left the union outside the reach of the Sherman Act. Labor acting in concert with business eliminated *Hutcheson* as the controlling precedent.

Hunt v. Crumboch (1945), decided a week before *Allen-Bradley*, produced a different result. Hunt was a trucking partnership that had a long-term contract with Great Atlantic and Pacific Tea Company (A&P) to transport its merchandise, 85 percent of which was trucked interstate. The union called for a strike of truckers working for A&P for the purpose of enforcing a closed shop. Hunt refused to unionize and attempted to operate during the strike. The strike was violent, a striking worker was killed, and a partner in the trucking firm was prosecuted for homicide, although he was subsequently acquitted. The strike eventually produced a closed-shop contract with A&P, and all the truckers hauling for A&P either joined the union or entered closed-shop agreements with it. The union, however, failed to negotiate with Hunt or admit any of Hunt's drivers to union membership, still believing the partner responsible for the death of the union striker, his acquittal notwithstanding. As a result, A&P canceled its contract with Hunt, and the trucker, unable to obtain other trucking contracts, eventually went out of business.

In a 5–4 decision, the Stone Court concluded the union's action did not violate the Sherman Act because Congress "manifested no purpose to make any kinds of refusal to accept personal employment a violation of anti-trust laws." The Sherman Act, said Justice Black, did not "purport to afford remedies for all torts committed by or against persons engaged in interstate commerce" (*Hunt*, 826). Justice Jackson disagreed. He acknowledged that strikes aimed at compelling an employer to accept its demands fall outside the reach of the Sherman Act. But in this case the employer had already yielded and the union achieved its objectives. The union could not, in Jackson's view, consistently with the Sherman Act, "refuse to enjoy the fruits of its victory and deny peace terms to an employer who has unconditionally surrendered" (*Hunt*, 831).

The Stone Court also freed unions from the provisions of the Anti-Racketeering Act of 1934 in *United States v. Local 807, International Brotherhood of Teamsters* (1942). Justice Byrnes, speaking for everyone except Chief Justice Stone, concluded that Teamsters union members had engaged in criminal extortion but confined the reach of the antiracketeering law to organized crime exclusively. In the Court's view, Congress had intended to afford organized labor "ample protection" by distinguishing union activities from the kind of criminal conduct falling within the purview of the law.

By the time the Court began its first term with Stone as chief justice, the two most significant federal labor statutes, the National Labor Relations Act and the Fair Labor Standards Act, had already been found constitutional by the Hughes Court. Nonetheless, the Stone Court had extensive opportunity to review actions taken by the administrative agencies created under those statutes—the National Labor Relations Board and the Wage and Hour Administration in the Labor Department. According to C. Herman Pritchett, the NLRB was before the Court in fifty-nine cases from the time the board was established in June 1935 to March 1947, the point at which the decade of the Roosevelt Court came to an end. The Court set aside only two NLRB orders and enforced nine others with some modification. The remaining forty-eight NLRB orders were "enforced in full" (Pritchett 1948, 199).

In addition to NLRB and FLSA cases, there were cases involving other labor issues, such as worker's compensation. As expected, Justices Murphy and Black were the most labor-supportive justices, voting on the labor side of issues in 94 percent and

93 percent of the cases, respectively. Justices Rutledge (88 percent) and Douglas (86 percent) were very closely positioned behind them. Justice Reed typically provided the fifth vote, supporting labor in 66 percent of the cases, followed in order by Jackson (52 percent), Frankfurter (44 percent), Stone and Burton (32 percent), and Roberts (5 percent) (Pritchett 1948, 208).

The Stone Court typically deferred to NLRB judgments concerning collective bargaining obligations of employers. An employer, for example, may not bargain with employees in such a way that undermines the collective bargaining process or impairs employee decision making. An employer violates the NLRA if the employer unilaterally offers wage increases in a way that bypasses the established bargaining channels. Such action tends to diminish employees' perception of the union. Furthermore, once a collective bargaining agreement has been secured, individual hiring contracts are subordinate. In *J. I. Case Co. v. NLRB* (1944), Justice Jackson said that individual hiring agreements are "subsidiary to the terms of the trade agreement and may not waive any of its benefits" (*J. I. Case Co.*, 336).

Similarly, an employer may not approach union members before bargaining officially begins with an offer of a pay increase on the condition that they give up their union memberships. In *Medo Photo Supply Corp. v. NLRB* (1944), Chief Justice Stone said that bargaining carried on by the employer directly with employees who have not "revoked their designation of a bargaining agent, would be subversive of the mode of collective bargaining which the [NLRA] has ordained" (*Medo Photo*, 685).

An NLRB case that severely tested the Stone Court's support for labor came in *Wallace Corp. v. NLRB* (1944). Employees of the Wallace Corporation were to determine which of two unions, one affiliated with the CIO and the other independent, would become their bargaining agent. Both unions agreed prior to the election that each would insist on a closed shop. The independent union was chosen and obtained a closed-shop contract. It then refused to admit to the union employees who had been members of the competing union. These employees were all terminated by the Wallace Corporation. The NLRB found the company guilty of an unfair labor practice, concluding that the independent union was actually controlled by the company and that the closed-shop agreement was a device by which it could discharge members of the CIO-affiliated union. In a 5–4 decision, the Court upheld the NLRB. No employee, said Justice Black, can be "deprived of his employment because of his prior affiliation with any particular union." One of the principal objectives of the NLRA was to "wipe out such discrimination." The provision of the NLRA authorizing a closed-shop contract should not be seen as congressional intent to "authorize a majority of workers and a company . . . to penalize minority groups of workers by depriving them of that full freedom of association and self-organization which it was the prime purpose of the Act to protect for all workers" (*Wallace Corp.*, 256).

The dissenters, Justices Jackson, Frankfurter, and Roberts and Chief Justice

Stone, were of the view that the NLRA could not require employers, even in combination with a union, to monitor the fairness of closed-shop practices. The NLRB was not given "any power to supervise union membership or to deal with union practices, however unfair they may be." Furthermore, Jackson suggested that it would be a "strange contradiction" if the NLRA, "whose chief purpose was to sterilize the employers and to free workmen of the influence they exerted through control of the right to work" if an employer could monitor union membership (*Wallace Corp.*, 268, 270).

The NLRB orders occasionally got very close to impairing the free expression rights of employers. In *NLRB v. Virginia Electric & Power Co.* (1941), the Court reviewed an NLRB finding that a bulletin issued by a power company and speeches by its officials had "coerced" the company's employees in exercising their organizing rights. The Stone Court unanimously concluded that the NLRB's cease and desist order did not violate the free speech interests of the employer, as it did not prevent the employer from "expressing its view on labor policies or problems." It was, instead, the employer's "total activities," its conduct, though "evidenced in part by speech," that produced a level of coercion requiring the NLRB to take protective action on behalf of the employees (*NLRB v. Virginia Electric*, 477). The Court was uncomfortable with the NLRB finding based exclusively on the speeches and bulletins the company had issued, and it remanded the case to the NLRB for it to broaden the basis of its findings—to examine the "whole course of company conduct." The NLRB did so, and the Court supported the NLRB's enforcement order in *Virginia Electric & Power Co. v. NLRB* (1943).

The cases arising from the Fair Labor Standards Act were somewhat different from the NLRA cases, although the Stone Court typically responded in similar, labor-supportive ways. The FLSA was a more tightly focused law than the Wagner Act. FLSA cases most often required the Court to make statutory interpretations and determine, for example, which classes of employees might be covered by the FLSA and which were not. The line of distinction was sometimes blurred, but in general the Stone Court found employee groups to fall within rather than outside the reach of the FLSA. That is, the work done for the employer had a sufficiently close connection to interstate commerce to be subject to FLSA regulations. A similar though less compelling prolabor pattern was found in the FLSA cases heard by the Roosevelt Court. The wage and hour administrator was upheld in about two-thirds of those cases. Isolating the Stone Court terms, Pritchett found that 68 percent of the rulings were favorable to labor.

In *Mabee v. White Plains Publishing Co.* (1946), the Court found employees of a newspaper covered by the FLSA even though it circulated less than 1 percent of its daily papers out of state. *Mabee* reflected the expansive regulatory scope the Court sustained by Stone's final year. Viewing the economy as national rather than local in character justified this extended reach of federal regulatory power. Justice Douglas said that in enacting the FLSA, Congress had recognized that in "present day industry, competition by a small part may affect the whole and that the total effect of the competition of many small producers may be great." He pointed out that Congress had eliminated the "substantial" standard from earlier drafts, indicating it wished to make no distinctions based on volume of business. The Court rejected the argument that free press considerations applied in *Mabee*. Rather, the press has "business aspects" and has "no special immunity from laws applicable to business in general" (*Mabee*, 182, 184).

Several cases further illustrate the Stone Court's strong inclination to find employee groups within the reach of the FLSA. In *Kirschbaum v. Walling* (1942), the Court found that service employees in a building used for light manufacturing were covered. Justice Frankfurter said that the work of these employees had a "close and immediate tie with the process of production for commerce" (*Kirschbaum*, 525–526). Justice Roberts was the single dissenter, concluding that when Congress enacted the FLSA it had not intended to reach employees who were engaged in "purely local" activities. Later in 1942, employees of an oil well drilling firm were found covered in *Warren-Bradshaw Drilling Co. v. Hall*, by the same 8–1 vote. Drilling wells, said Justice Murphy, is a "necessary part of the productive process to which it is intimately related." The connection between the drillers' activities and the "capture of oil is quite substantial." The activities of these drillers bear as "close and immediate tie to production" as did the services of the workers in *Kirschbaum* (*Warren-Bradshaw*, 91). Justice Roberts, as in *Kirschbaum*, protested the "extravagant application" of the FLSA to the drillers. Congress did not mean to extend the FLSA to purely local activities "on the pretext that everything everybody does is a contributing cause to the existence of commerce between the states, and in that sense necessary to its existence" (*Warren-Bradshaw*, 88).

Operators of a drawbridge over a navigable waterway were similarly found to be within the reach of the FLSA in *Overstreet v. No. Shore Corp.* (1943). Justice Murphy again spoke for the Court. The road leading to the bridge and the bridge itself "afford passage to an extensive movement of goods and persons" between Florida and other states. Furthermore, if not operated properly, the bridge "presents an obstacle to interstate traffic [using] the Intercoastal Waterway if not properly operated." Thus, the operating and maintenance activities of these workers "are vital to the proper functioning of these structures as instrumentalities of interstate commerce (*Overstreet*, 130).

The servicing of buildings housing businesses and their employees produced some fine-line distinctions regarding FLSA-covered workers. In *Borden Co. v. Bordella* (1945), the Court found that service employees working in a building owned by an interstate company were a necessary part of the company's interstate business and were thus covered by the act. The building housed the headquarters of the company and was occupied exclusively by Borden personnel. Unlike *Kirschbaum*, production was managed from the building, though no goods were actually produced in the building. Justice Murphy acknowledged that no products were "processed or sold" in the building, but such matters as the purchase of all supplies, methods of production, workforce characteristics, budgeting, and finance questions were "all directed from this building." Production includes "all activity directed to increasing the number of scarce economic goods." Murphy deemed various management activities as "equally a part" of the production process. The person who "conceives or directs a productive activity is as essential to that activity as the one who physically performs it" (*Borden Co.*, 683). Chief Justice Stone, joined by Justice Roberts, dissented. Stone argued that Congress had not intended, by a "house-that-Jack-built chain of causation," any activity that eventually results in the production of goods for interstate commerce (*Borden Co.*, 685).

At the same time, the Stone Court found in some cases that employees were not within the reach of the FLSA. In *10 East 40th Street Building v. Callus* (1945), a case decided on the same day as *Borden Co.*, the Court was presented with a situation the closely resembled that of *Borden Co.* Notwithstanding the similarities, a five-justice majority ruled that the service employees of the building did not qualify for FLSA coverage. The case involved a forty-eight-story office building. Space in the building was leased to more than 100 tenants "pursuing a great variety of enterprises," but none of the tenants was engaged in manufacturing of any kind. Renting office space in a building entirely set aside for an "unrestricted variety" of office work, suggested Justice Frankfurter, "spontaneously satisfies the common understanding of what is local business and makes the employees of such a building engaged in local business." Although separation of an activity from the physical production process does not necessarily place it outside the reach of the FLSA, the "remoteness" of a particular activity is a "relevant factor in drawing the line." Operating an office building as an "entirely independent enterprise is too many steps removed from the physical process of the production of goods." An office building "exclusively devoted to the purpose of housing all the usual miscellany of offices," Frankfurter concluded, "has many differences in the practical affairs of life from a manufacturing building, or the office building of a manufacturer" (*10 East 40th*, 581, 583). Justices Murphy, Black, Douglas, and Rutledge viewed the case as "indistinguishable" from *Kirschbaum* and *Borden Co.*

In *McLeod v. Threlkeld* (1943), the Court ruled 5–4 that a cook working for a company with a contract to provide meals to right-of-way workers of an interstate railroad was not covered. Justice Reed said for the Court that the employee provided for the "personal needs" of the right-of-way workers. Furthermore, the food was "consumed apart from their work." The furnishing of board seemed to the Court "as remote from commerce . . . as in the cases where employees supply themselves"

(*McLeod*, 497). Murphy spoke in dissent for Justices Black, Douglas, and Rutledge, saying that the statutory phrase "engaged in commerce" was meant to extend the benefits of the FLSA to employees "throughout the farthest reaches of the channels of interstate commerce" (*McLeod*, 498).

The *McLeod* majority ruled in *Western Union Telegraph Co. v. Lenroot* (1945) that the FLSA did not apply to Western Union messengers under the age of sixteen. A federal court restrained Western Union from transmitting messages in interstate commerce until they had ceased employment of messengers under the age of sixteen for thirty days. Western Union successfully challenged the order. The Court concluded that telegram messages are "goods" and that transmission of messages is "shipment" within the meaning of the FLSA. It also concluded, however, that Western Union's "handling" of messages was not the equivalent of "production" of goods for interstate shipment. Justice Jackson said that if the term "producing" is defined to include handling or working on, then every "transporter, transmitter, or mover in interstate commerce" is a "producer" of any goods they carry. In the Court's view, it leads to results that "Congress could not have intended" (*Western Union*, 503).

Further, Jackson indicated that it was "beyond the judicial power of innovation to supply a direct prohibition by construction." The Court should not try to reach the same result "by a series of interpretations so far-fetched and forced as to bring into question that candor of Congress as well as the integrity of the interpretive process" (*Western Union*, 508). Justice Murphy, in dissent, charged the majority with "reading into" the FLSA an unintended exception resulting in "special dispensation" for Western Union to use the "channels of interstate commerce while employing admittedly oppressive child labor." However much a justice might "dislike imposition of Congressional sanctions," Murphy concluded, the judicial function "does not allow us to disregard that which Congress has plainly and constitutionally decreed and to formulate exceptions which we think . . . Congress might have made had it thought more about the problem" (*Western Union*, 509, 514).

The Stone Court upheld the use of administrative subpoenas by the wage and hour administrator in *Oklahoma Press Publishing Co. v. Walling* (1946). This case (and a companion, *News Printing Co. v. Walling*) raised two issues—the newspaper publishers' claims that the First Amendment shielded them from coming under the provisions of the FLSA and the scope of the administrator's power to subpoena records during the course of his investigations against the Fourth and Fifth Amendment interests of the publishers. Over the single dissent of Justice Murphy, the Court ruled against the newspapers. The First Amendment does not preclude Congress from "strik[ing] directly" at the "evils" of low wages and long hours "when they adversely affect commerce." The First Amendment, said Rutledge, does not forbid any regulation that "ends in no restraint upon expression or in any other evil outlawed by its terms and purposes" (*Oklahoma Press*, 193).

The Court also dispatched the Fourth and Fifth Amendment claims. These cases presented "no question of actual search and seizure, but raise [a] question whether orders of court for the production of specified records have been validly made." The Court saw no reason to set aside the orders to produce the records. The Court also found it "impossible to conceive" a self-incrimination violation. The records sought were corporate and "no possible element of self-incrimination" was presented. Furthermore, it was "not to be doubted" that Congress could authorize investigation of the issues under inquiry by the wage and hour administrator (*Oklahoma Press*, 195, 210). Finally, the Court concluded that the administrator possessed subpoena power comparable to that of a grand jury or court to obtain information necessary to secure enforcement of the FLSA. Justice Murphy differed from the Court on this point—he could not support the use of subpoenas issued by administrative agents as opposed to the courts. Four years earlier, Murphy had provided the decisive vote in *Cudahy Packing Co. of Louisiana v. Holland* (1942). There the question what whether the wage and hour administrator could delegate his authority to issue subpoenas. The Court held he could not on a 5–4 vote.

The most difficult FLSA issue for the Stone Court was portal-to-portal pay. The FLSA required that employees who work more than a forty-hour week must be paid overtime wages. The statute did not further define "workweek." The Court decided in *Tennessee Coal, Iron & Railroad Co. v. Muscoda Local 123* (1944) that the workweek of underground iron miners included the time spent going from the mine entrance to the underground work area and back again. Justice Murphy described the process by which iron miners were transported to the mining site—a trip that presented substantial risk of injury. Indeed, the "exacting and dangerous" conditions in the mines "stand as mute, unanswerable proof that the journey from and to the portal involves continuous physical and mental exertion as well as hazards to life and limb" (*Tennessee Coal*, 598). The purpose of the FLSA, he suggested, is both "remedial and humanitarian." In this case the Court was not dealing with "mere chattels or articles of trade" but rather with the "rights of those who toil, of those who sacrifice a full measure of their freedom and talents to the use and profit of others." Those are the rights Congress sought to protect with the FLSA, and as a result the law should not be interpreted or applied in a "narrow, grudging manner." The extracting of iron ore from the mines requires the miners' dangerous travel to the sites where "production" actually takes place. Such hazardous travel is "essential" to the production on the mine owner's property. Murphy suggested that it "did not matter" that travel to the work site was, "in a strict sense, a nonproductive benefit." Nothing in the FLSA "demands that every moment of an employee's time devoted to the service of the employer shall be directly productive" (*Tennessee Coal*, 597–598). Chief Justice Stone and Justice Roberts disagreed with Murphy's "broad[ly] humanitarian" approach to interpreting the statute. The Court ought not "construe legislation so as to accomplish what we deem worthy objects." The Court ought utilize, suggested Roberts, the "traditional" approach to determining what Congress has enacted and not "what we wish it had enacted" (*Tennessee Coal*, 606).

The Stone Court made the obvious extension of the *Tennessee Coal* reasoning from iron ore miners to coal miners in *Jewell Ridge v. Local 6167* (1945). As in *Tennessee Coal*, the issue was whether the FLSA requires that miners' travel time to the actual work site—the "portal-to-portal principle"—must be compensated. The Court again concluded that miners must be paid for travel time.

The case split the Court more widely, however, as Justices Frankfurter and Jackson joined Stone and Roberts in dissent. The five-justice majority concluded that the case presented no "factual or legal" difference from *Tennessee Coal*. The dissenters disagreed because applying the portal-to-portal principle in this case either "invalidate[d]" or "ignore[d]" collectively bargained agreements. The Court unanimously denied without opinion a petition for rehearing of the case several weeks later. Justice Jackson issued a brief concurring opinion that focused on the issue of the qualification of a justice to hear any particular case. His comment was prompted by Justice Black's participation in the case, in which he cast the decisive fifth vote. Jackson felt strongly that Black should have disqualified himself because the United Mine Workers local was represented by Black's former law partner. The disagreement between Black and Jackson was later to take on feudlike proportions at the time a successor to Chief Justice Stone was under consideration by President Truman.

The most extreme application of the portal-to-portal principle came in *Anderson v. Mt. Clemens Pottery* (1946), where the Court, in a 5–2 decision, ruled that employees of a pottery business were entitled to compensation for the time spent going from the time-clock location to the work station as well as the time for any preparation required to begin work. The statutory workweek, said Justice Murphy, includes "all time during which an employee is required to be on the employer's premises, on duty or at a prescribed workplace." The time spent "in these activities," in the Court's view, must be compensated (*Anderson*, 690). "Trifl[ing]" or "negligible" amounts of time were excluded in the Murphy opinion, but even these exclusions could not forestall a flood of back pay claims that had commenced following the *Jewell Ridge* decision. Congress eliminated the portal-to-portal concept by amending the FLSA, suggesting that the Court had departed from traditional labor management practices on the issue, and the Vinson Court retreated to a less expansive view of the FLSA.

Antilabor sentiment eventually developed in the United States, but legislative responses to this sentiment appeared first at the state level. Several Stone Court cases involving picketing as a mode of expression were discussed earlier in this chapter from a First Amendment perspective. There were additional expression and picketing cases involving labor unions. Most of these cases entailed review of state law rather than federal law. The labor cases that touched upon expression and the right to picket were typically though not always decided in favor of unions by the Stone Court. In the case most reflective of the value assigned to unions, *Thomas v. Collins* (1945), the Court set aside the conviction of a labor organizer who had not complied with a state law requiring that he obtain state permission before engaging in membership solicitation. The five-justice majority found the state restriction "so destructive of the right of public discussion" that it could not be sustained in the absence of a "grave and imminent threat" to the public interest" (*Thomas*, 537). *Thomas*, however, came later rather than earlier in the Stone Court period.

Thornhill v. Alabama (1940) brought peaceful picketing within the reach of the First Amendment as free speech. *Thornhill* drew together the Court's priorities of protecting both civil liberties and the rights of labor. But picketing is more than a form of communication. It is likely that many people respect picket lines simply to avoid trouble or charges of being antiunion, not because they are persuaded by the signs picketers carry. On the picket lines the purpose is not so much publicity as it is economic pressure. Moreover, picketing in labor situations carries the potential for violence. As a result, *Thornhill* could not be viewed as a blank check for union picketing. The Stone Court did not immediately build on *Thornhill* but qualified and limited it. This course was in fact begun in the last Hughes Court decision on the question, *Milk Wagon Drivers Union v. Meadowmoor Dairies* (1941), where an Illinois court injunction was upheld against picketing in a labor dispute marked by frequent episodes of violence. Justice Frankfurter's opinion suggested the state courts were justified in enjoining picketing in disputes with so much past violence that future picketing without more violence was improbable. Justices Black, Douglas, and Reed dissented. The dissenters reiterated the picketing-as-speech theme from *Thornhill* (Reed), and Black argued that the injunction was overly broad.

The Stone Court provided its take on the subject beginning in early March 1942, when it decided a number of cases that examined either state court injunctions or state statutes regulating picketing. The initial rulings did not support unions and expressive tactics like picketing notwithstanding *Thornhill*. Indeed, the Stone Court's early rulings seemed to severely limit the reach of *Thornhill*. The first case was *Hotel Employees' Local v. Wisconsin Employment Relations Board* (1942). A Wisconsin statute prohibited picketing except in strike situations. A state agency issued an order pursuant to this statute forbidding a union from picketing, but the order was somehow interpreted by the state supreme court as allowing peaceful picketing. Accepting the state court's judgment, the Stone Court unanimously (Justice Roberts not participating) upheld the order as forbidding only violence and permitting nonviolent picketing by the union.

Three additional picketing rulings were announced on March 30, 1942. The same Wisconsin statute examined in *Hotel Employees' Local* was the origin of *Allen-Bradley Local 1111 v. Wisconsin Employment Relations Board*. A union had been ordered not to engage in a number of actions, including picketing. A unanimous Supreme Court ruled that the Wagner Act did not preclude states from regulating union actions such as picketing. The only actions forbidden by the Wisconsin board in this case were mass picketing, threatening employees who wished to work, and obstructing access to the factory or surrounding streets. Justice Douglas said for the Court that there had been no showing that any employee "was deprived of rights protected or granted by the [NLRA] or that the status of any of them under the [NLRA] was impaired." If the provisions of the Wisconsin law invoked in this case were invalid because they conflicted with the NLRA, Douglas concluded, "then so long as the [NLRA] is on the books it is difficult to see how any State could under any circumstances regulate picketing or disorder growing out of labor disputes of companies whose business affects interstate commerce" (*Allen-Bradley Local 1111*, 751).

On the same day, the Stone Court struck down a New York court injunction against picketing in *Bakery and Pastry Drivers Local v. Wohl*. A union representing truck drivers who delivered bakery goods picketed a bakery that sold goods to nonunion or independent delivery drivers. Although Justice Jackson's majority opinion said that the picketing involved in this case was neither "excessive" nor "otherwise unlawful or oppressive," he said that a state is "not required to tolerate in all places and all circumstances even peaceful picketing by an individual" (*Bakery and Pastry Drivers Local*, 775). Justices Black, Douglas, and Murphy issued a concurring opinion that distanced themselves from the reasoning contained in Justice Jackson's majority opinion. They were concerned that if Jackson's opinion meant that a state can prohibit picketing "when it is effective but may not prohibit it when it is ineffective," then the Court has made a "basic departure" from *Thornhill* (*Bakery and Pastry Drivers Local*, 775).

A third case decided on March 30, 1942, *Carpenters and Joiners Union v. Ritter's Café*, appeared earlier in this chapter. A state court had enjoined a union from picketing in front of a restaurant whose owner had a building project at another site using a nonunion contractor. In a 5–4 ruling, the Stone Court decided that the state could restrict picketing by limiting First Amendment protection of picketing to particular areas directly related to the labor dispute. Justice Jackson distinguished *Ritter's Café* from *Bakery and Pastry Drivers* because the picketing of Ritter's Café had no "nexus" to the building dispute. The Texas law on which the injunction was based was designed to "localize" industrial disputes by prohibiting the "exertion of concerted pressure directed at the business, wholly outside the economic context of the real dispute." The state had not, in the Court's view, attempted to "outlaw whatever psychological pressure may be involved in the mere communication by an individual of the facts relating to his differences with another" (*Ritter's Café*, 726–727).

The Stone Court became more receptive to the arguments of labor on the picketing issue with the appointment of Justice Rutledge. He represented the fifth and consistently decisive vote in a number of cases involving organized labor. A more *Thornhill*-like ruling came in *Cafeteria Employees Union v. Angelos* (1943), as the Court set aside a state court order enjoining a union from picketing a cafeteria in an attempt to organize it. A state, said Justice Frankfurter, cannot "exclude working men in a particular industry from putting their case to the public in a peaceful way by drawing the circle of economic competition between employers and workers so small as to contain only an employer and those directly employed by him." The right to free speech in the future "cannot be forfeited because of dissociated acts of past violence." Even less can the right to picket be "taken away" because there may have been "isolated incidents of abuse falling far short of violence occurring in the course of that picketing" (*Cafeteria Employees*, 296).

References

Abraham, Henry J. *The Judiciary: The Supreme Court in the Governmental Process*, 9th edition. Madison, Wisc.: Brown & Benchmark, 1994.

Epstein, Lee, Jeffrey A. Segal, Harold J. Spaeth, and Thomas Walker. *The Supreme Court Compendium: Data, Decisions, and Developments*. Washington, D.C.: Congressional Quarterly Press, 1994.

Pritchett, C. Herman. *The Roosevelt Court: A Study in Judicial Politics and Values, 1937–47*. New York: Macmillan, 1948.

Renstrom, Peter G. "The Dimensionality of Decision Making of the 1941–1945 Stone Court: A Computer-Dependent Analysis of Supreme Court Behavior." Ph.D. dissertation, Michigan State University, 1972.

Schubert, Glendon A., Jr. *The Presidency in the Courts*. Minneapolis: University of Minnesota Press, 1957.

tenBroek, Jacobus, Edward N. Barnhart, and Floyd W. Matson. *Prejudice, War and the Constitution: Causes and Consequences of the Evacuation of the Japanese Americans in World War II*. Berkeley: University of California Press, 1970.

Urofsky, Melvin I. *Division and Discord: The Supreme Court under Stone and Vinson, 1941–1953*. Columbia: University of South Carolina Press, 1997.

4

Legacy and Impact

The Stone Court era coincided with World War II, and in many respects the decisional record of the Stone Court carries the heavy imprint of that war. Indeed, many of the Stone Court's most important decisions focused either directly or indirectly on the dimensions of the government's war power. The Stone Court, as Courts that preceded it, recognized extraordinarily broad power to meet the exigencies of a world war. At the same time, the Stone Court moved civil liberties issues into a prominent position on its agenda. The Hughes Court had been preoccupied with matters associated with federal management of an integrated national economy. An extremely small proportion of the Hughes Court's rulings, on the order of 3–5 percent for any year during the 1930s, addressed individual rights issues. By contrast, individual rights cases made up 20–25 percent of the Stone Court's decisions in its last three terms. More important, the Stone Court decided upwards of two-thirds of these cases in favor of those asserting individual rights claims. In all of the five Stone Court terms, the proportion of decisions favoring individual rights were above 50 percent, and in three of the five terms decisions supporting civil liberties positions exceeded 70 percent. In the words of Robert McCloskey, the Stone Court was "more devoted to the protection of the helpless and the oppressed, to the values of free thought, free utterance, and fair play" than any Court to that point in American history (McCloskey 1972, 49).

When Harlan Fiske Stone became chief justice in June 1941, President Franklin Roosevelt had already remade the Court. At the beginning of the 1941 term, eight of the justices sitting on the Court were Roosevelt appointees (counting Stone as a "Roosevelt justice" by virtue of Roosevelt's having elevated him to chief justice). Indeed, the Court had become the "Roosevelt Court." These justices were expected to have much in common. The Roosevelt justices certainly shared a commitment to the New Deal economic programs and the constitutional interpretations required to sustain them. This should have been a group able not only to refine the post-1937 "revolution" doctrines requiring clarification but perhaps even to break doctrinal new ground as well. With seven New Deal appointees on a Court presided over by a chief justice of sympathetic views, it was expected that the new jurisprudence that had developed in the last four years of the Hughes Court would continue. Instead, the Stone Court's five terms were characterized by William Swindler as "turbulent." Reflected in this turbulence was the power and independent thought of the Stone Court justices: They may have been "Roosevelt's justices," but they were no one's "rubber stamp," at least on some issues (Swindler 1974, 123).

Much was expected of the Stone Court. It was a "time of great justices" who were perhaps unmatched in their collective excellence. In the words of David Currie, seldom had "so many gifted justices graced the institution at the same time" (Currie 1990, 333). Excluding Byrnes and Burton from the group because each served only one term on the Stone Court, six of the remaining nine justices are regarded as having "great" or "near great" stature. Although there were moments when the Stone Court approached the level of aggregate greatness, there were moments when this Court fell short not only of greatness but even of what was expected of it.

There were important cases in which the Stone Court advanced the cause of individual rights protection and did so with clear and powerful language—*Duncan v. Kahanamoku, Cramer v. United States, West Virginia State Board of Education v. Barnette,* and *Smith v. Allwright* are among the obvious examples. Other significant rulings of the Stone Court spoke to such constitutional issues as congressional power to regulate interstate commerce, executive authority in wartime, and the Court's proper role in a democratic political system. The Stone Court made an effort to keep the exercise of governmental authority during wartime within limits, and it succeeded to a degree.

Certain decisions, however—such as *Quirin, Yamashita, Hirabayashi,* and *Korematsu*—history does not treat kindly, and these rulings are often accorded disproportionate weight in assessments of the Stone Court's overall record. Each of these cases is a stark reminder that there are both legal and political limits on judicial power, especially in times of national emergency. Apart from the war context, the Stone Court let slip away some opportunities to take rights protection further than it did. It failed to build on *Smith v. Allwright* when it chose in *Colegrove v. Green* to leave the problem of malapportionment to its successors, for example. The Stone Court also failed to expand constitutional guarantees to state criminal cases in cases such as *Betts v. Brady*. Instead, it was left to the Warren Court to give full effect to criminal rights provisions of the Bill of Rights.

There is a Stone Court legacy, but it is a legacy with qualifications. It is a legacy of unmet expectations, and it is a legacy without significant consequence until the second decade of the Warren Court era. A number of factors speak to the unfulfilled expectations or "underachievement" of the Stone Court. For one, Stone died before the end of his fifth year as chief justice. It is very difficult for a Court, even one composed of extraordinary justices, to compile a correspondingly extraordinary record in a limited period of time. Five years was simply too short for the Stone Court to fashion its own distinctive jurisprudence, particularly with the enormous distraction of the war.

Second, the Court's membership had changed too extensively and too quickly in the months prior to the beginning of Stone's tenure as chief justice. Stone and Owen Roberts were the only members of the Court who had participated in the doctrinal "revolution" of 1937. Seven new justices between 1937 and 1941 altered the Court almost as much as the revolution itself. After 1941 the Court had to deal with the new, "postrevolution" constitutional fabric and, in addition, wrestle with the fundamental problem of what its own role should be—the activism versus self-restraint question. With the exception of Stone and Roberts, the Stone Court justices had virtually no judicial experience, and they disagreed with one another about the Court's role and the basis upon which justices should make their judgments. Justices Black and Frankfurter defined the two poles of thought on the Stone Court, and the philosophical conflict between justices of such stature virtually guaranteed jurisprudential disarray. The Stone Court was never able to find the right intellectual chemistry to enable it to find common ground needed to heighten its impact.

A third factor in the Court's limited success was the manifest incompatibility of specific individuals among the new justices, an interpersonal chemistry that could not be managed effectively. Personal animosities plagued the Stone Court. The feud between Justices Black and Jackson was the most public and significant, but other Stone Court justices were not inclined to negotiate with one another in search of consensus. The rate of disagreement is reflected in the number of split decisions, which during the Stone Court period reached unprecedented levels.

Fourth, the Stone Court's work was disrupted by the demands of World War II. Justice Roberts was called away in early 1942 to participate in the inquiry over Pearl Harbor, and a few months later Byrnes resigned to become "assistant president," as the director first of the Office of Economic Stabilization and then the Office of War Mobilization. At the end of the conflict, Jackson was "borrowed" from the Court to participate in the war crimes trials in Nuremberg. Stone was extremely upset about the loss of Jackson. He and Jackson had come to share common jurisprudential ground and typically voted with one another. Jackson's absence forced the Court to function with only eight justices for an entire year, and, to Stone's mind, this inflicted institutional damage on the Court.

Stone's leadership style presented a fifth obstacle: Because he was either unwilling or unable to lead his Court effectively, his was a divided and discordant Court. Prior to his elevation to chief justice, Stone had been a major contributor to U.S. constitutional development—the architect of the 1937 "constitutional revolution" in the minds of some observers. Stone's most significant opinions, such as the *Carolene Products* concurrence, the *Gobitis* and *Butler* dissents, and the majority opinion in *Darby Lumber*, all predated his becoming chief justice. Stone disliked the role of chief justice once he assumed it. Not only was he unhappy during the period, but his distinctive contributions to U.S. constitutional law seemed to diminish as well.

But the fault for the Court's shortcomings cannot be attributed to Stone alone. In addition to the war, it was a time in which more focused and particular disagreements existed among the justices, most notably over reconciling the self-restraintist approach with the judicial scrutiny required to give effect to the "preferred position" doctrine. To an extent, Stone's *Carolene Products* thinking had begun to take hold by the time of Stone's death in 1946, but it would not reach its fullest acceptance until Justice Frankfurter left the Court in 1962. As leading spokesmen on the issue, Justices Black and Frankfurter defined the intense debate over the question of how judicial review should be conducted for another sixteen years after Stone's death.

The intense differences over the degree to which the Court ought to intervene in individual rights cases was, at least in part, a product of Roosevelt's criteria in selecting his nominees for the Court. A central objective was to bolster support on the Court for the New Deal programs—"absolute loyalty to the principles of the New Deal, particularly to governmental authority," according to Henry Abraham (Abraham, 1992, 212).

That end had been achieved, albeit tenuously, before Roosevelt nominated his first justice. By the time Stone became chief justice, the new jurisprudence of the "postrevolution" period was already cast in concrete. The Roosevelt justices were put on the Court to resolve the constitutional conflict relating to New Deal initiatives, but no real disagreement was left on those issues once Roosevelt's nominees joined the Court. Since only doctrinal mop-up remained on New Deal–related issues, the Stone Court justices pursued their own agendas. Most of the issues after the New Deal were relatively new, and the limited number of prior decisions provided very little guidance. This was particularly true with respect to individual rights questions. The constitutional "revolution" of 1937 was about the Court's deferring to legislative judgments on managing the national economy. The self-restraintist approach presumed that legislative initiatives were constitutional. The Stone Court did not extend this presumption to government actions involving individual rights, however. To the contrary, if Bill of Rights provisions were to have "preferred position" status, as Stone suggested in *Carolene Products*, the Court would have to approach rights issues with great suspicion about governmental actions and subject those actions to the closest judicial scrutiny. The Stone Court justices' concerns about civil liberties often clashed with the restraintist value of legislative deference.

The legacy of the Stone Court is also muted for another reason: the modest record of the Vinson Court that followed it. The Stone Court era was brief. Its place in history would be more prominent had the Stone Court been followed immediately by the Warren Court. Some of the more important Warren Court individual rights rulings were influenced by decisions of the Stone Court. Certainly Warren Court opinions drew extensively on the language found in the opinions of Stone Court justices. The delayed effect of these influences was caused by the seven years of the Vinson Court, between 1946 and 1953. The Vinson Court, particularly after the deaths of Justices Murphy and Rutledge in 1949, simply did not have the votes to develop an individual rights jurisprudence suggested by some of the Stone Court's rulings. Sitting as it did during the outset of the cold war, the Vinson Court was not prepared to venture further on individual rights issues, especially those involving street-corner speech and political associations. Further, the personnel changes that took place in the late 1940s diminished the number of justices who might be receptive to civil liberties arguments. Justices Murphy and Rutledge, two zealous civil libertarians, were replaced by Tom Clark and Sherman Minton, neither of whom was so inclined. Indeed, from 1949 until Earl Warren succeeded Fred Vinson as chief justice, strong civil liberties positions were advanced only by Justices Black and Douglas. More important, the reduction of the activist bloc to only Black and Douglas meant that often there were not the required four votes to get certain issues before the Court via the writ of certiorari.

Finally, there was the war. It dominated everything else. The exigencies of war simply do not provide occasions for judicial intervention. War requires executive leadership, and the Stone Court felt it necessary to let Roosevelt, Congress, and the military win the war. The most noteworthy and troublesome example of the Stone Court's noninterventionist approach to war-related issues was, of course, the relocation of the Japanese. Although it was extremely distasteful for the Stone Court justices, the Court saw fit to sustain the relocation nonetheless. The Court eventually concluded that the War Relocation Authority could not confine loyal Japanese Americans, but its unwillingness to challenge the military necessity rationale for relocation skewed the Stone Court's individual rights record.

World War II

The New Deal had called for profound expansion in the size and reach of the federal government. It produced a vast increase of regulatory activity at the federal level through the agencies implementing the New Deal programs. The New Deal, in fact, enlarged the executive branch, and it also dramatically augmented the authority of the president to initiate and revise many government policies and practices. By the end of the 1930s, the fundamental rules of constitutional law had done a complete about-face from interpretations that had come prior to the 1937 revolution. This had significant consequences: The commerce and taxing powers of Congress became a foundation for comprehensive federal authority, the liberty of contract concept was no longer invoked as a device to further the objectives of the laissez-faire agenda, and the status of organized labor had been elevated to a point where it could effectively function as a counterweight to capital interests. In the four years between the "revolution" and the beginning of the Stone Court period, the Hughes Court had completely abandoned the old laissez-faire constitutionalism.

The demands of World War II led to additional regulatory measures beyond those stemming from the New Deal. The Stone Court supported all reasonable assertions of legislative or executive authority in the face of national emergency. For example, it upheld in every instance the Emergency Price Control Act of 1942 and the actions of the Office of Price Administration it created. With the war still in progress, the Court ruled that Congress should determine the degree of latitude an administrator or agency should possess.

The Supreme Court has typically deferred to the political branches of government in times of war. No Court has wished to jeopardize efforts to successfully prosecute a war, and the Stone Court was no different. In fact, several Stone Court justices chafed at not taking an even more active part in the war effort. Justice Murphy, for example, would have preferred to leave the Court and serve in active combat. Justice Byrnes resigned the Court to accept a position essential to management of the war effort. The wartime needs of the country came before all else, and the Stone Court frequently yielded to assertions of military necessity throughout the war.

The war crimes trials and the Japanese evacuation cases demonstrate that military exigencies can create compelling justifications for the exercise of governmental power. In times of war the norm is judicial ratification of actions taken by the legislative and executive branches. The Stone Court clearly adhered to this norm as it approved virtually all war initiatives it had an opportunity to review.

The *Quirin* and *Yamashita* cases posed the question of extending constitutional protections to members of the enemy military. These Stone Court rulings convey that the civilian courts are not responsible for safeguarding the procedural protections of enemy defendants. *Quirin* and *Yamashita* also reaffirmed the immensity of presidential war power. The Court ruled that Roosevelt's authority as commander in chief, powers conferred by Congress in several statutes, and power derived from the articles of war enabled him to establish military tribunals for the trial of captured enemy forces. This power not only allowed him to create military courts but also permitted them to operate on the basis of standards adopted by the tribunal itself. The Stone Court concluded that the designated military tribunals need not adhere to the constitutional protections afforded criminal defendants undergoing trial in a civilian court but were free to set their own procedural standards.

The Court's reasoning centered on the exigencies of wartime. Since the alleged crimes of *Quirin* and *Yamashita* were war crimes, it was necessary for the American military to have jurisdiction to prosecute. In the case of the German saboteurs, the Court held that those who "surreptitiously" enter the country for the purpose of destroying life and property acquire the status of "unlawful combatants." A military tribunal is the appropriate place for such defendants to be tried. *Yamashita* went further because it extended the *Quirin* reasoning to a trial occurring after hostilities had formally ended. The primary consequence of *Quirin* and *Yamashita* is affirmation of seemingly unconditional presidential discretion to create military commissions. Once created, these military commissions are not subject to the same procedural protections applicable in civilian courts. The Stone Court established no outer limits for the action of either the president or military commissions.

Neither Quirin nor Yamashita was a U.S. citizen, but the Stone Court did decide two treason cases, both involving American citizens and both stemming from the case of the German saboteurs. The outcomes were somewhat different, however. The Constitution defines the offense of treason in Article 3 as levying war against the United States or adhering to the country's enemies, giving them "aid and comfort." The Constitution further provides that a treason conviction requires the testimony of two witnesses "to the same overt act." The Stone Court interpreted these provisions in a manner that imposed a substantial burden of proof on the government. In setting aside Anthony Cramer's treason conviction in *Cramer v. United States* (1945), the Court held that the government must demonstrate that any overt act of the accused reflects clear intent to commit treason. Cramer's actions suggested no such treasonous intent. The Stone Court wanted to ensure that actions such as making speeches critical of the government and the "hundred other things which may impair our cohesion and diminish our strength" do not necessarily constitute adherence to the enemy or reflect treasonous intent. When coupled with the two-witness requirement for any overt act, the *Cramer* decision made treason a difficult, though not impossible, crime to prove.

The treason conviction of Hans Haupt, a case decided during the first term of the Vinson Court, backtracked on the overt act point. Haupt, the father of one of the saboteurs, argued that his actions did not reflect treasonous intent, but the Vinson Court concluded that his acts provided sufficient aid to the enemy to constitute treason. Had the *Haupt* ruling come before *Cramer* and been decided by the Stone Court, the result would have been different. As it was, the Vinson Court decision to uphold Haupt's conviction opened the door for a number of treason prosecutions of Americans who had given assistance to Axis agents during the war. The cold war mentality, which was to weigh so heavily during the Vinson Court era, seemed already evident in the *Haupt* ruling.

The cases involving denaturalization and Selective Service Act violations were distinguishable from the treason cases. The Stone Court valued citizenship very highly and was extremely suspicious of government attempts to revoke it. Justices Murphy and Rutledge were, in fact, most emphatic in the view that the government could not denaturalize anyone under any circumstances. Other justices, such as Black, Frankfurter, and Douglas, took the position that denaturalized citizens could not be treated as second-class citizens, with citizenship conditioned on compliance with certain restrictions that did not apply in a comparable way to natural-born citizens. It is in these cases, among others, that the Stone Court attempted to draw a line that permitted less political repression than had occurred during World War I.

Most of the Stone Court cases of this type were decided in favor of the political defendant. *Schneiderman, Baumgartner,* and *Hartzel* are representative of strongly worded Stone Court rulings on behalf of politically active citizens. Schneiderman was both a naturalized citizen and a Communist. The government sought to strip him of his citizenship some twelve years after his naturalization. Murphy's opinion for the Court restricted the use of citizenship revocation and clearly placed political beliefs beyond the scope of denaturalization. The Court was also troubled by a process that imposed a badge of inferiority on naturalized citizens. This was one instance in which several of the Roosevelt justices did not defer to legislative judgments and on the actions of executive agencies, choosing instead to subject denaturalization to the closest judicial scrutiny. Similarly, in *Baumgartner,* a unanimous Stone Court indicated that it must be particularly vigilant so that citizenship, once bestowed, should not be too easily placed in jeopardy by making political leanings the basis for determining whether citizenship status had been fraudulently obtained. In *Hartzel,* the Espionage Act case, Murphy once again argued that an American citizen, native-born or naturalized, has the right to discuss political matters even by employing "immoderate and vicious invective."

There were, of course, Stone Court rulings that permitted outcomes adverse to individual rights. These were cases in which military necessity was so compelling or evidence of criminal conduct was so overwhelming that convictions had to be sustained. Examples of the former are *Falbo* and *Estep,* in which the Court chose not to interfere with administration of the selective service laws because of the urgent need to mobilize citizens for military service. Judicial review could only jeopardize those objectives. *Knauer* speaks to the evidentiary point. The Stone Court agreed with the lower court finding that Knauer had falsely sworn allegiance to the United States and that his denaturalization was based on more than mere political utterances. Notwithstanding the national crisis brought on by World War II, the Stone Court left its mark on the need to protect certain rights in the wake of governmental response to a war emergency.

The Stone Court decisions sustaining exclusion of those of Japanese ancestry from "military zones" on the West Coast (*Hirabayashi* and *Korematsu*) reveal deference to the elective branches carried to excessive lengths. Although the Court eventually found the exclusion of the Japanese and the imposition of martial law in Hawaii to be constitutionally defective, it did not do so until the war emergency was over. In other words, it chose to err on the side of government authority during wartime despite the individual liberty implications. The opinions in *Endo* and *Duncan* contain strong language, however, and they became precedents that are quite protective to individual rights notwithstanding their tardy release from the Stone Court.

With the military government in Hawaii came suspension of all civilian governmental functions, including the writ of habeas corpus and the operation of civil courts. Ultimately, the Stone Court held that military government in Hawaii had been unconstitutional, saying that legislatures and courts are not merely "cherished" institutions but "indispensable" as well. Accordingly, the Court must be constantly vigilant against any excessive use of military power that might end in the "needless destruction of our rights and liberties" (*Duncan*, 335). These were powerful statements, but they would have been more powerful deterrents to future misuse of military authority had they been offered before rather than after the war ended. As with the relocation of the Japanese, however, earlier intervention by the Stone Court might simply be expecting too much of a Court in a time of national crisis.

In fact, the Stone Court had precedent for its nonintervention—the Supreme Court had done much the same thing in the Civil War, striking down test oaths and the military trial of civilians only after the cessation of hostilities. In the retrospective view of most, the Stone Court had carried judicial self-restraint to the point of judicial "abdication" in the Japanese evacuation cases. In *Hirabayashi* and *Korematsu*, the Court sustained a "drastic act of military government over citizen civilians within the country without inquiring into the factual justification" (tenBroek et al. 1970, 220–223). The basic proposition underlying the curfew, relocation, and detention was that alien residents and American citizens of Japanese ancestry were a greater danger to the national security than those of other ancestry. In addition, the war conditions of the Pacific Coast following Pearl Harbor were such that persons of Japanese heritage could not feasibly be isolated and dealt with individually. Neither of these propositions received judicial examination. In *Korematsu* the Court attributed to the military a conclusive determination that the curfew and other existing methods were inadequate protection against espionage and sabotage and that the relocation program was militarily necessary.

The Stone Court eloquently declared that distinctions among citizens solely because of their ancestry "are by their very nature odious to a free people whose institutions are founded upon the doctrine of equality" (*Hirabayashi*, 100). This was both an obvious and important point to register. Despite this observation, however, the Court upheld the broader evacuation program in *Korematsu*. Korematsu had been convicted for remaining in a military area contrary to the civilian exclusion order of the military commander. Such an order, said the Court, could lawfully be issued by military authorities given the particular situation confronting them on the West Coast after Pearl Harbor. The military authorities faced the real possibility of a Japanese follow-up attack, and Japanese Americans could rationally be set apart from citizens who had no particular associations with Japan. Residents who have ethnic affiliations with an invading enemy may be a greater source of danger than those of a different ancestry. Accordingly, it could not be said that the exclusion order bore no reasonable relation to the demands of military necessity. It was not until December 1944 that the Court ordered the release of Japanese Americans from relocation centers.

Although detention immediately following Pearl Harbor could be justified by military necessity, the same level of necessity did not remain three years after Pearl Harbor, when the government had ample opportunity to determine the loyalty of individual Japanese Americans. The impact of the Court's rulings in the *Hirabayashi* and *Korematsu* cases and the suspect nature of the policy was lost in the hysteria about the war; to the extent the public was aware of the scope of the relocation program, most thought it was justified. Attempts to redress the injury suffered by those detained gained momentum in 1980, when Congress established a blue-ribbon Commission on Wartime Relocation and Internment of Civilians. The commission gave much weight to the Stone Court's conclusions in *Endo*, and the government eventually paid compensation to the survivors of the relocation program..

The Roosevelt administration met the challenge of total war between 1941 and 1945 in much the same way as Lincoln and Wilson had in 1861 and 1917. Similar constitutional problems in all three war crises magnified the tension between the nature of constitutional government and the requirements of national security and military policy. In each case the executive solved the problem of the effective conduct of the war by establishing an emergency government grounded on a combination of statutory grants and the presidential prerogative as commander in chief in wartime.

During World War II the Stone Court generally confirmed the actions taken by the government to deal with the war emergency. There was also interference with civil liberties in the name of the war effort, but the Stone Court was not quite willing to affirm these actions across the board. In World War II this interference was primarily limited to the exclusion of the Japanese and the imposition of military government on Hawaii. These exceptions, particularly the relocation of the Japanese, are the most regrettable legacy of the Stone Court. In fairness, however, it must be pointed out that the Stone Court was able to maintain individual rights during wartime, particularly in the denaturalization cases, to a greater degree than any Court preceding it.

World War II, like wars before it, created circumstances that allowed the exercise of greatly expanded executive powers. Many of these powers, used in both domestic and foreign contexts, remained with the president even after the war. Indeed, on the foreign policy side Congress expanded these powers even further during the Vinson Court period. Roosevelt based his foreign policy on the theory of magnified presidential prerogative in a national emergency. Like Wilson before him, Roosevelt created a vast executive mechanism for the conduct of the war. Many of the wartime agencies were located within the Office of Emergency Management. Established by executive order in May 1940, the OEM drew its authority from the

Reorganization Act of 1939 and served as a central location for agencies Roosevelt could not conveniently assign elsewhere. The OEM quickly became a kind of coordinating agency for the wartime executive structure. The Stone Court reviewed none of these actions.

It did, however, rule on several issues stemming from the Emergency Price Control Act and sustained comprehensive federal authority over private property. The primary objective of the EPCA, adopted by Congress in 1942, was to control inflation. It was the most extensive program of price-fixing ever attempted in U.S. history—the prices of almost all goods and services were directly controlled from Washington. The Office of Price Administration was established to implement the provisions of the EPCA; the price administrator had the authority to fix maximum prices for all commodities. The Stone Court's most important ruling on the EPCA came in *Yakus v. United States* (1944), which examined the validity of price control provisions of the act. It was contended by Yakus (and others receiving OPA price orders) that Congress delegated excessive authority to the price administrator. The delegation of legislative power contentions resembled those successfully asserted in the challenge of the National Industrial Recovery Act in *Schechter Poultry Corp. v. United States* (1935). The Stone Court concluded that Congress had established objectives and guidelines with sufficient clarity in the EPCA to overcome any claim of the excessive delegation. The rationale offered by Chief Justice Stone was certainly grounded in the special needs created by the war, a point that could not be made in *Schechter.* More generally, however, Stone spoke of the realities of the legislative process and in doing so used judicial self-restraint principles. Congress, he argued, cannot be expected to fill in every detail as it sets national policy. Rather, Congress must have "ample latitude" to direct administrative officers to make independent determinations when giving effect to legislation. His words reaffirmed the jurisprudence that emerged from the "revolution" of 1937 and had lasting consequences even outside the war context.

Although *Yakus* may have been the most important EPCA ruling, the Court recognized even greater administrative authority in *Steuart & Bros. v. Bowles* (1944). Roosevelt had delegated to the price administrator the authority to ration fuel oil. The OPA issued a suspension order against Steuart and Brothers for its failure to comply with its rationing regulations. Steuart and Brothers argued that the suspension order was the equivalent of a penalty. Since the EPCA did not expressly provide for such orders, this penalty was established by the price administrator and not Congress. The Stone Court did not view the order as an arbitrary administrative penalty, concluding instead that the order was a necessary means to achieving the objective of Congress. The suspension order was inseparable from the power to allocate fuel oil, a power explicitly conveyed to the OPA by Congress. In Justice Douglas's words, if the power to allocate ration levels did not also embrace the power to issue enforcement orders, "it would be a feeble power indeed." Thus, the power given to the president to allocate materials during World War II was used extensively to withhold materials from those who disobeyed the economic control orders. The OPA suspension order, which effectively put the fuel oil dealer out of business (at least for the period of the suspension order), was sustained, although the power to impose such a sanction was nowhere conferred by Congress. Legislative deference clearly, but remarkable deference to the executive bureaucracy as well.

The Stone Court did little to restrain the drastic restrictions upon property rights that took place during World War II. The war power, of course, had an extreme impact upon property as well as persons. That should not be altogether surprising. At a time when the law mandated that citizens may be drafted and possibly lose their lives in combat, it should be expected as well that citizens may be required to yield their property if deemed necessary.

Regulatory Authority Independent of the War: The Commerce Power

The federal commerce and taxing powers were the focal points of the new constitutionalism. The "revolution" that occurred in 1937 produced interpretations of constitutional authority that allowed Congress to reach virtually any aspect of the national economy. The Stone Court clearly would have come to the same conclusion about the federal commerce power had it heard such Hughes Court cases as *NLRB v. Jones & Laughlin Steel Corp.* (1937). As Roosevelt justices were added to the Hughes Court, at least half a dozen New Deal statutes were upheld and many of the Court's own pre-1937 restrictive rulings were reversed. Suffice it to say, the Stone Court was completely committed to the restraintist, proeconomic regulation jurisprudence begun in 1937. *United States v. Darby Lumber Co.* (1941), decided a year before Stone was elevated to chief justice, is particularly revealing in this light.

Darby Lumber was a unanimous decision. In a sense, *Darby* is a "virtual" Stone Court ruling; the replacement of Hughes with Jackson was the only change in the Court's composition between the *Darby* ruling and Stone's elevation to chief justice. Six Roosevelt justices joined the three carryover justices from *Jones & Laughlin Steel* in voting to uphold the provisions of the Fair Labor Standards Act. The act established minimum wages and maximum hours of work for employees of businesses whose products were shipped in interstate commerce; the Wage and Hour Division was created to administer the requirements of the act. The Stone Court reviewed a number of cases stemming from rulings of the wage and hour administrator after the Hughes Court sustained the act against broader constitutional challenge.

The principal issue in *Darby* was whether Congress had the authority to prohibit the interstate shipment of products made by employees whose hours of work exceeded or whose wages were lower than the standard set by statute. Darby Lumber argued that the wage and hour provisions of the FLSA did not regulate interstate commerce at all but was instead an attempt to regulate production. Prior to 1937, production was viewed as separate from commerce—production preceded and was completed before commerce could begin. Justice Stone suggested that Congress intended that interstate commerce should not be made the "instrument of competition" in the distribution of goods produced under "substandard labor conditions." In upholding the act, Justice Stone said that the commerce power extends to any local or intrastate activities that "affect" interstate commerce. Even local businesses may be impaired by unfair competition through interstate commerce. The wage and hour regulations of the FLSA were directed at the suppression of a kind of competition deemed "unfair" in the NLRA and reflected the reality that in "present day industry, competition by a small part may affect the whole." Accordingly, legislation "aimed at the whole embraces all its parts" (*Darby*, 123).

Justice Stone also took aim at the application of the Tenth Amendment that had effectively limited the commerce power on state sovereignty grounds. The Tenth Amendment, in the Court's view, could no longer be used to insulate production workers from federal law. The Tenth Amendment was not intended, said Stone, to deprive the national government of the power to use any "appropriate and plainly adapted" means to safeguard interstate commerce regulation. Far from a device to curtail proper use of the commerce power, Stone indicated, the Tenth Amendment simply "states but a truism that all is retained [to the states] which has not been surrendered." The amendment is merely "declaratory" of the relationship between the federal and state governments. Its role was to generally "allay fears" that the federal government would exercise powers not granted to it (*Darby*, 124).

Darby had several consequences that carried the imprint of the justices who would sit on the Stone Court. *Darby* stated that judicial inquiry into congressional motives in exercising the commerce power was inappropriate. Second, *Darby* sustained the contention that prohibiting items from entering interstate commerce was an acceptable regulatory form. Third, *Darby* reiterated the conclusion that activities at the production stage were within reach of the federal commerce power; the old production-commerce distinction was abandoned. Finally, the Court rejected the previously effective dual federalism doctrine, which had defined certain activities, including production, as local and subject to the exclusive control of the states. The Stone Court was left little opportunity to expand or otherwise modify this interpretation of the commerce power. The views contained in *Darby* would maintain through the end of the century.

If there was any question about the extent to which the Stone Court would sustain the federal commerce power, it was emphatically answered in *Wickard v. Filburn* (1942). *Wickard* offered the most expansive interpretation of federal commerce power in the Court's history. Sustained in *Wickard* were quotas on agricultural production under the Agricultural Adjustment Act, a conclusion that required no broader interpretation of the commerce power than *Darby*. The extended reach of the commerce power came with the Court's sustaining a penalty for growing wheat on less than twelve acres more than the limit set by the federal regulation. By growing 239 bushels of wheat more than he was allowed, Filburn failed to comply with the quota set for the production of wheat on his farm, and he was fined. He argued that his overproduction was infinitesimal when measured on a national scale—the overproduction was so small that it could affect neither the national market conditions for wheat or interfere with the congressional objective of stabilizing commodity prices. The Stone Court disagreed, concluding that Filburn and his 239 extra bushels of wheat had a substantial influence on price and market conditions. Even a cursory reading of Justice Jackson's opinion in *Wickard v. Filburn* reveals that the Stone Court recognized a virtually limitless federal commerce power. Even though the Stone Court's opinions in cases such as *Wickard* supported expansive federal power, the doctrinal impact of these cases was modest because this view of the federal commerce power was not new in 1942, nor was the legislative deference necessary to sustain the agricultural regulations in *Wickard*.

One of the more effective approaches to limiting federal commerce power before 1937 was to define a variety of activities as local in character and thus not subject to federal regulation. Following the "revolution" of 1937, most economic activities were seen as parts, however small, of an integrated national economy. A question that appeared before the Stone Court was whether the states had any regulatory authority at all when interstate commerce was involved. The simple answer would have been that federal authority was now viewed as exclusive and that the states had no regulatory role: Whether Congress had acted or not, states were prohibited from taking any action affecting commerce. The Stone Court saw the federal commerce power as plenary and free from state interference.

But the Court did recognize a small zone within which states could regulate commerce. In *Parker v. Brown* (1943), for example, the Stone Court upheld a state agricultural marketing policy. The grant of commerce power to Congress did not absolutely preclude state regulation of matters that remained local in character and where uniform national regulation was not required or preferred. Although this view recognized a narrow zone for state regulation, the Stone Court found state initiatives that "coincided" or complemented federal policy to be constitutionally permissible. More often, however, the Stone Court was inclined to see the need for uniform national regulation, which could come only from Congress. The impact of the Stone Court in this policy area strongly affirmed the "postrevolution" jurisprudence initiated by the Hughes Court.

Civil Liberties

First Amendment

The most significant legacy of the Stone Court was in the area of individual rights. Glimpses of this are seen in cases involving denaturalization and other war-related individual rights issues, but the Stone Court advanced the cause of individual rights protection more extensively in cases unrelated to the war, especially on First Amendment and equal protection issues. Furthermore, it provided a foundation from which the Warren Court could launch its more comprehensive expansion of constitutional protections.

Ruling in *Thornhill v. Alabama* (1940), the Hughes Court had made it clear that the Court's restraintist approach would not automatically transfer to cases involving individual rights claims. Instead, *Thornhill* revealed that the "preferred position" doctrine would inevitably lead to a more aggressive judicial scrutiny of governmental actions raising constitutional rights issues, especially freedom of expression claims. According to Currie, *Thornhill* provides one of the Court's earliest statements that some constitutional provisions are "more equal than others" because they occupy a "preferred position" (Currie 1997, 90). The First Amendment protections easily met Stone's "preferred position" conditions for enhanced judicial scrutiny—the First Amendment contains explicit prohibitions regarding impairment of expression, and free expression is an essential component of a democratic political process. Indeed, the "preferred position" doctrine defined a significant part of the Court's agenda for the remainder of the century.

The "preferred position" doctrine required the post-1937 Hughes Court and the Stone Court to draw away from the legislative deference of the judicial self-restraint approach. The Court had to adopt a double standard with respect to judicial review, as it could not defer to legislative judgments and act as the principal and vigilant guardian of constitutional rights at the same time. The Stone Court justices were not in complete agreement on the judicial activism the "preferred position" doctrine requires. The question of how much deference ought to be accorded to the other branches of government in First Amendment cases arose in many Stone Court cases. As many as six Stone Court justices believed they should give stricter scrutiny to First Amendment claims. Some Stone Court justices, including Justice Frankfurter, were of the view that different scrutiny levels for different constitutional provisions could not be justified. These justices believed that judicial deference to reasonable legislative judgments should occur across the board. Justice Frankfurter rejected the double standard, arguing instead that the Constitution did not give the Court a greater "veto power" when dealing with one constitutional position as opposed to another.

The difference in outlook between the "preferred position" justices, led by Justice Black, on the one side and Justice Frankfurter on the other reflected what Currie has called the basic "ambiguity" in the 1937 constitutional "revolution." The conclusion in the turnaround cases of 1937 and thereafter was that the Court had not been deferential enough to legislative and executive branch actions. Although both Black and Frankfurter deferred to legislative judgments for the New Deal programs in the 1930s, they split when confronted by the civil liberties and political process cases of the 1940s. In Currie's words, Black had a "narrow conception of substantive due process," whereas Frankfurter had a "narrow conception of judicial review" (Currie 1997, 94). The differences of view on this point defined, at least in part, the individual rights debate into the 1960s.

A number of Stone Court decisions were favorable to the protection of civil liberties. Among the most significant were the rulings on free exercise of religion. A seemingly endless stream of cases involving Jehovah's Witnesses reached the Court during the 1940s, giving the Stone Court ample opportunity to define in some detail the protections afforded by the free exercise clause. The Hughes Court ruled against the Witnesses in 1940 in the first of the compulsory flag salute cases *(Minersville School District v. Gobitis)*, but the Stone Court overturned this ruling in *West Virginia State Board of Education v. Barnette* (1943). The Stone Court upheld a local tax on door-to-door solicitations against the religious freedom claims of the Witnesses in 1942 but reversed itself on this issue a year later. The only case in which the Court ruled against Witnesses (excepting those cases where the Court subsequently reversed the outcome) was in *Prince v. Massachusetts* (1944), a case in which the Court had to choose between free exercise of religion and a state's interest in protecting the welfare of minor children, a unique tension in these religious freedom cases.

The free exercise cases produced some of the most noteworthy opinions issued by the Stone Court. Perhaps the most memorable was Justice Jackson's majority opinion in *Barnette*. The Court saw the refusal to participate in the flag salute ceremony as a "form of utterance" that did not produce a danger sufficient enough to justify "muffling the expression" of those choosing to remain silent. Jackson described as a "fixed star in our constitutional constellation" that government could not "prescribe what shall be orthodox in politics, nationalism, religion, or other matters of opinion" *(Barnette*, 641–642).

The cases concerning a tax on door-to-door solicitation (license tax) also produced very powerful free exercise opinions. In addition to explicitly reaffirming the "preferred position" doctrine, Justice Douglas said in *Murdock v. Pennsylvania* that door-to-door distribution of religious tracts was a long-standing form of "missionary evangelism." Indeed, he believed carrying a religious message door-to-door occupied the "same high estate under the First Amendment as do worship in the churches and preaching from the pulpit." The Stone Court recognized that the power to impose even the most minimal tax brings with it the potential to suppress religion; the government can make religious exercise "so costly as to deprive it of the resources necessary for its maintenance" (*Murdock*, 111–112).

The compulsory flag salute and license tax had been sustained initially under the general secular purpose doctrine, which directs that religious beliefs cannot relieve any individual from obeying laws applicable to all that are aimed at neither promotion nor restriction of religious views. The Stone Court concluded that this doctrine produced results that too harshly restricted religious exercise rights. Beginning with *Barnette*, the Stone Court's free exercise rulings abandoned the general secular purpose doctrine, using instead a much more protective approach to free exercise of religion. The Stone Court's record from *Barnette* on was a clear precursor of the free exercise jurisprudence of the Warren Court as defined in cases such as *Sherbert v. Verner* (1963).

The Stone Court's rulings in the picketing cases distinguished between "pure" speech and expression requiring conduct—speech "plus" some action. In *Thornhill* the Hughes Court ruled that peaceful picketing is constitutionally protected expression. The protection of picketing, however, is conditional. The Stone Court was neither the first nor the last to view expression rights as less than absolutely protected. Picketing that is violent, for example, can certainly be regulated. Still, a state, in Justice Jackson's words, is not required to allow picketing "in all places and all circumstances" (*Bakery and Pastry Drivers v. Wohl*, 775). For the most part, however, the Stone Court protected picketing, particularly as it applied to labor unions. In *Cafeteria Employees Union v. Angelos* (1943), for example, the Court set aside a court order prohibiting a union from picketing a business as it attempted to organize the business's employees. The Court said a state cannot exclude working people from "putting their case to the public in a peaceful way" (*Cafeteria Employees*, 296).

One of the Stone Court's most significant free expression rulings came in *Thomas v. Collins* (1945). *Thomas v. Collins* did not involve picketing but rather an attempt by Texas to subject union organizing activity to a permit process. The state law required that any union organizer register with the state before attempting to solicit new members. The Stone Court struck down the Texas scheme and sent two extremely significant messages. The first involved the "preferred position" doctrine. Justice Rutledge spoke of the Court's duty to be particularly vigilant where First Amendment freedoms are involved. State regulations may not, said Rutledge, "trespass upon the domain set apart for free speech and free assembly" (*Thomas*, 530). The second message involved labor unions, a favored constituency of both the Roosevelt administration and the Stone Court. State legislation may not limit labor leaders to discussion of only "innocuous and abstract" matters (*Thomas*, 535). When it does so, it impairs the right of public discussion.

Rights of the Accused

A number of Stone Court justices were receptive to one or another of the incorporation positions—that some or all of the Bill of Rights provisions should apply not only to the federal government but to state governments as well. The split on the Stone Court in criminal rights cases was about incorporation rather than lack of commitment to procedural fairness as such. Enacting and administering criminal laws—exercising something called the police power—had been primarily a state function from the outset of American constitutional history. Since state cases amount to more than 99 percent of all criminal prosecutions, connecting the Bill of Rights was required if the federal constitutional protections were to have effect on the states, where the overwhelming majority of criminal cases are handled. No matter how important particular procedural rights were to the Stone Court justices, the difficulty was overcoming the argument that the administration of criminal justice was the exclusive domain of the states.

It was Justice Black's position that ratification of the Fourteenth Amendment had made the entire Bill of Rights applicable to the states. Frankfurter headed the bloc of justices who believed the Fourteenth Amendment's due process language applied only where fundamental fairness was denied. As a result, rights of the accused provisions of the Bill of Rights applied only to federal prosecutions, a handful of cases compared to the numbers of criminal cases in state court systems. This was an area where a more favorable rights expansion position might have been expected of the Stone Court, but it chose not to take one, leaving the states in virtually full control of criminal justice practices in their respective jurisdictions.

The Stone Court was occasionally receptive to claims of procedural rights violations, but only in federal cases. A limited exception involved involuntary or coerced confessions. In addition to a federal case in which a defendant was subjected to lengthy interrogation prior to arraignment (*McNabb v. United States* [1943]), the Stone Court reversed several state convictions on coerced confession grounds. In one of these cases, *Malinski v. New York* (1945), the Court upheld New York's rule requiring the trial judge to exclude confessions that were patently involuntary and allow a jury to determine the voluntariness and truthfulness of confessions in questionable cases. Although the Court decided cases like *Malinski* in favor of a state defendant, it was not prepared to apply the self-incrimination clause to the states in all cases. Cases such as *Malinski* were forerunners, albeit very limited and tentative, of such landmark Warren Court involuntary confession rulings as *Escobedo v. Illinois* (1964) and *Miranda v. Arizona* (1966).

The best example of the Stone Court's reluctance to intervene on criminal rights issues in state proceedings is *Betts v. Brady* (1942). The Hughes Court had ruled in *Powell v. Alabama* (1932) that states must provide counsel for indigent defendants in capital cases. *Powell* did not extend the assistance of counsel provision of the Sixth Amendment to the states, however. Rather, it reached its conclusion by applying the due process clause of the Fourteenth Amendment directly to death penalty cases. Six years later, in *Johnson v. Zerbst*, the Hughes Court required appointment of counsel for indigents in any felony-level prosecution.

Zerbst, however, applied only to federal defendants. *Betts v. Brady* involved an indigent defendant in a state felony case and provided the Stone Court with an opportunity to extend the assistance of counsel provision to all state felony cases. Once again, it chose not to do so, and Justice Roberts's opinion strongly emphasized the need for maintaining state control on administration of justice matters. Instead, the Court applied a case-specific fairness standard and concluded that state trials where indigent defendants are not provided with defense counsel are not inherently unfair. Only Justices Black, Douglas, and Murphy disagreed. Roberts suggested that state trial courts were free to appoint counsel in the "interest of justice" if they wished but said that the Supreme Court would not "straight-jacket" the states by imposing a categorical requirement that counsel be appointed (*Betts*, 472). Stone voted with the majority in *Betts v. Brady*, suggesting that his "preferred position" approach distinguished among individual rights—that all constitutionally protected rights are not equally important to achieving fundamental fairness in criminal cases.

Equal Protection

Justice Stone's *Carolene Products* footnote indicated that when legislation is aimed at "discrete and insular" minorities, the Court must engage in a more searching inquiry. Furthermore, the Stone Court subsequently stated in *Korematsu* that all legal restrictions that curtail the civil rights of a single racial group are "immediately suspect" and therefore "courts must subject them to the most rigid scrutiny." These statements seem to reveal that the Stone Court was perhaps prepared actively to pursue the objectives of equal protection. This was true at least to a degree. Although the Stone Court did not revisit the "separate but equal" doctrine from *Plessy v. Ferguson* (1896), which served as the legal foundation for racial segregation, it differed from its predecessors in its willingness to give fuller effect to the equal protection clause.

The most widely known of the Stone Court's race discrimination rulings outlawed the so-called white primary, but the Court also addressed racially discriminatory jury selection methods and segregation in interstate transportation. In addition, the Stone Court ruled that states could not discriminate against nonresidents by creating barriers to the movement of citizens across its borders. On balance, it is reasonable to suggest that part of the Stone Court's legacy is its contribution to contemporary equal protection jurisprudence.

The "white primary" case of *Smith v. Allwright* (1944) was significant because it removed a discriminatory practice from state election processes. More important, *Smith v. Allwright* indicated that the Court was willing to take a more aggressive approach in dealing with the "state action" requirement. Since the late nineteenth century, the Court had required that states must be party to discriminatory acts in order to trigger the provisions of the equal protection clause. As a result of this requirement, private acts of discrimination were outside the reach of the clause. The private character of political parties had long insulated the "white primary" practice from successful equal protection challenge. The Stone Court connected the actions of the Democratic Party of Texas, though technically a private entity, to the election apparatus of the state of Texas, thus meeting the state action requirement. In other words, the actions of the parties in nominating candidates for public office were viewed as part of the state's "machinery for choosing officials." Although the Stone Court did not consider doing away with the state action requirement itself, it signaled the beginning of a more diligent search for the linkage between discriminatory acts and state policies and practices.

The Stone Court also concluded that state segregation laws impermissibly impaired the interstate movement of travelers. The basis of the Court's ruling in *Morgan v. Virginia* (1946) was not the equal protection clause but rather the commerce clause. It was the Court's conclusion that the cumulative effect of state segregation laws burdened free travel and that a single, uniform national policy was necessary to protect interstate travel. *Morgan* would have been a stronger ruling had it been based on the equal protection clause, but it was a precursor of Warren Court decisions dealing with racial segregation.

The Stone Court also used the commerce clause in *Edwards v. California* (1941) to strike down a state law prohibiting the transport of an indigent person into the state. Justice Byrnes's opinion emphasized a national perspective in dealing with issues such as poverty. A state cannot "isolate itself" from the remaining states and the problems "common to all" states. This national vantage point would be used again in cases involving discriminatory state policies. A more significant consequence of *Edwards* was the view advanced by Justices Black, Douglas, and Murphy that a more effective way to deal with discriminatory policies was to use the Fourteenth Amendment—either the privileges and immunities or the equal protection clause. The Warren and Burger Courts would eventually expand the reach of the equal protection clause to classifications other than race, subjecting "suspect" classifications to the strictest judicial scrutiny. The thinking of several Stone Court justices influenced the evolution of equal protection jurisprudence during the Warren and Burger Court eras.

The Vinson Court Follows

Chief Justice Stone died in April 1946. The Court had been functioning with only eight justices through the 1945 term because of Justice Jackson's extended participation in the Nuremberg war crimes trials. Stone's death brought the Court's number to seven for the final weeks of the term.

Jackson and Douglas seemed the most likely to replace Stone. As more time passed without a selection, however, it became obvious that neither would be chosen. Selection of Jackson might have aggravated the Court's already deep division—it was rumored that as many as three of the justices had threatened to resign if Jackson were elevated. President Truman eventually picked Frederick M. Vinson in the hope that Vinson could better cope with the badly fractured Court. These hopes were immediately dashed following Jackson's transatlantic outburst directed at Justice Black.

Vinson's failure to achieve consensus on his Court are reflected in the increased number of nonunanimous decisions. After Stone's death, the percentage of split decisions rose to 64 percent in the 1946 term, 74 percent in 1948, and a record 81 percent in the 1952 term, the last under Vinson. Stone had called his Court a "team of wild horses"; McCloskey said it was "doubtful that Vinson's team was any more domesticated" (McCloskey 1972, 57). The Court remained stable in its membership after Stone's elevation to chief justice in 1941 until Vinson's death in 1952. During that period only five new justices joined the Court. Two particularly critical changes, however, were brought about by the deaths of Justices Murphy and Rutledge in 1949.

Readily identifiable voting blocs existed during the Stone and Vinson eras. Throughout their tenure on the Stone and Vinson Courts, Justices Black and Douglas formed a consistently liberal voting pair. In the 1941 term Black and Douglas were joined by Murphy and had an agreement rate of 82 percent. Two years later these three plus Rutledge faced a conservative bloc formed by the remainder of the Stone Court: Roberts (or Burton), Reed, Frankfurter, Stone, Byrnes (in the 1941 term only), and Jackson. Throughout the last three years of the Stone Court era (1943–1945), the liberal bloc broke into two pieces, with Black and Douglas forming one discrete bloc and Murphy and Rutledge the other. In 1946–1948 two identifiable conservative blocs emerged, with Vinson, Reed, and Burton in one and Frankfurter and Jackson in the other.

When Justices Minton and Clark replaced Murphy and Rutledge for the 1949–1952 terms, they joined the Vinson-Reed-Burton bloc. The conservative pair of Frankfurter-Jackson and the liberal pair of Black-Douglas remained. Truman's appointments of Vinson, Burton, Clark, and Minton significantly tilted the Vinson Court's balance in favor of the Frankfurter bloc. To Frankfurter and those voting with him, judicial restraint was the appropriate approach for a nonelected judiciary, regardless of the nature of the asserted interest(s) in particular cases. Failure to defer to legislative judgments was wholly incompatible with the basic presuppositions of representative democracy.

There was a clear difference of value orientation between the Vinson and Stone Courts, and this gap revealed itself almost immediately following Stone's death. A shift on constitutional rights issues began during Vinson's first term as chief justice. Following the lead of Justice Frankfurter, the Vinson Court took a decidedly less interventionist approach to civil liberties decision making and was much less receptive to asserted civil liberties violations. The proportion of decisions favorable to the individual rights claims was above 50 percent for each of the five years of the Stone Court, but the Vinson Court produced support of individual rights levels above 50 percent in only one of its seven terms. Across its five years, the Stone Court found for the individual in 65 percent of the cases, whereas the Vinson Court found for the government in only 42 percent of individual rights cases.

Vinson may have been the least effective chief justice in the Supreme Court's history. Appointed in 1946 after Stone's sudden death, Vinson had been a congressman and circuit judge and had served in executive positions, including a period as secretary of treasury. In fact, the justices regarded the new chief justice as only marginally equipped to handle the job. Stone had been criticized for his inability to effectively preside over the Court's conference session, although there was never any doubt about his intellectual capacity. Vinson was apparently even more inept in leading the conference, and he was regarded by some justices as having a "second-class" mind. His case presentations in conference were regarded as "shallow" and touching only the "obvious points." Throughout his tenure, many justices displayed their contempt for Vinson, some even suggesting a rotating chief justiceship. As Vinson's law clerk recalled it, several of Vinson's colleagues "would discuss in his presence the view that the Chief's job should rotate annually and . . . made no bones about regarding him—correctly—as their intellectual inferior" (Schwartz 1957, 253–254). Such a chief justice could scarcely be expected to lead the badly divided Court. If anything, the division among the justices intensified and, all too often, degenerated into personal animosity during Vinson's service.

The Stone Court had been profoundly influenced by the national emergency of World War II; the Stone Court era and the war are inseparable. The Vinson Court, in turn, was significantly influenced by the cold war that followed World War II. The Vinson Court decided a number of cases involving some aspect of the red scare—the growth of international communism around the world and the threat of Communist subversion within the United States. The most representative case is *Dennis v. United States* (1951), in which the Vinson Court upheld the Smith Act conviction of national leaders of the Communist Party of the United States. In *Dennis* the Court concluded that the advocacy of forcible overthrow of the government was constitutionally punishable. In upholding the convictions of Dennis and his fellow Communists, the Vinson Court modified the clear and present danger standard, which resulted in a heightened likelihood of governmental success in prosecuting "subversive" political activists. Just as the Stone Court had acquiesced in the Japanese relocation situation, the Vinson Court acquiesced in the face of the so-called red menace.

Compared to the Hughes and Stone Courts, the Vinson Court withdrew from the governmental spotlight and pursued a course of passive self-restraint. The Vinson Court was reluctant to press forward with individual rights issues, at least at the same pace as the Stone Court. This was most obvious in First Amendment cases. That is not to say, however, that the Vinson Court wholly abandoned the civil liberties legacy of the Stone Court. During the cold war the Vinson Court demonstrated a bias toward governmental authority and misgivings about the exercise of judicial power as a check on the elective branches of government. Nonetheless, there were significant jurisprudential developments in the areas of the church-state relationship and segregated public education. It was the Vinson Court that incorporated the establishment clause of the First Amendment in *Everson v. Board of Education of Ewing Township* (1947) and set the stage for overturning the "separate but equal" doctrine in *Sweatt v. Painter* (1950). The Warren Court expanded on both *Everson* and *Sweatt* as it fashioned a strict separationist establishment jurisprudence and abandoned "separate but equal" in *Brown v. Board of Education* (1954).

On balance, however, the Vinson Court disappointed those who hoped that the judiciary would "single-handedly lead America to a libertarian promised land." There were doubts about the Court's proper role in the American governance scheme during the Stone Court period, and those doubts "deepened" in the Vinson Court era. At the same time, the Vinson Court "maintained the essential continuity of modern constitutional law. It kept the light of freedom alive through a dark hour in the country's history; that light could now be passed on to the care of its successor" (McCloskey 1972, 126).

Conclusion

The Stone Court began an important transition in the kinds of cases that would make up the Court's docket. Over the next several decades, this transition would mark a dramatic change in the types of issues to which the Court would assign highest priority. There was, during the Stone Court years, a drop in the number of cases involving federal regulatory authority based on the commerce power. There was also a decrease in the number of cases reviewing federal taxing and spending initiatives. By the end of the Stone Court era, roughly a quarter of its docket was devoted to cases raising constitutional questions about individual rights. This compares to a level of about 3 percent during the Hughes Court period. A central element of the Stone Court legacy, then, was its redefining of the Court's priorities—or at least its start down that road. Economic regulation and property rights questions remained primary during World War II, but issues focusing on constitutional protections became increasingly prominent. The Vinson Court would continue this shift in priorities, though seemingly without the same enthusiasm. Nonetheless, the shift would provide the foundation for the individual rights jurisprudence of the Warren Court.

A more important aspect of the Stone Court legacy is the quality of debate it provided on a number of critical questions. Some of the finest minds in the Court's history sat on the Stone Court. These justices were in fundamental disagreement on such issues as judicial role—the activism-restraint issue—but such considerations as "preferred position" and incorporation were more explicitly added to the debate. The quality of the exchanges among the Stone Court justices did not result in resolution of their disagreements, but the thinking of these justices informed the views of jurists for the remainder of the century, particularly the justices of the Warren Court.

The debate about the appropriate role of the Court vis-à-vis the elective branches of government did not begin with the Stone Court. Justices Holmes and Brandeis in particular discussed this point extensively. A quarter century before *Darby Lumber*, in *Hammer v. Dagenhart* (1918), Holmes defended the congressional judgment to ban from interstate commerce items produced by child labor. He argued that the wisdom of such legislative policy determinations were outside the scope of judicial review. Brandeis would subsequently extend this view to issues of policy implementation—the means by which the burgeoning federal bureaucracy administered federal regulations and programs. Holmes and Brandeis believed that the Court ought to exercise closer scrutiny in individual rights cases, but Stone's *Carolene Products* footnote expressly suggesting the "preferred position" doctrine followed their service on the Court. Furthermore, divergent perspectives on such matters were not advanced as effectively by those with whom Holmes and Brandeis served as was true during the Stone Court period. Discussions on individual rights and the Court's role in protecting them had not featured the participation of as many legal philosophical giants as Justices Stone, Frankfurter, Black, Jackson, and Douglas, with Murphy and Rutledge contributing valuable perspectives as well. Holmes and Brandeis shared common viewpoints, whereas more diverse thoughts on these issues were represented in the Stone Court. This provided compelling point-counterpoint to an unprecedented extent.

The most prominent philosophical protagonists were Justices Frankfurter and Black. Frankfurter attempted to find specific constitutional limits on judicial power, arguing that legislatures were better qualified than the judiciary to make judgments about such matters as school administration, legislative redistricting and reapportionment, and even threats posed by subversives. Frankfurter's view was also favorable to assertions of state sovereignty and reflected the belief that the growth of the judicial power of the national government potentially threatened the federal-state balance. When utilized in concrete cases, Frankfurter's principles tended to favor outcomes that preserved both established legal doctrines and legislative judgments.

Like Frankfurter, Black doubted the judicial capacity to make national policy, but unlike Frankfurter, he contended that the Constitution's text itself precludes certain judicial choices. In addition, Black retained the populism of many New Dealers. He distrusted the abstract legal doctrines that were so important to Frankfurter. Black consistently argued for a literal interpretation of the Constitution's prohibitions. By the time the Vinson Court period had ended, Black was arguing that the language of the First Amendment placed an "absolute" prohibition on Congress that prevented legislative action in these areas. He also believed that the due process clause of the Fourteenth Amendment imposed the same limitations on the states. In his view, when legislatures seek to limit such things as expression, association, or religion, constitutional mandates rather than the judiciary restrain them. Black believed that judges simply have no competence to evaluate policy judgments of the elective branches of government outside the areas referred to by the Constitution.

Black's position more closely corresponded to the "preferred position" doctrine, in which Stone had declared that judicial scrutiny of laws that affected freedoms of expression and association should be most stringent. This position is the immediate intellectual precursor of the Warren and, to a degree, the Burger Courts' use of "strict judicial scrutiny" to protect "insular minorities" and "fundamental freedoms." Frankfurter and those sharing his views were quick to point out that this approach to constitutional interpretation was both simplistic and a device to mask substantive policy objectives of the Court. As they saw it, the meaning of such constitutional terms as "due process" required judicial interpretation, and the "preferred position" approach was too subjective and lacking in clear standards to guide the Court's interpretive function.

The activism-restraint debate was redefined by the introduction of the "preferred position" concept. The justices could agree that deference to legislative judgments was desirable in matters relating to regulation of the national economy and property rights. There were years of protracted battle on this point prior to the 1937 "revolution," but this issue was largely resolved by the time Stone became chief justice. The "preferred position" concept, in contrast, was incompatible with the legislative deference approach. Preferred position created the need for a departure from the legislative deference value. The Court could not aggressively protect the rights of individuals against impermissible government action without elevating the likelihood that legislative judgments would be struck down. This seemed paradoxical. What was required was what Abraham referred to as the "double standard," one approach for matters involving constitutionally protected rights and another for everything else. The justifications for such a double standard would be fully embraced by the Warren Court.

Finally, the incorporation question had received discussion since the ratification of the Fourteenth Amendment, but more seriously in the 1920s as the Taft Court concluded in *Gitlow v. New York* (1925) that the First Amendment's free speech provision applied to the states. The Hughes Court carried the debate further and offered, in *Palko v. Connecticut* (1937), a means by which certain Bill of Rights provisions might be selectively extended to the states. The Stone Court did not formally add to the list of selectively incorporated rights, but the views expressed in several coerced confession and assistance of counsel cases allowed the debate to be carried into the Warren Court period, when many constitutional protections, particularly those pertaining to criminal justice, were formally incorporated.

More should not be made of the Stone Court's legacy than its record warrants. The Stone Court was part of the transition from the period of judicial supremacy that existed until the 1937 "revolution" to one of judicial restraint. The Stone Court rulings stemming from the war emergency substantially reinforced the norm of restraint. At the same time, the Stone Court wrestled with the question of the Court's giving effect to constitutional rights. Where that would lead was not clear in 1946, when Chief Justice Stone died, or even during the seven years of the Vinson Court. A conclusion would finally be reached by the Warren Court. The Stone Court is perhaps best regarded as a bridging Court, one that facilitates the transition from one time and jurisprudence to another. In that capacity the Stone Court served well.

References

Abraham, Henry J. *Justices and Presidents: A Political History of Appointments to the Supreme Court.* 3rd edition. New York: Oxford University Press, 1992.

Currie, David P. "The New Deal Court in the 1940s: Its Constitutional Legacy." *Journal of Supreme Court History* 87, 1997: 87–98.

———. *The Constitution in the Supreme Court: The Second Century, 1888–1986.* Chicago: University of Chicago Press, 1990.

McCloskey, Robert G. *The Modern Supreme Court.* Cambridge: Harvard University Press, 1972.

Schwartz, Bernard. *The Supreme Court: Constitutional Revolution in Retrospect.* New York: Ronald Press, 1957.

Swindler, William F. *Court and Constitution in the Twentieth Century: The New Legality, 1932–1968.* Indianapolis, Ind.: Bobbs-Merrill, 1974.

tenBroek, Jacobus, Edward N. Barnhart, and Floyd W. Matson. *Prejudice, War and the Constitution: Causes and Consequences of the Evacuation of the Japanese Americans in World War II.* Berkeley: University of California Press, 1970.

PART TWO

Reference Materials

Key People, Laws, and Events

Agricultural Adjustment Acts (AAA)

The Agricultural Adjustment Act (AAA) of 1933 was the first of Franklin Roosevelt's New Deal programs addressing agricultural relief. It was enacted near the end of the famous Hundred Days at the outset of Roosevelt's first term. American farmers were suffering from extremely low prices for their commodities largely as a result of oversupply. The AAA of 1933 sought to stabilize prices for agricultural commodities by regulating production. The law levied a tax on agricultural processors and used the proceeds to subsidize farmers for letting acreage remain unplanted or shifting it to nonsurplus crops—the program created incentives to reduce or eliminate the planting of potentially surplus crops. The Hughes Court invalidated the AAA of 1933 in *United States v. Butler* (1936) by a 6–3 vote. The *Butler* decision revealed how bitterly divided the justices were on crucial constitutional issues raised by New Deal proposals. Justice Owen Roberts argued for the majority that the processing tax was in reality part of a program to regulate agricultural production. Although Congress could subsidize farmers through general welfare expenditures, the regulations contained in the AAA of 1933 impermissibly encroached on state power over agriculture and thus violated the Tenth Amendment. The design for regulation, Roberts contended, was no less real for being disguised under supposedly voluntary crop controls.

Following the *Butler* decision, Congress enacted the Agricultural Adjustment Act of 1938 aimed at price maintenance for cotton, wheat, corn, tobacco, and rice. Constitutionally justified by the effect of agricultural production on interstate commerce, the law provided for a system of marketing quotas to be imposed by the secretary of agriculture, subject to approval by referendum of two-thirds of the producers concerned. The Supreme Court struck down the 1933 act on state sovereignty grounds essentially but upheld the 1938 act in *Mulford v. Smith* (1939) as a permissible use of the federal commerce power. The Supreme Court held that Congress could limit the amount of a crop sold in interstate commerce and that Congress had issued sufficiently precise objectives as it delegated authority to the secretary of agriculture to implement the act.

Alien Registration Act of 1940 (Smith Act)

The first federal regulation of expression and association since the Alien and Sedition Acts of 1798, the Alien Registration Act, more commonly known as the Smith Act, required aliens living in the United States to register with the federal government. Any alien found to be associated with a subversive organization could be deported. The primary objective of the statute, however, was its restrictions on certain kinds of political expression even by U.S. citizens. The Smith Act prohibited, among other things, advocacy of the violent overthrow of the government, the publication of materials espousing forcible overthrow, and the organizing of groups dedicated to revolution.

The Vinson Court validated the Smith Act in *Dennis v. United States* (1951). Dennis was the head of the Communist Party of the United States. The criminal charges brought against him and other party leaders were confined to illegal advocacy and conspiracy. The Vinson Court upheld the convictions. Chief Justice Vinson, reshaped the "clear and present danger" test and suggested that in cases such as these courts must ask whether the "gravity of the evil, discounted by its improbability, justifies . . . invasion of free speech." Vinson said the severity of the danger in this case was great enough that it need not be imminent. Regarding imminence, he reasoned, "obviously, the words of the test cannot mean that before the Government may act, it must wait until the putsch is about to be executed, the plans have been laid, and the signal is awaited." Not only is governmental response allowed in such a situation, but it is required if the government is "aware that a group aiming at its overthrow is attempting to indoctrinate its members and to commit them to a course whereby they will strike when the leaders feel the circumstances permit." The likelihood that the threat will succeed is not required either. An attempt to overthrow the government by force, even though doomed from the outset, is a "sufficient evil for Congress to prevent it" (*Dennis*, 509–510).

Atlantic Charter

A joint statement issued by President Franklin Roosevelt and Prime Minister Winston Churchill on August 14, 1941, the Atlantic Charter was the product of several days of meetings between the two held on the USS *Augusta* as it lay anchored in the North Atlantic just off the coast of Newfoundland. The charter contained eight principles upon which at least short-term U.S. and British foreign policy would be based. The United States and Britain both agreed to forgo any territorial aggrandizement and expressed the hope that no other territorial changes occurred inconsistent with the "freely expressed wishes of the peoples concerned," a mutual commitment to the principle of self-determination. The charter also expressed the hope that international trade and economic development could be fostered with the "fullest collaboration" among all nations. Finally, the charter called for world peace and disarmament following the "final destruction of the Nazi tyranny." The principles contained in the charter allowed Roosevelt to commit to a framework on which U.S. and Allied policy could be based both during and after any war. Churchill had hoped that Roosevelt would formally declare war against Germany and issue a strong and joint warning to Japan. Roosevelt chose to do neither. Although he agreed to provide naval escort supply ships partway across the North Atlantic, he promised nothing further, preferring instead to let subsequent events determine whether the United States would further escalate its involvement. As for the Japanese, Roosevelt issued a guarded unilateral statement instead of joining Churchill in a stronger, joint warning.

Biddle, Francis B.

A Philadelphia-born corporate trial attorney, Francis Biddle became a significant figure in Franklin Roosevelt's final two terms as president. Biddle was educated at Harvard, earning his B.A. cum laude in 1909 and his LL.D. cum laude in 1911. Biddle served as private secretary to Supreme Court justice Oliver Wendell Holmes in 1912 before returning to Philadelphia, where he was associated with two prestigious law firms. He spent several years as special assistant to the U.S. attorney for the Eastern District of Pennsylvania from 1922 to 1926. Although a Republican in the 1920s, he switched parties when Roosevelt was elected president in 1932 and eventually became an ardent New Dealer. In late 1934 he became the chair of the National Labor Relations Board established by the National Industrial Recovery Act. When the NIRA was struck down by the Hughes Court, he returned to Philadelphia and resumed private practice. He left his practice three years later to became a judge of the U.S. Court of Appeals for the Third Circuit. The following year, however, he resigned the life-tenure judgeship to become solicitor general. Biddle subsequently became attorney general when Robert Jackson was appointed to the Supreme Court. He oversaw the successful prosecution of the German saboteurs in 1942. Biddle provided both legal and political counsel to Roosevelt during World War II, but his advice against mass evacuation of the Japanese was not heeded. He retired from government service after Roosevelt's death in 1945.

Bituminous Coal Act of 1935 (Guffey-Snyder Act)

The Bituminous Coal Act created a National Bituminous Coal Commission and gave it the authority to regulate coal prices. The act used the same industrial code-making design as the National Industrial Recovery Act of 1933, setting district boards in coal-producing regions to write code provisions. It also levied a 15 percent tax on all coal sold at the mine head, nine-tenths of which was remitted to producers who accepted the code provisions. A separate section guaranteed collective bargaining between mine owners and miners and provided that when negotiated wages covered more than half the country's miners, the wage levels would be binding upon the entire industry. In *Carter v. Carter Coal Co.* (1936), the Court declared the act unconstitutional in a 6–3 decision. Justice Sutherland, citing *United States v. E. C. Knight Co.* (1895), held the labor provisions void on the ground that they regulated an aspect of production having only an indirect effect on interstate commerce. Despite the expressed intention of Congress to separate the labor and price-fixing sections of the law, Sutherland contended that the legislature would not have enacted the other sections without the labor provisions. The "bone and sinew" of the law were gone, so the price-fixing provisions were unconstitutional as well. Reduced to simplest terms, Sutherland's argument was that price-fixing was unconstitutional because it was too closely bound up with matters directly reserved to the states.

Bowles, Chester

A New York advertising man who headed the Office of Price Administration during World War II, Chester Bowles was an ardent New Dealer. The administrative and public relations skills he exhibited during his tenure as head of the Connecticut Office of Price Control brought him to Roosevelt's attention. He became Roosevelt's federal price administrator in late 1943, replacing Leon Henderson. As price administrator, Bowles attempted to contain inflationary pressures and developed strong public and congressional backing for the fiscal controls necessitated by the war. Later he served as Truman's director of the Office of Economic Stabilization, then as a special consultant to the secretary-general of the United Nations until 1948, when he was elected governor of Connecticut. An early supporter of John Kennedy, he became Kennedy's principal foreign policy adviser during the campaign, then special adviser on African, Asian, and Latin American affairs after a brief period as undersecretary of state. In 1963 he was appointed ambassador to India, a post he held until April 1969, when he retired from public life.

Brandeis, Louis D.

Brandeis began a private law practice in Boston following graduation from Harvard Law School. He redefined the attorney's role from the outset of his practice. He was the first to do pro bono legal work, for example, and he introduced the "Brandeis brief" when he argued on behalf of a state ten-hour work law for women in *Muller v. Oregon* (1908). He assisted in fashioning Woodrow Wilson's New Freedom program, the term used to describe Wilson's reform agenda. The New Freedom program was intended to ensure competitiveness within a market economy and included, among other things, such economic reforms as tariff reduction and strengthening of antitrust sanctions.

Wilson thought of making Brandeis his solicitor general but instead nominated him to the Supreme Court to succeed Joseph R. Lamar in 1916. The nomination triggered a four-month confirmation battle during which conservative opponents unsuccessfully sought to defeat the nomination.

Brandeis believed that judges should defer to legislative judgments in matters of economic policy, although he took a different approach when governmental actions affected individual liberties. Brandeis suggested in *Gilbert v. Minnesota* (1920) that the liberty guaranteed by the Fourteenth Amendment went beyond property rights to include personal freedoms as well, the first time that a justice had suggested that the Bill of Rights impose limits on the states through the Fourteenth Amendment. Brandeis is perhaps best known for his advocacy of limited judicial intervention in policymaking; such restraint was a key element of his jurisprudence. Brandeis believed it was both undemocratic and unwise for judges to substitute their views for those of elected legislators. Perhaps his most comprehensive statement about the limits of judicial review came in *Ashwander v. TVA* (1936).

Bridges, Harry

A labor leader on the West Coast, Harry Bridges was the central party in two Court decisions in the early 1940s. Australian by birth, Bridges came to the United States in 1920 and eventually was elected president of the West Coast district of the International Longshoremen's Association (ILA). Bridges was seen by much of the public, employers, and government officials as a power-hungry figure with disturbing connections to the Communists, and an investigation was conducted to determine if Bridges could be deported for "affiliating" with the Communists. The deportation initiative failed. Soon thereafter, a state court ruled against the ILA in a dispute with another union. While a motion for a new trial was pending, Bridges sent a communication to the secretary of labor threatening a strike across the entire Pacific Coast if enforcement of the state court's ruling were attempted. The state court cited Bridges for contempt for attempting to interfere with the judicial process by threatening a strike even before the court ruled on the pending motion. The Stone Court reversed the contempt citation in *Bridges v. California* (1941), however, concluding that there was no "clear and present danger" of improper influence on the state court. The second case arose out of yet another government effort to deport Bridges for his alleged Communist affiliations. Bridges and others were ordered deported, but the Stone Court set aside the orders in *Bridges v. Wixom* (1945), concluding that the deportation hearings lacked procedural fairness by admitting hearsay and otherwise unreliable statements adverse to Bridges.

Brown v. Board of Education (1954)

In *Brown v. Board of Education*, the Supreme Court overruled the "separate but equal" doctrine and declared that racial segregation in public schools was unconstitutional. The *Brown* case came from the Topeka, Kansas, schools, but companion cases from school districts in Delaware, Virginia, South Carolina, and the District of Columbia were decided with *Brown* as well. All the cases raised the common legal question of whether de jure (mandated by law) racial segregation in public elementary and secondary schools was constitutional. After taking arguments in December 1952, the Court postponed a decision and ordered reargument the following December. During the intervening year, Earl Warren replaced Fred M. Vinson as chief justice. The Court's unanimous decision, which came in May 1954, was accompanied by a single opinion written by the new chief justice. Warren declared that constitutional status of de jure segregation is determined by "examining the effect of racial segregation on the public educational process." In making this judgment, the Court is obliged to consider public school "in the light of its full development and its present place in American life" (*Brown I*, 492). Given the fundamental nature of education, opportunity to acquire it must be available to all on equal terms. The controlling question was whether segregation deprived minority children of equal educational opportunity. The Court concluded that it did. The basis of the Court's judgment was extensive psychological evidence, which showed that segregation negatively affected the educational development of minority students. "To separate them from others of similar age and qualifications solely because of their race generates a feeling of inferiority as to their status in the community that may affect their hearts and minds in a way unlikely ever to be undone." The doctrine of "separate but equal has no place in public education," and separate educational facilities are "inherently unequal" (*Brown I*, 494–495).

The *Brown* case returned to the Court the following year for consideration of implementation. In *Brown v. Board of Education* (1955), known as *Brown II*, the Court concluded that "full implementation may require solution of varied local school problems." Lower federal courts were given the responsibility of monitoring desegregation efforts at the local level. Locally devised plans were to be compatible with the requirements of *Brown I*, and local authorities were expected to make "prompt and reasonable start toward full compliance." Although no deadline was set, the Court indicated that constitutional violations must be relieved "with all deliberate speed" (*Brown II*, 301).

Butler, Pierce

Pierce Butler was raised in rural Minnesota, and although a lifelong Democrat, he was extremely conservative ideologically. He served as special prosecutor in several antitrust cases, but most of his private practice was devoted to defending railroads from government regulation. Butler's nomination to the Supreme Court in 1923 was marked by controversy and political maneuvering. His legal conservatism attracted powerful Republicans, such as Chief Justice William Howard Taft, on whose recommendation President Warren Harding nominated Butler. Catholic and business groups backed him strongly, but labor and progressive organizations opposed him with equal vigor. Despite extensive Senate debate, only eight senators actually voted against Butler's confirmation, although twenty-seven others abstained. He was one of the Court's last advocates of substantive due process as a means of protecting property rights, a constitutional doctrine that failed to achieve a majority during his final three years on the Court. Butler was one of the dogmatic laissez-faire justices on the Hughes Court. Known as the "Four Horsemen," these justices opposed all of Roosevelt's New Deal proposals during the 1930s.

Cardozo, Benjamin Nathan

Benjamin Cardozo was nominated in 1914 by the newly formed anti–Tammany Hall Fusion Party as a candidate for the New York Supreme Court. He was elected by the slimmest of pluralities. Only a month after taking his seat, he was appointed to a vacancy on the New York Court of Appeals, where he remained until his appointment to the U.S. Supreme Court in 1932. As chief justice of the New York Court of Appeals, Cardozo achieved national recognition. When Justice Holmes left the Court, Cardozo was widely regarded as the most suitable successor, and President Herbert Hoover was lobbied strongly to nominate Cardozo to the Supreme Court. Once nominated, Cardozo won quick and unanimous Senate confirmation. As Holmes before him, he joined Justices Brandeis and Stone in advocating deference to congressional policy choices. He delivered the majority opinions in *Steward Machine Co. v. Davis* (1937) and *Helvering v. Davis* (1937), in which the Court upheld provisions of the Social Security Act as constitutional uses of congressional taxing and spending power. One of Cardozo's most important opinions came in *Palko v. Connecticut* (1937), where he defined a process of "selective incorporation" for determining which Bill of Rights provisions apply to the actions of state governments. Cardozo was a liberal, but his belief in judicial restraint led him to defer to legislative judgments in most instances. He supported the expansion of federal power and typically voted to uphold Roosevelt's New Deal programs. He died on July 9, 1938, after serving only seven terms on the Supreme Court.

Civilian Conservation Corps (CCC)

A New Deal relief program established in 1933, the Civilian Conservation Corps aimed at putting young people to work. The CCC was Roosevelt's first step in providing emergency unemployment relief and was one of the most popular New Deal initiatives. It placed more than 3 million youth in jobs before it was phased out in 1942. A related program, the Federal Emergency Relief Administration (FERA), was created at the same time to coordinate distribution of federal unemployment assistance to the states. World War II brought an end to the CCC and other New Deal relief agencies as the war economy diminished the need for such programs on a national level.

Clark, Tom Campbell

Tom Clark was a U.S. attorney general and Supreme Court justice. His legal career began in Texas, where he had both a private practice and was an assistant district attorney. Clark took a position with the U.S. Department of Justice in 1937, and he was transferred to the Antitrust Division as chief of its Wage and Hours Unit a year later. Following the attack on Pearl Harbor, Clark was designated the civilian relocation coordinator, a job that involved handling the legal aspects of the relocation and internment of Japanese Americans. He took charge of the Antitrust Division's War Frauds Unit in late 1942 and worked closely with Senator Harry Truman. His work in this unit impressed not only Truman but also Attorney General Francis Biddle, who promoted Clark to assistant attorney general. Clark headed the Antitrust Division until late 1943, when Biddle reorganized the Justice Department and Clark became director of the Criminal Division. Clark supported Truman for the vice presidential nomination at the 1944 Democratic National Convention. The next year Truman succeeded Roosevelt as president. Biddle, with whom Truman had political differences, resigned, and Truman appointed Clark attorney general.

During his tenure as attorney general, Clark fostered civil rights for African Americans. He was also one of the principal architects of the Truman administration's domestic anti-Communist program, and he authorized the 1948 prosecution of the top leaders of the American Communist Party under the Smith Act. The following year Truman nominated Clark for the Supreme Court. When Earl Warren replaced Fred Vinson as chief justice, the Court took a more liberal direction, and Clark did so as well, but only briefly. The appointment of liberal justices in the 1960s made Clark a permanent member of the conservative minority on internal security and criminal rights issues. He maintained, however, his support of civil rights initiatives and consistently supported the Warren Court's efforts to advance the interests of racial minorities. He spoke for the Court in both *Heart of Atlanta Motel v. United States* and *Katzenbach v. McClung* (1964), rulings that upheld the Title II (public accommodations) provisions of the Civil Rights Act of 1964. Clark also supported the Warren Court's intervention into legislative districting as well as its decisions on prayer and Bible reading in public schools. Clark, the former prosecutor, often disagreed with the Warren Court's liberal majority in the area of rights of the accused. In 1967 Lyndon Johnson appointed Clark's son Ramsey attorney general. Clark believed that his continued presence on the Court would compromise his son's work, and he resigned. Following his retirement, he frequently acted as a trial judge and later served as the first director of the Federal Judicial Center.

Cohen, Benjamin V.

Cohen earned a degree from Harvard Law School in 1916. At Harvard Cohen attracted the attention of Felix Frankfurter, a member of the law faculty, and on Frankfurter's recommendation Cohen became one of Roosevelt's principal advisers. Cohen initially worked on securities legislation with Thomas Corcoran and James Landis, two other Frankfurter protégés. Cohen then served under the supervision of Interior Secretary Harold Ickes as associate general counsel for the Public Works Administration (PWA) and counsel for the National Power Policy Committee. Cohen was a highly skilled legislative craftsman and had a particularly productive partnership with Corcoran. He and Corcoran participated in writing such significant New Deal proposals as the Securities Exchange Act of 1934, the Public Utilities Holding Company Act, and the Fair Labor Standards Act of 1938. Foreign policy issues came to occupy more of Roosevelt's attention after the 1940 election, and Corcoran provided counsel to Roosevelt on the 1940 destroyers-for-bases deal with Britain and helped draft the Lend-Lease Act. In 1941 he left the Department of Interior and became counsel to the U.S. ambassador to the Court of St. James. Beginning in 1943, he acted as general counsel to the Office of War Mobilization and helped draft the Dumbarton Oaks agreement, which provided the basis for the United Nations Charter. After Cohen spent a brief period outside the government, Truman appointed him general counsel to the State Department, and Cohen became one of Secretary of State James F. Byrnes's closest aides.

Corcoran, Thomas G.

Thomas Corcoran was a member of Franklin Roosevelt's inner circle of political advisers. At Harvard Law School, Corcoran and Benjamin Cohen were among Felix Frankfurter's protégés. Graduating at the top of his class at Harvard, Corcoran served as secretary to Justice Oliver Wendell Holmes. After a period of private practice in New York City, Corcoran joined the Reconstruction Finance Corporation in 1932. Soon thereafter, Roosevelt was elected, and Corcoran and Cohen teamed up to write a number of Roosevelt's New Deal proposals. Among others, Cohen and Corcoran were responsible for the Securities Tax of 1933, the Securities Exchange Act of 1934, and the Public Utility Holding Company Act of 1935. In addition, they worked on the judicial reorganization (Court-packing) plan, wages and hours legislation, the Tennessee Valley Authority, and the Electric Farm and Home Authority. Corcoran suffered some during the second term because of his association with such measures as the

Court-packing proposal and Roosevelt's unsuccessful attempt to purge conservative congressional Democrats in the midterm election of 1938. He resigned from the RFC in 1940 to serve on Roosevelt's campaign. After Roosevelt's reelection, Corcoran began a private law practice through which he established himself as one of the first lobbyists who used political connections to represent clients in their dealings with the government.

Cummings, Homer S.

A Chicago-born attorney who served as Franklin Roosevelt's attorney general from 1933 to 1939, Cummings completed his legal education at Yale, graduating in 1893. He began private practice with Charles D. Lockwood soon thereafter in Stamford, Connecticut. Cummings was regarded as an outstanding trial attorney and was extensively involved in local politics. After an unsuccessful candidacy for secretary of state in Connecticut in 1896, he was elected mayor of Stamford three times beginning in 1900. He failed in bids to win election to the U.S. House of Representatives and Senate but served as a state's attorney from 1914 to 1924. Cummings was extensively involved with the national Democratic Party. He was a national committeeman from Connecticut and national chair of the party from 1914 to 1920. Cummings was instrumental in Roosevelt's gaining the party's presidential nomination in 1932. In exchange for his support, Roosevelt offered to appoint Cummings governor-general of the Philippines. Just prior to his inauguration, however, Roosevelt's choice for attorney general died suddenly and Roosevelt selected Cummings as the replacement. Cummings served as U.S. attorney general for seven years. During his tenure he was responsible for a number of administrative changes in the Department of Justice, including broadening the department's criminal jurisdiction. More important, Cummings and his department defended many of the New Deal programs in the courts. Although he was successful in expanding the federal role in the criminal process, Cummings did not keep the courts from striking down many of the economic reforms of the New Deal. In 1935–1936 Roosevelt suffered a number of judicial reversals of such central New Deal programs as the NIRA, AAA, and Guffey-Snyder Act. Like Roosevelt, Cummings saw the 1936 election as a mandate both for Roosevelt and the New Deal, and he sought to exact some revenge on the Supreme Court. At Roosevelt's urging, but without wider consideration by Roosevelt's other legal and political advisers, Cummings fashioned the Judicial Reform Act—the so-called Court-packing proposal—which provided for the naming of additional judges to the federal courts. Roosevelt and Cummings persisted until the proposal was killed in the Senate. Cummings resigned from the Roosevelt administration in 1939 and pursued a private legal practice in Washington, D.C., until his death in 1956.

DeWitt, General John L.

Head of the Western Defense Command during World War II, John DeWitt was in charge of the Japanese relocation on the West Coast. He had been commandant of the Army War College in Washington until November 1939, when he was promoted to the rank of lieutenant general. On February 19, 1942, President Franklin Roosevelt issued Executive Order No. 9066, which authorized the War Department to designate "military areas" from which any persons, including citizens, might be excluded. The mass evacuation of the Japanese began in March 1942 under DeWitt's direction. Ironically, the very absence of real evidence of espionage or sabotage fueled fears about the Japanese on the West Coast. In September 1943 DeWitt was made commandant of the Army and Navy Staff College in Washington, D.C., where he remained until he retired from the military in 1947. The detention of the Japanese ended the following year.

Economic Stabilization, Office of (OES)

The Office of Economic Stabilization was created by executive order in October 1942 to coordinate efforts to achieve national economic stability during World War II. The agency's name changed to the Office of War Mobilization less than a year later, and Roosevelt picked Supreme Court justice James F. Byrnes to direct it. The Byrnes appointment reflected Roosevelt's recognition of the highly political character of economic mobilization. Byrnes was a skillful negotiator, popular with members of Congress, and completely loyal to Roosevelt. Controlling the cost of living was critical to the success of the OES, and Byrnes believed controlling the flow of scarce resources was essential to achieving that objective. Less than a month after his appointment, Byrnes put into effect something called the Controlled Materials Plan, which established a priorities system for three vital materials: steel, copper, and aluminum.

Emergency Management, Office of (OEM)

Created by Franklin Roosevelt on May 25, 1940, the Office of Emergency Management was intended to be the agency through which Roosevelt directed the effort to mobilize for war; Roosevelt's action was based on authority derived from the Defense Act of 1916, passed by Congress to enable President Woodrow Wilson to more effectively manage the nation's interests in World War I. The OEM was one of a number of wartime agencies established by administrative order, an approach that facilitated Roosevelt's creation of defense organizations structurally outside the regular executive departments.

Emergency Price Control Act of 1942 (EPCA)

The EPCA became law on January 30, 1942. The legislation authorized an expanded price-control program, which was seen as essential in bringing inflation under control. Its principal purpose was to stabilize prices by preventing unwarranted increases in prices and rents. The EPCA was also intended to assure that military appropriations were not affected by excessive prices and to prevent any collapse of price structure following the war. The EPCA directed that it "shall be the policy of the departments and agencies of the government dealing with wages, within the limits of their authority and jurisdiction, to work toward a stabilization of prices, fair and equitable wages, and cost of production." The administration of the act was located with the Office of Price Administration, which could issue such regulations and orders thought necessary to achieve the objectives of the act. The OPA's price administrator had authority to impose ceilings on a broad range of consumer items, from raw materials to finished goods, and to sanction those who did not comply with the ceilings. The EPCA also set up an Emergency Court of Appeals, the only court with jurisdiction to enjoin price control orders or regulations; it was limited to permanent injunctions. The EPCA and actions of the OPA were the only components of the war program challenged before the Supreme Court, albeit unsuccessfully.

Executive Order 9066

Franklin Roosevelt issued Executive Order 9066 on February 19, 1942. The order authorized the War Department to designate "military areas" from which specified persons might be removed or excluded. Secretary of War Henry Stimson implemented the order only on the West Coast and only against those of Japanese ancestry. Roosevelt established a civilian agency, the War Relocation Authority, to manage the evacuation and internment of persons of Japanese ancestry. Under its authority, evacuation centers were set up where evacuees could be settled for the duration of their internment. Beginning in March 1942, the evacuations were carried out gradually through a series of civilian evacuation orders from General John L. DeWitt. The orders were based on the military's insistence that widespread evacuation was necessary for the defense of the West Coast. The Court deferred to military judgment in the belief that the military should have full authority to defend the country in time of war. As the war progressed and the danger to the nation diminished, the Supreme Court in the *Ex parte Endo* (1944) decision ruled that the War Relocation Authority could not detain Japanese Americans whose loyalty was not in doubt. (Selected documents pertaining to the evacuation of the Japanese, including the text of Executive Order No. 9066, appear in the appendices to this volume.)

Executive Reorganization Act of 1939

Franklin Roosevelt created a commission on administrative management in 1936 known as the Brownlow Commission, which was to offer recommendations aimed at improving administrative policymaking. The commission proposed a number of reforms that would enable Roosevelt more effectively to meet the policymaking needs of a modern national government. In January 1937 the commission's recommendations were presented to Congress in a bill for executive reorganization (along with the Court reform bill) but was not taken up by the Senate until the following year. Senate and House differences on the initial proposal prompted a revised and narrower reorganization bill, which was approved in 1939. Even in its more restricted version, the act provided the foundation for the modern presidency. In the short term it gave Roosevelt the authority to consolidate already existing administrative agencies. Under terms of the act, Roosevelt created the Executive Office of the President, transferred the Bureau of the Budget out of the Treasury Department to the new office, and enlarged the White House staff.

Fair Labor Standards Act of 1938 (FLSA)

The FLSA established national standards for wages and hours of work. The law was based on congressional power to regulate interstate commerce and covered all employees either directly involved in such commerce or in the production of items for interstate commerce. It closed interstate commerce to products of firms violating the wage provisions or employing child labor in the production of goods for interstate shipment. A unanimous Supreme Court upheld the FLSA in *United States v. Darby Lumber Co.* (1941). Darby Lumber challenged the FLSA, contending that it was only "nominally" a commerce regulation and that its real objective was to regulate production conditions. The Court disagreed. Justice Stone said that the purpose of the regulation was to "make effective" the congressional objective that interstate commerce should not be made the "instrument of competition" in the distribution of goods "produced under substandard labor conditions." The Court concluded that Congress could reasonably find such competition "injurious" to interstate commerce and found the wage and hour regulations closely enough related to interstate commerce to bring them within congressional reach. Indeed, Chief Justice Stone said that the commerce power extends beyond interstate commerce as such to intrastate activities that "affect" interstate commerce.

Federal Emergency Relief Administration (FERA)

Created in 1933 to coordinate the distribution of direct federal unemployment assistance, FERA was initially charged with dispensing some $500 million in federal relief money through grants to state and local governments for public projects. Approximately half this amount went to the states on a matching basis—one federal dollar for three state dollars. With FERA the federal government took its first steps into direct relief programming, a step that started the United States on a course toward the modern welfare state. FERA elevated to national visibility Harry Hopkins, one of Roosevelt's administrators from New York who became the federal relief administrator. But soon after the creation of FERA, the administration realized that a relief program alone would not solve the massive unemployment problem. When FERA's initial appropriation was exhausted, the agency was replaced by the Civil Works Administration, which operated through the Public Works Administration.

Four Horsemen

The four justices associated with unbending conservatism in the interpretation of the U.S. Constitution during the 1920s and 1930s were collectively called the Four Horsemen. The first, Willis Van Devanter, was appointed to the Court by President William Howard Taft in 1910. James McReynolds joined the Court in 1914, a nominee of President Woodrow Wilson. The third and fourth horsemen were George Sutherland and Pierce Butler, both of whom were put on the Court in 1922 by President Warren Harding. The Four Horsemen were known as unyielding advocates of substantive due process, and they categorically rejected the economic and social initiatives of the New Deal.

Garner, John Nance

John Nance Garner served two terms in the Texas Assembly from 1898 to 1902. While in the assembly, he chaired the redistricting committee and fashioned a congressional district from which he was elected to Congress. Garner held this seat continuously from 1902 until he became vice president in 1933. During the Republican administrations of Harding and Coolidge, Garner was ranking member of the House Ways and Means Committee, and his reports formed the basis on which the Democrats articulated their opposition. Garner became Speaker when the Democrats took control of the U.S. House of Representatives in the election of 1930. He sought the presidential nomination in 1932 but eventually released his delegates to Roosevelt and was rewarded with the vice presidential nomination.

Garner was more conservative than Roosevelt and most New Dealers, differing from them on a number of issues, including diplomatic recognition of the Soviet Union. He supported most of the New Deal proposals out of party loyalty, however, and Roosevelt often consulted him on the domestic legislative program. Garner remained on the ticket in 1936 but distanced himself on such issues as Roosevelt's deficit-spending policies and the attempt to pack the Supreme Court. The split widened in 1938, when

Roosevelt unsuccessfully tried to purge a number of congressional Democrats for insufficient support of his programs; Roosevelt actively worked for their defeat in the 1938 elections. Garner became increasingly outspoken in his opposition as he realized that Roosevelt would seek a third term in 1940. Garner left Washington for Texas shortly after the 1941 inauguration and played no further role in national affairs.

German-American Bund

An organization of pro-Nazi groups that operated in the United States from the mid-1930s until the start of World War II, the German-American Bund followed the New Friends of Germany as the principal communicator of Nazi propaganda. The Bund was a small, isolated, yet vocal sociopolitical group. Its primary objective was not of a revolutionary nature; at no time did it advocate the forcible overthrow of the U.S. government. Rather, it was a body of people who were culturally alike, generally recent German immigrants who wished for the safety and comfort found in their ethnic tradition. The Bund's long-range purpose was to unify the community known as the German America, leading to a "united Germandom." The short-term goal was to combat the unfavorable image of Germany under the National Socialists. Nazi overtures to German America were based on the notion that allegiance to Germany was stronger than U.S. citizenship. Across the country, anti-Nazi organizations sprang up, and German Americans, rather than flocking to the support of the Bund's, sought to distance themselves from the Bund and its objectives. The leading Bund members, virtually all native Germans, did not understand how extensively the melting-pot philosophy had affected the lives of those they were attempting to attract.

The Bund was created and sustained during the 1930s by Fritz Julius Kuhn, the self-designated führer in the United States. Although Kuhn never attracted more than 25,000 followers, his pronouncements and media visibility engaged the public's attention. Noise volume notwithstanding, the Bund movement never posed a serious threat to U.S. security, though it did become the subject of congressional investigation led by the House Un-American Activities Committee. In May 1939 the Bund movement in the United States received a fatal blow when Kuhn was indicted for the embezzlement of Bund funds and sentenced to prison. When the United States entered World War II and declared war on Germany in late 1941, few Germans in the United States retained sympathy for or supported the National Socialist regime.

Great Depression of 1929

A depression is an economic slump that typically occurs when production facilities and credit have been overextended. The U.S. economy has suffered several depressions, but they do not compare to the Great Depression of the 1930s. Most historians mark the beginning of the Great Depression with the crash of the stock market in October 1929. Once started, the Great Depression impacted the entire country and produced such catastrophic consequences as lost savings, bankruptcies, failed banks, rising debt, declining purchases, diminished production, job layoffs, and shrinking real estate values. The Hoover administration initially underestimated the seriousness of the depression and as a result was largely ineffective in responding to it. The Great Depression led to the realignment of political party affiliation, which brought about the election of Franklin Roosevelt in 1932 and, with him, a Democratic majority in Congress. In the first 100 days of his administration, Roosevelt and Congress enacted several far-reaching economic regulatory initiatives, components of Roosevelt's New Deal program. Despite much governmental activity, the Great Depression did not end until the U.S. economy geared up for World War II.

Griswold v. Connecticut (1965)

In *Griswold v. Connecticut* the Warren Court identified a constitutional entitlement to privacy. A Connecticut law made it a crime to use birth control devices or provide counsel on their use. Griswold, who operated a birth control clinic in New Haven, was convicted for violating this 1879 law. The Warren Court struck down the law, although members of the majority differed about the constitutional bases of a right to privacy. Justice Douglas, writing for the Court, said the law "operated directly on an intimate relation of husband and wife and their physician's role in one aspect of the relation." The Court intervened here because "various guarantees create zones of privacy" (*Griswold*, 492, 494). These zones are formed by "emanations" from specific Bill of Rights guarantees. The emanations produce penumbras that give effect to Bill of Rights provisions. The several constitutional guarantees on which the privacy right are grounded include the First Amendment right of association; the privacy of the home, which comes from the Third and Fourth Amendments; the self-incrimination provision of the Fifth Amendment; and the Ninth Amendment.

Henderson, Leon

Leon Henderson, a central member of Franklin Roosevelt's administrative organization, began his public life in Pennsylvania, where he was in charge of state personnel and job classification. He organized the state retirement system and later became deputy secretary of the Commonwealth. National Recovery Administration director general Hugh Johnson persuaded Henderson to leave his position with the Russell Sage Foundation in 1934 to head the Division of Research and Planning of the NRA. Henderson was a strong advocate of consumer purchasing power theory, which would become a key component of New Deal economic policy. He urged Roosevelt to use direct relief and a comprehensive regulation of business practices as a means to achieve economic recovery. Henderson was a member of the National Industrial Recovery Board and an economic adviser to the Senate committee on manufacturers when the Supreme Court struck down the law on which the NIRB was based. After serving as economic adviser for the Democratic National Committee, Henderson became a consulting economist for Harry Hopkins and the Works Progress Administration from 1933 to 1938. He was executive secretary for the newly created Temporary National Economic Committee (TNEC) until 1939, when he was appointed to the Securities and Exchange Commission to fill the vacancy left when William O. Douglas was appointed to the Supreme Court. In 1941 he was appointed to the Office of Emergency Management. As the threat of inflation increased, Roosevelt created an Office of Price Administration in 1942 and named Henderson to head the agency. Negative response to rationing became so strong, however, that Henderson eventually was replaced as head of OPA by Chester Bowles. Henderson held no subsequent government office, instead working as an economic consultant and becoming one of the founders of the Americans for Democratic Action.

Hoover, Herbert C.

Herbert Hoover was the thirtieth president of the United States. He became a nationally visible figure during World War I for heading the Commission for Relief in Belgium, directing voluntary rationing efforts for Woodrow Wilson's administration, and serving as director general of the American Relief Administration. Both major parties pursued him as a possible presidential nominee in 1920, but he refused to run. Instead, Hoover served as secretary of commerce in the administrations of Warren Harding and Calvin Coolidge. When Coolidge decided not to seek reelection in 1928, Hoover won the Republican nomination and defeated Alfred Smith in the general election. Although he successfully completed his first several months in office, his performance slipped with the stock market crash in October 1929 and the severe economic depression that followed. The depression ended his hopes for a progressive reformation of the United States as well. Underestimating the severity of the economic situation, he initially suggested a variety of locally sponsored self-help strategies. Hoover reluctantly turned to more aggressive initiatives when the Democrats took control of Congress in 1930. He signed the Federal Economic Stabilization Act of 1931, which created a board with the authority to address job fluctuations through public construction projects. The Emergency and Relief Construction Act, passed the following year, appropriated federal money for public works projects and provided funding for state programs furnishing direct relief and work relief to the unemployed. Hoover eventually modified a World War I entity known as the War Finance Corporation and created the Reconstruction Finance Corporation as the mechanism through which to channel economic recovery initiatives, making him the first U.S. president to use a federal agency to intervene in a peacetime economy. For the thirty years following his defeat in the election of 1932, Hoover advocated policies that would avoid military conflict or engagement of U.S. troops abroad. He opposed the NATO alliance and U.S. involvement in the Korean War. He was, of course, opposed to Roosevelt's New Deal initiatives and the U.S. cold war foreign policy. Both parties ignored him until Truman and Eisenhower decided to use his skills as head of the Commissions of Organization of the Executive Branch of Government, later called the Hoover Commissions. The first Hoover Commission, established in 1947, addressed exclusively structural and process issues that had been prompted by the expansion of the federal executive branch during World War II. Its report, issued in 1949, led to a substantial reorganization of the federal executive branch.

Hopkins, Harry

Harry Hopkins came to the Roosevelt administration with extensive experience in human services. He worked in a New York City settlement house, handled widows' pensions for the New York City Board of Child Welfare, directed the southern division of the Red Cross, was assistant director of the Community Service Society of New York City, and headed the New York Tuberculosis Association. He first met Franklin Roosevelt in 1928 and during Roosevelt's tenure as governor of New York was appointed director of the Temporary Emergency Relief Administration (TERA), which provided jobs for New York's unemployed. When Roosevelt became president in 1933, he expanded TERA to a national scale and brought Hopkins to Washington to run it. In 1935 Hopkins was put in charge of the Works Progress Administration. During his almost five years as head of federal relief, Hopkins was one of Roosevelt's inner circle of advisers. As the importance of the WPA increased, Hopkins moved closer to Roosevelt. After the president's reelection in 1936, Roosevelt seriously considered Hopkins as a successor. Indeed, Roosevelt's appointment of Hopkins as secretary of commerce in December 1938 was seen by some as an indication that Roosevelt was positioning him for a 1940 presidential run. The thought was made moot by Roosevelt's decision to seek a third term. Hopkins became executive secretary of the U.S. War Cabinet, was one of Roosevelt's key national defense advisers, and was given the responsibility of administering the lend-lease program. Hopkins's health began to fail, however, and he resigned his Commerce Department position in late 1940.

Hughes, Charles Evans

Hughes graduated first in his class at Columbia Law School and completed the New York bar exam with a record high score. He was admitted to practice in 1884 at the age of twenty-two. Hughes had a successful private practice and earned a reputation as a leader of the corporate bar. He also gained recognition for his trust-busting work. His reputation as an independent-minded Republican led to his election as governor of New York in 1906. President Taft nominated Hughes to the Supreme Court in 1910. Hughes was on the Court with Oliver Wendell Holmes and developed a close intellectual relationship with him. Hughes's national stature made him an attractive choice to run against incumbent president Woodrow Wilson, and in June 1916 he resigned from the Court to engage in what would turn out to be an unsuccessful presidential campaign. After the election he returned to private practice and active participation in the civic affairs of the period. From 1921 to 1925, Hughes served as secretary of state under Presidents Harding and Coolidge. He strongly advocated U.S. participation in the League of Nations, international arms reduction, and the World Court. He briefly served on the International Court of Justice before 1930 when President Hoover nominated him to the chief justiceship to replace Taft.

Hughes's nomination was opposed by progressives, who saw Hughes as a Republican corporate lawyer. The Senate confirmed his nomination by a small majority, with twenty-six opposed and eighteen abstaining. Once on the Court, Hughes joined with the conservatives—Justices Van Devanter, Sutherland, Butler, and McReynolds—in overturning state and federal regulatory measures designed to foster the country's economic recovery. In 1937 Hughes responded to Roosevelt's Court-packing proposal by sending a letter to the Senate Judiciary Committee in which he countered Roosevelt's rationale for the proposal. The letter was instrumental in defeating the proposal. Hughes also changed his voting behavior following the Court-packing episode and became more receptive to some of the regulatory initiatives his Court had rejected before the confrontation with Roosevelt. Doctrinal change aside, Hughes led the Court through an extremely significant period of U.S. history.

Hull, Cordell

Cordell Hull was elected to the Tennessee legislature in 1893 and served until his appointment as judge of the Fifth Tennessee Circuit in 1903. Four years later Hull went to Congress from the state's Fourth District. He was not a charismatic politician, but he was a skilled consensus builder. In Congress Hull became known as an advocate of low tariffs and a graduated income tax. He served on the Ways and Means Committee for eighteen years and was leader of those sponsoring Wilson's economic program. Hull announced his support for Franklin Roosevelt in early 1932 and became secretary of state in Roosevelt's administration, a position he retained until 1945. Hull strongly believed in free trade and was a leading opponent of tariffs, preferring reciprocal free trade agreements instead. All of this influenced Roosevelt's selection, but it was particularly useful to Roosevelt to have a secretary who was popular on the Hill and with the public. In March 1934 he succeeded in getting Congress to pass the Reciprocal Trade Agreements Act, which set the pattern for tariff reduction by executive agreement on a most-favored-nation basis. This act was a forerunner to the 1948 General Agreement on Tariffs and Trade (GATT). Roosevelt described Hull as the "father of the UN"; recognition of his key role in the establishment of that international organization came with his winning the Nobel Prize in 1945.

Ickes, Harold

Harold Ickes was originally a Republican but switched his affiliation to support Franklin Roosevelt's candidacy in 1932. He was instrumental in convincing Midwest Republicans to support Roosevelt. In 1933 Ickes became Roosevelt's secretary of interior, a position he retained until 1946. He also headed the Public Works Administration during the late 1930s. Ickes was a leading spokesman for the administration, often saying things that Roosevelt was not in a position to say; he was known to some as Roosevelt's hatchet man. Ickes played a pivotal role in Roosevelt's campaign for a third term. He wrote the party platform, delivered the keynote speech at the convention, developed the overall campaign strategy, and outlined most of the campaign speeches. Ickes was one of the most forceful personalities in Washington, and in his capacity as the custodian of national resources he perhaps carried more responsibilities than any other cabinet member of the time. During the war Ickes was the petroleum administrator and established what was virtual government control of the U.S. oil industry. Ickes was argumentative and contentious, and his relations with other Roosevelt cabinet members were less than cordial. He resigned in February 1946 after a dispute with President Harry Truman.

Johnson, General Hugh S.

A West Point graduate, Hugh Johnson rose to the rank of brigadier general in the U.S. Army and became an important figure in the mobilization effort for both world wars. In 1917 he worked on developing and implementing the Selective Service System. As the army representative on the War Industries Board (WIB), he helped to organize the institutional network coordinating military procurement with WIB operations. Johnson became assistant to Bernard Baruch in 1927. Baruch, a wealthy financier, provided economic policy counsel to both Presidents Herbert Hoover and Franklin Roosevelt. Johnson remained with Baruch until 1932, when he became part of Roosevelt's inner circle. Johnson helped write the National Industrial Recovery Act in 1933 and was chosen by Roosevelt to head the National Recovery Administration to manage the system of fair-trade codes developed under the law. In part the program was an attempt to resurrect the system of business-government cooperation once handled by the old WIB. The program was ineffective, however, and tended to produce market restrictions that delayed recovery rather than promoted it. In September 1934, as the NRA was breaking down, Roosevelt eased Johnson out. Following his departure from the NRA, Johnson wrote his memoirs, served briefly as works progress administrator in New York City, and began a career as a syndicated columnist and radio commentator. He continued to support Roosevelt for a time but viewed the president's policy agenda changes in 1935–1936 as misguided departures from the original objectives of the New Deal. His "Hugh Johnson Says" column became more and more critical of Roosevelt after mid-1937, and Johnson actively worked for the election of Wendell Willkie in the 1940 presidential campaign.

Lend-Lease Act of 1941

In 1940 President Roosevelt urged that the United States attempt to meet the needs of the European nations who were defending themselves against Axis aggression. The Neutrality Act of 1933 and subsequent amendments to it restricted arms sales, but Roosevelt provided assistance nonetheless, particularly to Great Britain. More than a year before Pearl Harbor, Roosevelt concluded an executive agreement with Great Britain whereby the United States would supply the British with destroyers in exchange for long-term leases to British naval bases located in strategic places around the world. The Lend-Lease Act grew out of the "destroyers for bases" agreement. The purpose of the law was to enable the president to sell, exchange, lease, lend, or otherwise dispose of any defense article to the government of any country whose defense seemed vital to the defense of the United States. Intended primarily to aid Great Britain, it became the basis for extensive help to the Soviet Union and other countries. Supplying Britain with military weapons on credit was precisely what isolationists of the period feared; it was seen as leading inevitably to U.S. involvement in war. Roosevelt effectively sold the plan to Congress and the public. He compared lend-lease to a water hose one lends to a neighbor whose house is on fire. Despite the isolationists' opposition, lend-lease passed with relative ease. The production priorities set up under the act were extended when the United States became an active participant in the war. In the first year the United States provided materials to Great Britain valued at over $2.5 billion. The act was renewed several times following the attack on Pearl Harbor and provided Roosevelt with virtually unlimited executive authority to deliver war supplies to U.S. allies.

Lewis, John L.

A labor leader from the coalfields of Iowa and southern Illinois, John Lewis became president of the United Mine Workers of America (UMWA) following a series of appointed and elected promotions. A decline in UMWA membership in the late 1920s led Lewis to look to government action to help advance the interests of labor. Government support was slow in materializing, but the Great Depression and election of Franklin Roosevelt produced significant gains for organized labor. Lewis was instrumental in formulating the labor sections of the National Industrial Recovery Act, which had protective provisions. As the UMWA revived, Lewis played a larger role in the labor movement nationally. He saw unprecedented opportunity for the American Federation of Labor (AFL) to expand from its craft union base to mass production workers. In November 1935 a group formally constituted itself as the Committee for Industrial Organization (CIO) within the AFL, providing support to workers seeking to organize along industrial lines. For the next five years, Lewis and the CIO dominated the U.S. labor scene, and the CIO established permanent unions in the automobile, steel, rubber, and electrical appliance industries. The passage of the National Labor Relations Act in July 1935 underscored the importance of having a labor-friendly administration in Washington and industrial state capitals. In 1936 Lewis created Labor's Non-Partisan League, through which he channeled more than $500,000 in UMWA-CIO funds to Roosevelt's reelection campaign. The league was the forerunner of contemporary political action committees.

The CIO broke away from the AFL in late 1938 and reconstituted itself as the Congress of Industrial Organizations, an autonomous labor federation. Lewis was increasingly at odds with others in the CIO leadership, and he grew more critical of Roosevelt as well. He regarded Roosevelt's support of Western allies and program of accelerated defense production as dangerous, inevitably drawing the country into a world war. Lewis eventually endorsed Wendell Willkie, the Republican candidate, in the presidential election of 1940. Lewis stepped down as CIO president a month after the election, and by early 1942 Lewis had taken the UMWA out of the CIO. Lewis felt the Roosevelt administration was keeping labor from making legitimate claims for higher wages in the face of an escalating cost of living. He led the soft-coal miners in a series of strikes in 1943. Although these strikes were of short duration and did not threaten the war effort, they were widely criticized. Congress responded by passing the War Labor Disputes (Smith-Connally) Act, which subjected unions to tighter regulation. Lewis continued his confrontational approach, and soft-coal strikes occurred frequently into the late 1940s. The UMWA remained apart from the rest of the labor movement throughout this period. As demand for bituminous coal diminished in the 1950s, leadership of the UMWA shifted to Lewis's administrative assistant, a power transfer that began Lewis's complete withdrawal from UMWA activities.

McReynolds, James Clark

James McReynolds graduated as valedictorian from Vanderbilt, established a practice in Nashville, and returned to the Vanderbilt law faculty in 1900. Despite his affiliation with the Democratic Party, McReynolds was appointed assistant attorney general by President Theodore Roosevelt in 1903. Four years later McReynolds left the Justice Department and joined a prestigious law firm in New York City. In 1913 Wilson made McReynolds his U.S. attorney general. The following year Wilson nominated him to succeed Justice Horace Lurton on the Supreme Court. Some Court observers initially expected him to join the liberal wing of the Court, but by the 1930s he became its most conservative member. As a Supreme Court justice, McReynolds opposed the growing social and economic regulatory power of government and believed that the Constitution committed the nation to a policy of laissez-faire capitalism.

McReynolds is probably best remembered, along with Justices Sutherland, Butler, and Van Devanter, as one of the so-called Four Horsemen who consistently voted as a bloc against New Deal legislation. From the "constitutional revolution" of 1937 until his retirement in 1941, McReynolds became a dissenting voice on the Court, protesting what he considered to be unconstitutional exercises of power by the federal government. In fact, he dissented from every major decision that sustained New Deal legislation. He was the last of the Four Horsemen to leave the Court, retiring after Roosevelt won his third term in 1940.

Moley, Raymond

Raymond Moley was one of Franklin Roosevelt's principal political advisers and founder of the famous Roosevelt brain trust. He was both a teacher and administrator in Ohio for several years before returning to school to obtain an M.A. in political science from Oberlin College in 1913. He earned his Ph.D. from Columbia University five years later. While serving on the faculty at Western Reserve University, Moley was strongly influenced by the reform politics of Woodrow Wilson and Cleveland mayor Tom Johnson. His published work as well as his public lectures advocated an expanded role for the federal government in social planning. Moley was appointed director of the Cleveland Foundation in 1919, a position in which he gained national visibility. He joined the faculty of Barnard College in 1923 and published a number of highly regarded studies of urban crime. On the basis of this research, Moley was appointed research director of the New York State Crime Commission. While in this position Moley met Roosevelt political adviser Louis M. Howe and began writing speeches for Roosevelt during his 1928 gubernatorial campaign in New York. In early 1932 Moley offered his services to the Roosevelt presidential campaign. Moley and a number of faculty from Columbia University, including Rexford Tugwell and Adolf Berle, were recruited as political advisers. Howe was to name the group the "brain trust." Moley served as Roosevelt's interpreter of the ideas offered by Tugwell, Berle, and others. Much of the content of the initial New Deal proposals was developed in this manner, and it was Moley who coined the term "new deal," which Roosevelt used in accepting the Democratic Party's nomination in 1932. As assistant secretary of state during the first year of Roosevelt's presidency, Moley was the president's principal contact with Congress in the development of the Hundred Days' initiatives. Moley's insistence that Roosevelt remain focused on domestic solutions to the economic problems brought him into direct conflict with Secretary of State Cordell Hull, who preferred the international trade approach to American economic recovery. In mid-1933 Moley was transferred from the State Department to the Justice Department at Hull's insistence. Although Moley remained a presidential adviser until early 1936, an ideological rift developed with Roosevelt, and Moley left the administration. He argued that Roosevelt had lost sight of the initial New Deal objective and had moved into the camp of the anticorporate, prolabor group, which included Thomas Corcoran. Moley soon moved toward the Republican Party and endorsed Wendell Willkie in the 1940 presidential election. Moley later provided counsel to such Republican presidential hopefuls as Robert Taft, Barry Goldwater, and Richard Nixon. Moley died in February 1975.

National Industrial Recovery Act (NIRA)

The National Industrial Recovery Act was the most innovative and constitutionally dubious of Roosevelt's New Deal proposals. Drafted by members of his administration as well as representatives from business and labor, the NIRA attempted to establish comprehensive federal coordination of the economy. Congressional power to enact such legislation was based on Roosevelt's declaration of a national economic "emergency," an emergency that could justify the use of unprecedented federal regulatory power. The ambitious objectives of the NIRA included stimulating industrial production, decreasing unemployment, stabilizing prices and wages, improving industrial working conditions, and regulating certain business practices through the use of codes of fair competition. Congress delegated extensive lawmaking authority to the executive branch, and the National Recovery Administration was the key enforcement mechanism. The NRA was charged with overseeing a comprehensive program of government controls over virtually every sector of the economy. The NRA was the most conspicuous of the New Deal agencies and best reflected the early New Deal's economic philosophy and antidepression strategy. The NRA served as the framework through which the U.S. economy might be reformed and regulated.

The NIRA conveyed legislative powers to the president and delegated legislative power to representatives of business and trade associations as well. The codes contained, among other things, regulations on maximum hours and minimum wages for each industry. The NIRA also established the right of industrial workers to organize and pick their own representatives to engage in collective bargaining. Passage of the NIRA brought to an end the period known as the Hundred Days, during which Congress enacted fifteen major pieces of federal law in response to the postdepression economic emergency.

The Hughes Court struck down the NIRA in *Schechter Poultry Corp. v. United States* (1935). The case involved an appeal from a conviction for violation of the code of fair competition for the live poultry industry of New York City. The Court examined whether the law was justified "in the light of the grave national crisis with which Congress was confronted," whether the law illegally delegated legislative power, and whether the act exceeded the limits of the interstate commerce power. Chief Justice Hughes ruled that even "[e]xtraordinary conditions do not create or enlarge constitutional power" (*Schecter*, 528). The delegation required the Court to consider whether Congress had set adequate "standards of legal obligation" in calling for the codes of fair competition. The Court concluded it had not. Hughes said the codes embraced whatever "the formulators would propose, and what Roosevelt would approve, or prescribe, as wise and beneficent measures for the government of trades and industries" (*Schechter*, 535). In other words, trade groups had been given a blank check in developing codes for their particular industries. Finally, the Court concluded that Congress had sought to regulate intrastate commercial transactions through the codes and that the federal commerce power could not reach such transactions— since all Schechter's business was local, it had no direct effect upon interstate commerce.

National Labor Relations Act (NLRA; Wagner Act)

The National Labor Relations Act, known also as the Wagner Act, was a major component of the so-called second New Deal period. It guaranteed the right of labor to organize and bargain collectively through designated representatives. The NLRA imposed extensive controls on industrial labor-management relations. In doing so, it regulated a key aspect of production, an area previously regarded outside the reach of the federal commerce power. The Court upheld the act in *NLRB v. Jones & Laughlin Steel Corp.* (1937). Chief Justice Hughes used the "stream of commerce" doctrine as the foundation of his opinion. Jones and Laughlin Steel drew its raw materials from interstate commerce and placed its finished products back into interstate commerce. The *Jones & Laughlin* ruling recognized for the first time the highly integrated character of the U.S. economy. Economic activities once viewed as isolated and local came to be seen as having economic effects that transcended state lines. As a result, the consequences of a protracted labor dispute in the steel industry were considered potentially "catastrophic" rather than remote or indirect, and Congress could legitimately intervene. The National Labor Relations Board, designed after the National Labor Board under the NIRA, was created to administer the Wagner Act and provisions of the Taft-Hartley and Landrum-Griffin Acts when those laws were passed. The principal functions remain certification of bargaining agents and fact-finding regarding alleged unfair labor practices by employers. The NLRB consists of five members appointed by the president, with the Senate's consent, for five-year terms. The NLRB is authorized to issue cease-and-desist orders, hold bargaining representative elections, and seek court injunctions and other enforcement orders. The act significantly altered labor-management relations in the United States, and its primary purpose of protecting the collective-bargaining process remains basic policy.

National War Labor Board (NWLB)

Roosevelt called a conference in 1941 to develop recommendations for regulating wartime labor-management relations. The conference suggested the creation of the NWLB without precisely determining its jurisdiction, although it eventually included the issues of union security and wage rates. Soon after Pearl Harbor, Roosevelt secured a no-strike/no-lockout agreement with labor and management. The NWLB was then established in January 1942 to head off labor conflicts that might impair the war effort. By the end of the war, the NWLB had imposed settlements in some 20,000 wage disputes affecting more than 20 million workers and had approved 415,000 wage agreements. In a few instances the government took over plants shut down by work stoppages. The NWLB fostered union membership growth through the use of a "maintenance of membership" policy that required that in any workplace already under a collective bargaining contract, any new employees would be automatically enrolled in the union. Unions of the time were inclined to accept marginal wage increases as a trade-off for the membership gains. Like the Mediation Board that preceded it, the NWLB was composed of representatives from labor, industry, and the public but had no independent power to enforce its rulings.

Neutrality Acts

Many people in the United States believed the country's participation in World War I was a mistake, and in the 1930s there was substantial public sentiment against getting involved in another "European" war. President Franklin Roosevelt was not an isolationist as such, but he was sufficiently occupied with domestic policy and economic recovery that he back-burnered foreign policy issues. Congress, however, sought to ensure that the United States would not intervene in foreign conflicts by passing a series of neutrality laws. The Neutrality Act of 1935 required an embargo on most war-related items if the president determined that a state of war existed. Two years later further restraints were added, including a ban on arming U.S. merchant ships traveling to ports of belligerents. In late 1937 Congress narrowly voted down a proposal that called for a majority vote of the public before the United States could go to war, unless the country was invaded. Although the defeat of this proposal maintained some presidential discretion in the conduct of foreign affairs, the restrictive provisions of the 1937 statute continued severely to limit presidential capacity in the field of international relations. Following the German invasion of Poland in September 1939, Roosevelt was required by the 1937 law to impose an arms embargo on U.S. allies as well as the Axis powers. Congress later amended the act to allow sale of war goods to the Allies even though U.S. ships could not enter war zone waters. As world war became imminent, Roosevelt gained expanded executive authority that Roosevelt exercised by entering into a number of executive agreements. Perhaps the most significant of these, at least in terms of the Neutrality Acts, was the "destroyers-for-bases" agreement, under which the United States provided military vessels to Great Britain in exchange for use of British bases located throughout the world. The Lend-Lease Act of 1941 repealed much of the 1939 Neutrality Act and authorized Roosevelt to supply any materials necessary to the defense of any nation determined to be critical to U.S. security.

New Deal

The New Deal, a legislative program of President Franklin Roosevelt, was designed to achieve national economic recovery following the Great Depression. The term "New Deal" was coined by political adviser Raymond Moley and first used by Roosevelt when he accepted the Democratic Party's nomination for president in 1932. The economic problems facing the nation in the early 1930s were extensive. The stock market crash of 1929 was only the beginning. Banks and businesses failed, farm property was foreclosed, and workers lost their jobs. Roosevelt viewed the economic crisis as one that had to be dealt with as though it were a war. Using the wartime analogy, Roosevelt created an emergency- or crisis-driven government through unilateral executive actions and executive leadership of Congress.

Shortly after his inauguration, Roosevelt called Congress into special session, and what followed was a period of extraordinary legislative action that became known as the Hundred Days. The package of legislation contained a variety of measures initiated by Roosevelt, his political and economic advisers, and Congress itself. The first priority was stabilization of the banking industry. Roosevelt called a bank "holiday" to stop depositors from withdrawing their savings. The Emergency Banking Act, passed on March 9, 1933, subjected banks to federal regulation. In addition, the Federal Reserve Board was given authority to regulate lending practices, and the Federal Deposit Insurance Corporation was created to insure bank deposits. The Securities Act imposed full disclosure requirements on the securities industry, and the Securities and Exchange Commission was created to more fully oversee the sale of securities.

The New Deal included measures to manage various sectors of the U.S. economy and the needs of the unemployed. The Agricultural Adjustment Act was aimed at stabilizing commodity prices by regulating production. The National Industrial Recovery Act set up the National Recovery Administration, which was to implement codes of practice across a number of economic sectors. Included in the codes were minimum wage provisions and support for the workers' right to join labor unions. Relief for the unemployed was provided through several agencies such as the Civilian Conservation Corps, Federal Relief Administration, and Public Works Administration. The Hundred Days ended in mid-June 1933, and many of the programs created by legislative enactments in this time were subsequently struck down by the Hughes Court. A second period of heightened legislative activity, which became known as the second New Deal, occurred in 1935. Among the important measures from this period were the National Labor Relations Act, Social Security Act, and Works Progress Administration. The only legislation regarded as part of the New Deal enacted after mid-1935 was the Housing Act of 1937 and the Fair Labor Standards Act of 1938.

Norris-LaGuardia Anti-Injunction Act of 1932

Norris-LaGuardia was one of the first federal laws designed to advance labor interests. The law prohibited yellow-dog contracts by which workers would agree not to join unions and limited the use of the injunction in labor disputes. The principal purpose of Norris-LaGuardia was to protect organized labor from the more successful strategies used against it in the 1920s. The act was instrumental in providing a climate in which labor could develop as an economic power. Norris-LaGuardia was followed three years later by the passage of the Wagner Act, a statute that guaranteed the right of labor to organize and bargain collectively. The Court upheld the Norris-LaGuardia Act in *Lauf v. E. G. Shinner & Co.* (1938). In *United States v. Hutcheson* (1941), the Hughes Court ruled that the Norris-LaGuardia Act had greatly limited the use of criminal prosecutions against labor unions for Sherman Antitrust Act violations. The Court also indicated in *Hutcheson* that business should no longer expect judicial support when it sought to obtain injunctive relief in labor-management disputes.

Perkins, Frances

Frances Perkins began her professional life as a social worker and in 1907 became general secretary of the Philadelphia Research and Protective Association, a group that helped immigrant girls and newly arrived southern blacks. In the meantime, she studied economics and sociology at the University of Pennsylvania. A Sage Foundation fellowship brought Perkins to New York for further study, and she later accepted the position of executive secretary of the New York Consumer's League. While with the Consumer's League, she formed the Committee on Safety of the City of New York and eventually became its executive secretary. An experienced lobbyist, Perkins worked with New York Assembly leaders like Al Smith and Robert Wagner as well as trade unionists such as Samuel Gompers for industrial and labor regulation. In 1919 then Governor Smith named Perkins to the Industrial Commission of the State of New York. Her tenure was interrupted when Smith lost his 1920 bid for reelection, but in 1923 he returned to office and named her chair of a reorganized commission. Smith's successor as governor of New York was Franklin Roosevelt, who appointed Perkins head of the state labor department.

President-elect Roosevelt nominated Perkins for secretary of labor in 1933. She was easily confirmed and served until July 1945. She participated in writing the sections of the National Industrial Recovery Act dealing with public works and collective bargaining and played a significant role in the formulation of the Social Security and Fair Labor Standards Acts. After Roosevelt's death in April 1945, Perkins remained as secretary of labor for several months. Later that year Truman appointed her to the Civil Service Commission, where she remained until the beginning of the Eisenhower administration. She concluded her career with a visiting professorship in the School of Industrial and Labor Relations at Cornell University.

"Preferred Position" Doctrine

The "preferred position" doctrine of judicial review requires laws affecting fundamental constitutional rights to be more closely scrutinized than other laws. The doctrine suggests that certain laws call for the most stringent review because they affect such rights as free speech or voting rights. Any enactment that impinges on such rights must serve a compelling state interest. In applying strict scrutiny, the burden rests with the government to demonstrate justification for limiting a preferred position freedom. The doctrine was first articulated by Justice Stone in *United States v. Carolene Products Co.* (1938). A lesser presumption of constitutionality exists when legislation "appears on its face to be within a specific prohibition such as those of the first ten amendments." Stone further suggested that if legislation restricts corrective action through the political processes, courts must engage in a "more exacting judicial scrutiny" when reviewing such enactments. (The text of Justice Stone's footnote four, outlining the preferred position doctrine, is contained in Appendix II.)

Price Administration, Office of (OPA)

Roosevelt created the Office of Price Administration and Civilian Supply in April 1941. This agency assumed the functions of the former Price Stabilization Division of the National Defense Advisory Commission, which included closely monitoring price trends. The OPA possessed more than the merely advisory powers of the agency it replaced, however. It was authorized to issue maximum price orders as a means of preventing price spiraling, rising costs of living, profiteering, and other inflationary pressures. In August 1941 its name was shortened to "Office of Price Administration," but the change did not affect its power over price control. Leon Henderson headed the OPA and aggressively sought to control the domestic economy during the war. Henderson initially established controls on prices and rents, but by early 1942 he imposed a general price freeze. The OPA also undertook rationing of such scarce commodities as meat and gasoline. Henderson's approach generated opposition from many quarters, including business, labor, and agriculture. Henderson became a political liability to the Roosevelt administration, and he was replaced by Chester Bowles in early 1943. The OPA was able to cap the cost of living for the duration of the war.

Public Works Administration (PWA)

A New Deal agency established in 1933 by Congress as the Federal Administration of Public Works, the PWA was one of the three major components of the National Industrial Recovery Act. The PWA was designed to complement the National Recovery Administration, which was to generally overhaul the national economy. Roosevelt and his advisers believed that stabilizing employment and increasing purchasing power across the country were essential to economic recovery. The PWA administered the construction of various public works projects, such as public buildings, bridges, dams, and housing projects. Interior Secretary Harold Ickes served as director of the PWA and over its eight-year duration put more than 8 million people to work on more than $11 billion worth of projects.

Reconstruction Finance Corporation (RFC)

The Reconstruction Finance Corporation was the most innovative component of President Herbert Hoover's response to the economic difficulties caused by the Great Depression. Hoover first attempted to address the economic problems through the National Credit Association, but private-sector actions through the association were insufficient to revive the failing banks. The Reconstruction Finance Corporation, established in January 1932, was patterned after the War Finance Corporation, created in 1918 to finance construction of military plants. The RFC was designed to make federal funds available directly to private financial institutions, providing emergency loans to banks, building-and-loan societies, railroads, and agricultural stabilization corporations. Congress capitalized the new agency at $500 million and authorized it to borrow up to $1.5 billion more.

Robinson, Joseph Taylor

Joseph Robinson was elected to the Arkansas General Assembly before his admission to the state's bar. He established a private law practice at the end of a single term in the legislature but resumed political life in 1902 when he was elected to Congress. He was reelected to the U.S. House four times. Though a Democrat, Robinson aligned himself with progressive Republicans; he favored the regulation of child labor and railroads, a federal income tax, and women's suffrage. Robinson was elected governor of Arkansas in 1912, but the death of U.S. senator Jeff Davis created a vacancy that Robinson himself filled less than two weeks after his inauguration as governor. He was reelected to the Senate in 1918 and 1924. He supported the major initiatives of his party and President Woodrow Wilson and was strong advocate of the League of Nations. Robinson was elected Democratic minority leader in 1920 and led the opposition to the Republican policies of the Harding, Coolidge, and Hoover administrations. He was seriously considered for the Democratic presidential nomination in 1924 and was the vice presidential candidate in 1928. During his fourth Senate term, he became majority leader, was Roosevelt's main connection with southern Democrats, and guided the New Deal program through the Senate. He strongly supported Roosevelt's controversial Court-packing proposal as well. It was expected that Roosevelt would appoint him to the Court, but as Justice Van Devanter left the Court, creating the first vacancy, Robinson died. Van Devanter was replaced by Robinson's Senate colleague Hugo Black.

Roosevelt, Franklin D.

Franklin Roosevelt passed the New York bar exam without completing his degree at Columbia Law School. He joined a practice with a prominent New York City law firm but spent a great deal of time at Hyde Park, the family home. He was urged to run for the New York Senate, and although he ran as a Democrat in a heavily Republican district, he won by a small margin. He was reelected to a second term in 1912. He also worked on the presidential campaign of Woodrow Wilson in 1912 and later became assistant secretary of navy in the Wilson administration. After a failed vice presidential campaign in 1920, he became vice president of the Fidelity and Deposit Company, a position he kept until 1928. Struck with infantile paralysis in 1921, Roosevelt was nevertheless elected governor of New York in 1928 and 1930 and two years later became the Democratic presidential nominee. As president he surrounded himself with a number of economists, academics, and others experts, a group known as his brain trust. He took office at a time when business was stagnant, millions were unemployed, and banks were failing. Congress was in session for 104 days in the spring of 1933, during which time fifteen major pieces of Roosevelt-sponsored legislation were enacted. Following the midterm elections of 1934, Roosevelt successfully pressed for adoption of additional social legislation. Congress passed the National Labor Relations Act, the Utility Holding Company Act, the Guffey-Snyder Bituminous Coal Act, the Social Security Act, and measures providing more aid to agriculture. In 1940 Roosevelt was elected to a third term, during which he took on the role of commander in chief. Roosevelt acquiesced to party leaders in 1944 and replaced Vice President Henry Wallace with Missouri senator Harry Truman. Roosevelt died less than three months after he began his fourth term. Achievements of the Roosevelt administration rank among the most important of any presidency in U.S. history. Roosevelt's political coalition brought about a long-term realignment that produced Democratic majorities in the Congress, and he formed new agencies that significantly and permanently expanded the role of the federal government.

Selective Service Act of 1940

The Selective Service Act was an attempt by the Roosevelt administration and Congress to develop a policy on military manpower for war needs. The act was based on the constitutional provisions giving Congress the authority to "raise" armies and "provide" a navy. A military draft has been used in one form or another since the Civil War for wartime or emergency service. The 1940 act authorized the executive to inaugurate a comprehensive system of military conscription even though the United States was still at peace. The preamble of the act stated the principle that the "obligations and privileges" of military service should be "shared generally" according to a "fair and just system of selectivity." This standard was adhered to throughout the war and proved an effective method for supplying the armed services with manpower.

Sherman Antitrust Act

The principal federal anti-monopoly statute. The Sherman Act forbids "every contract, combination . . . or conspiracy in the restraint of trade or commerce." The Sherman Act reflected a recognition by Congress that governmental intervention in the market place is essential to preserve competition. The effectiveness of the act was limited by two Supreme Court rulings, *United States v. E.C. Knight Co.* (1895) and *Standard Oil Co. v. United States* (1911). In *E.C. Knight*, the Court held that manufacturing trusts were not engaged in commerce and therefore could be regulated only by the states. In *Standard Oil*, contrary to explicit language in the act, the Court set forth a "rule of reason" by which not every combination in restraint of trade was illegal, but only those unreasonably so. Congress reinforced the provisions of the Sherman Act with the Clayton Act of 1914, a statute intended, among other things, to minimize the effects of the *E.C. Knight* and *Standard Oil* decisions. Enforcement of the Sherman Act is achieved through a combination of criminal penalties, civil remedies with triple damages to injured parties, injunctions, and property seizures. Responsibility for enforcement resides with the Antitrust Division of the Department of Justice.

Social Security Act of 1935

A federal law enacted in 1935 as part of Roosevelt's "second" New Deal, the Social Security Act set up a federal program of old-age retirement benefits and a joint federal-state program for compensating the unemployed. In addition, the act provided funding at the state level for such programs as vocational rehabilitation, public health services, and child welfare services, along with assistance to the elderly and the handicapped. The act created a system of mandatory old-age insurance, which issues benefits in proportion to the previous earnings of persons over sixty-five and established a reserve fund financed through payroll taxes on employers and employees. Only employees in industrial and commercial occupations were originally eligible for protection under the act, but numerous amendments have expanded the categories of coverage.

The Supreme Court upheld the Social Security Act in two decisions. In *Steward Machine Co. v. Davis* (1937), the Court upheld the unemployment insurance feature of the act. The Court reasoned that Congress had the power to levy a tax for relief of the unemployed to provide for the national welfare and that the states were not coerced to join the plan. Similarly, in *Helvering v. Davis* (1937), decided the same day as *Steward Machine*, the Court upheld the old-age, survivors, and disability insurance provisions. The Court recognized the broad power of Congress to promote the general welfare and said that determination of what the general welfare might require was a matter of legislative judgment. These rulings established the legal framework for an extensive system of social welfare measures carried on by the national government with the cooperation of state and local governments.

Stimson, Henry

Henry Stimson was Franklin Roosevelt's secretary of war during World War II. Trained at Harvard Law School, Stimson was appointed U.S. attorney for the Southern District of New York in 1906 by President Theodore Roosevelt. He resigned to become the Republican candidate for governor of New York in 1910. Following his defeat, he became President Taft's secretary of war on the recommendation of Elihu Root, who had been secretary of war for William McKinley and secretary of state for Theodore Roosevelt. Stimson left government in 1915 and spent the next twelve years in a successful private practice. In 1927 he arbitrated a dispute involving the president of Nicaragua and then served as the governor-general of the Philippines for the following two years. President Hoover named him secretary of state in 1929. Stimson brought a strongly interventionist view to the position, and albeit conservative, he later supported many New Deal objectives. In June 1940 Secretary of War Henry Woodring resigned and Roosevelt chose Stimson to replace him. He was an outspoken advocate of a comprehensive national service policy, and one of his first actions as secretary of war was to press for adoption of a selective service system. Stimson played a central role in approving the decision to intern more than 100,000 Japanese, and he also oversaw the Manhattan Project, the top-secret program to develop an atomic bomb.

Sutherland, George

George Sutherland was born in Buckinghamshire, England, in 1862. He received his law degree from the University of Michigan Law School and was admitted to the Michigan bar in 1883. Sutherland joined a prestigious law firm in Salt Lake City and became active in Utah politics, serving in the territorial legislature and as a state senator prior to his 1900 election to the U.S. House. A Republican, he advocated protective tariffs and maintained his protectionist position throughout his two terms in the U.S. Senate. In 1917 Sutherland resumed private law practice in Washington and was elected president of the American Bar Association. President Warren Harding nominated him to fill the Court seat vacated by Justice John Clarke in 1922.

Sutherland's conservatism was evident throughout his tenure on the Court. As was most evident in the substantive due process cases, he was a laissez-fairist. He was a zealous defender of property rights and immediately identified with the views of Chief Justice Taft, and Justices Van Devanter and Butler. Though best known as one of the Four Horsemen who opposed Roosevelt's New Deal initiatives, Sutherland developed a record on the Court more complex than the Four Horseman association might suggest. Sutherland not only registered objections to intrusions on property and contract rights but strongly defended free press and the rights of the accused as well. Sutherland's use of the Fourteenth Amendment provided the Court's conservative bloc with the foundation to sustain its resistance to state laws perceived as unreasonable social and economic legislation. Sutherland was ready to leave the Court in 1936, but Roosevelt's Court-packing proposal led him to wait: He wanted to stay on as long as the Court was under attack from Roosevelt and the New Dealers. The Court's "new majority" in *West Coast Hotel v. Parrish* (1937) persuaded him that the fight was over, and he resigned two months later. If one focuses exclusively on his substantive due process jurisprudence and the intransigence of the Four Horsemen, Sutherland's legacy is fairly mediocre. He did, however, fashion and present his arguments with great skill.

Taft-Hartley Act of 1947

Formally known as the Labor Management Relations Act, the Taft-Hartley Act sought to neutralize some of the gains made by organized labor under the Wagner Act of 1935. Taft-Hartley limited certain union practices such as closed-shop agreements, secondary boycotts, collection of excessive dues, and political campaign expenditures. Taft-Hartley retained the Wagner Act provisions on unfair practices by employers against unions. It also permitted unions and employers to sue each other for contract violations and provided for the use of injunctions and other "cooling-off" procedures in strikes that threaten the national welfare. Taft-Hartley was a reaction to growing union strength, allegations that the Wagner Act and the National Labor Relations Board favored unions over employers, and allegations of communism and corruption in some unions. President Truman saw the law as antiunion and vetoed it, but his veto was overridden by Congress. Under Section 14(b) of the act, a number of states have passed right to work laws that have curtailed the union shop in workplaces outside the reach of federal law.

Truman, Harry S.

Harry Truman was the thirty-second president of the United States. He was a student of military history and obtained an appointment to West Point but was later rejected because of defective vision. He held a variety of jobs, spending twelve years as a farmer before being appointed postmaster of Grandview, Missouri. After military service overseas, he returned to Missouri to join the political machine of Tom Pendergast, a local politician in Kansas City. Pendergast was responsible for Truman's appointment to an administrative body comparable to a county board of commissioners. Eight years later, Truman was elected to the U.S. Senate from Missouri; he was reelected in 1940.

There was little doubt at the 1944 Democratic National Convention that Roosevelt would be nominated to run for a fourth term; interest at the convention centered on the selection of a running mate. Roosevelt replaced his third-term vice president, Henry Wallace, with Truman, who was to serve only eighty-three days before he succeeded to the presidency on Roosevelt's death. Truman presided over the conclusion of World War II and established himself as a strong advocate of U.S. postwar global involvement and a strong United Nations. Extensive erosion of his public approval ratings and Republican control of the House limited Truman's presidency. He vetoed Taft-Hartley as damaging to the interests of labor, the only constituency still loyal to him. He fashioned the Truman Doctrine, a foreign policy designed to contain the spread of international communism; NATO was established as a component of the doctrine's objectives. After winning reelection in 1948 against seemingly overwhelming odds, Truman embarked on a domestic program called the Fair Deal. As the country became mired in the Korean War and the cold war, however, attention and support for his Fair Deal proposals waned. He announced in March 1952 that he would not run for reelection and retired to his home in Independence, Missouri.

Van Devanter, Willis

Willis Van Devanter moved to Wyoming three years after he completed his law degree at Cincinnati Law School. He quickly became involved in public life as city attorney of Cheyenne, a territorial legislator, and chief judge of the territorial court. Van Devanter's involvement in Republican Party politics led to his appointment as assistant attorney general in the Department of Interior. President Theodore Roosevelt appointed him to the Eighth Circuit Court of Appeals in 1903, and seven years later President Taft chose him to replace retiring Supreme Court justice William Moody. Van Devanter's service on the Court was distinguished by his performance in the Court's conference sessions and as a critic of his colleague's opinions. Van Devanter is known primarily for the opinions he wrote or joined that subscribed to principles of limited government. He was dogmatically opposed to the use of the federal commerce and taxing powers, and he used substantive due process to insulate private property and business from state regulation. He, along with Justices McReynolds, Sutherland, and Butler, were known collectively as the Four Horsemen, who categorically rejected New Deal economic and social programs. He was Taft's confidant and was instrumental in writing judicial reform proposals that Taft saw through to approval. Historians have referred to Van Devanter as "unimaginatively conservative," with strengths largely in negotiation and knowledge of judicial procedure. Indeed, he has been ranked as one of the "failures" among Court justices. Others, however, have suggested that evaluations of Van Devanter were unfairly downgraded because of his laissez-faire views. His decision to retire in 1937 gave Roosevelt the opportunity to change the Court beginning with the appointment of Hugo Black.

Vinson, Frederick Moore

Vinson earned an L.L.B. at Centre College and returned to his hometown of Louisa, Kentucky, to serve as city attorney. In 1921 he was elected district attorney and three years later was elected to Congress. After a defeat in the Republican landslide of 1928, Vinson was returned to Congress in 1930, where he served four more terms. A member of both the House Appropriations and Ways and Means Committees and a key supporter of the New Deal initiatives, Vinson was highly regarded in Congress, which was valuable in his later confirmation proceedings. Roosevelt nominated Vinson for the Court of Appeals for the District of Columbia in 1937. Vinson resigned the judgeship in May 1943 to become Roosevelt's director of economic stabilization. Vinson then served as Truman's treasury secretary before he was nominated to replace Harlan Fiske Stone as chief justice.

Vinson usually voted with the conservative justices (Jackson, Frankfurter, Burton, and Reed), the wing of the Court that was solidified with the appointments of Tom Clark and Sherman Minton in 1949. Vinson did not possess a broad or systematic view of the Constitution or the judicial role. He was instead a judicial pragmatist. Experts were generally unimpressed with Vinson, and a 1970 poll of law school deans and faculty rated Vinson's performance as a "failure." Vinson's tenure was shorter than most of his counterparts (seven years), and he presided over a Court divided by ideology and personality. Truman hoped that the strength of Vinson's personality would help unite his badly divided Court, but like his immediate predecessor, Stone, Vinson was unable to unify his Court.

Vinson inherited many of the difficulties that had split the Stone Court, especially the questions about judicial role and the extent to which the Court should defer to the elected branches of government. Expansion of the federal commerce clause and protecting federal authority from state encroachment were repeated themes in Vinson's opinions. Individual rights were generally subordinate to governmental authority. Vinson's Court offered little protection for those called to testify before congressional committees, executive investigations, or criminal prosecutions. One of his most famous opinions was his dissent in *Youngstown Sheet & Tube Co. v. Sawyer* (1952). In *Youngstown*, Vinson vigorously disagreed with the Court's decision to strike down President Truman's order to seize control of the country's private steel mills. Vinson's cold war concerns were best exemplified in *Dennis v. United States* (1951), which affirmed convictions against leaders of the American Communist Party for Smith Act violations.

Vinson remained in close contact with members of the Truman administration after his appointment, and there was even some speculation that he would leave the Court to assume a major position in the executive branch. He stayed in the Court, however, until his unexpected death on September 8, 1953.

Wallace, Henry Agard

Henry Wallace was Franklin Roosevelt's agriculture secretary until 1940 and vice president during Roosevelt's third term. Wallace's extensive familiarity with the farm scene made him a natural choice for secretary of agriculture. Wallace earned a degree in agriculture and following his graduation worked on the staff of *Wallace's Farmer*, published by his father (who had been agriculture secretary for President Harding in the early 1920s). He eventually became the magazine's editor. A Republican initially,

Wallace changed party affiliation to back Al Smith in 1928. He actively supported Franklin Roosevelt's candidacy in 1932, and some believed Wallace was a factor in Roosevelt's carrying Iowa. He joined the Roosevelt administration as secretary of agriculture and was responsible for drafting the Agricultural Adjustment Act of 1933. When the AAA was declared unconstitutional, Wallace revised it in the Agricultural Adjustment Act of 1938, which remains the foundation of contemporary U.S. agricultural policy.

Wallace resigned his secretaryship in August 1940 to become Roosevelt's running mate. As Roosevelt's vice president, he expanded the office beyond its traditional limits. He served as Roosevelt's goodwill ambassador, traveling extensively in the Far East and Latin America. Party conservatives opposed Wallace's renomination in 1944, and Roosevelt instead placed Senator Harry Truman on the national ticket. Wallace served as secretary of commerce for the next two years, but he broke with the Democratic Party in 1946 over foreign policy issues. He resigned from the Truman administration and became editor of the *New Republic*. He helped form a new left-wing political alliance called the Progressive Party and became its presidential nominee in 1948.

War Labor Disputes Act (Smith-Connally Act)

The conservative Seventy-eighth Congress enacted, over Roosevelt's veto, the War Labor Disputes Act of 1943, which was also known as the Smith-Connally Act. The act was prompted at least in part by rising public anger over wartime strikes, especially by John L. Lewis's United Mine Workers of America. The objective of Smith-Connally was to prevent strikes from disrupting production, and it authorized executive seizure of plants closed by strikes or other labor disputes. Although regarded as a wartime measure, Smith-Connally, a precursor to the Taft-Hartley Act of 1947, imposed restraints on organized labor that had been on the conservative agenda since passage of the Wagner Act in 1935. The law required unions to give notice of a strike, mandated a thirty-day cooling-off period, provided penalties for illegal work stoppages, and enhanced presidential power to seize war plants. Although never as harmful as many union leaders feared, the Smith-Connally Act restricted both the economic and political activities of unions and was a major setback to the labor movement.

War Powers Acts of 1941 and 1942

When war broke out, Congress rushed through the first of two War Powers Acts. The 1941 act reinstated the provisions of the Overman Act from World War I. It authorized Roosevelt to reorganize executive departments, expedite the awarding of government contracts for war supplies, and seize enemy properties, among other things. This expansion of executive power allowed Roosevelt to make some administrative changes, which had not been politically feasible before the war emergency. The first War Powers Act was written in language so sweeping that it gave Roosevelt the authority not only to shuffle functions among old agencies but also to create new agencies for war purposes.

The War Powers Act of 1942 contained a combination of components that further expanded the emergency power of the chief executive. Among the items included were plant-requisitioning power, control of overseas communications and alien property, and the allocation of war-related materials and all defense contracts. The act provided that the president "may exercise any power, authority, or discretion conferred on him by this section, through such department, agency or officer of the Government as he may direct, and in conformity with any rules and regulations which he may procure." The second act complemented the first by broadening controls over interstate transportation, expediting the naturalization process for foreign-born members of the armed services, and redefining censorship power.

War Relocation Authority (WRA)

Following the attack on Pearl Harbor, the Justice Department was responsible for dealing with Japanese who lived in the United States and might immediately threaten national security. Cases were handled on an individual basis, with the FBI conducting investigations and gathering evidence against particular suspects. At the same time, the attorney general established curfew zones for all Japanese Americans on the West Coast. Many believed the curfew was an insufficient response, and on February 20, 1942, the military was given broader jurisdiction. On March 3, 1942, General John DeWitt issued Proclamation Number 1 outlining a plan for the gradual evacuation of all persons of Japanese ancestry. To administer the plan, President Roosevelt set up the War Relocation Authority, which arranged to receive the evacuees at centers where they were settled for the duration of the war. (The text of Roosevelt's Executive Order 9102 creating the War Relocation Authority and other selected relocation documents are contained in Appendix I.)

Wheeler, Senator Burton K.

Born in Massachusetts, Wheeler earned his law degree at the University of Michigan before moving west and settling in Butte, Montana, where he began a private practice. An active Democrat, Wheeler served in the U.S. House of Representatives for a term before accepting appointment in the Wilson administration as the U.S. attorney for Montana, a position he held from 1913 to 1918. After an unsuccessful bid for governor of Montana in 1920, Wheeler was elected to the U.S. Senate in 1922; he served four terms. Wheeler was the vice presidential candidate on the Progressive Party ticket in 1924 as the running mate of Robert LaFollette. Had Franklin Roosevelt not chosen to seek a third term, Wheeler would have been a contender for the Democratic presidential nomination in 1940. Wheeler aggressively represented the interests of labor, farmers, and small business owners. A constant adversary throughout his political career was the Anaconda Copper Mining Company. Wheeler was one of the first Democrats to support Franklin Roosevelt's candidacy for the 1932 Democratic presidential nomination and was one of Roosevelt's political advisers in fashioning much of the New Deal program. Although Wheeler and Roosevelt differed on some issues during Roosevelt's first term, Wheeler campaigned for his reelection in 1936. Wheeler and Roosevelt parted company, however, when Roosevelt proposed packing the courts. Wheeler in fact led the fight against the proposal and was the Senate member to whom Chief Justice Hughes directed his letter opposing the Roosevelt proposal. Wheeler and the opponents of the plan prevailed, and the Roosevelt-Wheeler relationship was never the same afterward. Wheeler further distanced himself from Roosevelt on foreign policy bases. He felt such Roosevelt initiatives as lend-lease was drawing the United States into war. Prior to Pearl Harbor, he led opposition to Roosevelt's "aid-short-of war" policies and was one of the most highly sought-after speakers at the rallies of the America First Committee, a noninterventionist organization. Following Pearl Harbor, however, Wheeler supported the U.S. war effort and reluctantly backed U.S. membership in the United Nations. His isolationist views damaged his political reputation, and he was defeated in the Democratic Senate primary in 1946. During the 1946 campaign, his opponents used vicious smear tactics, including representation of his isolationism as disloyal and pro-Nazi. Once his long tenure in the Senate ended, he practiced law with his son in Washington, D.C., until his death in 1975.

Works Progress Administration (WPA)

The Works Progress Administration was a component of President Roosevelt's New Deal program. Created in May 1935, the WPA was the largest agency established under the Emergency Relief Appropriation Act; it was renamed the "Works Projects Administration" in 1939. WPA director Harry Hopkins felt that government relief resources should go into wages, and the WPA put more than 3 million people to work in its first year. During the eight years of the agency's life, it placed 8.5 million persons at a total cost of $11 billion. The majority of the WPA workforce built and renovated bridges, post offices, schools, public swimming pools, and airport runways. Along with its endorsers, the WPA had its critics, who claimed that WPA projects involved work that did not really need to be done. Roosevelt, however, felt that giving unemployed workers jobs and wages was better for the workers' morale than simply giving them welfare checks. Within the WPA, there were three fine arts projects: the Federal Theater Project, the Federal Writer's Project, and the Federal Art Project. Although the WPA was a federal program, it recognized the proposition that all politics is local. Roosevelt used it to build up local organizations that would support his national programs. Republicans complained that it was simply a gigantic federal patronage machine, operated for the sole benefit of the Democratic Party.

Yamashita, General Tomoyuki

General Yamashita, the son of a doctor, began preparing for a military career when he was still a child. After completing work at a series of military academies, he was commissioned second lieutenant in the Japanese army in 1908. By 1932, at the age of forty-seven, he became section chief of military affairs in the Japanese War Ministry and seemed destined to become war minister or even premier. When Japan entered the war against the Allies, Yamashita was placed in charge of the Twenty-fifth Army, and in October 1944 Yamashita took full command of all Japanese forces in the Philippines. Once the Allies, under the command of General Douglas MacArthur, regained control of the Philippines, the retreating Japanese troops committed a number of atrocities, including massacring civilians. Yamashita was captured and charged with war crimes as the officer responsible for the actions of his troops. Yamashita was tried and convicted of the charges and hanged on February 23, 1946. In *In re Yamashita* (1946) the Supreme Court ruled that the military proceedings under which Yamashita was tried, convicted, and sentenced were constitutional.

Youngstown Sheet & Tube Co. v. Sawyer (1952)

Youngstown was the Supreme Court decision that struck down a presidential order directing governmental seizure and management of privately owned steel mills, an order prompted by a labor dispute in the steel industry. After failing to achieve resolution of the dispute through other means, President Harry Truman ordered Commerce Secretary Charles Sawyer to "take possession of a number of steel mills and keep them operating" because he believed that a steel strike would curtail steel production, which in turn would jeopardize production of supplies for the Korean War effort. The steel companies sought to enjoin the seizure. The Court was asked in *Youngstown* to permit the exercise of inherent or aggregate executive power. A six-justice majority was not persuaded that the president possessed such authority even under these circumstances. Each of the majority's six members authored an individual opinion.

Justice Black noted the absence of statutory authorization for the seizure. Indeed, he pointed out that Congress had "refused to adopt that method of settling labor disputes." Black felt that the authority to order the seizure must "be found in some provisions of the Constitution," and he rejected the contention that power can be implied from the "aggregate" of presidential powers (*Youngstown*, 586). Justice Frankfurter acknowledged that the president's constitutional authority is not as "particularized" as that of Congress but warned that "unenumerated powers do not mean undefined powers" (*Youngstown*, 610). Justice Douglas's concurring opinion was also grounded on separation of powers. Emergencies do not "create" power or suspend checks and balances. The separation doctrine was not intended to "promote efficiency, but to preclude the exercise of arbitrary power" (*Youngstown*, 629). Justice Jackson more directly rejected the inherent power arguments as based on the "unarticulated assumption . . . that necessity knows no law." Jackson felt that constitutional authors consciously withheld such emergency power because crises are a "ready pretext for usurpation" and that possession of emergency power "would tend to kindle emergencies" (*Youngstown*, 650). The concurring opinions of Justices Burton and Clark also noted the lack of legislative authorization for the seizure, but they suggested that procedures under the Taft-Hartley Act were still available to Truman. A dissent written by Chief Justice Vinson urged that "flexibility as to mode of execution to meet critical situations is a matter of practical necessity" (*Youngstown*, 702). Presidents must possess sufficient authority to respond to emergencies. Vinson also cited historical precedent for the action and placed the seizure wholly within the bounds of executive action previously established.

Appendix I: Selected Documents on the Relocation of the Japanese

Executive Order No. 9066
(Creation of Military Areas)

Whereas, The successful prosecution of the war requires every possible protection against espionage and sabotage to national-defense material, national-defense premises and national-defense utilities. . . .

Now therefore, by virtue of the authority vested in me as President of the United States, and Commander in Chief of the Army and Navy, I hereby authorize the Secretary of War, and the Military Commanders whom he may from time to time designate, whenever he or any designated Commander deems such action necessary or desirable, to prescribe military areas in such places and of such extent as he or the appropriate Military Commander may determine, from which any or all persons may be excluded, and with respect to which, the right of any person to enter, remain in, or leave shall be subject to whatever restriction the Secretary of War or the appropriate Military Commander may impose in his discretion. The Secretary of War is hereby authorized to provide for residents of any such area who are excluded therefrom, such transportation, food, shelter, and other accommodations as may be necessary, in the judgment of the Secretary of War or the said Military Commander, and until other arrangements are made, to accomplish the purpose of this order. The designation of military areas in any region or locality shall supersede designations of prohibited and restricted areas by the Attorney General under the Proclamation of December 7 and 8, 1941, and shall supersede the responsibility and authority of the Attorney General under the said Proclamations in respect of such prohibited and restricted areas.

I hereby further authorize and direct the Secretary of War and the said Military Commanders to take such other steps as he or the appropriate Military Commander may deem advisable to enforce compliance with the restrictions applicable to each Military area hereinabove authorized to be designated, including the use of Federal troops and other Federal Agencies, with authority to accept assistance of state and local agencies.

I hereby further authorize and direct all Executive Departments, independent establishments and other Federal Agencies, to assist the Secretary of War or the said Military Commanders in carrying out this Executive Order, including the furnishing of medical aid, hospitalization, food, clothing, transportation, use of land, shelter, and other supplies, equipment, utilities, facilities, and services.

This order should not be construed as modifying or limiting in any way the authority heretofore granted under Executive Order No. 8972, dated December 12, 1941, nor shall it be construed as limiting or modifying the duty and responsibility of the Federal Bureau of Investigation, with respect to the investigations of alleged acts of sabotage or the duty and responsibility of the Attorney General and the Department of Justice under the Proclamations of December 7 and 8, 1941, prescribing regulations for the conduct and control of alien enemies, except as such duty and responsibility is superseded by the designation of military areas hereunder.

Franklin D. Roosevelt
February 19, 1942

Executive Order 9102 (Establishment of the War Relocation Authority)

By virtue of the authority vested in me by the Constitution and statutes of the United States, as President of the United States and Commander in Chief of the Army and Navy, and in order to provide for the removal from designated areas of persons whose removal is necessary in the interests of national security, it is ordered as follows:

1. There is established in the Office of Emergency Management of the Executive Office of the President the War Relocation Authority, at the head of which shall be a director appointed by and responsible to the President.

2. The Director of the War Relocation Authority is authorized and directed to formulate and effectuate a program for the removal, from areas designated from time to time by the Secretary of War or appropriate military commander under the authority of Executive Order No. 9066 of February 19, 1942, of the persons or classes of persons designated under such Executive Order, and for their relocation, maintenance, and supervision.

3. In effectuating such program the Director shall have authority to:

(a) Accomplish all necessary evacuation not undertaken by the Secretary of War or appropriate military commander, provide for the relocation of such persons in appropriate places, provide for their needs in such manner as may be appropriate, and supervise their activities.

(b) Provide, insofar as feasible and desirable, for the employment of such persons at useful work in industry, commerce, agriculture, or public projects, prescribe the terms and conditions of such public employment, and safeguard the public interest in the private employment of such persons.

(c) Secure the cooperation, assistance, or services of any governmental agency.

(d) Prescribe regulations necessary or desirable to promote effective execution of such program, and, as a means of coordinating evacuation and relocation activities, consult with the Secretary of War with respect to regulations issued and measures taken by him.

(e) Make such delegations of authority as he may deem necessary.

(f) Employ necessary personnel, and make such expenditures, including the making of loans and grants and the purchase of real property, as may be necessary, within the limits of such funds as may be made available to the Authority.

4. The Director shall consult with the United States Employment Service and other agencies on employment and other problems incident to activities under this order.

5. The Director shall cooperate with the Alien Property Custodian appointed pursuant to Executive Order No. 9095 of March 11, 1942, in formulating policies to govern the custody, management, and disposal by the Alien Property Custodian of property belonging to foreign nationals removed under this order or under Executive Order No. 9066 of February 19, 1942; and may assist all other persons removed under either of such Executive Orders in the management and disposal of their property.

6. Departments and agencies of the United States are directed to cooperate with and assist the Director in his activities hereunder. The Departments of War and Justice, under the direction of the Secretary of War and the Attorney General, respectively, shall insofar as consistent with the national interest provide such protective, police and investigational services as the Director shall find necessary in connection with activities under this order.

7. There is established within the War Relocation Authority the War Relocation Work Corps. The Director shall provide, by general regulations, for the enlistment in such Corps, for the duration of the present war, of persons removed under this order or under Executive Order No. 9066 of February 19, 1942, and shall prescribe the terms and conditions of the work to be performed by such Corps, and the compensation to be paid.

8. There is established within the War Relocation Authority a Liaison Committee on War Relocation which shall consist of the Secretary of War, the Secretary of the Treasury, the Attorney General, the Secretary of Agriculture, the Secretary of Labor, the Federal Security Administrator, the Director of Civilian Defense, and the Alien Property Custodian, or their deputies, and such other persons or agencies as the Director may designate. The Liaison Committee shall meet at the call of the Director, and shall assist him in his duties.

9. The Director shall keep the President informed with regard to the progress

made in carrying out this order, and perform such related duties as the President may from time to time assign to him.

10. In order to avoid duplication of evacuation activities under this order and Executive Order No. 9066 of February 19, 1942, the Director shall not undertake any evacuation activities within military areas designated under said Executive Order No. 9066, without the prior approval of the Secretary of War or the appropriate military commander.

11. This order does not limit the authority granted in Executive Order No. 8972 of December 12, 1941; Executive Order No. 9066 of February 19, 1942; Executive Order No. 9095 of March 11, 1942; Executive Proclamation No. 2525 of December 7, 1941; Executive Proclamation No. 2526 of December 8, 1941; Executive Proclamation No. 2527 of December 8, 1941; Executive Proclamation No. 2533 of December 29, 1941; or Executive Proclamation No. 2537 of January 14, 1942; nor does it limit the functions of the Federal Bureau of Investigation.

Franklin D. Roosevelt
March 18, 1942

Public Law 503 (Criminal Penalties for Violation of Restrictions)

To provide a penalty for violating restrictions or orders with respect to persons entering, remaining in, leaving, or committing any act in military areas or zones.

Be it enacted by the Senate and House of Representatives of the United States of America in Congress assembled, That whoever shall enter, remain in, or commit any act in any military area or military zone prescribed, under the authority of an Executive Order of the President, by the Secretary of War, contrary to the restrictions applicable to any such area or zone or contrary to the order the Secretary of War or any such military commander, shall, if it appears that he knew or should have known of the existence and extent of the restrictions or order and that his act was in violation thereof, be guilty of misdemeanor and upon conviction shall be liable to a fine not to exceed $5,000 or to imprisonment for not more than one year, or both, for each offense.

March 21, 1942

Public Proclamation 5 (Establishment of War Relocation Centers)

To: The people within the States of Washington, Oregon, California, Montana, Idaho, Nevada, Utah, Arizona, and the Public Generally:

Whereas, by Public Proclamation No. 1, dated March 2, 1942, this headquarters, there were designated and established Military Areas Nos. 1 and 2 and Zones thereof; and

Whereas, by Public Proclamation No. 2, dated March 16, 1942, this headquarters, there were designated and established Military Areas Nos. 3, 4, 5, and 6 and Zones thereof; and

Whereas, the present situation within these Military Areas and Zones requires as a matter of military necessity the establishment of certain regulations, as set forth hereinafter:

Now Therefore, I, J. L. DeWitt, Lieutenant General, U.S. Army, by virtue of the authority vested in me by the President of the United States and by the Secretary of War and my powers and prerogatives as Commanding General, Western Defense Command, do hereby declare and establish the following regulations covering the conduct to be observed by all alien Japanese, all alien Germans, all alien Italians, and all persons of Japanese ancestry residing or being within the Military Areas above described:

Prior to and during the period of exclusion and evacuation of certain persons or classes of persons from prescribed Military Areas and Zones, persons otherwise subject thereto but who come within one or more of the classes specified in (a), (b), (c), (d), (e), and (f), below, may make written application for exemption from such exclusion and evacuation. Application Form WDC-PM 5 has been prepared for that purpose and copies thereof may be procured from any United States Post Office or United States Employment Service office in the Western Defense Command by persons who deem themselves entitled to exemption.

The following classes of persons are hereby authorized to be exempted from exclusion and evacuation upon the furnishing of satisfactory proof as specified in Form WDC-PM 5:

(a) German and Italian aliens seventy or more years of age.

(b) In the case of German and Italian aliens, the parent, wife, husband, child of (or other person who resides in the household and whose support is wholly dependent upon) an officer, enlisted man, or commissioned nurse on active duty in the Army of the United States (or any component thereof), U.S. Navy, U.S. Marine Corps, or U.S. Coast Guard.

(c) In the case of German and Italian aliens, the parent, wife, husband, child of (or other person who resides in the household and whose support is wholly dependent upon) an officer, enlisted man, or commissioned nurse who on or since December 7, 1941, died in the line of duty with the armed services of the United States indicated in the preceding paragraph.

(d) German and Italian aliens awaiting naturalization who had filed a petition for naturalization and who had paid the filing fee therefor in a court of competent jurisdiction on or before December 7, 1941.

(e) Patients in hospitals, or confined elsewhere, and too ill or incapacitated to be removed therefrom without danger to life.

(f) Inmates of orphanages and the totally deaf, dumb, or blind.

The applicant for exemption will be required to furnish the kinds of proof specified in Form WDC-PM 5 in support of the application. The certificate of exemption from evacuation will also include exemption from compliance with curfew regulations, subject, however, to such future proclamations or orders in the premises as may from time to time be issued by this headquarters. The person to whom such exemption from evacuation and curfew has been granted shall thereafter be entitled to reside in any portion of any prohibited area, including those areas heretofore declared prohibited by the Attorney General of the United States.

Lieutenant General J. L. DeWitt, Commander
Western Defense Command
March 30, 1942

Appendix II: Footnote Four to United States v. Carolene Products Co.

There may be narrower scope for operation of the presumption of constitutionality when legislation appears on its face to be within a specific prohibition of the Constitution, such as those of the first ten amendments, which are deemed equally specific when held to be embraced within the Fourteenth. See *Stromberg v. California*, 283 U.S. 359 (1931); *Lovell v. Griffin*, 303 U.S. 444 (1938).

It is unnecessary to consider now whether legislation which restricts those political processes which can ordinarily be expected to bring about repeal of undesirable legislation, is to be subjected to more exacting judicial scrutiny under the general prohibitions of the Fourteenth Amendment than are most other types of legislation. On restrictions upon the right to vote, see *Nixon v. Herndon*, 273 U.S. 536 (1927); *Nixon v. Condon*, 286 U.S. 73 (1932); on restraints upon dissemination of information, see *Near v. Minnesota*, 283 U.S. 697 (1931); *Grosjean v. American Press Co.*, 297 U.S. 233 (1936); *Lovell v. Griffin*, supra; on interferences with political organizations, see *Stromberg v. California*, supra; *Fiske v. Kansas*, 274 U.S. 380 (1927); *Whitney v. California*, 274 U.S. 357 (1927); *Herndon v. Lowry*, 301 U.S. 242 (1937); and see Holmes in *Gitlow v. New York*, 268 U.S. 652 (1925); as to prohibition of peaceful assembly, see *DeJonge v. Oregon*, 299 U.S. 353 (1937).

Nor need we enquire whether similar considerations enter into the review of statutes directed at particular religious, *Pierce v. Society of Sisters*, 268 U.S. 510 (1925), or national, *Meyer v. Nebraska*, 262 U.S. 390 (1923); *Bartels v. Iowa*, 262 U.S. 404 (1923); *Farrington v. Tokushige*, 273 U.S. 284 (1927), or racial minorities, *Nixon v. Herndon*, supra; *Nixon v. Condon*, supra; whether prejudice against discrete and insular minorities may be a special condition, which tends seriously to curtail the operation of those political processes ordinarily to be relied upon to protect minorities, and which may call for a correspondingly more searching judicial inquiry. Compare *McCulloch v. Maryland*, 4 Wheat. 316 (1819); *South Carolina State Highway Department v. Barnwell Bros.*, 303 U.S. 177 (1938).

Justice Harlan Stone

Chronology

1933

March 4   Franklin Roosevelt inaugurated for first term.

March 6   Roosevelt issues a proclamation closing all banks and stopping all gold transactions until Congress can meet in special session.

March 9   Emergency Banking Relief Act gives Roosevelt broad discretionary power over national banks and Federal Reserve banks and provides support for Roosevelt's closing of all banks.

March 16   Beginning of the first hundred days, a period during which Roosevelt made a number of specific legislative proposals to Congress—the first initiatives of the New Deal program.

March 31   Civilian Conservation Corps—initial unemployment relief act of the New Deal—creates 250,000 jobs for men in such areas as conservation and road construction.

May 12   Agricultural Adjustment Act—first statutory program for agricultural relief.

           Federal Emergency Relief Act—second major unemployment relief statute of the Roosevelt period—provides for grants to local governments for state-administered work programs.

May 18   Tennessee Valley Authority Act—intended to address flood control, power generation, and general economic recovery of the region.

May 27   Federal Securities Act regulates stock market practices and imposes

May 27, 1933 *cont.*	such requirements as full disclosure of all pertinent information to prospective investors.
June 13	Home Owners Refinancing Act creates Home Owners Loan Corporation to refinance home mortgages for nonfarm families.
June 16	National Industrial Recovery Act enacted at the end of the Hundred Days, seeking to promote industrial recovery by imposing a series of codes of fair competition. Establishes the right of workers to organize and creates the National Recovery Administration and National Labor Board as the principal means of implementation.
	Emergency Railroad Transportation Act seeks to deal with the problem of railroad bankruptcies and brings railroads and rate-making processes under the surveillance of the ICC.
1934	
January 8	*Home Building & Loan Association v. Blaisdell* sustains the Minnesota mortgage moratorium law on the ground that the economic welfare of the state and legislation to protect it are within reserved powers of the state.
March 5	*Nebbia v. New York* holds that any business is subject to reasonable regulation; upholds a New York law setting prices for milk producers.
June 19	Communications Act replaces the Federal Radio Commission with the FCC.
	Labor Disputes Joint Resolution creates the first NLRB.
June 27	Railroad Retirement Act requires all interstate railroads to participate in funding a program of unemployment compensation and retirement benefits.
1935	
January 7	*Panama Refining Co. v. Ryan*—first major New Deal case invalidating a section of the NIRA, relating to petroleum production controls. This "hot oil" decision focuses on delegation of legislative power to the president.

April 1   *Norris v. Alabama*—second "Scottsboro case" where criminal conviction is reversed for discriminatory jury selection.

April 8   Emergency Relief Appropriations Act—first legislation in the so-called second New Deal period, creates the Works Progress Administration, which attempts to put the unemployed to work on public projects.

May 6   *Railroad Retirement Board v. Alton Railroad Co.* overturns a major New Deal statute seeking to establish a social security system within the railroad industry.

May 27   *Schechter Poultry Corp. v. United States* invalidates Title I of the NIRA on excessive delegation of legislative power grounds.

        Humphrey's Executor v. United States denies the president the power to remove an administrative appointee without Senate consent.

July 5   National Labor Relations (Wagner) Act creates the second NLRB with broadened authority to certify election of bargaining representatives, adjudicate complaints of unfair labor practices by employers, and order employers to end practices deemed unfair.

August 14   Social Security Act creates system for unemployment compensation, levies a payroll tax to fund a broad program of old-age insurance, and provides funding to state programs for dependent children and the disabled.

August 23   Banking Act imposes controls on lending practices.

August 26   Public Utility Holding Company Act empowers the FPC to regulate interstate transmission of electric power by such holding companies and broadens SEC powers over financial practices.

August 30   Bituminous Coal Conservation Act (first Guffey-Snyder Act) creates "little NRA" to preserve the effective elements of the production, price, and labor codes established under the NIRA.

1936

January 6   *United States v. Butler* invalidates the first AAA, holding that agriculture is a purely local subject.

1936 *cont.*

February 17   *Grosjean v. American Press Co.* holds an advertising tax on major newspapers in Louisiana is unconstitutional impairment of free press.

Brown v. Mississippi overturns state conviction on coerced confession grounds.

Ashwander v. TVA upholds the TVA, the Court ruling that the government has constitutional power to construct dams to provide power for wartime munitions as well as improve navigability of waterways. A by-product of these activities, such as electricity, is a disposable property of the government.

May 18   *Carter v. Carter Coal Co.* invalidates the first Bituminous Coal Conservation Act as an invasion of states' rights.

June 1   *Morehead v. New York ex rel. Tipaldo* strikes down New York minimum wage law for women as infringing upon the constitutional rule against impairment of contract rights.

1937

January 4   *DeJonge v. Oregon* invalidates Oregon criminal syndicalism law as infringing upon free speech rights.

January 20   Roosevelt inaugurated for second term.

March 1   Supreme Court Retirement Act, first congressional response to judiciary reform bill, provides for justices to retire on guaranteed income eliminating any economic reason against retirement.

March 29   *West Coast Hotel Co. v. Parrish* upholds Washington state law fixing minimum wages for women, specifically overruling *Adkins v. Children's Hospital* (1923) and essentially overruling the *Morehead* decision of the previous June.

April 12   *NLRB v. Jones & Laughlin Steel Corp.* upholds all the key features of the National Labor Relations Act.

April 26   Bituminous Coal (Guffey-Vinson) Act reenacts the basic provisions of the first Guffey Act invalidated in *Carter v. Carter Coal Co.* (1936).

May 24   *Steward Machine Co. v. Davis* upholds the unemployment compensation feature of the Social Security Act.

                Helvering v. Davis upholds the old-age benefits of the Social Security Act.

June 3   Agricultural Adjustment Act, encouraged by the reversal of judicial position on constitutional questions after the Court-packing plan, reenacts basic provisions of the AAA struck down in *United States v. Butler* (1936).

October 4   Hugo L. Black replaces Justice Willis Van Devanter.

December 6   *Palko v. Connecticut* sets out the standard by which certain federal Bill of Rights provisions could be applied to the states through the Fourteenth Amendment.

1938
January 31   Stanley F. Reed replaces Justice George Sutherland.

February 14   *South Carolina Highway Department v. Barnwell Brothers* upholds a state regulation on interstate transportation by setting the maximum size of trucks.

April 25   *Erie Railroad Co. v. Tompkins* overrules *Swift v. Tyson* (1842) and denies the existence of federal common law, directing that in the absence of federal or state statutes federal courts are to apply the common law of the state in which the federal court sits.

                United States v. Carolene Products Co. upholds a federal statute on food standards and provides the occasion for Justice Stone to offer the "preferred position" doctrine.

May 23   *Johnson v. Zerbst* holds that the Sixth Amendment requires the federal courts to appoint counsel for indigent criminal defendants.

June 25   Fair Labor Standards (Wage-Hour) Act, complementing the Wagner Act, establishes a minimum wage, fixes a forty-hour limit to the workweek, and prohibits child labor.

December 12   *Missouri ex rel. Gaines v. Canada,* one of the early cases in the dis-

December 12, 1938 *cont.*	mantling of the separate but equal doctrine, holds that a state must provide students similar higher education opportunities irrespective of their race.
1939 January 20	Felix Frankfurter succeeds Justice Benjamin Cardozo.
March 27	*Graves v. New York ex rel. O'Keefe* upholds the right of states to tax income of federal employees, overruling *Collector v. Day* (1871).
April 13	Administrative Reorganization Act consolidates presidential control over the executive branch and enables the president to consolidate and regroup administrative agencies under reorganization plans subject to congressional review.
April 17	William O. Douglas succeeds Justice Louis Brandeis.
	Mulford v. Smith upholds the second AAA.
June 7	Administrative Office Act creates the Administrative Office of the United States Courts, a managerial service for the federal courts. Provides for executive officer for the Judicial Conference.
November 4	Neutrality Act amended to permit the cash-and-carry export of arms to belligerent nations.
1940 February 5	Frank Murphy succeeds Justice Pierce Butler.
April 22	*Thornhill v. Alabama* strikes down a state antipicketing statute on First Amendment grounds.
May 20	*Cantwell v. Connecticut* strikes down state law forbidding the sale of religious literature without a license; incorporates the free exercise clause to the states.
May 27	*Apex Hosiery Co. v. Leader* holds that the Sherman Act does not apply to union activity manifestly aimed at improving working conditions and not effecting a monopoly in trade.
June 3	*Minersville School District v. Gobitis* upholds compulsory flag

salute in public schools, the first of two such cases, with the second ruling reversing the first.

June 28   Alien Registration (Smith) Act aims at the surveillance of resident aliens by fingerprinting and periodic registrations.

September 16   Selective Training and Service Act, the first peacetime draft law in national history, provides for a one-year program of registration and selection of 2 million men.

October 14   Immigration and Nationality Act tightens the immigration and naturalization laws and, as amended, provides for the loss of citizenship in the case of desertion in time of war.

1941

January 6   Roosevelt delivers his "four freedoms" speech as his State of the Union address.

January 20   Roosevelt inaugurated for third term.

February 1   Justice James C. McReynolds resigns.

February 3   *United States v. Darby Lumber Co.* and *Opp Cotton Mills v. Administrator* uphold the FLSA.

                 United States v. Hutcheson reiterates union exemption from Sherman Act restraint of trade provisions.

February 10   *Milk Wagon Drivers Union v. Meadowmoor Dairies* sustains state authority to regulate union picketing if it provokes violence.

March 11   Lend-Lease Act authorizes lending of war materials to Great Britain and provides Roosevelt with a bypass of the limits of the Neutrality Act.

May 26   *United States v. Classic* holds that federal civil rights laws extend to the electoral process, including primary elections.

June 2   Chief Justice Charles Evans Hughes resigns.

1941 *cont.*

June 6   Roosevelt nominates James Byrnes to the Court; the Senate confirms him.

June 12   Roosevelt nominates Stone for chief justice and Jackson for associate justice.

June 22   Senate confirms Harlan F. Stone as chief justice.

July 7   Robert H. Jackson confirmed as associate justice.

August 14   Atlantic Charter issued.

October 21   *Edwards v. California* strikes down state law that prohibits bringing indigent persons into the state.

December 7   Attack on Pearl Harbor; martial law declared in Hawaii.

December 8   *Bridges v. California* and *Times-Mirror Co. v. Superior Court* overturn contempt citations for directing criticism at a court while a case is still pending.

December 18   First War Powers Act authorizes the president to extensively reorganize executive agencies to facilitate prosecution of the war.

1942

January 14   President orders all resident aliens to register with government.

January 19   *Glasser v. United States* holds that the same attorney may not be appointed to represent two defendants jointly if one objects.

January 30   Emergency Price Control Act passes, creating Office of Price Administration, with authority to fix prices and ration vital commodities.

February 2   *United States v. Pink* rules that executive agreements have the force of law.

February 19   Roosevelt issues Executive Order 9066, starting the process leading to the internment of 112,000 Japanese Americans.

February 20   Roosevelt authorizes the secretary of war to exclude persons from military areas on the West Coast.

March 9   *Chaplinsky v. New Hampshire* upholds state law that prohibits use of insulting or provocative language in public.

March 16   *FPC v. Natural Gas Pipeline Co.* extends federal power to control prices for interstate transit of natural gas.

March 18   Roosevelt executive order creates the War Relocation Authority.

March 21   Congress passes law embracing Roosevelt's Executive Order 9066, which authorizes evacuation of persons from designated military areas.

March 27   Second War Powers Act supplements first law by broadening executive control of interstate transportation and expediting naturalization process for foreign-born members of the armed services, among other things.

By proclamation General DeWitt orders that all Japanese nationals and citizens of Japanese ancestry remain within designated military areas.

March 30   *Allen-Bradley Local 1111 v. Wisconsin Employment Relations Board* upholds a state law regulating union picketing.

April 27   *Goldman v. United States* rules that neither the Fourth Amendment nor the Communications Act is violated when federal officers use a detectaphone against the wall of an adjoining room to overhear conversations.

Goldstein v. United States holds that an individual's protection against wiretapping applies only when the person is a party to the conversation.

May 9   All Japanese nationals and citizens of Japanese ancestry are excluded from designated military areas and sent to relocation centers.

June 1   *Kirschbaum v. Walling* extends federal control over production to a point where very few employees are outside reach.

June 1, 1943 *cont.*	*Betts v. Brady* rules that the assistance of counsel clause of the Sixth Amendment does not apply to the states.
	Skinner v. Oklahoma invalidates state law that allows for the sterilization of felons convicted of moral turpitude.
June 8	*Jones v. Opelika* sustains Alabama municipal law that licenses street vendors against expression and religion claims.
July 31	*Ex parte Quirin* rules that enemy saboteurs may be tried by military tribunals under military rules of justice.
October 3	Justice James Byrnes resigns.
October 4	*Wickard v. Filburn* allows Congress to pass laws setting production quotas to stabilize agricultural prices.
November 9	*Warren-Bradshaw Drilling Co. v. Hall* broadens the scope of the commerce clause to include operators of oil well drilling rigs.

1943

January 11	Roosevelt nominates Wiley B. Rutledge to replace Justice Byrnes.
February 1	*Tileston v. Ullman* upholds Connecticut anticontraceptive law.
February 8	Senate confirms Justice Rutledge.
March 1	*McNabb v. United States* rules that an accused must be taken before a judicial officer without unreasonable delay following arrest.
May 3	*Murdock v. Pennsylvania* overrules *Jones v. Opelika* and strikes down license fees on door-to-door salespeople, including religious practitioners.
May 10	*Lockerty v. Phillips* upholds wartime price controls and the creation of the Office of Price Administration.
May 27	Former justice Byrnes becomes director of war mobilization.
June 14	*West Virginia State Board of Education v. Barnette* reverses *Gob-*

itis and rules that compulsory participation in flag salute exercises in public schools violates the First Amendment.

June 21   *Hirabayashi v. United States* sustains constitutionality of wartime curfew applied to Japanese Americans.

               Schneiderman v. United States reverses a denaturalization order on grounds that the government failed to establish that the individual was a dangerous subversive.

June 25   Over Roosevelt's veto, Congress passes War Labor Disputes (Smith-Connally) Act requiring that unions in war plants must give a thirty-day notice of an intention to strike.

December 20   *Magnolia Petroleum Co. v. Hunt* rules the full faith and credit clause requires that the final judgment from a court in one state can prevent an action on the same issue in the courts of another state.

1944

January 3   *Falbo v. United States* upholds conviction of a conscientious objector to military draft for failure to report for alternate service.

               FPC v. Hope Natural Gas Co. expands federal government's authority to regulate utilities.

March 27   *Yakus v. United States* upholds Emergency Price Control Act of 1942, which created the Office of Price Administration to fix prices.

               Bowles v. Willingham—upheld rent control powers of the OPA.

               Tennessee Coal, Iron & Railroad Co. v. Muscoda Local 123 upholds principle of portal-to-portal pay.

April 3   *Smith v. Allwright* ends the "white primary" practice of excluding African Americans from party nominating elections or conventions.

May 1   *Ashcraft v. Tennessee* sets aside criminal conviction on coerced confession grounds.

May 15   *McLeod v. Dilworth* strikes down an Arkansas law that levied a tax on goods sold in another state.

1944 *cont.*

May 22   *Steuart & Bros. v. Bowles* upholds OPA sanctions on a fuel distributor who did not comply with rationing procedures.

June 5   *United States v. South-Eastern Underwriters Association* rules that insurance business is interstate in character and subject to Sherman Act.

                Polish National Alliance v. NLRB places insurance industry under commerce power regulation.

June 12   In *Hartzell v. United States* Court holds that convictions under the Espionage Act of 1917 require evidence of clear and present danger. *Baumgartner v. United States* reverses a deportation order based on contention that a naturalized citizen had not renounced his allegiance to a foreign government.

December 18   *Korematsu v. United States* upholds the Japanese evacuation against equal protection challenge.

1945

January 8   *Thomas v. Collins* strikes down Texas law that enjoined labor organizers from engaging in membership solicitations without first obtaining a state-issued license.

January 20   Roosevelt inaugurated for fourth term.

April 12   Roosevelt dies and is succeeded by Harry Truman.

                United Nations Charter language approved by United Nations conference in San Francisco.

April 23   *Cramer v. United States* overturns a treason conviction by narrowing definition of an "overt act."

May 7   *Jewell Ridge Coal Corp. v. Local No. 6167 of the United Mine Workers of America* reaffirms the portal-to-portal pay principle (with Jackson arguing that Black should not have participated in the case). *Screws v. United States* holds that criminal acts could be prosecuted under federal civil rights laws.

June 6   *Akins v. Texas* rules that no racial or other population group is enti-
                tled to proportional representation on a particular jury.

June 18   *Southern Pacific Railroad Co. v. Arizona* strikes down state law
                limiting length of trains on interstate commerce grounds.

                Associated Press v. United States rules that an exclusive member-
                ship provision of a wire news association is a conspiracy to restrain
                trade and therefore federal regulation of the practice does not vio-
                late the free press protection.

                Bridges v. Wixom upholds a militant labor leader's petition for
                habeas corpus review of deportation order.

July 28   U.S. Senate approves U.S. membership in United Nations by 89–2 vote.

August 14   Japan surrenders.

September 18   Justice Harold H. Burton replaces Justice Roberts.

1946
January 14   *New York v. United States* rules that sale of mineral water by the
                state of New York is a business, not a governmental function, and
                subject to federal taxes.

January 25   *Duncan v. Kahanamoku* rules that trials before military tribunals in
                Hawaii are unconstitutional, as martial law cannot supplant civil law
                when civil courts are operating.

February 4   *In re Yamashita* rules that an enemy commander may be tried in a
                military court on war crimes charges.

April 22   *Girouard v. United States* overrules *United States v. Schwimmer*
                (1929) and other previous decisions that conscientious objectors are
                ineligible for citizenship.

                Chief Justice Stone dies.

June 3   *Morgan v. Virginia* invalidates a state law requiring racial segrega-
                tion on public transportation that crosses state lines.

1946 *cont.*

June 6   Truman nominates Fred Vinson to replace Stone as chief justice.

June 10   *Colegrove v. Green* rules that courts ought not intervene in a congressional apportionment case.

              Anderson v. Mt. Clemens Pottery, another portal-to-portal case, holds that workers are entitled to pay for preparation time.

Table of Cases

Brown v. Board of Education (Brown I), 347 U.S. 483 (1954)

Brown v. Board of Education (Brown II), 349 U.S. 294 (1955)

Brown v. Maryland, 12 Wheaton 419 (1827)

Brown v. Mississippi, 297 U.S. 278 (1936)

Bunting v. Oregon, 243 U.S. 426 (1917)

Cafeteria Employees Union v. Angelos, 320 U.S. 293 (1943)

Cantwell v. Connecticut, 310 U.S. 296 (1940)

Carpenters' and Joiners' Union v. Ritter's Café, 315 U.S. 722 (1942)

Carter v. Carter Coal Co., 298 U.S. 238 (1936)

Carter v. Virginia, 321 U.S. 131 (1944)

Chambers v. Florida, 309 U.S. 227 (1940)

Chaplinsky v. New Hampshire, 315 U.S. 568 (1942)

Cloverleaf Butter Co. v. Patterson, 315 U.S. 148 (1942)

Colegrove v. Green, 328 U.S. 549 (1946)

Collector v. Day, 11 Wallace 113 (1871)

Cramer v. United States, 325 U.S. 1 (1945)

Cudahy Packing Co. of Louisiana v. Holland, 315 U.S. 357 (1942)

DeJonge v. Oregon, 299 U.S. 353 (1937)

Dennis v. United States, 341 U.S. 494 (1951)

Douglas v. Jeannette, 319 U.S. 157 (1943)

Duncan v. Kahanamoku, 327 U.S. 304 (1946)

Edwards v. California, 314 U.S. 160 (1941)

Endo, Ex parte, 323 U.S. 283 (1944)

Erie Railroad Co. v. Tompkins, 304 U.S. 64 (1938)

Escobedo v. Illinois, 378 U.S. 478 (1964)

Estep v. United States, 327 U.S. 114 (1946)

Everson v. Board of Education, 330 U.S. 1 (1947)

Falbo v. United States, 320 U.S. 549 (1944)

Federal Communications Commission v. National Broadcasting Co., 319 U.S. 239 (1943)

Federal Power Commission v. Hope Natural Gas Co., 320 U.S. 591 (1944)

Federal Power Commission v. Natural Gas Pipeline Co., 315 U.S. 575 (1942)

Follette v. McCormick, 321 U.S. 573 (1944)

Gibson v. United States, 329 U.S. 338 (1946)

Gideon v. Wainwright, 372 U.S. 335 (1963)

Gilbert v. Minnesota, 254 U.S. 325 (1920)

Girouard v. United States, 328 U.S. 61 (1946)

Gitlow v. New York, 268 U.S. 652 (1925)

Glasser v. United States, 315 U.S. 60 (1942)

Goldman v. United States, 316 U.S. 129 (1942)

Marbury v. Madison, 1 Cranch 137 (1803)

Marsh v. Alabama, 326 U.S. 501 (1946)

Martin v. Struthers, 319 U.S. 141 (1943)

Mayo v. United States, 319 U.S. 441 (1943)

McCulloch v. Maryland, 4 Wheaton 316 (1819)

McLeod v. Dilworth, 322 U.S. 327 (1944)

McLeod v. Threlkeld, 319 U.S. 491 (1943)

McNabb v. United States, 318 U.S. 332 (1943)

Medo Photo Supply Corp. v. National Labor Relations Board, 321 U.S. 678 (1944)

Milk Wagon Drivers Union v. Meadowmoor Dairies, 312 U.S. 287 (1941)

Milligan, Ex parte, 4 Wallace 2 (1866)

Minersville School District v. Gobitis, 310 U.S. 586 (1940)

Miranda v. Arizona, 384 U.S. 436 (1966)

Missouri ex rel. Gaines v. Canada, 305 U.S. 337 (1938)

Mitchell v. United States, 313 U.S. 80 (1941)

Morehead v. New York ex rel. Tipaldo, 298 U.S. 587 (1936)

Morgan v. Virginia, 328 U.S. 373 (1946)

Mulford v. Smith, 307 U.S. 38 (1939)

Muller v. Oregon, 208 U.S. 412 (1908)

Murdock v. Pennsylvania, 319 U.S. 105 (1943)

National Labor Relations Board v. Jones & Laughlin Steel Corp., 301 U.S. 1 (1937)

National Labor Relations Board v. Virginia Electric & Power Co., 314 U.S. 469 (1941)

Near v. Minnesota, 283 U.S. 697 (1931)

Nebbia v. New York, 291 U.S. 502 (1934)

New York v. United States, 326 U.S. 572 (1946)

News Printing Co. v. Walling, 327 U.S. 186 (1946)

Nippert v. Richmond, 327 U.S. 416 (1946)

Norman v. Baltimore & Ohio Railroad, 294 U.S. 240 (1935)

Norris v. Alabama, 294 U.S. 587 (1935)

North American Co. v. Securities and Exchange Commission, 327 U.S. 686 (1946)

Northwest Airlines v. Minnesota, 322 U.S. 292 (1944)

Nortz v. United States, 294 U.S. 317 (1935)

Oklahoma Press Publishing Co. v. Walling, 327 U.S. 186 (1946)

Olmstead v. United States, 277 U.S. 438 (1928)

Opp Cotton Mills v. Administrator, 312 U.S. 126 (1941)

Overstreet v. North Shore Corp., 318 U.S. 125 (1943)

Palko v. Connecticut, 302 U.S. 319 (1937)

Panama Refining Co. v. Ryan, 293 U.S. 388 (1935)

Parker v. Brown, 317 U.S. 341 (1943)

United States v. Classic, 313 U.S. 299 (1941)

United States v. Curtiss-Wright Export Corp., 299 U.S. 304 (1936)

United States v. Darby Lumber Co., 312 U.S. 100 (1941)

United States v. E. C. Knight Co., 156 U.S. 1 (1895)

United States v. Hutcheson, 312 U.S. 219 (1941)

United States v. Local 807, International Brotherhood of Teamsters, 315 U.S. 521 (1942)

United States v. Macintosh, 283 U.S. 605 (1931)

United States v. Pink, 315 U.S. 203 (1942)

United States v. Schwimmer, 279 U.S. 644 (1929)

United States v. South-Eastern Underwriters Association, 302 U.S. 533 (1944)

Viereck v. United States, 318 U.S. 236 (1943)

Virginia Electric & Power Co. v. National Labor Relations Board, 319 U.S. 533 (1943)

Wallace Corp. v. National Labor Relations Board, 323 U.S. 248 (1944)

Warren-Bradshaw Drilling Co. v. Hall, 317 U.S. 88 (1942)

West Coast Hotel v. Parrish, 300 U.S. 379 (1937)

West Virginia State Board of Education v. Barnette, 319 U.S. 624 (1943)

Western Union Telegraph Co. v. Lenroot, 323 U.S. 490 (1945)

Wickard v. Filburn, 317 U.S. 111 (1942)

Williams v. North Carolina (Williams I), 317 U.S. 287 (1942)

Williams v. North Carolina (Williams II), 325 U.S. 226 (1945)

Wolf v. Colorado, 338 U.S. 25 (1949)

Yakus v. United States, 321 U.S. 414 (1944)

Yamashita, In re, 327 U.S. 1 (1946)

Youngstown Sheet & Tube Co. v. Sawyer, 343 U.S. 937 (1952)

Glossary

adversary proceeding   A legal process that involves a contest between two opposing parties. Formal notice is served on the party against whom an action has been filed to allow that party an opportunity to respond. This system is generally regarded as the most effective means for the evaluation of evidence.

advisory opinion   An opinion of a court indicating how it would rule on an issue if the issue were presented in an actual case—although no real case exists to present the legal question; an interpretation of law without binding effect.

affirmation   An appellate court ruling that upholds the judgment of a lower court—that maintains the judgment of the lower court is correct and should stand.

amicus curiae (lit., "friend of the court")   A person or group not a party to a case that submits a brief detailing its views on a case. The purpose of an amicus brief is to direct a court's attention to an issue or argument that might not be developed in the same way by the parties themselves.

appeal   A process by which a final judgment of a lower court ruling is reviewed by a higher court.

appellate jurisdiction   Authority of a superior court to review decisions of inferior courts. Appellate jurisdiction empowers a higher court to conduct such a review and affirm, modify, or reverse the lower court decision. Appellate jurisdiction is conveyed through constitutional or statutory mandate. Federal appellate jurisdiction is granted by Article 3 of the Constitution, which says that the Supreme Court possesses such jurisdiction "both as to law and fact, with such exceptions and under such regulations as the Congress shall make."

appellee   The party who prevails in a lower court and against whom an appeal of the judgment is sought; in some situations called a "respondent."

assembly, right to   A fundamental right provided by the First Amendment that the people are entitled peaceably to gather and petition the government for "redress of grievances." It includes the right to protest governmental policies as well as to advocate particular, even distasteful, views. The government can impose regulations on the time, place, and manner of assembly, provided that substantial interests, such as preventing threats to public order, can be shown.

balancing test   A judicial decision-making approach where interests on one side are weighed against interests on another, based on the traditional idea that individual freedoms and governmental authority must be kept in equilibrium. This approach is used most frequently where courts are reviewing individual rights issues. An individual's free speech interests, for example, may be balanced against a societal interest for national security to determine if the speech is protected from regulation or not.

brief   A document containing arguments on a matter under consideration by a court. A brief submitted to a court by an attorney typically contains, among other things, points of law from previous rulings.

case law   Precedent created as courts resolve disputes. Case law is made by judges as they rule on a specific set of facts. Common law is similar to case law but judicially incorporates accepted traditional community values, usages, and customs into court decisions. Statutory law, by contrast, is enacted by a legislative body.

case or controversy   A constitutional requirement that disputes or controversies be definite and concrete and involve parties whose legal interests are truly adverse. This requirement, contained in Article 3 of the Constitution, establishes a bona fide controversy as a precondition for adjudication by federal courts.

certification   A process by which judges in one court state uncertainty about the rule of law to apply in a case and request instructions from a higher court.

certiorari (lit., "to be informed of, to be made certain in regard to")   A writ or order to a court whose decision is being challenged on appeal to send up the records of the case to enable a higher court to review the case. The writ of certiorari is the primary means by which the U.S. Supreme Court reviews cases from lower courts.

citizenship   A legal status that entitles a person to all the rights and privileges guaranteed and protected by the Constitution of the United States. All persons born in the United States or to parents who are U.S. citizens possess U.S. citizenship. Others may obtain citizenship through naturalization, a process established by Congress.

civil liberties   Those liberties spelled out in a bill of rights or a constitution that guarantee the protection of persons, opinion, and property from the arbitrary interference of government officials. Civil liberties create immunities from certain governmental actions that interfere with an individual's protected rights.

civil rights   Positive acts of government designed to protect persons against arbitrary and discriminatory treatment by government or individuals. Civil rights guarantees may be found in constitutions but more frequently take the form of statutes.

class action   A legal action in which one or more persons represent both themselves and others who are similarly situated. All members of a class must share a common legal interest and meet particular requirements in order to proceed as a class or collective action.

comity   Legal principle that prompts a court to defer to the exercise of jurisdiction by another court. Comity is a rule of judicial courtesy rather than a firm requirement of law, and it suggests that a court that first asserts jurisdiction will not undergo interference by another court without its consent.

commerce clause   Provision found in Article 1, section 8 of the U.S. Constitution that empowers Congress to "regulate commerce with foreign nations, and among the several states, and with the Indian tribes." Since the 1930s the commerce power has been the basis for extensive federal regulation of the economy and, to a limited extent, federal criminal law.

common law   A body of principles that derive their authority from court judgments that are grounded in common customs and usages. Common law consists of principles that do not have their origin in statute and as such is distinct from law created by legislative enactments.

concurrent jurisdiction   Authority that is shared by different courts and may be exercised at the same time over the same subject matter.

concurring opinion   An opinion by a judge that agrees with the decision of the majority but disagrees with the majority's rationale—in other words, has arrived at the same conclusion but for different reasons.

conference   A closed meeting of Supreme Court justices in which the justices conduct all business associated with deciding cases—determining which cases to review, discussing the merits of cases after oral argument, and deciding by vote which party to a case will prevail.

constitutional court   A federal court created by Congress under authority conveyed by Article 3. Judges of constitutional courts serve for the duration of good behavior (life tenure) and are protected from having their salaries reduced by the legislature.

declaratory judgment   A ruling of a court that clarifies rights of the parties or offers an opinion or a legal question and is invoked when a plaintiff seeks a declaration of his or her rights. It differs from a conventional action in that no specific order is issued nor is any relief or remedy granted.

decree   A judgment or order of a court.

de facto (lit., "from the fact")   Something that exists or is actual, but unlike de jure, is not caused by any official or state action. For example, racial segregation that is not legally mandated, but exists nonetheless, is referred to as de facto segregation.

defendant   The party who is sued in a civil action or charged in a criminal case; the party responding to a civil complaint. A defendant in a criminal case is the person formally accused of criminal conduct.

de jure (lit., "by right")   A de jure action occurs as a result of law or official government action.

demurrer   An allegation by a defendant that even if the facts alleged were true, their legal consequences are not such as to require an answer or further proceedings in the cause. Under contemporary rules of civil procedure, a motion to dismiss a case for failure to establish a claim is more commonly used to accomplish the same objective.

dissenting opinion   The opinion of a judge that disagrees with the result reached by the majority.

diversity jurisdiction   Authority conveyed by Article 3 of the Constitution empowering federal courts to hear civil actions involving parties from different states.

due process   Government procedures that follow principles of essential or fundamental fairness. Provisions designed to ensure that laws will be reasonable both in substance and in means of implementation are contained in two clauses of the Constitution. The Fifth Amendment prohibits deprivation of "life, liberty, or property, without due process of law." It sets a limit on arbitrary and unreasonable actions by the federal government. The Fourteenth Amendment contains parallel language aimed at the states. Due process requires that actions of government occur through ordered and regularized processes.

en banc (lit., "on the bench")   A proceeding in which all the judges of an appellate court participate, as distinguished from a proceeding heard by a panel of three judges.

enjoin   To require to perform or refrain from a specified action. A party is enjoined by a court issuing an injunction or a restraining order.

equity   A system of remedial justice administered by certain courts empowered to order remedies based on principles as well as precedent.

exclusive power   Authority that is assigned to either the national or state level of government but not exercised by both.

executive order   A regulation issued by the president, a state governor, or some other executive authority for the purpose of giving effect to a constitutional or statutory provision. An executive order has the force of law and is one means by which the executive branch implements laws.

ex parte (lit., "on one side")   Done for, on behalf of, or on the application of one party only.

federal question   An issue arising out of provisions of the Constitution, federal statutes, or treaties. A federal court has authority to hear federal questions under powers conferred by Article 3.

federalism   A political system in which a number of sovereign political units join together to form a larger political unit that has authority to act on behalf of the whole. A federal system or federation preserves the political integrity of all the entities that compose the federation. Federal systems are regarded as weak if the central government has control over very few policy questions and strong if the central government possesses authority over most significant policy issues. Authority that is not exclusively assigned may be shared by the two levels and exercised concurrently. The supremacy clause of the Constitution requires that conflicts arising from the exercise of federal and state power are resolved in favor of the central government. Powers not assigned to the national government are "reserved" for the states by the Tenth Amendment.

grand jury   A panel of twelve to twenty-three citizens who review prosecutorial evidence to determine if there are sufficient grounds to formally accuse an individual of criminal conduct. The charges a grand jury issues are contained in a document called an indictment.

habeas corpus (lit., "you have the body")   Habeas corpus was a procedure in English law designed to prevent the improper detention of prisoners. The habeas process forced jailers to bring a detained person before a judge who would examine the justification for the detention. If the court found the person was being improperly held, it could order the prisoner's release by issuing a writ of habeas corpus.

implied power   Authority that is possessed by inference from expressed provisions of a constitution and deduced from circumstances, general language, or the conduct of parties rather than conveyed by explicit language.

in camera (lit., "in a chamber")   In private; a hearing conducted with no spectators present.

incorporation   The question of whether the federal Bill of Rights extends as a limitation on state governments. The issue has been largely resolved and most federal Bill of Rights provisions now operate at the state as well as the federal level. Several differing schools of thought on incorporation have existed historically. The most sweeping position was that all Bill of Rights provisions connect to the states through the due process clause of the Fourteenth Amendment, which prohibits a state from denying liberty without due process. Those advocating total incorporation viewed the term "liberty" as an all-inclusive shorthand for each of the rights enumerated in the Bill of Rights. A second opinion rejected any structural linkage of due process to the Bill of Rights and held simply that the due process clause requires states to assure fundamental fairness. Due process is assessed under this standard by criteria of immutable principles of justice, or, as Justice Cardozo suggested in *Palko v. Connecticut* (1937), elements that are "implicit in the concept of ordered liberty." Application of such standards would occur on a case-by-case basis. The third opinion is a hybrid of the first two and is known as "selective" incorporation. The selective approach resembles the fundamental fairness position in that it does not view as identical those rights contained in the Bill of Rights and those rights fundamental to fairness. Unlike the fundamental fairness approach, however, the selective view holds that rights expressly contained in the Bill of Rights, if adjudged fundamental, are incorporated through the Fourteenth Amendment and are applicable at the state level regardless of the circumstances of a particular case.

indictment   A written accusation presented by a grand jury to a court, charging that a person has done some act or omission that by law is a punishable offense.

injunction   An order prohibiting a party from acting in a particular way or requiring its specific action. An injunction allows a court to minimize injury to a person or group until the matter can otherwise be resolved, or it may prevent injury altogether. Failure to comply with an injunction constitutes contempt of court. Once issued, an injunction may be annulled or quashed, and it may be temporary or permanent. Temporary injunctions, known as interlocutory injunctions, are used to preserve a situation until the issue is resolved through normal processes of litigation. A permanent injunction may be issued upon completion of full legal proceedings.

in re (lit., "in the matter of")   The usual manner of entitling a judicial proceeding in which there are no adversary parties as such but some issue requiring judicial action.

judgment of the court   The final conclusion reached by a court—the outcome as distinguished from the legal reasoning supporting the conclusion.

judicial activism   An interventionist approach or role orientation for appellate decision making that has the appellate courts playing an affirmative policy role. Judicial activists are inclined to find more constitutional violations than those who see a more restrained role for courts; activists are more likely to invalidate legislative and executive policy initiatives. Critics regard judicial activism as legislating by justices to achieve policy outcomes compatible with their own social priorities.

judicial notice   The act by which a court, on its own initiative, recognizes the existence and truth of certain facts not offered as evidence by either party.

judicial review   The power of a court to examine the actions of the legislative and executive branches with the possibility of declaring those actions unconstitutional. Judicial review was discussed extensively at the Constitutional Convention of 1787, but it was not included in the Constitution as an expressly delegated judicial function. The Supreme Court first asserted the power of judicial review in *Marbury v. Madison* (1803).

judicial self-restraint   A role view of appellate court decision making that minimizes the extent to which judges apply their personal views to the legal judgments they render. Judicial self-restraint holds that courts should defer to the policy judgments made by the elected branches of government.

jurisdiction   The boundaries within which a particular court may exercise judicial power; the power of a court to hear and decide cases. The jurisdiction of federal courts is provided in Article 3 of the Constitution in the case of the Supreme Court and in acts of Congress in the case of the lower federal courts. Federal judicial power may extend to classes of cases defined in terms of substance and party as well as to cases in law and equity stemming directly from the federal Constitution, federal statutes, treaties, or those cases falling into the admiralty and maritime category. Federal judicial power also extends to cases involving specified parties; regardless of the substance of the case, federal jurisdiction includes actions where the federal government itself is a party, between two or more states, between a state and a citizen of another state, between citizens of different states, between a state and an alien, between a citizen of a state and an alien, and where foreign ambassadors are involved. State constitutions and statutes define the jurisdiction of state courts.

jurisprudence   A legal philosophy or the science of law; the course or direction of judicial rulings. Jurisprudence draws upon philosophical thought, historical and political analysis, sociological and behavioral evidence, and legal experience; it is grounded on the view that ideas about law evolve from critical thinking in a number of disciplines. Jurisprudence enables people to understand how law has ordered both social institutions and individual conduct.

jus belli (lit., "law of war")   The rights and legal obligations of those nations engaged in warfare as well as the status of neutral nations.

justiciable   Appropriate for a court to hear and decide.

laissez-faire   An economic theory that advocates the government ought not interfere with the dynamics of a free market economy—government should stay out of economic matters. Those subscribing to the laissez-faire view reject any form of government control or regulation of the economy. The decisions of the U.S. Supreme Court from the 1890s through 1937 frequently reflected laissez-faire values.

legislative court   A court created by Congress under authority of Article 1 of the Constitution. Legislative courts may be assigned administrative functions in addition to or instead of judicial functions in order to facilitate development of some level of specialization in a court system. Judges of federal legislative courts may be granted life tenure by Congress but do not have the same level of protection as judges of Article 3 or constitutional courts.

liberty of contract   A laissez-faire doctrine used to free private agreements from governmental regulation. The liberty of contract concept holds that individuals have a right to assume contractual obligations affecting their personal affairs. This includes the right of employers and employees to agree about wages, hours, and conditions of work without government interference. The concept was a central element of substantive due process in which the courts closely examined the reasonableness of governmental regulations. The liberty of contract concept was used to strike down laws establishing minimum wages and maximum hours of work.

litigant   A party to a lawsuit.

mandamus (lit., "we command")   A writ issued by a court of superior jurisdiction to an inferior court or governmental official commanding the performance of an official act.

martial law   Military government established over a civilian population during an emergency. Under martial law, military decrees supersede civilian laws and military tribunals replace civil courts. Martial law can be invoked by the president when necessary for the security of the nation. State governors, as commanders in chief of state militias, may declare martial law during an emergency occasioned by internal disorders or natural disasters.

mootness doctrine   A principle that applies if a question presented in a lawsuit cannot be answered by a court either because the issue has resolved itself or conditions have so changed that the court is unable to grant the requested relief.

motion   A request made to a court for a certain ruling or action.

natural law   Laws considered applicable to all nations and people because they are basic to human nature. Contrasts with positive law.

naturalization   Legal procedure by which an alien is admitted to citizenship. Congress is authorized by Article 1, section 8 of the Constitution to establish uniform rules for naturalization. An individual over eighteen may be naturalized after meeting certain qualifications, including residence in the United States for five years; ability to read, write, and speak English; and proof of good moral character. The residence requirement is lowered for spouses of citizens and for aliens who serve in the armed services. Minors become citizens when their parents are naturalized.

obiter dictum (lit., "something said in passing")   Statement contained in a court's opinion that is incidental to the disposition of the case. Obiter dicta often are directed to issues upon which no formal arguments have been heard, thus the positions represented there are not binding on later cases.

opinion of the court   The statement of a court that expresses the reasoning, or *ratio decidendi*, upon which a decision is based. The opinion summarizes the principles of law that apply in a given case and represents the views of the majority of a court's members. Occasionally the opinion of a court may reflect the views of less than a majority of its members; it is then called a plurality opinion.

order   A written command issued by a judge.

original jurisdiction   The authority of a court to hear and decide a legal question before any other court. Original jurisdiction typically is vested with trial courts rather than appellate courts, although Article 3 of the Constitution extends very limited original jurisdiction to the Supreme Court. Trial courts are assigned specific original jurisdiction defined in terms of subject matter or party.

per curiam opinion (lit., "by the court")   An unsigned written opinion issued by a court.

petitioner   A party seeking relief in court.

plaintiff   The party who brings a legal action to court for resolution or remedy.

plurality opinion   An opinion announcing a court's judgment and supporting reasoning in a case but not endorsed by a majority of the justices hearing the case.

police power   Authority that empowers government to regulate private behavior in the interest of public health, safety, and general welfare. In the U.S. constitutional system, police power resides with the state, not the federal government. It is a comprehensive power, and states possess substantial discretion for its exercise, but it is limited by various provisions of the U.S. Constitution and state constitutions and must conform to the requirements of due process.

political question   An issue that is not justiciable, or appropriate for judicial determination, because it is primarily political or involves a matter directed toward either the legislative or executive branch by constitutional language. The political question doctrine is sometimes invoked by the Supreme Court not because the Court is without power or jurisdiction but because the Court adjudges the question inappropriate for judicial response. In the Court's view, to intervene or respond would be to encroach upon the functions and prerogatives of one of the other two branches of government.

preemption doctrine   The notion that federal laws supersede, or preempt, state laws in certain policy areas. Grounded in the supremacy clause of Article 6, the preemption doctrine applies where the federal regulatory interest is so dominant or pervasive as to allow no reasonable inference that room is left for states to act. Congress may state explicitly such a preemptive interest, or the courts may interpret the intent of Congress fully to occupy the field.

preferred position doctrine   The concept that legislative enactments that affect First Amendment rights must be scrutinized more carefully than legislation that does not, since they affect fundamental rights such as free speech. The burden is clearly on the state to demonstrate justification for limiting a preferred position freedom. The preferred position doctrine is attributed to Justice Stone, who said in a footnote to his opinion in *United States v. Carolene Products Co.* (1938) that a lesser presumption of constitutionality exists when legislation "appears on its face to be within a specific prohibition such as those of the first ten amendments."

prior restraint   A restriction placed on a publication before it can be published or circulated. Prior restraint typically occurs through a full prohibition on publication or a licensure or censorship process that involves the state's review of materials for objectionable content. Prior restraint poses a greater threat to free expression than after-the-fact prosecution because government restrictions are imposed in a manner that precludes public scrutiny. The First Amendment therefore prohibits prior restraint in most instances, though it may be justified if the publication threatens national security, incites overthrow of the government, is obscene, or interferes with the private rights of others. Prior restraint is heavily suspect, and the First Amendment therefore prohibits it under most circumstances. It may be justified, however, if publication threatens national security, incites overthrow of the government, is obscene, or interferes with the private rights of others.

procedural due process   Fundamental fairness in the means by which governmental actions are executed. Procedural due process demands that before any deprivation of liberty or property can occur, a person must be formally notified and provided an opportunity for a fair hearing. Procedural due process—including access to legal counsel, the ability to confront witnesses against the accused, and a trial by jury—must also be accorded persons accused of crimes.

recusal   The process by which a judge is disqualified from hearing or reviewing a case when such participation might be inappropriate because of self-interest or bias. Disqualification may be initiated by a party to a case or by the judge himself or herself.

remand   To send a case back to an inferior court for additional action, such as correcting a specified error.

removal jurisdiction   The power to transfer a case, before trial or final hearing, from one court to another.

republicanism (guaranty clause) Government by representatives chosen by the people. A republic is distinguished from a pure democracy, where the people make policy decisions themselves rather than through an elected representative. Article 4, section 4 of the Constitution provides that the national government shall guarantee to each state a "republican form of government."

respondent The party against whom a legal action is filed.

reversal An action by an appellate court setting aside or changing a decision of a lower court. The opposite of an affirmation.

right A power or privilege to which a person is entitled. A right is legally conveyed by a constitution, statutes, or common law and may be absolute, such as one's right to believe, or conditional so that the acting out of one's beliefs will not injure other members of a political community.

ripeness A condition in which a legal dispute has evolved to the point where the issue(s) it presents can be determined by a court.

separation of powers The principle of dividing the powers of government among several coordinate branches to prevent excessive concentration of power. Separation of powers is designed to limit abusive exercise of governmental authority by partitioning power and then assigning that power to several locations. In distributing powers the U.S. Constitution functionally distinguishes between the government and the people and between legislative, executive, and judicial branches. Although the Constitution creates three separate branches, it also assigns overlapping responsibilities that makes the branches interdependent through the operation of a system of checks and balances.

sovereignty The supreme power of a state or independent nation free from external interference. Sovereignty is exercised by government, which has exclusive and absolute jurisdiction within its geographical boundaries.

standing The requirement that a real dispute exists between the prospective parties in a law suit before it can be heard by a court. As a result, courts typically are unable to respond to hypothetical questions. If a party does not have standing to sue, the matter is not justiciable.

stare decisis (lit., "to let the decision stand") The doctrine that once a principle of law is established for a particular fact situation, courts should adhere to that principle in similar cases in the future. The case in which the rule of law is established is called a precedent. Precedents may be modified or abandoned if circumstances require, but the expectation is that rules from previously adjudicated cases will prevail, creating and maintaining stability and predictability in the law.

state action   An action taken by an agency or official of government. The state action concept is used to determine whether an action complained of has its source in state authority or policy. The concept is critically important in cases presenting allegations of discrimination, as the equal protection clause typically cannot be applied to private acts of discrimination but only to conduct that occurs "under color" of governmental authority.

substantive due process   Fundamental fairness in the content or substance of government policy. Substantive due process review requires courts to examine the reasonableness of legislative enactments—that laws be fair and reasonable in substance as well as application. Substantive due process is distinguished from procedural due process.

summary judgment   A decision by a court made without a full hearing or without receiving briefs or oral arguments.

taxing power   The authority granted Congress in Article 1, section 8 of the Constitution to "lay and collect taxes, duties, imposts and excises" and to provide for the "common defense and general welfare" of the United States. The scope of federal power to tax and spend has depended at least in part on the Court's interpretation of the "general welfare" phrase.

Tenth Amendment   Provision added to the U.S. Constitution in 1791 that retains, or "reserves," for the states powers not assigned to the federal government. The Tenth Amendment has frequently been used to limit the actions of the federal government.

vested right   A right that so completely applies to a person that it cannot be impaired by the act of another person. Such rights must be recognized and protected by the government.

warrant   A judicial order authorizing an arrest or search and seizure.

writ   A written order of a court commanding the recipient to perform certain specified acts.

Annotated Bibliography

Abraham, Henry J. *The Judiciary: The Supreme Court in the Governmental Process.* 9th edition, Madison, Wisc.: Brown & Benchmark, 1994.

An excellent introduction to the Supreme Court and its role in the American governmental process. Includes three extremely valuable chapters dedicated to a discussion of "fundamental freedoms," including the incorporation process by which Bill of Rights freedoms are made applicable to state governmental action.

———. *Justices and Presidents: A Political History of Appointments to the Supreme Court.* 3rd edition. New York: Oxford University Press, 1992.

Written by a preeminent constitutional scholar, an analysis of the process used to select Supreme Court justices. Abraham discusses every nomination, successful or not; the motivations and expectations of the nominating president; and the Senate review and characterizes the on-bench performance of each justice.

Ackerman, Bruce. *We the People: Transformations.* Cambridge: Harvard University Press, 1998.

This second volume in a planned trilogy examines constitutional change and argues that the Constitution undergoes "revolutionary transformation" in response to such crises as the Civil War and the Great Depression.

Asch, Sidney H. *The Supreme Court and Its Great Justices.* New York: Arco, 1971.

Brief discussion of fifteen justices, including Stone Court justices Harlan Fiske Stone, Felix Frankfurter, Robert H. Jackson, Hugo L. Black, and William O. Douglas.

Baker, Leonard. *Brandeis and Frankfurter: A Dual Biography.* New York: New York University Press, 1984.

A combined biographical discussion of Louis Brandeis and his successor on the Court, Felix Frankfurter. Baker's examination of the two justices provides valuable insights into the political environment of the Court during the periods each served.

———. *Back to Back: The Duel between FDR and the Supreme Court.* New York: Macmillan, 1967.

Detailed account of the struggle between Franklin Roosevelt and the Supreme Court, the "reform" proposed in response (Roosevelt's so-called Court-packing plan), and the consequences of this initiative on executive-judicial relations.

Baker, Liva. *Felix Frankfurter.* New York: Coward-McCann, 1969.

An excellent biographical source on Frankfurter, with particularly valuable discussion of his years as one of Roosevelt's inner circle as well as his Court years.

Ball, Howard. *Hugo L. Black: Cold Steel Warrior.* New York: Oxford University Press, 1996.

A significant account of Black, his roots, his years in the political arena, and his thirty-four years on the Supreme Court. The volume provides a particularly valuable discussion of the values Black acquired throughout his life and how these values influenced his jurisprudence.

Berry, Mary Frances. *Stability, Security, and Continuity: Mr. Justice Burton and Decision-Making in the Supreme Court 1945–1958.* Westport, Conn.: Greenwood Press, 1978.

The only extended discussion of Burton's thirteen years on the Court. With the exception of the first chapter, which is dedicated to representing Burton's pre-Court life, the remainder of the volume examines Burton's jurisprudence and his fit on the Stone, Vinson, and Warren Courts.

Breen, Daniel L. "Stanley Forman Reed." In Melvin I. Urofsky, ed., *The Supreme Court Justices: A Biographical Dictionary.* New York: Garland, 1994, pp. 367–372.

Develops Reed's deference to federal power and decisions of the legislative and executive branches. Portrays Reed as a committed New Dealer, but not a judicial liberal, who was somewhat reluctant to support claims of rights violations.

Buchanan, A. Russell. *The United States and World War II.* 2 vols. New York: Harper & Row, 1964.

An examination of the American experience during World War II, both at home and abroad. Valuable for its discussion of federal agencies created in response to the conditions created by the war.

Bureau of the Budget. *The United States at War.* New York: DaCapo Press, 1972.

A comprehensive source on the agencies created to meet a broad array of war-related purposes. Produced by the Committee on Records of War Administration, a group of government employees appointed by the director of the Bureau of the Budget, this volume was intended as a government self-study of how the United States mobilized for war. The endeavor was guided by academics and evaluates those activities begun before as well as during the war.

Burner, David. "Owen J. Roberts." In Leon Friedman and Fred L. Israel, eds., *The Justices of the United States Supreme Court, 1789–1995: Their Lives and Major Opinions.* New York: Chelsea House, 1995, pp. 1117–1129.

Provides biographical background on Justice Roberts but offers valuable discussion of the pivotal role Roberts played on the Hughes Court, his switched positions on federal power to regulate the economy, and the marginalizing of Roberts during the Stone Court era.

Cardozier, V. R. *The Mobilization of the United States for World War II: How the Government, Military and Industry Prepared for War.* Jefferson, N.C.: McFarland & Company, 1994.

A recent attempt to examine how the United States mobilized for war following the attack on Pearl Harbor. The author argues that the American people, military, and industry responded effectively with both speed and efficiency. This response is seen as all the more remarkable in that "widespread antimilitarism" prevailed throughout the country during the 1930s, leaving the United States wholly unprepared for war.

Chandler, Ralph C., Richard A. Enslen, and Peter G. Renstrom. *Constitutional Law Dictionary: Governmental Powers.* Santa Barbara, Calif.: ABC-CLIO, 1987.

Summaries of Supreme Court decisions dealing with institutional authority. Volume also contains brief biographical entries on leading justices and discussions of selected legal terms and concepts.

Currie, David P. *The Constitution in the Supreme Court: The Second Century, 1888–1986.* Chicago: University of Chicago Press, 1990.

The second of two volumes that critically represents the constitutional decisions of the Supreme Court from 1888 to 1986. Currie breaks the second century at 1941, focusing on the rise and fall of substantive due process through the end of the 1930s and the evolution of individual rights protection thereafter.

Cushman, Clare, ed. *The Supreme Court Justices: Illustrated Biographies, 1789–1993.* Washington, D.C.: Congressional Quarterly Press, 1993.

A volume produced by the Supreme Court Historical Society under the direction of Clare Cushman. Each justice is profiled in a five-page essay that provides biographical background information. Although this volume does not intend to assess the jurisprudence of each justice, it does include a short description of the justice's most significant opinions.

Douglas, William O. *The Court Years, 1939–1975: The Autobiography of William O. Douglas.* New York: Random House, 1980.

Douglas's own recollections of his almost thirty-seven years on the Supreme Court, the second volume of his two-volume autobiography. Provides insights into his judicial activism and his observations of the political environment within which the Supreme Court functions.

Dunne, Gerald T. *Hugo Black and the Judicial Revolution.* New York: Simon & Schuster, 1977.

One of several excellent biographical discussions of Black. Dunne covers Black's Alabama and Senate years before engaging in a more lengthy examination of Black's tenure on the Court, divided into three parts—one part covering what Dunne calls the "great divide," the *Brown* decision, with each of the other two parts devoted to the period preceding and following *Brown.*

Epstein, Lee, Jeffrey A. Segal, Harold J. Spaeth, and Thomas Walker. *The Supreme Court Compendium: Data, Decisions, and Developments.* Washington, D.C.: Congressional Quarterly Press, 1994.

A comprehensive collection of information about the Supreme Court, including institutional history, decision-making processes, cases, caseload, and impact. It also supplies valuable information about the justices, such as background characteristics, opinions, and voting patterns.

Farber, Daniel A. "Robert Houghwout Jackson." In Melvin I. Urofsky, ed., *The Supreme Court Justices: A Biographical Dictionary.* New York: Garland, 1994, pp. 257–262.

Focuses on three of Jackson's most significant opinions—*Barnette, Wickard,* and *Youngstown.*

Fine, Sidney. *Frank Murphy: The Washington Years.* Vol. 3. Ann Arbor: University of Michigan Press, 1984.

An extraordinarily detailed discussion of Murphy's tenure on the Court, generally regarded as the definitive representation of Murphy's time on the Court. The two earlier volumes cover Murphy's political career in Detroit and the New Deal years.

Frank, John P. "Frank Murphy." In Leon Friedman and Fred L. Israel, eds., *The Justices of the United States Supreme Court, 1789–1995: Their Lives and Major Opinions.* New York: Chelsea House, 1995, pp. 2493–2506.

Helpful discussion of the most significant influences on Murphy's pre-Court life. Emphasis on what the author suggests is Murphy's "most distinguishing quality—the absoluteness of his devotion to civil liberties."

———. "Hugo L. Black." In Leon Friedman and Fred L. Israel, eds., *The Justices of the United States Supreme Court, 1789–1995: Their Lives and Major Opinions.* New York: Chelsea House, 1995, pp. 2321–2347.

Extensively represents Black's pre-Court background before systematically summarizing his jurisprudence. The author features Black's civil liberties record, of course, but develops as well Black's rejection of substantive due process, his "to-the-hilt" support of federal economic regulatory authority, and his willingness to permit states a significant role in economic regulation.

———. "William O. Douglas." In Leon Friedman and Fred L. Israel, eds., *The Justices of the United States Supreme Court, 1789–1995: Their Lives and Major Opinions.* New York: Chelsea House, 1995, pp. 2447–2470.

Informative biographical discussion. Frank overviews Douglas's Court record and presents several cases to illustrate what he calls Douglas's "most important function" during his almost four-decade tenure on the Court: his service as a "bridge from an old liberalism to a new."

Friedman, Leon, and Fred L. Israel, eds. *The Justices of the United States Supreme Court, 1789-1995: Their Lives and Major Opinions.* New York: Chelsea House, 1995.

A superb five-volume set containing extended essays on all of the Supreme Court justices. Each essay offers not only biographical background information but also substantial discussion of the justices' jurisprudence. Earlier editions contain a sample of two or three of each justice's major opinions.

Gerhardt, Michael J. "Hugo Lafayette Black." In Melvin I. Urofsky, ed., *The Supreme Court Justices: A Biographical Dictionary.* New York: Garland, 1994, pp. 5–14.

Sketches the essentials of Black's liberal-activist jurisprudence. Highlights those issues on which Black most influenced the Court's thinking but also those issues where his failures were as notable as his successes.

Gerhart, Eugene C. *America's Advocate: Robert H. Jackson.* Indianapolis, Ind.: Bobbs-Merrill, 1958.

Useful discussion although not a critical analysis of Jackson's tenure on the Court. The volume draws heavily on Jackson's own discussions of his unfulfilled quest for the chief justiceship.

Glancy, Dorothy J. "William Orville Douglas." In Melvin I. Urofsky, ed., *The Supreme Court Justices: A Biographical Dictionary.* New York: Garland, 1994, pp. 141–152.

Informative exploration of the values on which Douglas's judicial philosophy was grounded. Selects a number of his most significant opinions to reflect the breadth of his jurisprudence.

Goldman, Sheldon. *Constitutional Law: Cases and Essays.* 2nd edition. New York: HarperCollins, 1991.

Conventionally fashioned constitutional law casebook with two unusually valuable features: Goldman develops the political and historical context of the Supreme Court from 1789 to the present and discusses each justice as he or she joined the Court, the characteristics of the group interactions of each Court era, and the voting patterns of each individual justice.

Goodwin, Doris Kearns. *No Ordinary Time: Franklin and Eleanor Roosevelt: The Home Front in World War II.* New York: Simon & Schuster, 1994.

A delightful narrative of the home front and how it affected the course of World War II and in turn American life.

Gunther, John. *Roosevelt in Retrospect: A Profile in History.* New York: Harper and Brothers, 1950.

Biography with several informative chapters on the presidential years—Roosevelt's "peace presidency" and his "war presidency."

Hall, Kermit L. "Owen Josephus Roberts." In Melvin I. Urofsky, ed., *The Supreme Court Justices: A Biographical Dictionary.* New York: Garland, 1994, pp. 383–387.

Describes Roberts as a judicial moderate or centrist but without a defining judicial philosophy. Focuses on Roberts's early inclination to vote with conservatives prior to 1937 and his famous switch after the Court-packing episode.

———, ed. *The Oxford Companion to the Supreme Court.* New York: Oxford University Press, 1992.

A comprehensive single volume with informative entries on the Supreme Court, its principal decisions, and the justices.

Harper, Fowler Vincent. *Justice Rutledge and the Bright Constellation.* Indianapolis, Ind.: Bobbs-Merrill, 1965.

A detailed biographical discussion of Rutledge but lacking any critical analysis of Rutledge's Court years.

Hirsch, H. N. *The Enigma of Felix Frankfurter.* New York: Basic Books, 1981.

A biographical treatment that undertakes a provocative behavioral examination of Frankfurter derived from his Court opinions, scholarly work, correspondence, and other written records.

Howard, J. Woodford. *Mr. Justice Murphy: A Political Biography.* Princeton, N.J.: Princeton University Press, 1968.

A less detailed discussion of Justice Murphy than provided by Sidney Fine but more analytically rigorous.

Howard, John R. *The Shifting Wind: The Supreme Court and Civil Rights from Reconstruction to Brown.* Albany: State University of New York Press, 1999.

Traces the role of the Supreme Court in fashioning constitutional policy on civil rights. Excellent discussion of the Stone Court in the chapter "On the Road to *Brown.*"

Irons, Peter. "Francis (Frank) William Murphy." In Melvin I. Urofsky, ed., *The Supreme Court Justices: A Biographical Dictionary.* New York: Garland, 1994, pp. 331–336.

Focuses on Murphy's apprehension about joining the Court and the impact of that apprehension on his first two terms. Irons develops Murphy's commitment to individual rights and his zealous guardianship of constitutional rights.

Israel, Fred L. "Wiley Rutledge." In Leon Friedman and Fred L. Israel, eds., *The Justices of the United States Supreme Court, 1789–1995: Their Lives and Major Opinions.* New York: Chelsea House, 1995, pp. 2593–2601.

A brief biographical essay that overviews Rutledge's route to the Court and a broad overview of his civil liberties jurisprudence.

Jeffries, John W. *Wartime America: The World War II Home Front.* Chicago: Ivan Dee, 1996.

Written more than half a century after World War II, an assessment of the domestic impact of World War II and its significance on the American society, economy, and political system.

Johnson, John W. "Harlan Fiske Stone." In Melvin I. Urofsky, ed., *The Supreme Court Justices: A Biographical Dictionary.* New York: Garland, 1994, pp. 425–434.
Features Stone's largely minority position on the Hughes Court and his disappointing tenure as chief justice.

Kirkendall, Richard. "Harold Burton." In Leon Friedman and Fred L. Israel, eds., *The Justices of the United States Supreme Court, 1789–1995: Their Lives and Major Opinions.* New York: Chelsea House, 1995, pp. 1322–1333.
Highlights Burton's political background and his role on the badly divided Stone and Vinson Courts.

Konefsky, Samuel J. *Chief Justice Stone and the Supreme Court.* New York: Macmillan, 1945.
A thorough discussion of Stone's legal philosophy—on central constitutional issues such as the scope of federal regulatory authority, the federal commerce and its intersection with state power, and the protection of individual liberties.

Kurland, Philip B. "Robert H. Jackson." In Leon Friedman and Fred L. Israel, eds., *The Justices of the United States Supreme Court, 1789–1995: Their Lives and Major Opinions.* New York: Chelsea House, 1995, pp. 2543–2571.
Extensive background on Jackson's political life, especially his involvement with the Roosevelt administration prior to his nomination to the Court. Develops Jackson's judicial philosophy and his contributions to constitutional law. Centers on two reasons Jackson was dissatisfied with his Court service—his view that the Court's work was irrelevant when compared to the "struggle for freedom" taking place with the war and the level of conflict within the Court.

Larrowe, Charles P. *Harry Bridges: The Rise and Fall of Radical Labor in the United States.* New York: Lawrence Hill, 1972.
Biography of the labor leader Harry Bridges, whose activities and associations prompted the federal government to try to deport him. The volume provides perspective on the several law cases involving Bridges, two of which were ultimately decided by the Stone Court.

Lash, Joseph. *Dealers and Dreamers: A New Look at the New Deal.* New York: Doubleday, 1988.
A detailed account of the "350 odd men and women," the New Dealers, who helped President Roosevelt put through the "social transformation" of the 1930s. Lash, a Washington insider during this period, draws information from his own experiences and the papers of many of the central figures involved in the Roosevelt revolution.

Leonard, Charles A. *A Search for a Judicial Philosophy: Mr. Justice Roberts and the*

Constitutional Revolution of 1937. Port Washington, N.Y.: Kennikat Press, 1971.

Examines the voting record of the justice who was the pivotal vote on the Supreme Court in the mid-1930s and offers an explanation for the changes in Roberts's jurisprudence while he was a member of the Hughes Court.

Leuchtenburg, William E. *The Supreme Court Reborn: The Constitutional Revolution in the Age of Roosevelt.* New York: Oxford University Press, 1995.

Discusses the constitutional "revolution" emerging from the battle between the Court and Roosevelt over the New Deal initiatives. The author argues that the conflict changed the Court into the institution we see currently.

Maney, Patrick J. *The Roosevelt Presence: A Biography of Franklin Delano Roosevelt.* New York: Twayne, 1992.

An assessment of Roosevelt's political life. Maney concludes that Roosevelt was an effective and successful president but suggests that his stature was in large part a product of the political context, the demands of the period in which he served.

Mason, Alpheus T. "Harlan F. Stone." In Leon Friedman and Fred L. Israel, eds., *The Justices of the United States Supreme Court, 1789–1995: Their Lives and Major Opinions.* New York: Chelsea House, 1995, pp. 1099–1116.

———. *The Supreme Court from Taft to Burger.* 3rd edition. Baton Rouge: Louisiana State University Press, 1979.

An overview of the several Supreme Court eras beginning with the Taft Court of the 1920s. Mason identifies the principal characteristics of each Court and discusses what he finds to be the most significant aspects of the jurisprudence of each.

———. *Harlan Fiske Stone: Pillar of the Law.* New York: Viking, 1956.

The most authoritative work on Stone, offering as well essential insights into the Supreme Court as an institution.

McCloskey, Robert G. *The Modern Supreme Court.* Cambridge: Harvard University Press, 1972.

An excellent discussion of the "modern" Supreme Court—the Stone, Vinson, and Warren Court eras. Valuable treatment of the most important rulings of each of these Courts.

Mendelson, Wallace. *Justices Black and Frankfurter: Conflict on the Court.* Chicago: University of Chicago Press, 1966.

A brief comparative examination of Frankfurter's orientation of judicial restraint and Black's liberal activism across a number of constitutional issues.

Murphy, Walter F. "James F. Byrnes." In Leon Friedman and Fred L. Israel, eds., *The Justices of the United States Supreme Court, 1789–1995: Their Lives and Major Opinions.* New York: Chelsea House, 1995, pp. 1263–1281.

Examines Byrnes's one year on the Court in some detail, commenting insightfully on what Byrnes probably considered his least significant year of public service.

Nash, A. E. Kier. "Wiley Blount Rutledge." In Melvin I. Urofsky, ed., *The Supreme Court Justices: A Biographical Dictionary*. New York: Garland, 1994, pp. 391–393.

Suggests that several themes reflect Rutledge's six terms on the Court—broadened civil liberties, procedural fairness, expanded federal regulatory authority over the economy, and assistance to the interests of organized labor.

O'Brien, F. William. *Justice Reed and the First Amendment: The Religion Clauses*. Washington, D.C.: Georgetown University Press, 1958.

The best treatment of Reed's jurisprudence, although its focus is limited to First Amendment issues.

O'Neill, William L. *A Democracy at War: America's Fight at Home and Abroad in World War II*. New York: Free Press, 1993.

An account of U.S. participation in World War II. Focuses on the political relationships of Roosevelt and Congress and between the United States and its allies and argues that the country's war effort was hampered by its failure sufficiently to prepare for war, politicians' fears of asking for "too many sacrifices" from the public, and prejudice against refugees, blacks, Japanese Americans, and women.

Parrish, Michael E. "Felix Frankfurter." In Melvin I. Urofsky, ed., *The Supreme Court Justices: A Biographical Dictionary*. New York: Garland, 1994, pp. 171–181.

Not only effectively represents Frankfurter and his self-restraint orientation throughout his Court years but also develops Frankfurter's remarkable life prior to his appointment equally well.

———. *Felix Frankfurter and His Times: The Reform Years*. New York: Free Press, 1982.

A revealing discussion of Frankfurter's years on the Harvard Law School faculty, his students who later made their marks in Washington after Harvard Law, and his role in Roosevelt's inner circle.

Phillips, Cabell. *The 1940s: Decade of Triumph and Trouble*. New York: Macmillan, 1975.

Narrative on the 1940s by a former *New York Times* journalist.

Polenberg, Richard. *War and Society: The United States, 1941–45*. Philadelphia: J. B. Lippincott , 1972.

One of a series of volumes examining "critical periods" of history, presents a valuable discussion of the transition from the New Deal to mobilizing for war. Polenberg's volume devotes two chapters to the civil rights struggle and the relocation of the Japanese.

Pritchett, C. Herman. "Stanley Reed." In Leon Friedman and Fred L. Israel, eds., *The Justices of the United States Supreme Court, 1789–1995: Their Lives and Major Opinions*. New York: Chelsea House, 1995, pp. 1181–1198.

Describes Reed's route to the Court, his New Deal credentials, and his moderate position between the two poles of the Stone Court. Pritchett conveys Reed's reluctance to paint with the broad brush so often used by his Stone Court colleagues.

———. *Constitutional Law of the Federal System*. Englewood Cliffs, N.J.: Prentice-Hall, 1984.

One of a two-volume set, this volume discusses major themes of U.S. constitutional law as it applies to the institutions of the national government and the federal-state relationship.

———. *Civil Liberties and the Vinson Court*. Chicago: University of Chicago Press, 1954.

A follow-up to Pritchett's classic work on the Roosevelt Court. Here he examines the effect of judicial personality on the civil liberties decisionmaking of the Vinson Court.

———. *The Roosevelt Court: A Study in Judicial Politics and Values, 1937–47*. New York: Macmillan, 1948.

The first examination of the value orientations of Supreme Court justices and the influence of these values on judicial decisions.

Reel, A. Frank. *The Case of General Yamashita*. New York: Octagon Books, 1971.

Historical narrative of the life of Tomoyuki Yamashita, commander of the Fourteenth Army Group of the Imperial Japanese Army, and the details of the atrocities committed by those under his command that led to Yamashita's prosecution for war crimes following World War II.

Renstrom, Peter G. "The Dimensionality of Decision Making of the 1941–1945 Stone Court: A Computer-Dependent Analysis of Supreme Court Behavior." Ph.D. dissertation, Michigan State University, 1972.

A quantitative analysis of the structure and characteristics of the Stone Court's decision making.

Rise, Eric W. "Harold Hitz Burton." In Melvin I. Urofsky, ed., *The Supreme Court Justices: A Biographical Dictionary*. New York: Garland, 1994, pp. 77–80.

A brief overview of Burton's tenure on the Court. Suggests that Burton did not possess the well-developed judicial philosophy of many of his contemporaries, preferring instead to decide cases on narrow, fact-focused grounds.

Robertson, David. *Sly and Able: A Political Biography of James F. Byrnes*. New York: W. W. Norton, 1994.

An examination of Byrnes the political figure. Much more attention devoted to Byrnes's activities before and after his Supreme Court service, but one chapter provides useful discussion of the one term Byrnes served on the Court.

Rodell, Fred. *Nine Men: A Political History of the Supreme Court of the United States from 1790 to 1955*. New York: Vintage Books, 1955.

Overview of the Court's history with brief sketches of the justices who served prior to 1955.

Rudko, Frances Howell. *Truman's Court: A Study in Judicial Restraint*. New York: Greenwood Press, 1988.

An examination of the four Truman appointees—Justices Burton, Clark, Minton, and Vinson—and their judicial philosophies.

Sacks, Albert M. "Felix Frankfurter." In Leon Friedman and Fred L. Israel, eds., *The Justices of the United States Supreme Court, 1789–1995: Their Lives and Major Opinions*. New York: Chelsea House, 1995, pp. 2401–2417.

Examines Frankfurter's judicial philosophy and how it was shaped by his lengthy service as a faculty member at Harvard Law School, his advocacy for selected causes, and the counsel he provided President Roosevelt. The author skillfully presents the nuances of Frankfurter's distinctive restraint orientation.

Schubert, Glendon. *Dispassionate Justice: A Synthesis of the Judicial Opinions of Robert H. Jackson*. Indianapolis, Ind.: Bobbs-Merrill, 1969.

A collection of some of Jackson's most important and revealing opinions. The first chapter gives biographical information as well as a behavioral analysis of Jackson's decision making.

Schwartz, Bernard. *The Supreme Court: Constitutional Revolution in Retrospect*. New York: Ronald Press, 1957.

An excellent discussion of the how the Supreme Court has defined constitutional meaning, focusing at length on the "veritable revolution" in the Court's jurisprudence beginning in 1937 and the changed role of the Supreme Court.

Simon, James F. *Independent Journey: The Life of William O. Douglas*. New York: Harper & Row, 1990.

Thorough biographical discussion of Douglas, with particularly valuable chapters on his lengthy Court service. Volume provides a thought-provoking account of the essential qualities of Douglas's character.

Swindler, William F. *Court and Constitution in the Twentieth Century: The New Legality, 1932–1968*. 2 vols. Indianapolis, Ind.: Bobbs-Merrill, 1974.

A comprehensive narrative on the major constitutional developments through the end of the Warren Era. The second volume provides insights into the Stone and Vinson Court's role in the transition from the Hughes to the Warren Courts.

tenBroek, Jacobus, Edward N. Barnhart, and Floyd W. Matson. *Prejudice, War and the Constitution: Causes and Consequences of the Evacuation of the Japanese Americans in World War II*. Berkeley: University of California Press, 1970.

Product of a broad-scale study of the Japanese evacuation, the volume explores the long-standing anti-Japanese attitudes that influenced policy decisions during World War II. The third section is devoted to the constitutional issues and the role of the courts in the evacuation.

Urofsky, Melvin I. *Division and Discord: The Supreme Court under Stone and Vinson, 1941–1953.* Columbia: University of South Carolina Press, 1997.

Carefully examines the unusually high level of division within the Stone and Vinson Courts, which lasted only twelve years but were important "transitional" Courts in Urofsky's view.

———, ed. *The Supreme Court Justices: A Biographical Dictionary.* New York: Garland, 1994.

A collection of essays about each of the 107 justices who have served on the U.S. Supreme Court. The essays in this volume were prepared by an extremely distinguished collection of authors and provide valuable albeit summary analysis of the jurisprudence of the justices.

———. *Felix Frankfurter: Judicial Restraint and Individual Liberties.* Boston: Twayne, 1991.

An insightfully developed discussion that covers the origins of Frankfurter's judicial self-restraint philosophy and his application of this approach throughout his twenty-three years on the Supreme Court.

Walter, David O. *American Government at War.* Chicago: Richard D. Irvin, 1942.

Descriptive discussion of the period immediately preceding the U.S. entry into World War II and the mobilization activities following the attack on Pearl Harbor.

White, G. Edward. *The American Judicial Tradition: Profiles of Leading American Judges.* Oxford: Oxford University Press, 1976.

Group and individual portraits of selected Supreme Court justices. Particularly valuable to an understanding of the Stone Court are the chapters on the Four Horsemen of the 1930s, a comparative examination of Hughes and Stone as chief justices, and Jackson's jurisprudence and a profile of Black and Frankfurter as members of the Warren Court.

White, Graham, and John Maze. *Harold Ickes of the New Deal: His Private Life and Public Career.* Cambridge: Harvard University Press, 1985.

A historian (White) and a psychologist (Maze) examine the paradoxes between Ickes's public image and his private life. The work is based on Ickes's own extensive accounts of his experiences; indeed, the authors suggest that "few men can have left a more complete record of their public and private lives" than did Ickes.

Woeste, Victoria Saker. "James Francis Byrnes." In Melvin I. Urofsky, ed., *The Supreme Court Justices: A Biographical Dictionary.* New York: Garland, 1994, p. 87.

Brief sketch of Byrnes's single term on the Court.

Yarbrough, Tinsley E. *Mr. Justice Black and His Critics.* Durham: Duke University Press, 1988.

A systematic examination of and response to the most significant criticism of Justice Black's jurisprudence, which features both the academic critics as well as those with whom Black sat on the Supreme Court, in particular Justices Frankfurter, Jackson, and Harlan.

Young, Roland. *Congressional Politics in the Second World War.* New York: Columbia University Press, 1956.

Examines the role of Congress during World War II. Although Congress played a generally subordinate role to Roosevelt at the time, Young examines policy areas such as agriculture where initiatives came from Congress. Valuable discussion of the relationship and "pattern of politics" between Roosevelt and Congress.

Internet Sources

New Internet sites are introduced frequently. Readers who go to the addresses listed below are encouraged to explore the countless links to other sites provided at virtually every site.

There are a number of excellent sites with information about the U.S. Supreme Court, some of which are listed below. The full text of Court of decisions is available from some, but they are generally limited to cases decided since approximately 1900.

Emory University School of Law

http://www.law.emory.edu/LAW/refdesk/toc.html

The electronic reference desk initial menu offers several useful categories of information, including federal and state laws in the United States and selected representation of laws from over seventy other countries. This site contains a reference option as well as sections on law by subject, law schools, legal periodicals, legal career information, and selected law firms.

http://www.law.emory.edu/FEDCTS

This U.S. Federal Courts finder links the user to all federal appellate courts. Supreme Court link connects the user to Cornell's Legal Information Institute site. Excellent source for U.S. Court of Appeals decisions. Click any of the circuits on the U.S. maps to access rulings covering the last several years.

Federal Judicial Center

http://www.fjc.gov/

Home page for the Federal Judicial Center, the research and education agency of the federal judicial system. Features links to other courts, including the new Supreme Court site and the newly added link to the "History of the Federal Judiciary" site, which contains a biographical database of all federal judges since

1789, histories of the federal courts, and other historical materials related to the federal judicial branch.

Federal Judiciary Homepage

http://www.uscourts.gov/

> This page, maintained by the Administrative Office of the U.S. Courts, is a good source of information on the federal courts. The site contains a number of links to other valuable court- and law-related sites. There is also a link that features recent developments regarding the federal courts, including the latest on the status of federal judicial vacancies.

Federal Legal Information Through Electronics (FLITE)

wysiwyg://14/http://www.fedworld.gov/supcourt/index.htm

> Contains the full text of about 7,500 U.S. Supreme Court decisions from 1937 to 1975. Cases can be retrieved by case name or keyword. Also provides links to other sites.

Findlaw

http://www.findlaw.com/

> Extraordinarily valuable and comprehensive site. Among other things, the site has federal and state cases and codes, U.S. and state resources, news and reference, a legal subject index, and links to bar associations, lawyers, and law firms. Decisions of the U.S. Supreme Court back to 1893 can be accessed, as can federal courts or appeals rulings.

Jurist: The Legal Education Network

http://jurist.law.pitt.edu/supremecourt.htm

> Pittsburgh University Law School guide to the U.S. Supreme Court as an online introduction to the "jurisprudence, structure, history and Justices of America's highest court." Links the user to sites that contain Supreme Court decisions, news about the Court, biographies of the justices, the Court's procedures, and the latest media coverage of the Court.

Legal Information Institute (LII)

http://www.law.cornell.edu/index.html

> Cornell Law School site containing Supreme Court decisions since 1990, U.S. and state constitutions and codes, law by source or jurisdiction (including international law), "law about" pages providing summaries of various legal topics, and a "current awareness" page with news about the Court. LII provides a free email service that distributes syllabi of Supreme Court decisions within hours of their release.

Lexis-Nexis Academic Universe

http://web.lexis-nexis.com/universe/

> A subscription database that covers a wide range of news, business, and reference information. Free access can be obtained to Lexis-Nexis through Academic Universe, which is available through most educational institutions.

National Center for State Courts

http://www.ncsc.dni.us/

> A comprehensive site with extensive information on state courts, state judges, and state court caseloads. Links are provided for information about federal courts and international courts.

Oyez Project

http://oyez.nwu.edu/

> Northwestern University multimedia database that allows users to hear oral arguments from selected cases, obtain summaries of more than 1,000 Court opinions, access biographical information on all the justices who have served on the Court, and take a virtual-reality tour of the Supreme Court building.

Supreme Court

http://supremecourtus.gov/

> Offers an overview of the Supreme Court as an institution, its functions, traditions, procedures, court rules, docket, and calendar. Information on the justices and the Supreme Court building is available as well. Plug-in capability is required to access information from this site.

Westlaw

http://westlaw.com/

> One of the largest and most comprehensive legal and business databases available on the Internet. Subscription is required for access, but prospective subscribers are able to explore the site fully on a trial basis.

Yahoo Law

http://dir.yahoo.com/Government/Law/

> A search engine with a separate and extensive listing of law-related sites. An easy-to-use and comprehensive searching device.

A number of newspapers provide good coverage of the U.S. Supreme Court. Among the best are the *New York Times* (http://www.nytimes.com/), and the *Washington Post* (http://www.washpostco.com/).

Index

P eter G. Renstrom is a professor of political science at Western Michigan University. He is also a coauthor of ABC-CLIO's *The Constitutional Law Dictionary* (1987) and author of *Constitutional Law and Young Adults* (1992) and *Constitutional Rights Sourcebook* (1999).